MW01105869

Exposition of the Psalms

Exposition of the Psalms

An Interpretation and Application
Volume Two: Psalms 51–100

Frank R. Shivers

LIGHTNING SOURCE
1246 Heil Quaker Blvd.
La Vergne, TN

Copyright 2019 by
Frank Shivers Evangelistic Association
All rights reserved
Printed in the United States of America

Unless otherwise noted, Scripture quotations are from
The Holy Bible *King James Version*

Library of Congress Cataloging-in-Publication Data

Shivers, Frank R., 1949-
Exposition of the Psalms Vol. 2 / Frank Shivers
ISBN 978-1-878127-36-5

Library of Congress Control Number:
2018910734

Cover design by
Tim King of Click Graphics, Inc.

For Information:
Frank Shivers Evangelistic Association
P. O. Box 9991
Columbia, South Carolina 29290
www.frankshivers.com

Presented to

_____

By

_____

Date

_____

The law instructs, history informs, prophecy predicts, correction censures, and morals exhort. In the Book of Psalms, you find the fruit of all these, as well as a remedy for the salvation of the soul. The Psalter deserves to be called the praise of God, the glory of man, the voice of the church, and the most beneficial confession of faith.[1] ~ Ambrose

Here is a "Book of Devotion" for the ages. Here every heart chord is touched and tuned to holy melody. God is here in His natural and moral attributes. Christ is here in His divinity and humanity, humiliation and exaltation. The Gospel is here, sublime unfoldings of pardoning and purifying grace. Christian life is here: faith, hope, love—and even church history in outline.[2] ~ A. T. Pierson

If all the greatest excellences and most choice experience of all the true saints should be gathered from the whole church since it has existed and should be condensed into the focus of one book; if God, I say, should permit any most spiritual and gifted man to form and concentrate such a book, such a book would be what the Book of Psalms is, or like unto it. For in the Book of Psalms we have not the life of the saints only, but we have the experience of Christ Himself, the Head of all the saints. So that you may truly call the Book of Psalms a little Bible. Be assured that the Holy Spirit Himself has written and handed down to us this Book of Psalms as a Liturgy, in the same way as a father would give a book to his children. He Himself has drawn up this Manual for His disciples; having collected together, as it were, the lives, groans and experience of many thousands, whose hearts He alone sees and knows.[3] ~ James Hastings

There [Psalms] you look right down into the heart of saints and behold all manner of joys and joyous thoughts toward God and His love springing lustily into life! Again, you look into the heart of saints as into death and Hell! How gloomy and dark their mournful visions of God.[4] ~ Martin Luther

How varied and how splendid the wealth which this treasury [Psalms] contains it is difficult to describe in words; whatever I shall say, I know full well must fall far short of its worth.[5] ~ John Calvin

To

Phillip Roland, Sr., better known as "Big Daddy," for forty-five years of faithful friendship, unselfish sacrificial support and the dispensing of humorous medicine for the soul.

"Take Mark, and bring him with you: for he is profitable [useful] to me for the ministry." ~ 2 Timothy 4:11 AKJV

Contents

According to legend, renowned Yosemite Ranger Carl Sharsmith was once asked by a visitor, "If you had only one day in Yosemite, what would you do?"

The veteran ranger and Yosemite lover looked solemn and replied "Madam, if I could only have one day in Yosemite, I'd sit by the Merced River and cry."[6]

Attempting to survey the Psalms in three volumes is even more formidable. Nonetheless, with due diligence, ever seeking to follow the divine guidance of the "pillar of fire" by night and the "pillar of a cloud" by day (Exodus 13:21), effort was exerted to enter the vast caverns of the Psalms, hewing out choice nuggets of pure gold to extract its invaluable and inexhaustible inspiration and instruction.

I join with Charles Haddon Spurgeon in saying, "In these busy days, it would be greatly to the spiritual profit of Christians if they were more familiar with the Book of Psalms, in which they would find a complete armory for life's battles and a perfect supply for life's needs. Here we have both delight and usefulness, consolation and instruction. For every condition there is a Psalm, suitable and elevating. The Book supplies the babe in grace with penitent cries and the perfected saint with triumphant songs. Its breadth of experience stretches from the jaws of Hell to the gate of Heaven."[7]

With regard to the vast works on the Psalms, one discovers various emphases. It has been my purpose in these three volumes to make understandable the "hidden" meaning of the original Hebrew words in which the Psalms were written; to simplify historical settings when known, making connection between the Psalm and the event; and to grant insight into the Psalm's personal devotional application. You, the reader, will render verdict whether or not that objective was achieved.

Words cannot describe or express the joy, challenge and enrichment to my soul derived in this journey through the Psalms. Its laborious but delightful task, that daily required hours upon hours in isolation in the study, will but be counted worthwhile if the reader is blessed in similar measure. Walter Brueggermann, in the Preface to

Spirituality of the Psalms, states, "Any comment upon them is inevitably partial and provisional. There is simply more than can be touched and handled. So one finishes with a sense of inadequacy, of not probing enough. That, of course, is why the Psalms continue to nourish and nurture long after our interpretation has run its course."[8] I couldn't agree more. This work at best but touches the hem of the garment of the treasure-filled Psalms. May the Lord favor this writing presently and then long after my departure unto His glory, honor and praise.

The Hebrew word for the Book of Psalms means "praises,"[9] whereas the Greek word means "songs of praise."[10] J. L. Crenshaw states that the word *Psalter* "comes from the title in Alexandrinus...and indicates a musical instrument, presumably to accompany the singing of Psalms."[11] Elwell and Comfort say the Psalter is a compilation of "poems sung to musical accompaniment, originally the harp."[12] Marvin Tate said, "The title probably respresents a stage in Israel's past when the Psalms were used as a general hymnal, suitable for all occasions."[13]

Augustine gave himself to a lifetime study of the Psalms; Henry Martyn was comforted and encouraged in times of tremendous stress through memorizing portions of the Psalms; Matthew Henry's father instructed him to read a Psalm a day, for it would bring him to love the whole of Scripture; to John Ruskin, Psalm 119 was the most precious because of its great emphasis on the Word of God.[14] Charles Haddon Spurgeon wrote in the introduction to his classical work on the Psalms, *The Treasury of David* (a work that took twenty years to compose), "More and more is the conviction forced upon my heart that every man must traverse the territory of the Psalms himself if he would know what a goodly land they are. They flow with milk and honey, but not to strangers; they are only fertile to lovers of their hills and vales."[15]

The chiefest treasure of the Psalms belongs to him that excavates its vast mines not casually but rigorously, not shallowly but thoroughly, and not merely academically but spiritually. John Stott has written, "The psalms...speak the universal language of the human soul....Whatever our spiritual mood may be, there is sure to be a Psalm which reflects it— whether triumph or defeat, excitement or depression, joy or sorrow, praise or penitence, wonder or anger. Above all, the Psalms declare the greatness of the living God as Creator, Sustainer, King, Lawgiver, Saviour, Father, Shepherd and Judge."[16] Matthew Henry says, "There is no one book of Scripture that is more helpful to the devotions of the saints than this, and it has been so in all ages of the church, ever since it was written....So rich, so well made, are these divine poems, that they can never be exhausted, can never be worn threadbare."[17]

Willem VanGemeren, in the introduction to his work on the Psalms in *The Expositor's Bible Commentary,* states, "The Book of Psalms is God's prescription for a complacent church, because through it He reveals how great, wonderful, magnificient, wise and utterly awe-inspiring He is!"[18] J. J. S. Perowne states, "No single Book of Scripture, not even of the New Testament, has, perhaps, ever taken such hold on the heart of Christendom. None, if we may dare judge, unless it be the Gospels, has had so large an influence in moulding the affections, sustaining the hopes, purifying the faith of believers. With its words, rather than with their own, they have come before God. In these they have uttered their desires, their fears, their confessions, their aspirations, their sorrows, their joys, their thanksgivings. By these their devotion has been kindled and their hearts comforted. The Psalter has been, in the truest sense, the Prayer Book both of Jews and Christians."[19]

The book of Psalms is a book for the spiritually thirsty and hungry. Isaiah well could have said of it, "Is anyone thirsty? Come and drink—even if you have no money!...Come to me with your ears wide open. Listen, and you will find life" (Isaiah 55:1a, 3a NLT). Max Lucado is right. "This collection of hymns and petitions are strung together by one thread—a heart hungry for God."[20] Mueller testified, "The Psalms teach one to prize a much tried life...David yields me every day the most delightful hour. There is nothing Greek, nothing Roman, nothing in the West, nor in the land towards midnight, to equal David, whom the God of Israel chose to praise Him higher than the gods of the nations. The utterance of His mind sinks deep into the heart, and never in my life, never have I thus seen God."[21]

But only the sanctified soul can reap such benefit and pleasure in their reading. W. S. Plumer is correct to say, "If to any man these songs are unsavory, the reason is found in the blindness and depravity of the human heart."[22] Hengstenberg said, "The Psalms are expressions of holy feeling, which can be understood by those only, who have become alive to such feeling."[23] The Psalms, as with all the Books of the Bible, must be read through the "lenses" of a sanctified mind and a heart hungry for God in order to discover their vast jewels of knowledge and wisdom and experience their inspirational, invigorating and instructional delight. C. H. Spurgeon wrote, "Whenever we look into David's Psalms, we may somewhere or other see ourselves. I never get into a corner but I find David in that corner. I think I was never so low that I could not find that David was lower, or I never climbed so high that I could not find that David was up above me, ready to sing his song upon his stringed instruments, even as I could sing mine."[24]

Authorship. Psalms is one of only two books in the Bible written by multiple authors (Proverbs being the other). Its many authors under the inspiration and direction of the Holy Spirit include David, Asaph, the sons of Korah, Heman, Ethan, Moses and Solomon. Of the 150 Psalms, authorship is unknown for 50[25] (see 2 Peter 1:21). Psalms that were composed by David ("the sweet psalmist of Israel," 2 Samuel 23:1) were Holy Spirit inspired (Acts 4:25), as were those that were not from David. A. F. Kirkpatrick wrote, "The widest diversity of opinion prevails as to the date and authorship of the Psalms, and we must often be content to acknowledge that a Psalm cannot be assigned to a definite period, still less to a particular author, with any degree of certainty."[26]

The title ascribed to various Psalms. The Psalms usually carry a heading or superscription that includes one or more of the following catergories: identification of the author, historical setting, musical and liturgical details, and genre.[27] The Psalms without a superscription are called "Orphan Psalms." These are Psalms 1; 2; 10; 33; 43; 71; 91; 93-97; 99; 104–107; 111–119; 135–137; 146–150.[28] With regard to the author and historical setting of these Psalms, man can make only a reasonable "guess."

Psalm titles are ascribed to 116 of the 150 psalms (eighty-seven of the first 100) in the Hebrew Psalter.[29] Uncertainity exists as to the time these titles were affixed to numerous Psalms—at the time of composition or later.[30] However, evidence abounds to prove they have long been included in the Psalter text (canonical text).[31]

These titles prove invaluable in determining a Psalm's historical setting and authorship. The title used in the superscription preceeding each Psalm associating names with the Psalm does not necessarily indicate authorship, as readers of the English text think. For example, "of David" is literally "to David." The Psalm therefore may possess one of three distinct meanings: (1) Davidic authorship; (2) attributed to David by the opinion of others; (3) connected with David's life and experiences.[32] This makes definitive authorship difficult if not impossible.

Chrysostom's view of the authorship of the Psalms is mine: "How does it concern me whether David was the author of all the Psalms or whether some of them were written by others, since it is certainly known that they were all written by the inspiration of the Holy Spirit?"[33] (See 2 Timothy 3:16–17 and 2 Samuel 23:2–3.) W. S. Plumer notes the absence of the historical setting in some of the Psalms is because it didn't have one. He states, "We are not bound to hold that David wrote all the Psalms to suit particular times and events."[34] A. F. Kirkpatrick wrote, "Important as it is for the full interpretation of many Psalms to know the circumstances under which they were written, and for the elucidation of the religious history of Israel to determine the age to which they belong, the Psalms as a whole suffer less from this uncertainty than might be expected. Their interest is human and universal. They appeal to the experience of all ages."[35]

When the Psalms were written. Historical data within the Psalms clearly suggest they were written over a span of a thousand years—from the time of Moses to the time of David, Asaph and Solomon to the time of the Ezrahites that lived most likely after the Babylonian captivity.[36] The final compilation of Psalms was not complete until the latter half of the fifth century B.C. (the time of Ezra and Nehemiah).[37]

Elwell and Comfort state, "Ezra is traditionally credited with the final grouping and editing of the psalms, a hypothesis that appears reasonable in light of his vital contribution to the systematic reshaping of the national religious life."[38]

Divine inspiration of the Psalms. George Horne writes, "The right of the Psalter to a place in the sacred canon [Holy Scriptures] hath never been disputed, and it is often cited by our Lord and His apostles in the New Testament as the work of the Holy Spirit."[39] Keil and Delitzsch wrote, "Jesus Christ's exposition of the Psalms is the beginning and the goal of Christian Psalm-interpretation. This began, as that of the Christian church, and in fact first of all that of the Apostles, at Pentecost when the Spirit, whose instrument David acknowledges himself to have been (2 Samuel 23:2), descended upon the apostles as the Spirit of Jesus, the fulfiller and fulfilment of prophecy....He opened up to the disciples the meaning of the Psalms."[40]

Tholuck says, "Hilary, Chrysostom and Augustine state that these Psalms were frequently sung by the congregation, sometimes recited by separate individuals and repeated by the rest."[41] A. F. Kirkpatrick agrees with Franz Delitzsch that there is nothing which comes to light in the New Testament which does not already exist in germ in the Psalms.[42]

Five books of the Psalms. The Psalms may be categorized as follows: "(1) penitential Psalms (6; 32; 38; 51; 102; 130; 143), (2) praise Psalms (113–118), (3) imprecatory Psalms, i.e., Psalms which invoke evil upon one's enemies (35; 52; 58; 59; 69; 79; 83; 109; 137; 140), (4) songs of ascents or songs of degrees (120–134), (5) messianic Psalms (2; 8; 16; 22–24; 40-41; 45; 68-69; 72; 89; 96–99; 102; 110; 118; 132)"[43] and hallelujah Psalms (146–150). The "Five Books" or divisions of the Psalter: Book 1 (Psalms 1–41); Book 2 (Psalms 42–72); Book 3 (Psalms 73–89); Book 4 (Psalms 90–106); Book 5 (Psalms 107–150). Many have seen a parallelism between these five books and the Pentateuch (the first five books of the Bible). *Genesis Section*, Psalms 1–41: The fall and restoration of man. *Exodus Section*, Psalms 42–72: Man's ruin and deliverance by God. *Leviticus Section*, Psalms 73–89: The Temple, holy sanctuary and house of God; and sanctification, holiness and communion with God. *Numbers Section*, Psalms 90–106: Man's testing, danger and protection. H. A. Ironside considers this book the "darkest" in the Psalter, for they deal with some of the most horrendously bitter and difficult experiences of the Christian.[44] *Deuteronomy Section*, Psalms 107–150: The absolute truthfulness of God's Word, praise of and adherence to it; and the believer's triumph over life's sorrows and hardships through Jehovah. David, who was gifted in spiritual poetry and music (1 Samuel 18:10; 2 Samuel 1:17–18; 6:5; 1 Chronicles 6:31; 16:7; 25:1; 2 Chronicles 7:6; 29:30; Ezra 3:10; Nehemiah 12:24, 36, 45; Amos 6:5) composed at least half of the Psalms (75). It is thought that he also wrote some of the "Orphan Psalms."

Theology of the Psalms. Oetinger states there is no essential New Testament truth not contained in the Psalms (according to its unfolded meaning).[45] Keil and Delizsch say, "The Old Testament barrier encompasses the germinating New Testament life, which at a future time shall burst it....Everywhere, where it begins to dawn in this eschatological darkness of the Old Testament, it is the first morning rays of the New Testament sunrise which is already announcing itself."[46]

In the Psalms Jesus Christ is presented as: the Anointed King (Psalms 2; 45; 72; 110), God's Son (Psalm 2), God (Psalms 45; 68; 97; 102), Servant (Psalms 69; 86), Son of Man (Psalm 8), Priest (Psalm 110), the Stone the Builders Rejected (Psalm 118), King of Glory (Psalm 24) and Suffering Savior (Psalms 22; 34; 38; 69).[47] Harry Ironside said, "If anybody has any doubt as to the divine inspiration of Scripture, it seems to me that a careful study of the Book of Psalms alone ought to make clear to him that God has ordered all these things, even to the arrangement of this wonderful book."[48]

Psalm singing. Eskew and McElrath summarize the use of the Psalms through history this way: "From one standpoint the entire history of the hymn could be delineated according to its varying relationship to the Scriptures. Generally speaking, the line of evolution in that story, if it were retold, is from the actual singing of parts of the Bible (the Psalms, for example) through the strict paraphrasing of extended passages and the dutiful use of biblical allusion, language and figures of speech to the free expression of scriptural thought and teaching in contemporary terms."[49] Psalm singing was customary in the church.

Tholuck writes, "When our Lord instituted the holy Supper, He sung Psalms with His apostles (Matthew 26:30). He testified to His disciples that the traits of His fate were delineated in the Psalms (Luke 24:44). He referred His opponents to a prophetic Psalm as inspired by the Holy Ghost (Matthew 22:43). The extent to which His humiliation and exaltation were, mirrorlike, beheld by Him in the Psalms may be illustrated by the fact that even on the cross, when expressing the desertion of His soul, He used not His own words, but adopted the language of His typical ancestor (Matthew 27:46). Paul and Silas, at dead of night, praise God in Psalms from the dungeon (Acts 16:25). Paul exhorts the Christian Church to sing Psalms (Colossians 3:16; Ephesians 5:19). Tertullian mentions, in the second century, that Christians were wont to sing Psalms at the Agapæ, and that pious husbands and wives repeated them antiphonically, i. e., by alternate responses. The Psalms have, ever since the first century, formed an essential portion of Christian worship."[50] Regretably that "essential portion" is growing less and less.

The Psalter (hymnal) has served as a model for the church's hymnology or hymnal. Martin Luther (1483–1546) composed "A Mighty Fortress Is Our God" (based on Psalm 46) while Isaac Watts (1674–1748) and Charles Wesley (1707–1788) attempted to use the content of various Psalms with distinctively New Testament teaching infused into them.[51] "Jesus Shall Reign" from Psalm 72 and "O God, Our Help in Ages Past" from Psalm 90 are examples of the composition of Isaac Watts. Wesley conversely based hymns upon the Psalms as he did other Scripture (not their translation as Watts did). "Oh, for a Heart to Praise My God" uses the ideas of Psalm 51, while "Jesu, Mighty to Deliver" is Psalm 70 expanded as a Christian song of praise.[52]

"Let the peace of Christ rule in your hearts, since as members of one body you were called to peace. And be thankful. Let the message of Christ dwell among you richly as you teach and admonish one another with all wisdom through psalms, hymns, and songs from the Spirit singing to God with gratitude in your hearts" (Colossians 3:15–16 NIV). Paul emphatically states that the "word of Christ" must dwell in us richly. Various types of Christian songs, including Psalms, are regarded as "Christ's word."[53] It is to take up abode within our hearts that it may build us up in the faith and be utilized to teach others.[54]

The gist of the Psalms. George Horne encapsulates the whole of the Psalms: "Composed upon particular occasions, yet designed for general use; delivered out as services for Israelites under the law, yet no less adapted to the circumstances of Christians under the Gospel, they present religion to us in the most engaging dress; communicating truths which philosophy could never investigate, in a style which poetry can never equal, while history is made the vehicle of prophecy, and creation lends all its charms to paint the glories of redemption. Calculated alike to profit and to please, they inform the understanding, elevate the affections, and entertain the imagination. Indited ["compose" or "put down in writing"[55]] under the influence of Him to whom all hearts are known and all events foreknown, they suit mankind in all situations, grateful as the manna which descended from above and conformed itself to every palate. The fairest productions of human wit, after a few perusals, like gathered flowers wither in our hands and lose their fragrancy; but these unfading plants of paradise become, as we are accustomed to them, still more and more beautiful; their bloom appears to be daily heightened; fresh odors are emitted and new sweets extracted from them. He who hath once tasted their excellences will desire to taste them yet again, and he who tastes them oftenest will relish them best."[56]

The Word of God in the Psalms. All who visit the Psalms soon discover the place of prominence it gives to the Word of God. The longest Psalm and chapter in the Bible, Psalm 119, alone ascribes honor and homage over and over again to the Word of God, saying that it is pure, is unmixed with error and lasts forever. Matthew Henry states regarding this emphasis, "What a high value does this Book put upon the Word of God, His statutes and judgments, His covenant and the great and precious promises of it; and how does it recommend them to us as our guide and stay, and our heritage forever!"[57]

Prophecy in the Psalms. Standing on equal footing alongside the emphasis on the Bible as inerrant and infallible are its messianic prophecies. J. Vernon McGee wrote, "The Book of Psalms is a hymnbook and a HIM book—it is all about Him....He is the object of praise in every one of them....Although all of them have Christ as the object of worship, some are technically called Messianic Psalms."[58] Joseph Exell said, "Nearly half of all Messianic references in the New Testament originate from the Psalms."[59] Harry Ironside wrote, "If you are thinking only of yourself as you read these Psalms, you will never see what the book is really taking up, but once you understand something of God's prophetic counsel, once you enter into His purpose in Christ Jesus for the people of Israel and the Gentile nations, you will realize how marvelously this book fits in with the divine program."[60]

Jesus, prior to His ascension, reminded the disciples that "all things must needs be fulfilled, which are written in the law of Moses, and the prophets, and the Psalms, concerning me" (Luke 24:44 ASV). A study of Genesis to Malachi reveals the progressive message of Messiah's coming primarily cited through prophecies. Note that Jesus includes the Psalms among the writings containing such prophecies. Andrew Bonar wrote, "There is in almost every one of all these Psalms something that fitted them for the use of the past generations of the church and something that fits them admirably for the use of the church now, while also there is diffused throughout a hint for the future. There is, we might say, *a past, a present* and *a future* element. Few of them can be said to have no prophetic reference, no reference to generations or events yet to arise—a circumstance that gives them a claim upon the careful study of everyone who searches into the prophetic records, in addition to the manifold other claims which they possess."[61] See Acts 13:33.

The Messianic Psalms may be divided into five categories: "(1) purely messianic Psalms—e.g., Psalm 110, which refers to a future Davidic king who is the Lord; (2) eschatological Psalms—e.g., Psalms 96–99, which are usually entitled enthronement Psalms and describe the coming of the Lord and His kingdom; (3) typological-prophetic Psalms—e.g., Psalm 22, where the writer describes his own experience which is transcended by that of Jesus the Messiah; (4) indirectly Messianic—e.g., Psalms 2; 45; 72 which were penned for a king of Israel or a royal occasion in general, but their ultimate and climactic fulfillment is realized in Christ; and (5) typical Messianic Psalms—these are less obvious: the psalmist in some sense is a type of Christ (Psalm 34:20), but not all aspects of the Psalm necessarily apply to the Messiah (see also Psalm 109:8; Acts 1:20)."[62] Keil and Delitzsch state, "The Old Testament, according to its very nature, tends toward and centers in Christ. Therefore the innermost truth of the Old Testament has been revealed in the revelation of Jesus Christ, but not all at once: His passion, resurrection and ascension are three steps of this progressive opening up of the Old Testament and of the Psalms in particular."[63]

B. H. Carroll said of the Psalmist's vision of the Messiah, "He saw the uncreated Son, the second Person of the Trinity, in counsel and compact with the Father, arranging in eternity for the salvation of men: Psalm 40:6–8; Hebrews 10:5–7. Then he saw this Holy One stoop to be the Son of Man: Psalm 8:4–6; Hebrews 2:7–9. Then He was the Son of David, and then he saw Him rise again to be the Son of God: Psalm 2:7; Romans 1:3–4."[64] Included in the Psalmist's prophecy was Christ's atoning sacrifice (Psalm 40:6–8; Hebrews 10:5–7); final judgment (Psalm 6:8; Matthew 25:41); visit from the Magi (Psalm 72:9–10; Matthew 2); wilderness temptations (Psalm 91:11–12; Luke 4:10–11); triumphant

Exposition of the Psalms

entry into Jersualem (Psalm 118; Matthew 21:9); corrupt trial (Psalms 27:12; 35:15–16; 38:13; 69:19 and Matthew 26:57–68; 27:26–31); crucifixion (Psalm 22:14–17; Luke 23:33); garments being parted and His vesture being gambled for (Psalm 22:18; Matthew 27:35); thirst and the gall and vinegar being offered (Psalm 69:21; Matthew 27:34); prayers for His enemies (Psalm 109:4; Luke 23:34) and resurrection, victory over death and Hell, ascension into Heaven and exaltation at God's right hand (Psalm 16:8–11; 24:7–10; 68:18; 2:6; 111:1–4; 8:4–6 and Acts 2:25–36; Ephesians 1:19–23; 4:8–10).[65]

The messianic Psalms were fulfilled explicitly in the person and life of Jesus Christ, proving to the gainsayers that He is in fact the long-awaited Savior of the world sent from God the Father. "With regard to the Jews, Bishop Chandler very pertinently remarks that 'they must have understood David their prince to have been a figure of Messiah. They would not otherwise have made his Psalms part of their daily worship; nor would David have delivered them to the church to be so employed, were it not to instruct and support them in the knowledge and belief of this fundamental article. Was the Messiah not concerned in the Psalms, it were absurd to celebrate twice a day in their public devotions the events of one man's life who was deceased so long ago as to have no relation now to the Jews and the circumstances of their affairs, or to transcribe whole passages from them into their prayers for the coming of the Messiah.'"[66]

Composition of the Psalms. With regard to composition, its most important characteristic is its parallelism (a statement that is emphasized or extended by repetition).[67] Within the Psalms there are three forms of paralleisms: synonymous parallelism (the same thought is expressed at least twice in a different way, as in Psalm 49:1); antithetic (contrasted) parallelism (the truth of the first sentence is stressed by contrast in its final clause, as in Psalm 1:6); synthetic (connecting) parallelism (the final teaching of the Psalm completes and expands that of the first sentence, as in Psalm 22:4).[68]

J. M. Boice wrote about the complexity of the Psalms: "I do not know of any book of the Bible that requires more knowledge, more experience of life and more skill of interpretation to understand it well than the Book of Psalms. It is because the Psalms are so diverse. They cover the vast range of biblical theology and the full scope of human experience—from doubt to faith, suffering to jubilation, defeat to victory—and they do so in an amazing variety of poetic forms. The Psalms are so deep, so diverse, so challenging that I do not believe anyone can ever really master them. Moreover, as soon as the student begins to get hold of one type of Psalm and thinks he understands it, he is suddenly confronted with another that is entirely different."[69] Harry Ironside writes, "It is very remarkable the way the Psalms are arranged. They are arranged in divine order. In many instances we find the last verses of the one introducing the theme of the next."[70]

The imprecatory Psalms. The imprecatory Psalms are prayers directed against enemies of David and the Jewish nation but "are not expressions of personal resentment."[71] B. H. Carroll explains: "They are vigorous expressions of righteous indignation against incorrigible enemies of God and His people and are to be interpreted in the light of progressive revelation....These imprecations do not teach that we, even in the worst circumstances, should bear personal malice, nor take vengenance on the the enemies of righteousness, but that we should live so close to God that we may acquiesce in the destruction of the wicked and leave the matter of vengeance in the hands of a just God, to whom vengeance belongs (Romans 12:19–21)."[72]

Profitabilty of the Psalms. The Psalter is a combination praisebook, "how-to" cope handbook, devotional exposition, moral and ethical compass for living life, duty manual and treatise on the infallibility of the Holy Scriptures. It is a book of praise, prayer, precept and promise. Psalms will benefit personal and corporate worship. The Book of the Psalms "can revolutionize our devotional life, our family patterns, and the fellowship and the witness of the church of Jesus Christ."[73] Max Lucado writes, "Worship is a daunting task. For that reason, God gave us the Psalms....Some [Psalms] are defiant. Others are reverent. Some are to be sung. Others are to be prayed. Some are intensely personal. Others are written as if the whole world would use them. Some were penned in caves, others in temples. But all have one purpose—to give us the words to say when we stand before God. The very variety should remind us that worship is personal. No secret formula exists. What moves you may stymie another. Each worships differently, but each should worship."[74]

To maximize the Psalms' effect and impact in worship, personalize them. Make them your own.

J. Vernon McGee stated, "Someone has said that there are 126 psychological experiences....all of them are recorded in the Book of Psalms. It is the only book which contains every experience of a human being. The Psalms run the psychological gamut. Every thought, every impulse, every emotion that sweeps over the soul is recorded in this book."[75] Athanasius, Bishop of Alexandria in the fourth century, wrote: "To me, indeed, it seems that the Psalms are to him who sings them as a mirror, wherein he may see himself and the motions of his soul, and with like feelings utter them. So also one who hears a psalm read takes it as if it were spoken concerning himself, and either, convicted by his own conscience, will be pricked at heart and repent, or else, hearing of that hope which is to God-wards, and the succour which is vouchsafed to them that believe, leaps for joy as though such grace were specially made over to him, and begins to utter his thanksgivings to God."[76] As we read, absorb, and personalize the Psalms, life is lifted to a higher plane spiritually. How wondrous is the thought that the same Psalms that profit us benefited David and others hundreds of years ago when they were first written, as they have myriads since. Though their blossom has been squeezed over and over again by kings and peasants, rich and poor, saint and sinner, their sweet fragrance remains untarnished and undepleted.

Exposition of the Psalms is written in three volumes: Vol. One: Psalms 1–50; Vol. Two: Psalms 51–100; and Vol. Three: Psalms 101–150.

Included with each entry is an *Exposition* of the text; a *Homily*, discourse based upon the Psalm with regard to its application, and *The Bottom Line*, a concise statement or paragraph summarizing the gist of the selected text. The task in selection of the verse(s) to exegete and expound in a homily in each Psalm was daunting and most challenging. In all the expositions I sought to be theologically sound and simple, thorough in exegesis and applicable in homily. To simplify navigation through the Psalms for specific subject matters, each are entitled according to its general or specific theme.

Conservative theological scholars were heavily leaned upon for interpretation of the Hebrew language and its theological and cultural meaning. Such word pictures and meanings opened up the Psalms to new truths and applications not before seen. Spurgeon's observation on the use of commentators in studying Scripture I found encouraging: "In order to be able to expound the Scriptures, and as an aid to your pulpit studies, you will need to be familiar with the commentators: a glorious army, let me tell you, whose acquaintance will be your delight and profit. Of course, you are not such wiseacres as to think or say that you can expound Scripture without assistance from the works of divines and learned men who have labored before you in the field of exposition. If you are of that opinion, pray remain so, for you are not worth the trouble of conversion and like a little coterie [inner circle of friends] who think with you, would resent the attempt as an insult to your infallibility. It seems odd that certain men who talk so much of what the Holy Spirit reveals to themselves should think so little of what he has revealed to others."[77]

My aim in this work was not to do a thorough treatise of the Psalms but to exegete a text from each that is paramount in importance while providing its practical doctrinal and devotional insight and inspiration. It is intended that the intensity of the work upon each text will provide both the minister and teacher inspiration and sufficient foundational exegetical basis for the building of sermons and studies, while providing knowledge and devotional insight to them and to others. Effort was made to limit the repetition of themes to facilitate entry of more subjects.

Why another commentary on the Psalms when hundreds have been written? The bottom line is that it was undertaken out of divine leadership. It was an inescapable work. *Exposition of the Psalms* is different from other commentaries in its focus upon a specific text(s) within each Psalm and in its 4,700 insights gleaned from some of the greatest theologians of history. It is to be viewed not as a replacement for traditional conservative commentaries on the Psalms, but as a supplement. The commentary is based upon the *King James Version* of the Holy Bible.

We are in danger of losing the Book of Psalms in the church. They are being read and sung less in the church. But even sadder, they are being preached less. I was heartbroken to read of a homiletics professor who stated that the Psalms "do not want" to be preached from. He that neglects preaching from the Psalter robs his people of what C. H. Spurgeon called *The Treasury of David*. The Book of Psalms contains many "pearls of great price" that beg to be preached! In this work the minister is presented with the necessary "lumber" with which to build sound expository sermons upon them.

Major contributing theologians to this work include Charles Haddon Spurgeon, W. S. Plumer, J. J. S. Perowne, A. F. Kirkpatrick, Albert Barnes, Matthew Henry, Matthew Poole, Joseph Benson, John Gill, W. A. Criswell, John MacArthur, J. Montgomery Boice, William A. VanGemeren, William Barclay, George Rawlinson, Adam Clarke, Martin Luther, John Calvin, Charles John Ellicott, Robert Jamieson, Andrew Robert Fausset, David Brown, Alexander Maclaren , Charles Bridges, Charles Simeon, Robert Bratcher, William Reyburn, Leslie C. Allen, John Walvoord, Roy Zuck, George Horne, Karl F. Keil, Franz Delitzsch, J. A. Alexander, P. C. Craigie, D. Williams, L. J. Ogilvie, William MacDonald, E. E. Hinson, W. M. Kroll, Warren Wierbe, Billy Graham, John Stott, W. A. Elwell, T. W. Comfort, Adrian Rogers, M. E. Tate, Herbert Lockyer, E. W. Bullinger, Derek Kidner, Allen Ross, John Trapp, James Coffman, R. Ellinsworth, Daniel Whedon, Thomas Watson, R. Whitaker, F. Brown, S. R. Driver, R. L. Harris, G. L. Archer, B. K. Waltke, W. P. Holladay, L. Kohler, M. D. Futato, W. Gesenius, S. P. Tregelles, J. Swanson, G. M. Landes, J. Strong, W. E. Vine, M. F. Unger, W. White, Jr., Joseph Parker and J. I. Packer.

Untranslated Hebrew Words Used in the Titles of Some of the Psalms

From *Handbook to the Old Testament*
W. Scott, page 238.

Aijeleth-Shahar (Psalm 22)	The hind of the morning
Alamoth (Psalm 46)	Virginals
Al-taschith (Psalm 57, 58, 59, 75)	Destroy not
Degree (Psalm 120–134)	To go up, ascend
Gittith (Psalm 8, 81, 84)	The wine-vat
Higgaion (Psalm 9:16)	Meditation
Jonath-Elem-Rechokim (Psalm 56)	Dove dumb (among) stranger
Mahalath (Psalm 53)	Disease
Mahalath Leannoth (Psalm 88)	Bitter disease
Maschil (Psalm 32, 42, 44, 45, 52, 53, 54, 55, 74, 78, 88, 89, 142)	To instruct
Michtam (Psalm 16, 56–60)	Golden (psalm)
Neginah (Psalm 61)	A stringed instrument
Neginoth (Psalm 4, 6, 54, 55, 67, 76)	The stringed instruments
Nehiloth (Psalm 5)	The pipes
Selah (Psalm 3:2, 4, 8, etc.)	Pause [meaning is uncertain]
Sheminith (Psalm 6, 12)	Eight-stringed instrument
Shiggaion (Psalm 7)	Wandering ode
Shoshannim (Psalm 45, 80)	The lilies
Shushan Eduth (Psalm 60)	The lily of the testimony[78]

Psalms Quoted in the New Testament[79]

Psalm 2:1–2	Acts 4:25–26
Psalm 2:7	Acts 13:33
Psalm 2:9	Revelation 2:27
Psalm 4:4	Ephesians 4:26
Psalm 5:9	Romans 3:13
Psalm 6:8	Matthew 7:23
Psalm 8:2	Matthew 21:16
Psalm 8:4–6	Hebrews 2:6–8
Psalm 8:6	1 Corinthians 15:27
Psalm 10:7	Romans 3:14
Psalm 14:3	Romans 3:10
Psalm 16:8	Acts 2:25
Psalm 16:10	Acts 13:35
Psalm 18:49	Romans 15:9
Psalm 19:4	Romans 10:18
Psalm 22:1	Matthew 27:46
Psalm 22:7	Matthew 27:39
Psalm 22:8	Matthew 27:43
Psalm 22:18	John 19:24
Psalm 22:18	Matthew 27:35
Psalm 22:22	Hebrews 2:12
Psalm 24:1	1 Corinthians 10:26
Psalm 31:5	Luke 23:46
Psalm 32:1–2	Romans 4:7–8
Psalm 34:8	1 Peter 2:3
Psalm 34:12	1 Peter 3:10
Psalm 34:20	John 19:36
Psalm 35:19	John 15:25
Psalm 36:1	Romans 3:18
Psalm 37:11	Matthew 5:5
Pslam 38:11	Luke 23:49
Psalm 40:6–8	Hebrews 10:5–7
Psalm 41:9	John 13:18
Psalm 41:13	Luke 1:68
Psalm 42:5	Matthew 26:38
Psalm 44:22	Romans 8:36

Psalms Quoted in the New Testament

Psalm 45:6–7	Hebrews 1:8–9
Psalm 48:2	Matthew 5:35
Psalm 51:4	Romans 3:4
Psalm 53:1–3	Romans 3:10–12
Psalm 55:22	1 Peter 5:7
Psalm 62:12	Matthew 16:27
Psalm 68:18	Ephesians 4:8
Psalm 69:4	John 15:25
Psalm 69:9	Romans 15:3
Psalm 69:9	John 2:17
Psalm 69:22–23	Romans 11:9–10
Psalm 69:25	Acts 1:20
Psalm 72:18	Luke 1:68
Psalm 78:2	Matthew 13:35
Psalm 78:24	John 6:31
Psalm 82:6	John 10:34
Psalm 86:9	Revelation 15:4
Psalm 88:8	Luke 23:49
Psalm 89:10	Luke 1:51
Psalm 89:20	Acts 13:22
Psalm 90:4	2 Peter 3:8
Psalm 91:11–12	Matthew 4:6
Psalm 91:13	Luke 10:19
Psalm 94:11	1 Corinthians 3:20
Psalm 94:14	Romans 11:1–2
Psalm 95:7–11	Hebrews 3:7–11
Psalm 97:7	Hebrews 1:6
Psalm 98:3	Luke 1:54
Psalm 102:25–27	Hebrews 1:10–12
Psalm 103:17	Luke 1:50
Psalm 104:4	Hebrews 1:7
Psalm 105:8–9	Luke 1:72–73
Psalm 106:10	Luke 1:71
Psalm 106:45	Luke 1:72
Psalm 106:48	Luke 1:68
Psalm 107:9	Luke 1:53
Psalm 109:3	John 15:25

Psalm 109:8	Acts 1:20
Psalm 109:25	Matthew 27:39
Psalm 110:1	Matthew 22:44; Mark 12:36; Luke 20:42
Psalm 110:4	Hebrews 5:6
Psalm 111:9	Luke 1:68
Psalm 111:9	Luke 1:49
Psalm 112:9	2 Corinthians 9:9
Psalm 116:10	2 Corinthians 4:13
Psalm 117:1	Romans 15:11
Psalm 118:6	Hebrews 13:6
Psalm 118:22–23	Matthew 21:42
Psalm 118:26	Matthew 21:9
Psalm 132:5	Acts 7:46
Psalm 132:11	Acts 2:30
Psalm 132:17	Luke 1:69
Psalm 135:14	Hebrews 10:30
Psalm 140:3	Romans 3:13
Psalm 143:2	Romans 3:20
Psalm 146:6	Acts 4:24; 14:15

1. Repentance Psalm 51:1–4

"Have mercy upon me, O God, according to thy lovingkindness: according unto the multitude of thy tender mercies blot out my transgressions. Wash me throughly from mine iniquity, and cleanse me from my sin. For I acknowledge my transgressions: and my sin is ever before me. Against thee, thee only, have I sinned, and done this evil in thy sight: that thou mightest be justified when thou speakest, and be clear when thou judgest."—Psalm 51:1–4.

"Have mercy" (Bratcher and Reyburn say "it means to show favor, to be kindly disposed [see Psalm 4:1c, where the same verb is translated 'Be gracious'].")[80] Plumer says "equivalent to undeserved favor. It always implies pity to the miserable; commonly, grace to the guilty."[81]) upon "me" (The confession is deeply personal.) "O God" (Rawlinson says, "It is observable that the whole Psalm is addressed to God *[Elohim],* and not to Jehovah [the 'Lord' in verse 15 is *Adonai*], as though the Psalmist felt himself unworthy to utter the covenant name and simply prostrated himself as a guilty man before his offended Maker."[82]).

"According to thy lovingkindness" (Barnes says "the mercy of God."[83] Gill says "not according to his merits, nor according to the general mercy of God, which carnal men rely upon; but according to his everlasting and unchangeable love in Christ; from which as the source, and through whom as the medium, special mercy comes to the children of men"[84]). According unto "the multitude of thy tender mercies" (Kirkpatrick says "or, according to the abundance of thy compassions. See Psalm 25:6; Isaiah 63:7; Lamentations 3:32; 1 Peter 1:3."[85]).

"Blot out my transgressions" (Benson says, "The word properly signifies to wipe out, or to wipe anything absolutely clean, as a person wipes a dish."[86] It is to erase from a register or book, as in Exodus 32:32–33. See Psalm 69:28.[87] To blot out or erase a debt recorded in a book.[88] Poole says "either, out of my conscience and soul, where it hath left a stain and filthy character, or, out of Thy book of remembrance and accounts, in which all men's sins are written, and out of which all men shall be judged hereafter"[89]). Harman summarizes the cluster of words relating to sin and forgiveness in Psalm 51:1–2:

transgression: rebellious actions against authority;

iniquity: what is crooked or bent;

sin: missing the mark;

have mercy: request speaks of graciousness beyond expectation;

unfailing love: the term of covenantal commitment;

compassion: the word describing the tenderest love;

blot out: complete removal;

wash away: used of scrubbing clothes and removing all stains;

cleanse: a ritual term for pronouncing someone clean.[90]

"For I acknowledge" (Jennings and Lowe say "I am continually conscious of"[91]). "Transgressions" (The first of three words depicting sin. Bratcher and Reyburn say transgressions "are primarily acts of disobedience, of rebellion."[92] Implies "a willful throwing off of authority or restraint."[93] Jennings and Lowe say, "i.e., my acts of deliberate rebellion against Thee" [94]). "Wash me" (Bratcher and Reyburn say, "...'wash' represents sin as a stain that has to be washed out; the verb expresses the way in which clothes were washed by being beaten against rocks to remove the dirt."[95] Rawlinson says "wash me, as a fuller washes a fouled garment, not as a man washes his skin"[96]).

"Throughly" (Barnes says "suggests the idea of 'multiplying' or 'increasing.' The reference is to that which might need constant or repeated washings in order to remove a stain. The word is used, however, adverbially to denote intensity, or thoroughness."[97] Gill says, "David's sin had long lain upon him, the faith of it had as it were eaten into him, and spread itself over him, and therefore he needed much washing: 'wash me much,' all over, and thoroughly."[98]) "mine iniquity" (Bratcher and Reyburn say "is guilt, fault, a deliberate act of misconduct."[99]).

AND "cleanse me" (to make pure or completely "white" on the inside, which only the blood of Jesus Christ can do. See 1 John 1:7.) "from my sin" (missing the mark or straying off course of God's expectations and holy commands regarding righteousness or upright conduct.) For "I acknowledge" (Inwardly David knows his sinfulness, has faced up to the fact of it, and now does so to God.) "my transgressions" (Note the plural of the word. David's sin was multiple: the adultery with Bathsheba, the lies to and the murder of her husband.) AND "my sin is ever before me" (David's sin was relentlessly tormenting guilt to his conscience that was awakened by Nathan [2 Samuel 12:7].)

"Against thee only, I have sinned, and done this evil in thy sight" (Rawlinson says, "Though no sins could be more directly against man than adultery and murder, yet David feels that that aspect of them shrinks away into insignificance, and is as if it were not, when they are viewed in their true and real character, as offences against the majesty of God. Every sin is mainly against God."[100] See 2 Samuel 12:13 and Genesis 39:9. Benson says, "Which is not to be understood absolutely, because he had sinned against Bathsheba and Uriah, and many others; but comparatively. So the sense is, though I have sinned against my own conscience, and against others, yet nothing is more grievous to me than that I have sinned against thee."[101] David's sin for the moment seemed so enormous and heinous against God that "he lost sight of it considered in any other of its bearings. It 'was' a sin, as all other sins are, primarily and mainly against God; it derived its chief enormity from that fact. We are not to suppose that David did not believe and notice that he had done wrong to people, or that he had offended against human laws, and against the well-being of society. His crime against Uriah and his family was of the deepest and most aggravated character, but still the offence derived its chief heinousness from the fact that it was a violation of the law of God. The state of mind here illustrated is that which occurs in every case of true penitence."[102]).

THAT "thou mightest be justified when thou speakest, and be clear when thou judgest" (David is stating that the punishment that God renders for his sins is just and deserved and righteous. Poole paraphrases David, "This will be the fruit or consequent of my sin, that whatsoever severities thou shalt use towards me and mine, it will be no blemish to Thy benignity [quality of kindness], or righteousness, or fidelity, but the blame of all will rest upon my head as I desire it may, and Thy justice will be glorified by all men."[103] Patrick's paraphrase, "If thou shouldn't pronounce the heaviest sentence upon me for my crimes, and execute it with the greatest severity, I could not accuse Thee of too much rigor, but must still justify Thee in Thy proceedings, and clear Thee from all such unjust imputations."[104]).

Ironside says, "David prays, 'Take not Thy Holy Spirit from me." No well-instructed Christian would pray that today, for we know now that we have received the Holy Spirit to abide with us forever. We have been sealed Lord Jesus, by His sacrificial death upon the Cross, has rent the veil by the Holy Spirit until the redemption of the purchased possession. And then there are a great many of the prayers in the book of Psalms that imply a hidden God. But today God has come out into the light, since our and opened up the way into the immediate presence of God for poor sinners and enabled God to come out to man in all the perfection of His glorious Person."[105] (See Matthew 27:51; Hebrews 10:19–22.)

Homily

A Psalm of David. The Psalm is rightly called *The Sinner's Guide*.[106] It ought to be connected with 2 Samuel 11:2–12:24. Spurgeon says, "David's horrible sin had stained him and left him needing to be washed. I do not know where we have record [in Holy Scriptures] of a worse sin committed by one who yet was a true child of God. He had good reason to pray to the Lord, 'Wash me,' for he had a special and peculiar stain. The power of Jesus Christ to cleanse from sin must lie, first in the greatness of His person."[107] He was none other than the Son of God, the awesome Creator of all that exists who conquered death upon the cross to make possible the redemption of man. Jesus alone has power to make the blackest sinner "so clean they are 'whiter than snow.'"[108]

In Psalm 32 David bewails the consequence of adultery and murder. (See notes there.) Here, a year after the sins he is compelled to face them by Nathan and is crushed deeply beneath their weight. He had lost "joy and gladness." George Horne states, "Next to the blessing of forgiveness is to be desired that joy and comfort in the conscience which forgiveness only can inspire: the effect of this, in repairing the vigor of the spirit, decayed through sorrow and anguish, is compared to setting broken bones, and restoring them again to perfect strength."[109] The acknowledgement of the sins smites his conscience with burning, relentless guilt prompting genuine, heartfelt godly sorrow for them and the pleading with all his being for abundant ("multitude of thy tender mercies") mercy and grace for forgiveness and restoration. He engages in true repentance.

David uses three words to depict his wicked behavior. *Transgressions* depict rebellious behavior, acts of disobedience. *Iniquity* is waywardness;[110] "the perversion of right, depravity of conduct"[111]); *Sin* is failure[112]; "error, wandering from the right way, missing the mark in

4

life."[113] "Transgressions," "iniquity," "sin," cover every form of moral evil, and, united together, imply the deepest guilt.[114] The same three words David uses to express the sinfulness of his heart are the ones used by God in Exodus 34:7 when He declares Himself to be a sin-forgiving God.[115]

The Psalm denotes the biblical blueprint for repentance following sin. *Blot out my transgressions.* "'Transgressions' is plural—sins, trespasses. Discontent, ingratitude, covetousness, hardness of heart, selfishness, pride, worldliness, unbelief, adultery and murder were all chargeable to David in the matter of Uriah. A clear sight of one sin is sure to show us others."[116] *For I acknowledge.* Luther said, "That little word *for* must be so understood as not to imply that his sins must be forgiven him because he had confessed them; for sin is always sin, and deserving of punishment, whether it is confessed or not; still confession of sin is of importance on this account, that God will be gracious to no one, but to those who confess their sin; while to those who do not confess their sin, he will show no favor."[117] David exhibited a broken, crushed heart with regard to his sin.

My sin is ever before me. He did not cast blame upon another (i.e., "It was Bathsheba's fault.") but took full responsibility for his actions. There was no effort to excuse the sins or to vindicate his conduct.[118] Horne states, "The penitent's second plea for mercy is, that he doth not deny, excuse, or palliate [Dictionary.com says, 'to try to mitigate or conceal the gravity of (an offense) by excuses, apologies, etc.] his fault, but confesses it openly and honestly, with all its aggravations, truly alleging, that it haunts him night and day, causing his conscience incessantly to reproach him with his base ingratitude to a good and gracious Father."[119]

Against thee, thee only, have I sinned. David is neither forgetful nor unremorseful that his sinful conduct was against Bathsheba and Uriah but realizes that it especially, specifically was against Holy God, the supreme Ruler and Judge of the entire world. W. S. Plumer said, "All sin is against God in this sense that it is His law that is broken, His authority that is despised, His government that is set at naught."[120] Oswald Chambers wrote, "Very few of us know anything about conviction of sin. We know the experience of being disturbed because we have done wrong things. But conviction of sin by the Holy Spirit blots out every

5

relationship on earth and makes us aware of only one—'Against You, You only, have I sinned...(Psalm 51:4).'"[121] J. A. Alexander remarked, "Even murder, the highest crime that can be committed against man, is condemned and punished as the violation of God's image (Genesis 9:6). It is also possible to understand 'thee, thee only,' as opposed not to other objects, but to the sinner himself, as one of two contending parties. As if he had said, thou hast not sinned against me, but I have sinned against thee, thee only."[122] Scripture is clear that sin against others ought to be set right if possible (the thief on the cross with Jesus obviously did not have the opportunity to request forgiveness from those he had injured). See James 5:16 and Matthew 5:23–24.

Wash me thoroughly from mine iniquity and cleanse me from my sin. David pleads for the mercy and lovingkindness of God to *blot out* his sin (as a debt in a book that is erased or marked "paid in full"), *wash out* his sin (as a deep stain is washed away from a garment; pictures women at the river bank beating their soiled garments against the rocks until they are clean), and *cleanse out* his sin (sin is pictured as a moral leprosy that can only be healed by the direct pronouncement of God[123]). He wants God to pronounce him "clean." See Jeremiah 31:34.

Spurgeon makes a good observation with regard to David's cry to God to *wash me thoroughly*. "He would have God Himself cleanse him....The washing must be thorough, it must be repeated, therefore he cries, 'Multiply to wash me.'...The hypocrite is content if his garment is washed, but the true suppliant cries, '*Wash me.*'...[T]he truly awakened conscience desires a real and practical washing, and that of a most complete and efficient kind....He desires to be rid of the whole mass of his filthiness."[124] J. A. Alexander said, "The image here presented, therefore, is the same as in Jude 23, sin being represented as a stain, and the grace of God as purifying water."[125]

> Lord Jesus, let nothing unholy remain;
> Apply Thine own blood and extract every stain.
> To get this blest cleansing I all things forgo;
> Now wash me, and I shall be whiter than snow.
> Whiter than snow, yes, whiter than snow;
> Now wash me and I shall be whiter than snow.
> ~ William G. Fischer (1872)

David couches his repentance upon *thy lovingkindness* (God's unfailing love and mercy). Albert Barnes comments, "The only hope of a sinner when crushed with the consciousness of sin is the mercy of God; and the plea for that mercy will be urged in the most earnest and impassioned language that the mind can employ."[126] And secondly it is based upon *thy multitude of thy tender mercies*. David pleads plenteous and extraordinary mercy based upon all God's prior work in that regard toward man. Albert Barnes says this was "a ground of hope that his appeal would not be rejected. So to us: every instance in which a great sinner has been forgiven is evidence that we may be forgiven also, and is an encouragement to us to come to God for pardon."[127]

David wanted the mercy of God. Adam Clarke remarked, "Without mercy I am totally, finally ruined and undone."[128] John Gill observes, "The Psalmist makes mention of the multitude of the mercies of God, because of the multitude of his sins, which required a multitude of mercy to forgive, and to encourage his hope of it."[129] J. A. Alexander states, "Here again there is a tacit admission of the greatness of his guilt, as requiring infinite mercy to forgive it."[130]

Then will I teach transgressors thy ways; and sinners shall be converted unto thee. See Psalm 51:13. Upon restoration David exclaims that he will witness of God's grace and goodness to others. Matthew Henry wrote, "When Solomon became a penitent he immediately became a preacher, Ecclesiastes 1:1. Those are best able to teach others the grace of God who have themselves had the experience of it: and those who are themselves taught of God ought to tell others what he has done for their souls (Psalm 66:16) and so teach them."[131]

The heartfelt penitent prayer of the Psalmist results in cleansing and restoration. See Psalm 32:1–2. South said, "True repentance has a double aspect; it looks upon things past with a weeping eye, and upon the future with a watchful eye."[132]

With Barnes, I can't help but wonder why the heinousness of David's double sin did not trouble him "before" Nathan's confrontation. It but goes to show that people may be guilty of enormous sins without impact on their conscience for months or years, only to burn with relentless guilt once awakened by the Holy Spirit that nothing will calm.[133]

Such mandates the preaching against sin by its particular names that it will be as a "Nathan" to awaken the conscience to the wrong done.

The Bottom Line: David is proof there is life after even the most heinous sin. Man's basis for forgiveness of sin is *consciousness of it* (awareness of sin is the first step to repentance and restoration), *contrition over it* (brokenness and sorrow for it), *confession and petition about it* (acknowledgement to God of the sin couched in pleas for His undeserved and unmerited mercy, pity, and grace for its forgiveness provided through the blood of Jesus Christ). As David, exhibit *confidence or trust in the Lord* that in thus praying you will be purged of the sin and be made clean and "shall be whiter than snow" (Psalm 51:7). "Christ receiveth sinful men, even me with all my sin." Hallelujah! See 1 John 1:7–10. Matthew Henry urges caution: "Many mourn for their sins that do not truly repent of them; weep bitterly for them, and yet continue in love and league with them."[134]

2. The Consequences of Sin Psalm 51:2–3, 8, 10, 12–13, 15

"Wash me thoroughly from mine iniquity, and cleanse me from my sin....[M]y sin is ever before me....Make me to hear joy and gladness; that the bones which thou hast broken may rejoice....Create in me a clean heart, O God; and renew a right spirit within me. Restore unto me the joy of thy salvation; and uphold me with thy free spirit. Then will I teach transgressors thy ways; and sinners shall be converted unto thee....O Lord, open thou my lips; and my mouth shall shew forth thy praise."—Psalm 51:2-3, 8, 10, 12–13, 15.

"Wash me thoroughly from mine iniquity, and cleanse me from my sin....[M]y sin is ever before me." (See notes on Psalm 51:1–4). Make me to "hear joy and gladness" (Alexander says, "The joy here anticipated is that of pardoned sin....He expects to hear it, as communicated or announced by God."[135] David is confident that God will answer.) "that the bones which thou hast broken" (Alexander says that in the Hebrew the term is an "emphatic figure, *crushed or broken*, which expresses, in a very lively manner, the disorder and distress produced by consciousness of aggravated and unexpiated guilt."[136]) may rejoice.

"Create" (Spurgeon says, "I, in my outward fabric, still exist; but I am empty, desert, void. Come, then, and let Thy power be seen in a new creation within my old fallen self."[137] Horne says, "The purification and renovation of the heart and spirit of a man is a work to which that power only is equal which, in the beginning, created all things, and, in the end, will create all things new."[138] Benson says, "Seeing I have not only defiled myself by these actual sins, but also have a most unclean heart, corrupt even from my birth, which nothing but Thy almighty, new-creating power can purify; I beseech Thee to exert that power to produce in me a new and holy frame of heart, free from those impure inclinations and vile affections, the effects of which I have too fatally felt."[139])

In me a clean heart, O God; AND "renew a right spirit within me" (Alexander says, "The word *renew* implies a previous possession of it, derived not from nature but from grace, and interrupted by his yielding to temptation. Though his faith and love could not utterly fail, his fixedness of purpose was destroyed for the time, and could only be recovered by a new conversion [not as in salvation but in heart disposition], as in the case of Peter."[140] Smith says, "Renew within me a steadfast mind, a mind steady in following the path of duty, an unyielding spirit. To have a mind always set on God!"[141])

"Restore unto me" (Vine, Unger & White say "'to return or go back, bring back....The basic meaning of the verb is movement back to the point of departure."[142]) "the joy of thy salvation" (Poole says "'the comfortable sense of thy saving grace and help, promised and vouchsafed to me, both for my present and everlasting salvation."[143]).

AND "uphold me with thy free spirit" (Rawlinson says, "And uphold me with thy free spirit. There is no 'thy' in the original; and it is his own spirit, not God's Spirit, of which the Psalmist here speaks. 'Uphold me,' he says; 'preserve me from falling, by giving me a "free," or "generous," or "noble" spirit—the opposite of that "spirit of bondage" which the apostle says that Christians do not receive [Romans 8:15].'"[144]).

"Then will I teach transgressors" (Horne says, "He that would employ his abilities, his influence, and his authority, in the reformation of others, must take care to reform himself, before he enters upon the work. 'When thou art converted,' said Christ to St. Peter, 'strengthen thy brethren' [Luke 22:32]. The history of David has 'taught' us many useful lessons; such as the frailty of man, the danger of temptation, the torment of sin, the nature and efficacy of repentance, the mercy and the judgments of God by which many 'sinners' have in all ages since been 'converted,' and many more will be converted, so long as the Scriptures shall be read, and the fifty-first Psalm recited in the church."[145]

Teach. Perowne says, "The form is optative, and expresses that which he desires to do, as an evidence of his gratitude, and as knowing how greatly his sin must have been a stumbling-block to others. Terrible had been the fruit of his sin, not only in the wasting of his own soul, but in the injury done to others. Terrible was his punishment in witnessing this; and therefore the more anxious is he, though he cannot undo his own sin, to heal the breach, and repair the evil of sin in other souls."[146] *Transgressors.* Alexander says, "Transgressors, rebels, traitors, apostates."[147]) "thy ways" (Perowne says, "i.e., the ways of God's commandments, in which He would have men walk."[148]).

AND "sinners shall be converted unto thee" (Barnes says, "They would see from his case the evil of transgression; they would learn from his example that mercy might be found; they would be persuaded to flee from the wrath to come. The best preparation for success in winning souls to God, and turning them from the error of their ways, is a deep personal experience of the guilt and the danger of sin, and of the great mercy of God in its forgiveness. No man can hope to be successful who has not experienced this in his own soul; no one who has, will labor wholly in vain in such a work."[149]).

O Lord, "open thou my lips; and my mouth shall shew forth thy praise" (Perowne says, "His lips had been sealed by sin, but God, by His free forgiveness, would give him fresh cause of rejoicing, and so would open them. Calvin compares Psalm 40:4, where the Psalmist says that God had put a new song in his mouth. David thus prays God to be gracious, that he may be the loud herald of that grace to others, 'My mouth shall declare.'"[150] Spurgeon says, "He fears to speak till the Lord unstops his shame-silenced mouth. This prayer of a penitent is a golden petition for a preacher. But it may stand for anyone whose shame for sin

10

makes him stammer in his prayers, and when it is fully answered the tongue of the dumb begins to sing."[151]).

Homily

The Psalm depicts the consequences of the sin of the unrepentant (as was David for nearly a year). Chuck Swindoll wrote, "Some of the most difficult experiences for the Christian emerge in the backwash of sin. There are two kinds of suffering in the midst of the whirlwind: the kind of suffering we deserve because we were the ones who disobeyed; and the kind of suffering we don't deserve but experience in the backwash of someone else's transgression."[152] See Hosea 8:7 and Galatians 6:7–8.

David's sin with Bathsheba came with a bitter price both for her and himself. See 2 Samuel 11. What sin cost David, it will cost every man.

It costs a soiled heart. David prays "Wash me thoroughly from mine iniquity, and cleanse me from my sin" (Psalm 51:2). It is impossible to violate God's commandments without dirtying the heart with the filthiness of its abomination.

It costs a stinging conscience. "My sin is ever before me" (Psalm 51:3). When a "Nathan" (a sermon, witness, Holy Scripture) awakens the conscience to the wrong committed, as was David's through the agency of the Holy Spirit, the conscience is set on fire with burning guilt. Matthew Henry states, "David had such a deep sense of his sin that he was continually thinking of it, with sorrow and shame....His sin was committed against God, whose truth we deny by willful sin; with Him we deal deceitfully."[153] Albert Barnes says, "The memory of his guilt followed him; it pressed upon him; it haunted him. It was no wonder that this was so....Everything reminds the soul of it; and nothing will drive away its recollection. In such a state the sinner has no refuge—no hope of permanent peace—but in the mercy of God."[154]

It costs a sickened body. "Make me to hear joy and gladness; that the bones which thou hast broken may rejoice" (Psalm 51:8). Ellicott clarifies, "Through his whole being the Psalmist has felt the crushing weight of sin; to its very fibers, as we say, his frame has suffered."[155] Ross says, "Bones denotes one's whole physical structure, the person himself.

11

To say that one's bones are in agony is to say emphatically that his body is wracked with pain. This is often mentioned in the Psalms (Psalms 31:10; 32:3; 38:3; 42:10; 102:3, 5)."[156] The weight of sin upon the soul causes such mental anguish and stress, it effects the body.

It costs a spoiled testimony. Nathan told David, "Because by this deed thou hast given great occasion to the enemies of the LORD to blaspheme" (2 Samuel 12:14). What sin undoes to the reputation in moments takes years to restore. David is yet reeling from his double sin.

It costs a sad disposition. "Make me to hear joy and gladness" (Psalm 51:8). Under the weight of sin and its condemnation, joy is absent. All is despair and disgust. The backslider is the unhappiest person on earth. David prays similarly again in Psalm 51:12: "Restore unto me the joy of thy salvation."

It costs a shut mouth. "O Lord, open thou my lips; and my mouth shall shew forth thy praise....Then will I teach transgressors thy ways; and sinners shall be converted unto thee" (Psalm 51:15, 13). "'Open thou my lips,'" Benson says, "which are shut with shame, and grief, and horror. Restore unto me the opportunity, ability, and liberty which I formerly had of speaking to thee in prayer and praise, and to my fellow-creatures, by way of instruction, reproof, or exhortation, with freedom and boldness."[157] Sin seals the lips from testifying of the goodness of the Lord and from singing praises unto His name. Sin smothers and stifles testimony and praise.

It costs a severed fellowship with the Lord. "Renew a right spirit within me" (Psalm 51:10). "Renew—implies that he had possessed it; the essential principle of a new nature had not been lost, but its influence interrupted (Luke 22:32); for Psalm 51:11 shows that he had not lost God's presence and Spirit (1 Samuel 16:13), though he had lost the 'joy of his salvation' (Psalm 51:12), for whose return he prays."[158] Barnes says, "The language is that of one who had done right formerly, but who had fallen into sin, and who desired that he might be brought back into his former condition."[159] See John 15:5–7. Job prayed likewise, "Oh that I were as in months past...[w]hen his candle shined upon my head, and when by his light I walked through darkness" (Job 29:2–3).

The whirlwind of sin's backwash

David's baby was seriously ill, so he fasted and prayed unto God for the child's healing. The child died. Upon hearing the news, David took a bath, put on fresh garments, and went into the house of God and worshiped. Upon returning home, he broke his fast and enjoyed a good meal (2 Samuel 12:20–21). David's servants were puzzled, failing to understand how he so soon could return to some normalcy of life. "David said, 'I fasted and wept while the child was alive, for I said, "Perhaps the LORD will be gracious to me and let the child live." But why should I fast when he is dead? Can I bring him back again? I will go to him one day, but he cannot return to me.'" See 2 Samuel 12:22–23 NLT. You need to do what King David did following repentance in the backwash of sin.

David engaged in prayer.

Sorrow for sin and its consequences ought to bring us to our knees, for the believer's true source of healing, strength and comfort comes through prayer from the throne of God. David's time of prayer was alone in his house initially in total solitude. Chuck Swindoll makes great application from David's experience. "I learned that when I go through the whirlwind, I should be still and quiet. I should not announce or advertise everything I'm going through. We Christians tend to tell everything, just dump it all out, rather indiscriminately, when, really, it isn't everyone's business."[160]

David returned to church.

In addition to the worship of God, it provides support from fellow believers, some of whom have walked in similar steps. Lean heavy upon them for support and encouragement.

David also rested upon the Bible.

Chuck Swindoll says he "settled his case with God as he rested in the truth of God's Word."[161] Especially in the "storms" do not allow knee-jerk reactions of the flesh to direct your life. Rely upon the sure compass of Holy Scripture to guide and its promises to console. "There is no counsel like God's counsel, no comfort like His comfort, no wisdom more profound than the wisdom of the Scriptures!"[162]

> There is no counsel like God's counsel, no comfort like His comfort, no wisdom more profound than the wisdom of the Scriptures!

To summarize, the pleasure of sin for a "season" exacts a painful price. Just ask David. It is best before an act of sin to ponder its long-term consequences. Sin's cure is confession that leads to its cleansing. See notes on Psalm 51:1–4. Prompt penitent confession of sin may prevent its deplorable and devastating consequences. J. I. Packer comments, "Repentance is more than just sorrow for the past; repentance is a change of mind and heart, a new life of denying self and serving the Savior as King in self's place."[163] Ride out the storm in prayer, church and resting upon the Word of God.

> The Christian ministry is the only profession in the world in which the message and the messenger are inseparable.
> Dr. Ritson

The Bottom Line: Jeremy Taylor said, "It is the greatest and dearest blessing that ever God gave to men, that they may repent; and therefore to deny or to delay it is to refuse health when brought by the skill of the physician—to refuse liberty offered to us by our gracious Lord."[164] "The Christian ministry is the only profession in the world in which the message and the messenger are inseparable."[165]

3. The Slanderous Tongue   Psalm 52:2–4

"Thy tongue deviseth mischiefs; like a sharp razor, working deceitfully. Thou lovest evil more than good; and lying rather than to speak righteousness. Selah. Thou lovest all devouring words, O thou deceitful tongue."—Psalm 52:2–4.

The tongue "deviseth mischiefs" (VanGemeren says "plots destruction."[166] Bratcher and Reyburn say the "plotting of ruin of other people with lies."[167] Sins of the tongue include slander, lies, defamation and deceit.) like a "sharp razor" (Barnes says, "His slanders were like a sharp knife with which one stabs another. So we say of a slanderer that he 'stabs' another in the dark."[168] Kirkpatrick says "like a *whetted razor*, which cuts you before you are aware, as you handle it incautiously. The tongue and its words are elsewhere compared to swords and spears and arrows (Psalm 55:21, Psalm 57:4, Psalm 59:7, Psalm 64:3; Proverbs 26:18)."[169]).

"Working deceitfully" ("lying" [TEV]; "slander" [FRCL]; or "bad things" [SPCL]. Poole says "wherewith a man pretending only to shave off the hair, doth suddenly and unexpectedly cut the throat. So Doeg pretended only to vindicate himself from the imputation of disloyalty, [1 Samuel 22:8], but really intended to expose the priests, who were friends to David, to the king's fury and cruelty."[170] Clarke says, "His tongue was deceitful; he pretended friendship while his heart was full of enmity."[171]).

"Thou lovest evil more than good" (Kirkpatrick says "evil rather than good, evil and not good. The meaning is not merely that he has a preference for evil, but that he chooses evil instead of good, like the nobles censured in Micah 3:2, 'who hate the good and love the evil.'"[172] The wicked prefer to bring harm to others, instead of good.[173] Rawlinson says, "To 'love evil' is to have reached the lowest depth of depravity. It is to say, with Milton's Satan, 'Evil, be thou my good!'"[174]).

AND "lying rather than to speak righteousness" (Doeg before King Saul engaged in "lying rather than to speak righteousness; as appears by his affirming that Ahimelech inquired of the Lord for David, when he did not [1 Samuel 22:10]; and by suffering some things to pass for truths which were falsehoods, when it lay in his power to have disproved them."[175] *Speak righteousness*, Poole says "(i.e.) the whole and naked truth, without any such lying or malicious comment upon it."[176] "Selah" (Spiritually it may mean to take a moment to pause, to ponder what has been said.)

Thou "lovest all devouring words" (Ellicott says "literally, words of swallowing, such as swallow down [Psalm 5:9, where the throat is called 'an open sepulcher'] a neighbor's life, honor, and goods."[177] Spurgeon says, "There are words that, like boa-constrictors, swallow people whole;...these words evil minds are fond of."[178] Rawlinson says

15

"words that cause ruin and destruction."[179] It also may be taken to mean words that cause confusion.[180] Jennings and Lowe say "lit. 'words of swallowing up,' i.e. malicious conversation tending to undermine the character and reputation of others."[181]) O "thou deceitful tongue" (Spurgeon says, "Men can manage to say a great many furious things, and yet cover all over with the pretext of justice. They claim they are jealous for the right, but the truth is, they are determined to put down truth and holiness."[182]).

Homily

The occasion for the Psalm was David's flight to Nob to see the priest Ahimelech for food and weapon (1 Samuel 21:1–9). He received "hallowed bread" and the sword with which he had slain Goliath. Doeg the Edomite ("a servant of King Saul") witnessed what David requested and received. David, in fear that Doeg would tell Saul his hiding place, immediately fled to King Achish in Gath (verse10). Doeg did just what David supposed, informing Saul of seeing him in Nob and the food and sword that he received from the priest. Ahimelech and the other priests were summoned to appear before Saul. Being accused of aiding and abetting an enemy of Saul, they were sentenced to death on the spot (1 Samuel 22:13–16). Doeg slew Ahimelech and eighty-four other priests when others commanded to do so would not (verses 17–18). Additionally the entire city of Nob was destroyed (verse 19). Doeg in the betrayal of David (to gain favor with the King) lied by inferring David was Saul's enemy (which he was not), that Saul's suspicions were well-founded about him.[183]

A falsehood by implication is still a slanderous lie. Matthew Henry observes that David's words that Doeg loved lying lips "may refer to the information itself which he gave...against Ahimelech; for the matter of fact was, in substance, true, yet it was misrepresented, and false colors were put upon it, and therefore he might well be said to love lying, and to have a deceitful tongue. He told the truth, but not all the truth, as a witness ought to do; had he told that David made Ahimelech believe he was then going upon Saul's errand, the kindness he showed him would have appeared to be not only not traitorous against Saul, but respectful to him. It will not save us from the guilt of lying to be able to say, "There was some truth in what we said," if we pervert it, and make it to appear otherwise than it was."[184]

Ahimelech in contrast refused to defame David or present him as an enemy of the king. Rather he highly exalted him as an honorable man that was true and loyal (1 Samuel 22:14) to the king. Unwilling to shade the truth to appease King Saul as Doeg had done, he died. David says of Doeg, "You scheme catastrophe; your tongue cuts razor-sharp, artisan in lies. You love evil more than good, you call black white. You love malicious gossip, you foul-mouth" (Psalm 52:2–4 MSG).

A slanderer is a person who gives an evil or untrue report (verbal, gestures, writing, pictures, etc.) about another, forthrightly or by insinuation. W. S. Plumer writes, "The razor works most keenly and effectually when it is sharpest and makes least noise. So 'the words of a talebearer are as wounds, and go down into the innermost parts of the belly.'"[185] The Old Testament condemns slandering: "Do not spread false reports. Do not help a wicked man by being a malicious witness" (Exodus 23:1 NIV); as does the New Testament: "Brothers, do not slander one another. Anyone who speaks against his brother or judges him speaks against the law and judges it. When you judge the law, you are not keeping it, but sitting in judgment on it" (James 4:11 NIV).

"To judge another," states William Barclay, "is to take to ourselves a right to do what God alone has the right to do; and he is a reckless man who deliberately infringes the prerogatives of God. We might think that to speak evil of our neighbor is not a very serious sin. But Scripture would say that it is one of the worst of all because it is a breach of the royal law and an infringement of the rights of God."[186] Spurgeon says, "Slander, falsehood, insinuation, ridicule—these are poisoned arrows; how can we meet them? The Lord God promises us that, if we cannot silence them, we shall, at least, escape from being ruined by them. They condemn us for the moment, but we shall condemn them at last and forever. The mouth of them that speak lies shall be stopped, and their falsehoods shall be turned to the honor of those good men who suffered by them."[187]

"When Solomon wrote the Proverbs," Chuck Swindoll states, "he included the seven things the Lord hates. Among them, 'A false witness who utters lies' (Proverbs 6:19 NASB). Nevertheless, liars are still on the loose. If you have been the brunt of someone's lying tongue, more specifically, if you have been falsely accused, you don't need me to describe real pain. You've not only been there. You've discovered how difficult it can be to defend yourself. You try, but folks are hard to convince once they've heard convincing lies. The venom from a poisoned tongue has already taken its toll. Tragically, churches can be a feeding ground for loose lips and lying tongues. It takes courage to stand up to liars."[188]

The sure foundation of enduring slander is in knowing that God knows the truth and will in time put to silence those who falsely accuse. C. H. Spurgeon underscores this point in saying, "Are you the victim of slander? The Lord knows the truth. Though you have been sadly misunderstood, if not willingly misrepresented by ungenerous persons, yet God knows all about you; and His knowledge is of more importance than the opinion of dying men."[189]

James calls the tongue a fire, a world of iniquity, an unruly evil full of deadly poison that defiles the whole body that must be *bridled* (James 3:6, 8). Bridling the tongue however is extremely difficult, more so than steering a ship in a hurricane (verse 4). *Bridling the tongue* involves being careful what you say, when you say it and how you say it. Sometimes silence is golden. To speak rashly oft results in hurt to others and oneself. Mean, proud, obnoxious, deflating and debasing words *never* are to be spoken. Neither are you permitted to speak truthful words any way you want, to whomever you want. Even speaking truthfully about another must be done in an attitude and tone of love (Ephesians 4:15) and then only for their betterment, not disdain. "Set a watch, O Lord, before my mouth; keep the door of my lips" (Psalm 141:3).

A gossipy tongue is a dangerous thing,
    If its owner is evil at heart.
He can give whom he chooses many a sting
    That will woefully linger and smart.
But the gossipy tongue would be balked in its plan
    For causing heartburning and tears,
If it weren't helped out by the misguided man
    Who possesses two gossipy ears.

Oh, the gossipy ears are the ones that believe
    The evil reports they are told.
The sly, subtle tales which they gladly receive
    Would tarnish the purest of gold.
The cruel "they say" which goes floating about
    Like a hidden foe, fostering fears,
Would lose all its force were it firmly shut out
    By the man with the gossipy ears.

When the man with the gossipy tongue happens by
    With his stories of evil and strife,
We ought just to look him right square in the eye
    And ask him his mission in life.
We ought to refuse him a chance to retail
    The false, idle rumors he hears.
He ought to be locked up somewhere in jail
    With the man with the gossipy ears. ~ Nixon Waterman

A. B. Simpson said, "I would rather play with forked lightning, or take in my hand living wires with their fiery current, than speak a reckless word against any servant of Christ or idly repeat the slanderous darts which thousands of Christians are hurling on others, to the hurt of their own souls and bodies."[190]

The Bottom Line: To insinuate an untruth or tell a half-truth about another is still slanderous lying which God promises to punish severely (Psalm 52:5). Be named among the Ahimelechs that speak honorably of others rather than the Doegs that speak of them maliciously.

4. Just As I Am   Psalm 53:3

"There is none that doeth good, no, not one."—Psalm 53:3.

There is "none that doeth good." (Man is corrupt at the core of his being. He must attest with Paul, "In me...dwelleth no good thing" [Romans 7:18]. All have erred.) "No, not one." (The indictment includes the entire human race, without exception, for "all have sinned, and come short of the glory of God" [Romans 3:23].) See Romans 3:10; Psalm 14:3; and Isaiah 53:6.

Homily

This is a Psalm composed by David, similar to Psalm 14.

Man's problem. "There is no corruption so odious as moral corruption, no filthiness like the filthiness of sin."[191] Psalm 53:3 is the Old Testament Romans 3:12, which states, "They are all gone out of the way, they are together become unprofitable; there is none that doeth good, no, not one." John Gill remarks, "'They are all gone out of the way': that is, out of the way of God and His precepts, out of the way of holiness and righteousness, of light and life; into their own ways, the ways of sin, Satan, and the world of darkness, and of death."[192] Adam Clarke says, "The corruption of their hearts extends itself through all the actions of their lives. They are a plague of the most deadly kind; propagate nothing but destruction; and, like their father the Devil, spread far and wide the contagion of sin and death."[193]

They are unprofitable. Albert Barnes explains, "This word in Hebrew means to become 'putrid' and 'offensive,' like fruit that is spoiled. In Arabic, it is applied to 'milk' that becomes sour. Applied to moral subjects, it means to become corrupt and useless. They are of no value in regard to works of righteousness."[194] Man is so corrupt and depraved that he does not have the ability to do good. Bengel says, "They have not the power of returning to do good. And on the contrary, in all these particulars they cling to what is evil, either secretly, or even openly. They have become unfit for any useful purpose."[195]

None doeth good, no, not one. All mankind are under the guilt and penalty of sin, inapt to change their inherent sinful nature. Not most men are corrupt sinners, but *all.* Paul, to insure no misunderstanding, *states twice* that not even one person is right or justified in the eyes of God (Romans 3:10 and 12). John substantiates Paul's theology of the utter depravity of man in 1 John 1:8, 10, as do Jesus (Luke 18:19) and David (Psalm 51:5; Psalm 53:1-3).

A student continuously found himself before the same trial judge for crimes he had committed. The judge's patience finally waned, prompting the question to the youth, "Why is it that you cannot keep from doing wrong?"

"Your honor," the student replied, "I guess I was just born wrong."

> Sin consists not only of wrong doing, but in wrong being.
> —James Smith

Man was born wrong (sin), resulting in separation from God (Romans 3:23). Jesus Christ alone can reconcile sinful man to Holy God. "Sin consists not only of wrong doing, but in wrong being."[196]

Man's peril. The consequence of sin is temporal and eternal separation from God. Paul declares, "For the wages of sin is death; but the gift of God is eternal life through Jesus Christ our Lord" (Romans 3:23). Hell awaits the unrepentant at death. This awful place called Hell was originally created for Satan and the demons, not man. Unimaginable physical and mental torment will be experienced in Hell. There will be varying degrees of punishment in Hell (Matthew 10:15; 11:22, 24; Mark 6:11; Hebrews 10:29). "In one form or another the word 'torment' occurs [sixteen] times in the New Testament. In the case of Hell's torment, this suffering will last forever. Over 1,500 years ago, the great preacher John Chrysostom emphasized what this will mean. 'The damned shall suffer an end without end, a death without death, a decay without decay....They shall have punishment without pity, misery without mercy, sorrow without succor, crying without comfort, torment without ease.'[197] See Revelation 20:15.

Man's provision. Admission of sin is not enough to be reconciled to God. It must be cleansed from the heart. How? Not by anything you have done or may do (not baptism, religious work, goodness or church attendance). What you cannot do for yourself, God makes possible through His Son, the Lord Jesus Christ. "For when we were yet without strength, in due time Christ died for the ungodly" (Romans 5:6). "The blood of Jesus Christ his Son cleanseth us from all sin" (1 John 1:7). "I am the way, the truth, and the life: no man cometh unto the Father, but by me" (John 14:6). "For whosoever shall call upon the name of the Lord shall be saved" (Romans 10:13). Jesus died upon the cross and was raised from the dead to make possible divine forgiveness. Jesus is man's only bridge (Mediator) into the presence of God. He alone reconciles man with God, enabling a personal relationship instantly to take place. "For there is one God, and one mediator between God and men, the man Christ Jesus; Who gave himself a ransom for all, to be testified in due time" (1 Timothy 2:5–6). To summarize, man is saved by Jesus when he expresses godly sorrow over sin that results in a "turning away" from it (repentance) and a "turning toward" Christ (faith). Godly repentance coupled with faith results in salvation (Acts 20:21).

Man's promise. The good news of the Gospel is that salvation is available to one and all (Romans 10:13). No one is excluded from God's gift of eternal life, regardless of his baggage of sin or darksome past. But he must accept it on God's terms, not his own. The famous American evangelist D. L. Moody was preaching when a man stood and said, "I would come, but I cannot come. The ball chained to my feet won't let me."

Moody replied, "Pick up the ball and come."

To everyone Jesus says, "Pick up the ball of sin and bring it with you." "Christ receiveth sinful men—even me with all my sin."

W. A. Criswell, commenting on 1 John 2:2, states, "The death of Christ makes provision for the propitiation [cancellation of sin's effect] for the sins of the whole world. The universal extent of the atonement of Christ is nowhere clearer than here. Men may reject the Lord's substitutionary death, accepting condemnation instead, but Jesus died for all. The word [propitiation] may be translated 'satisfaction' in the sense that Christ's death satisfied the just demands of God's holy judgment of sin."[198] See 1 John 4:10.

> Come, ye sinners, poor and needy,
> Weak and wretched, sick and sore;
> Jesus ready stands to save you,
> Full of pity, love and power. ~ Joseph Hart (1712–1768)

On one occasion when Vice President Calvin Coolidge was presiding over a Senate meeting, one senator angrily told another to go "straight to Hell." The offended senator complained to Coolidge. Coolidge, having leafed through the rule book while listening to the heated debate, responded, "I've looked through the rule book. You don't have to go."[199] Neither you nor anyone else has to go to Hell. God has made a way of escape. It's up to you to take it. See John 1:12; John 3:16 and John 10:9–10.

Matthew Henry outlines the Psalm:

1. The fact of sin. God is a witness to it. He looks down from Heaven and sees all the sinfulness of men's hearts and lives (Psalm 53:2).

2. The fault of sin. It is iniquity (Psalm 53:1, 4); it is an unrighteous thing; it is that in which there is no good (Psalm 53:1, 3); it is going back from God (Psalm 53:3).

3. The fountain of sin. How comes it that men are so bad? Surely it is because there is no fear of God before their eyes; they say in their hearts, 'There is no God at all to call us to account, none that we need to stand in awe of' (See Psalm 53:1).

4. The folly of sin. He is a fool (in the account of God, whose judgment we are sure is right) who harbours such corrupt thoughts. The "workers of iniquity," whatever they pretend to, "have...no knowledge"; they may truly be said to know nothing, that do not know God (Psalm 53:4).

5. The filthiness of sin. Sinners are "corrupt" (Psalm 53:1); their nature is vitiated (*Cambridge Dictionary* says "to destroy or damage something) and spoiled; their iniquity is "abominable."

6. The fruit of sin. See to what a degree of barbarity it brings men at last! See their cruelty to their brethren! They "eat [them] up...as they eat bread." As if they had not only become beasts, but beasts of prey. See their contempt of God at the same time—they have not called upon Him, but scorn to be beholden to Him (Psalm 53:4).

7. The fear and shame that attends sin (Psalm 53:5). "There were they in great fear" who had made God their enemy; their own guilty consciences frightened them and filled them with horror. This enables the virgin, the daughter of Zion, to put them to shame and expose them, "because God hath despised them."[200]

The Bottom Line: Charlotte Elliot was visiting some friends in West London where she met a minister named Cesar Malan who at supper told her that he hoped she was a Christian. Charlotte took great offense in what he said. The preacher apologized and told her he hoped one day she would become a worker for Christ. The Lord orchestrated a meeting between these again three weeks later at a friend's home. Charlotte told Malan that she had been trying to find the Savior ever since he last spoke to her and wanted him to tell her how she might be saved. He told her, "Just come to Him as you are." This she did and was gloriously saved. Twelve years later, Charlotte Elliot wrote the beloved hymn *Just As I Am*. The way she came, every sinner must come to Christ, including you. Come to Him with your doubts, questions, and baggage of sin—just as you are. He stands eagerly awaiting to forgive and save you, even as He did Charlotte Elliot.

5. Prayer Works   Psalm 54:2

"Hear my prayer, O God; give ear to the words of my mouth."—Psalm 54:2.

Hear "my prayer, O God" (David addresses his prayer to the true and living God, Him that alone is able to answer in deliverance). Give "ear to the words of mouth" (Gill says, "the prayer which was conceived in his mind, and inwrought there by the Spirit of God, was expressed vocally."[201] Spurgeon says, "Vocal prayer helps the supplicant, and we keep our minds more fully awake when we can use our tongues as well as our hearts."[202]).

Homily

The Psalm is penned by David while a fugitive from King Saul hiding "on the hill of Hakilah" (1 Samuel 26:1 NIV). "Friends" of David betrayed him in revealing the location of the hiding place to Saul who immediately took three thousand soldiers "to seek David in the wilderness of Ziph" (1 Samuel 26:2). Their intent was clear: They "seek after my soul" (Psalm 54:3). Fortunately for David, Saul was needed elsewhere due to an invasion by the Philistines. Dickson said, "Mighty men will readily find more friends in an evil cause, than the godly find in a good one." [203] W. S. Plumer explains, "The reason is that an evil cause mortifies no vile affection and requires no self-denial."[204]

Derek Kidner says, "To be betrayed by Doeg the Edomite had been hardly a surprise (1 Samuel 22:22), but now David finds himself rejected by men of his own tribe [the Ziphites of Judah]."[205] With King Saul's huge army pursuing, friends betraying and ruthless people assaulting, David prays for divine intervention and deliverance. Adam Clarke remarks, "David was now in such imminent danger of being taken and destroyed, that no human means were left for his escape; if God therefore had not interfered, he must have been destroyed."[206] Matthew Henry says, "David has no other plea to depend upon than God's name, no other power to depend upon than God's strength, and these he makes his refuge and confidence."[207] Spurgeon comments, "This has ever been the defense of saints. As long as God has an open ear we cannot be shut up in trouble. All other weapons may be useless, but all-prayer is evermore available."[208] No enemy can stop this gun. Calvin said, "Surrounded as [David] was by hostile troops, and hemmed in on every side by apparently inevitable destruction, we cannot but admire the rare and heroical intrepidity, which he displayed in committing himself by prayer, to the Almighty."[209]

The prayer of David was graciously heard. Just as Saul's men were about to close a net in on David (1 Samuel 23:26) a messenger brought word to Saul that the Philistines had invaded the land (1 Samuel 23:27), forcing an end to the pursuit. David safely escaped to En-gedi (1 Samuel 23:29). As the Lord delivered David, He is ready to rescue all His children in their times of betrayal, despair, sorrow and enemy attack, when they pray for help.

Prayer is conversation with God. Jesus forthrightly issues the must of prayer in saying, "Men ought always to pray, and not to faint" (Luke 18:1). Believers live in an evil, polluted society. The only escape from its toxic fumes which promote spiritual fainting (drifting, backsliding, worldliness) is the intake of "pure air" from the atmosphere of Heaven which occurs in prayer. Prayer is to the believer what an oxygen mask is to those who work in hazardous waste facilities, an absolute essential to survival. Obviously, then, this oxygen mask for believers ought to be worn continuously ("always to pray"). The apostle Paul similarly states, "Pray without ceasing" (1 Thessalonians 5:17).

Christians should pray scripturally (in accordance with God's Word and will), passionately (earnestly, fervently), specifically (without vagueness), and confidently (not doubting, but fully trusting God to answer). Scripture indicates various postures of prayer: kneeling in prayer (1 Kings 8:54; 2 Chronicles 6:13; Psalm 95:6; Ephesians 3:14.); bowing and falling prostrate (Genesis 24:26; Matthew 26:39; Mark 14:35); spreading out the hands (1 Kings 8:22; Psalm 28:2; 1 Timothy 2:8); and standing (1 Samuel 1:26; Mark 11:25; Luke 18:11). No rule is specified with regard to the posture of the body in prayer. The only posture imperative in prayer is that of the heart. It must ever be kneeling in humility and submission in its approach to the throne room of a thrice holy God.

David cries out, "Save me, O God, by thy name" (Psalm 54:1). Spurgeon comments, "Thou art my Savior; all around me are my foes and their eager helpers. No shelter is permitted me....But thou, O God, wilt give me refuge and deliver me from all my enemies. By thy name, by thy great and glorious nature."[210]

The Bible instructs us to pray in Jesus' name. The invoking of Jesus' name is not a magical formula. "Praying in Jesus' name," declares John MacArthur, "is not simply tacking a phrase onto the end of prayers. To pray in Jesus' name is to seek what He seeks, to promote what He desires, to give Him glory. We can only rightly ask God for that which will glorify the Son."[211] Adrian Rogers said, "When asking in Jesus' name, first consider: His Approval—Does Jesus approve this thing? His Authorization—Is it something He has authorized? His Acclaim—Is it for His glory?"[212]

Does prayer work? James states, "The earnest prayer of a righteous person has great power and produces wonderful results" (James 5:16 NLT). Sometimes prayer results are seen instantly, while at other times they are delayed. Sometimes we receive exactly that for which we pray, while at other times God provides something far better (though we may not think so at the time). Henry Drummond tells of a little girl aboard a ship en route across the ocean who dropped her doll overboard. She ran to the captain asking if he might stop the ship to rescue her doll. His refusal led her to count him insensitive and cruel. Upon reaching port, the captain purchased the finest doll available and gave it to the girl. He had refused her request but gave her something far better.[213] God always can be trusted "to do exceeding abundantly above all that we ask or think" (Ephesians 3:20).

> There's a garden where Jesus is waiting;
> There's a place that is wondrously fair,
> For it glows with the light of His presence.
> 'Tis the beautiful garden of prayer.
>
> Oh, the beautiful garden, the garden of prayer,
> Oh, the beautiful garden of prayer!
> There my Savior awaits, and He opens the gates
> To the beautiful garden of prayer.
>
> There's a garden where Jesus is waiting,
> And I go with my burden and care.
> Just to learn from His lips words of comfort
> In the beautiful garden of prayer.
>
> There's a garden where Jesus is waiting,
> And He bids you to come meet Him there
> Just to bow and receive a new blessing
> In the beautiful garden of prayer. ~ Eleanor Allen Schroll (1920)

David testified that time spent in communion and fellowship with the Lord ("in the beautiful garden of prayer") filled him with "great" authentic joy. He says, "The LORD is my strength and my shield; my heart trusted in him, and I am helped: therefore my heart greatly rejoiceth; and with my song will I praise him" (Psalm 28:7). Prayer is a joy, brings joy. "Until now you have not asked for anything in my name. Ask and you will receive, and your joy will be complete" (John 16:24 NIV). Tim Keller says, "A triune God would call us to converse with him...because He wants to share the joy He has. Prayer is our way of entering into the happiness of God Himself."[214] George Mueller remarks, "The joy which answers to prayer give cannot be described, and the impetus which they afford to the spiritual life is exceedingly great. The experience of this happiness I desire for all my Christian readers. If you believe indeed in the Lord Jesus for the salvation of your soul, if you walk uprightly and do not regard iniquity in your heart, if you continue to wait patiently and believingly upon God, then answers will surely be given to your prayers."[215] Spurgeon stated, "Prevalence with God in wrestling prayer is sure to make the believer strong—if not happy. The nearest place to the gate of Heaven is the throne of the heavenly grace. Much alone, and you will have much assurance; little alone with Jesus, your religion will be shallow, polluted with many doubts and fears, and not sparkling with the joy of the Lord. Since the soul-enriching path of prayer is open to the very weakest saint, since no high attainments are required, since you are not bidden to come because you are an advanced saint but freely invited if you be a saint at all, see to it, dear reader, that you are often in the way of private devotion. Be much on your knees, for so Elijah drew the rain upon famished Israel's fields."[216]

The Berleberg Bible states, "We should learn from the example of David that even in the greatest danger we should resort to no forbidden means, nor grow faint, but should call upon the name of God, and commit to him all our concerns as to the Supreme Judge."[217] See 1 Samuel 26:8-12.

The Bottom Line: "The psalmist prays because he is ringed about by foes. God will hear because He is so surrounded. It is blessed to know that the same circumstances in our lot which drive us to God incline God to us."[218] E. M. Bounds said, "Four things let us ever keep in mind: God hears prayer, God heeds prayer, God answers prayer, and God delivers by prayer."[219]

6. Wounded by Betrayal of a Friend   Psalm 55:12–14

"For it was not an enemy that reproached me; then I could have borne it: neither was it he that hated me that did magnify himself against me; then I would have hid myself from him: But it was thou, a man mine equal, my guide, and mine acquaintance. We took sweet counsel together, and walked unto the house of God in company."—Psalm 55:12–14.

For it was "not an enemy" (It was not a person that was an avowed foe.[220]) that "reproached me" (Barnes says "refers to slander; calumny ['the act of uttering false charges or misrepresentations maliciously calculated to harm another's reputation'[221]]; abuse."[222]).

Then I could have "borne it" (Spurgeon says, "The slanders of an avowed antagonist are seldom so mean and dastardly as those of a traitor, and the absence of the elements of ingratitude and treachery renders them less hard to bear. We can bear from Shimei what we cannot endure from Ahithophel."[223] Calvin says, "I could then have met it, as one meets and parries off a blow, which is aimed at him. Against a known foe we are on our watch, but the unsuspected stroke of a friend takes us by surprise."[224]). NEITHER was it "he that hated me that did magnify himself against me" (Poole says, "I could and should easily have prevented or avoided the effects of his hatred."[225]).

Then I would have "hid myself from him" (as David hid from Saul). Gill says, "The sense may be that he would have shunned his company, refused conversation with him; much less would he have admitted him to his privy councils, by which means he knew all his affairs, and there was no hiding and concealing things from him."[226]). "But it was thou, a man mine equal" (Poole says "not in power and dignity, which could not be, but in reputation for his deep wisdom and excellent conduct, and the great influence which he had upon me, and upon all my people."[227]) "my guide" (companion. Spurgeon says "a counselor so sage that I trusted your advice and found it prudent to do so."[228]).

AND "mine acquaintance" (Barnes says, "The phrase 'mine acquaintance' is a feeble expression and does not convey the full force of the original, which denotes a more intimate friend than would be suggested by the word 'acquaintance.' It is language applied to one whom we thoroughly 'know,' and who 'knows us'; and this exists only in the case of very intimate friends. All the expressions used in this verse would probably be applicable to Ahithophel and to the intimacy between him and David.'[229] Edwards says, "But it is thou, a man whom I valued as my own self, my guide and acquaintance."[230] Green says, "But it is thou, the man whom I took for my guide and my friend."[231] Horsley says "But thou, a man, put upon a level with myself, my confidant, and my familiar friend."[232]).

29

We took "sweet counsel together" (*Counsel*. Perowne says "close intimate intercourse."[233] Spurgeon says, "The traitor had been treated lovingly, and trusted much. Solace, mutual and cheering, had grown out of their intimate communings."[234] Green says, "We sweetly communicated our secrets in private, and in public we walked to the house of God."[235]).

AND "walked unto the house of God in company" (Kirkpatrick says, "Ours was a habitual intimacy of the closest and most sacred kind, in confidential intercourse in private, in companionship in the worship of God in public."[236]).

Homily

David was the victim of betrayal by a servant of King Saul, Doeg the Edomite (Psalm 52), the Ziphites (Psalm 54) and now in Psalm 55 by an intimate friend named Ahithophel (see 2 Samuel 15:31). The former were somewhat understandable but certainly not the latter. All betrayal brings anguish of soul. But there is no anguish, hurt or sorrow comparable to that of the betrayal of one that is counted the dearest of friends. W. S. Plumer comments, "Were friendships sacred and never disgraced by treachery, some might doubt the depravity of man. But as things are, there is no room for incredulity ('the state of being unwilling or unable to believe something' [Oxford Dictionary])."[237] Alexander Maclaren writes, "The psalmist feels that the defection of his false friend is the worst blow of all. He could have braced himself to bear an enemy's reviling; he could have found weapons to repel, or a shelter in which to escape from, open foes; but the baseness which forgets all former sweet companionship in secret, and all association in public and in worship, is more than he can bear up against. The voice of wounded love is too plain in the words for the hypothesis that the singer is the personified nation."[238] T. W. Chambers remarked, "We can escape from open foes, but where can one find a hiding place from treachery? Hence the faithlessness of a professed friend is a form of sin for which there is not even the pretence of excuse."[239]

It is no wonder David moans, "My heart is sore pained within me: and the terrors of death are fallen upon me. Fearfulness and trembling are come upon me, and horror hath overwhelmed me" (Psalm 55:4–5).

Matthew Henry paraphrases David: "It was thou, a man, my equal, one whom I esteemed as myself, a friend as my own soul, whom I had laid in my bosom and made equal with myself, to whom I had communicated all my secrets and who knew my mind as well as I myself did—my guide, with whom I advised and by whom I was directed in all my affairs, whom I made president of the council and prime minister of state—my intimate acquaintance and familiar friend; this is the man that now abuses me. I have been kind to him, but I find him thus basely ungrateful. I have put a trust in him, but I find him thus basely treacherous; nay, and he could not have done me the one-half of the mischief he does if I had not shown him so much respect."[240]

David's spirit had been deeply wounded with an injury that was greater in pain than sword or spear could cause to the flesh. Spurgeon remarks, "It is a terrible wounding when he who should have been your friend becomes your foe, and when, like your Lord, you also have your Judas Iscariot. It is not easy to bear misrepresentation and falsehood, to have your purest motives misjudged....This is a very painful kind of wounded spirit."[241]

> It is a terrible wounding when he who should have been your friend becomes your foe, and when, like your Lord, you also have your Judas Iscariot. It is not easy to bear misrepresentation and falsehood, to have your purest motives misjudged....This is a very painful kind of wounded spirit.
> —Charles Spurgeon

To betray one means "to disclose a secret or confidence treacherously; to break a promise, or be disloyal to a person's trust; to disappoint the expectations of" (Collins). *YourDictionary.Com* defines betrayal as an attempt to lead astray, deceive, seduce, then desert. Betrayal comes in the forms of broken promises, revealed secrets, failure of family or friend(s) to give support in the time of crisis, the deceitful stealing one's spouse or boy/girlfriend, underhanded play to get the position or promotion instead of another, etc. Betrayal may result in broken relationships, emotional aliments like depression, abandonment, damaged reputation/character, injury to the cause of Christ at large and the local church, and the danger of "shell shock" (fear of its happening again) that prompts distrust of others. The consequences of betrayal are so painful and devastating that anyone with Christian love in his heart would never stoop to such an act.

Jesus warned there would be "many...offended, and shall betray one another" (Matthew 24:10). It is a crushing blow when a friend violates the trust placed in him or turns away in times of trouble or crisis. "A friend is forsaken," states C. H. Spurgeon, "by one upon whom he leaned, to whose very soul he was knit, so that their two hearts had grown into one; and he feels that his heart is broken, for the other half of himself is severed from him. When Ahithophel forsakes David, when the kind friend unto whom we have always told our sorrows betrays our confidence, the consequence may possibly be a broken heart."[242]

Jesus was betrayed by Judas to the chief priests (Matthew 26:14–15), and Delilah betrayed Samson to the Philistines (Judges 16:16–21) for the same reason (material gain). David betrayed Uriah to conceal his sin (2 Samuel 11:14–15); Absalom betrayed his father, King David, in an effort to steal the kingdom (2 Samuel 15:10–17); Haman betrayed the king and God's people in an effort to eradicate the Jews (Esther 3:8–11) and Peter betrayed Jesus for fear of persecution (John 18:15–27). As you see, reasons for betrayal are varied and originate in those that are close to us as a rule. Other reasons may include making another look bad so one may look better by comparison (An old proverb from India says, "Some men try to be tall by cutting off the heads of others."); positional advancement in the workplace or athletic arena; to relieve one's hurt by inflicting pain on another; to get even with the person; to damage the cause of Christ; and the notoriety of making known something that should ever be concealed.

Forgive the betrayer and move on with your life. In the Lord's Prayer, Jesus gave instruction to pray in this fashion, "And forgive us our debts, as we forgive our debtors" (Matthew 6:12). The Holy Spirit within you will enable (supernatural power) this forgiveness if you are living under His control. Paul declares, "For as many as are led by the Spirit of God, they are the sons of God" (Romans 8:14). A person cannot be on the outs with another and be right with God at the same time. Refusal to forgive allows the betrayer to win, for it allows the seeds of bitterness, ill will and depression to take root, wounding (damaging) the heart even further. Rely on Jesus for peace. He Himself alone is our peace—not source of peace, but peace. Isaiah declared, "Thou wilt keep him in perfect peace, whose mind is stayed on thee: because he trusteth in thee" (Isaiah 26: 3). It's impossible to know peace apart from knowing Jesus. The slogan is correct in stating, "Know Jesus; Know Peace. No Jesus; No peace." Jesus longs to fill your life with His presence, compassion and love so that you will know His peace. He is a true friend that will never betray you.

Chuck Swindoll writes, "When everything else fails and everybody else has turned away, there are precious few who will give you a call and say, 'I'm with you. I'm there. Count on me. Call on me anytime, day or night. I'll come. I won't kick you when you're down. I'm by your side. I understand.'"[243] Fortunately, though David had his backstabbing and deserting friends, he also had groves of friends that were as sheltering trees. All David's *real* friends came through for him when he needed them the most—big time. "They had no agenda, like gaining political clout. They were there to help with his physical and emotional needs."[244] It was these friends that enabled David to make it through the toughest of days and darkest of nights. Every person needs a sheltering tree.

Shortly before his death, Samuel Taylor Coleridge wrote the poem "Youth and Age" in which is depicted his old age, with that of his youth. In part, he writes,

> Flowers are lovely; Love is flower-like;
> Friendship is a sheltering tree.

Friendship is a sheltering tree. What descriptive language to describe true friends; what an image to describe intimate friendship! The words suggest taking shelter from the raging heat of a July day in an extremely hot place under a gigantic tree whose branches and foliage block the sun, providing a cool shade. Coleridge is right. True friends provide a refuge from the trials, tribulations and troubles of life inasmuch as possible by allowing us to sit under their massive sheltering shade to be refreshed in their encouragement, strengthened by their companionship and helped by their counsel.

33

Yes, we will have our share of Ahithophels that betray us. But thank God for the Jonathans that are as sheltering trees!

The Bottom Line: "False and hollow as are some professions of friendship, there are others of an opposite kind."[245] Matthew Henry says, "The true Christian must expect trials from professed friends, from those with whom he has been united; this will be very painful; but by looking unto Jesus we shall be enabled to bear it."[246] Regrettably there are Ahithophels among the Jonathans. See 1 Samuel 20.

7. Tears in a Bottle   Psalm 56:8

"Thou tellest my wanderings: put thou my tears into thy bottle: are they not in thy book?"—Psalm 56:8.

"Thou tellest" (Plumer says "tellest, countest, takest account of, payest attention to. The clause is a grateful recognition of God's kindness up to this hour, and implies confidence that it will be continued."[247]). "My wanderings" (David's life was spent primarily as a fugitive. Every step he took was observed and recorded by God as he fled the enemy from place to place seeking safety. "'My wanderings,' to Gath, 1 Samuel 21:10; to the cave of Adullam, 1 Samuel 22:1; to Mizpeh, in Moab, 1 Samuel 22:3; to the forest of Hareth, 1 Samuel 22:5; to Keilah, 1 Samuel 23:5; to the wilderness of Ziph, 1 Samuel 23:14; to the wilderness of Maon, 1 Samuel 23:25; to En-gedi, 1 Samuel 24:1–2."[248]).

"Put thou my tears" (tears he shed during the wanderings.[249] Perowne says, "He knows that each day of his wandering, each nook in which he has found shelter, each step that he has taken, every artifice by which he has baffled his foes—all have been numbered by his Heavenly Keeper. Yea, no tear that he has shed, when his eye has been raised to Heaven in prayer, has fallen to the ground. He asks God to gather them all in His bottle, and trusts that He will note them in His book."[250]).

"Into thy bottle" (Barnes says, "The word here rendered 'bottle' means properly a bottle made of skin, such as was used in the East; but it may be employed to denote a bottle of any kind. It is possible, and, indeed, it seems probable, that there is an allusion here to the custom of collecting tears shed in a time of calamity and sorrow, and preserving them in a small bottle or 'lachrymatory,' as a memorial of the grief. The Romans had a custom, that in a time of mourning—on a funeral occasion—a friend went to one in sorrow, and wiped away the tears from the eyes with a piece of cloth, and squeezed the tears into a small bottle of glass or earth, which was carefully preserved as a memorial of friendship and sorrow."[251]).

ARE "they not in thy book?" (Tate says of the Hebrew word for *book* "'count/record'—'reckoning/scroll-book' plays on the background idea of a divine 'scroll of remembrance'—God's book about the behavior of the righteous. See Psalm 69:28; Exodus 32:32–33; Isaiah 4:3; 65:6; Job 14:17; 19:23; Malachi 3:16; Daniel 7:10; and Revelation 20:12; 21:27."[252] God keeps record of not only wanderings but the tears shed in them.).

Homily

The title ascribes the Psalm to David when the Philistines took him in Gath. See 1 Samuel 21 and 1 Samuel 22:1. *Thou tellest my wanderings.* "The hunted fugitive feels that every step of his weary interlacing tracks, as he stole from point to point as danger dictated, was known to God."[253] Dilday and Kennedy said, "The persecuted psalmist was sustained by the conviction that God was concerned. Even his bitter tears would be treasured up and noted in the heavenly record (v. 8; Malachi 3:16)."[254]

The Psalmist states that God records life's tribulations (trials, trouble, and sorrow) in the book of remembrance and treasures up our tears they induce *in His* "bottle." Spurgeon says the text "implies that they are caught as they flow."[255] Matthew Henry comments, "David comforts himself, in his distress and fear, that God noticed all his grievances and all his griefs. God has a bottle and a book for His people's tears, both the tears for their sins, and those for their afflictions. He observes them with tender concern."[256] John Gill states the afflictions God's children bear "are in His book of purposes; they are all appointed by Him, their kind and nature, their measure and duration, their quality and quantity; what they shall be, and how long they shall last; and their end and use: and they are in His book of providence, and are all overruled and caused to work for their good; and they are in the book of His remembrance; they are taken notice of and numbered by Him, and shall be finished; they shall not exceed their bounds. These tears will be turned into joy, and God will wipe them all away from the eyes of his people."[257]

Ross states, "The image of *David's* tears being collected in a wineskin means that God did not forget his suffering."[258] "He observes them with compassion and tender concern; he is afflicted in their afflictions, and knows their souls in adversity. As the blood of his saints, and their deaths, are precious in the sight of the Lord, so are their tears, not one of them shall fall to the ground."[259] See 2 Kings 20:5. It is this knowledge of God's continual observation, concern and care that brings David comfort in the calamities and trouble he confronted (Psalm 56:11–13). Alexander Maclaren writes, "What does He keep them [tears] for? To show how precious they are in His sight, and perhaps to suggest that they are preserved for a future use. The tears that His children shed and give to Him to keep cannot be tears of rebellious or unmeasured weeping, and will be given back one day to those who shed them, converted into refreshment, by the same Power which of old turned water into wine."[260] Calvin remarked, "We may surely believe, that if God bestows such honor upon the tears of his saints, he must number every drop of their blood. Tyrants may burn their flesh and their bones, but the blood remains to cry aloud for vengeance; and intervening ages can never erase what has been written in the register of God's remembrance."[261]

It is okay to cry. With David, in my life's wandering I have been hurt by betrayal and injurious harsh words of Christian "friends" that caused tears of anguish and sorrow. Never have I known such pain or wept so grievously as then. Eugene Peterson remarks, "Jesus wept. Job wept. David wept. Jeremiah wept. They did it openly. Their weeping became a matter of public record. Their weeping, sanctioned by inclusion in our Holy Scriptures, [is] a continuing and reliable witness that weeping has an honored place in the life of faith."[262] Tears are a language that God understands. Not a *one* flows down the cheek unnoticed or unremembered or uncollected by Him. He counts every teardrop as a liquid jewel to be treasured.

We can only speculate as to why God saves our tears. In keeping with His nature I think He does so as a reminder of His constant awareness and compassionate concern regarding life's hurts. He bottles the tears shed in life's sorrows as in the death of a loved one and friend. He bottles the tears induced by rebellious children, the betrayal of friends, the yielding to a favorite sin (again), life's failures and disappointments, divorce, and abandonment by those whom we love. John Gill thinks tears are so stored by God "that they might be brought forth another day and shown, to the aggravation of the condemnation of wicked men, who by their hard speeches, and ungodly actions, have caused them."[263] Like Scrooge in Dickens' *Christmas Carol,* judgment is inescapable for him that mistreats another. A day is forthcoming when the bottle of your treasured tears will be opened before their inducers for the purpose of divine judgment.

If man is to give account for "every idle word" spoken (Matthew 12:36), he also will with regard to every teardrop of hurt caused. Matthew Henry agrees with Gill, stating, "The tears of God's persecuted people are bottled up and sealed among God's treasures; and, when these books come to be opened, they will be found vials of wrath, which will be poured out upon their persecutors, whom God will surely reckon with for all the tears they have forced from his people's eyes; and they will be breasts of consolation to God's mourners, whose sackcloth will be turned into garments of praise. God will comfort his people according to the time wherein he has afflicted them, and give to those to reap in joy who sowed in tears. What was sown a tear will come up a pearl."[264]

To paraphrase Maclaren, the same tears that are bitterly wept by His child will presently or in time be converted into tears of joy, peace and comfort by the same power which turned water into wine.[265] God makes sure they are not wasted but will work for our good. Our tears will be changed into songs of praise (Psalm 56:10). The fears that brought the tears will be banished through trust in God (Psalm 56:11). A future day is coming when the last tear shed will be wiped from the eye. See Revelation 21:4.

> Human tears may freely flow,
>   Authorized by tears Divine,
> Till Thine awful will we know,
>   Comprehend Thy whole design.

Jesus wept! and so may we;
>Jesus, suffering all Thy will,
Felt the soft infirmity,
>Feels His creatures sorrows still. ~ Charles Wesley (1767)

Wesley composed the hymn for his son who was battling small-pox (as was the case with many children in the eighteenth century). The child for whom he sings here, "a musical prodigy by all accounts," died.[266]

Paul Wesley Chilcote says, "The images that Charles creates in these lines are staggering. Jesus weeps with us in our sorrow. Jesus blends our tears with His own. The hymn concludes, not with a stoic resignation to the pain and agony of life, but with an affirmation that the One who has stood with us will never abandon us and loves every person with an undying love."[267] God stores our "tears" in a bottle of remembrance.

But let us as believers also put the tears of others into a bottle to show empathy, pity, love and comfort. Paul admonishes us to "weep with them that weep" (Romans 12:15). This Paul did in remembering Timothy's tears (2 Timothy 1:4). Go and do thy likewise.

The Bottom Line: God is mindful of our every tear, sorrow and trial. Arnd states, "Here lies a powerful consolation, that God gathers up such tears, and puts them into His bottle, just as one would pour precious wine into a flagon (*Meriam-Webster* says 'a large usually metal or pottery vessel [as for wine] with handle and spout and often a lid'), so precious and dear are such tears before God, and God lays them up as a treasure in the heavens; and if we think that all such tears are lost, lo! God hath preserved them for us a treasure in the heavens, with which we shall be richly consoled in that day."[268]

Allan Harman said, "God does not need a written record to remember his people and their needs, but the idea is used in the Old Testament as a reassuring way of speaking of God's knowledge of, and care for, his people."[269]

8. Ambushes   Psalm 57:6

"They have prepared a net for my steps; my soul is bowed down: they have digged a pit before me, into the midst whereof they are fallen themselves. Selah."—Psalm 57:6.

"They" (King Saul and his soldiers) have "prepared a net for my steps" (Clarke says, "A gin or springe ['a noose or snare for catching small game'[270]], such as huntsmen put in the places which they know the prey they seek frequents: such, also, as they place in passages in hedges, etc., through which the game creeps."[271] Gill says, "They laid snares for him, as the fowler does for the bird, in order to take him. It denotes the insidious ways used by Saul and his men to get David into their hands."[272] Plumer says, "Here and often the word points to the snares and artifices of wicked and crafty men, whereby they would inveigle ['persuade someone to do something by means of deception or flattery,' *Oxford Dictionary*] men into sin, folly, or ruin. Psalm 9:15; 10:9; 140:5; Micah 7:2."[273]).

My "soul is bowed down" (Poole says, "Mine heart was oppressed, and almost overwhelmed."[274]). They have "digged a pit before me" (A huge pit would be hewn in the ground, its mouth camouflaged with sticks and branches to entrap unsuspecting animals. Saul's men prepared such *pits* in the path they thought David would walk.).

"INTO the midst whereof they are fallen themselves" (Saul in setting traps for David falls into one himself at the cave of En-gedi. The cave happened to be the hiding place for David and his men. David treats Saul compassionately, sparing his life. See 1 Samuel 24:1–4, Psalm 7:15 and Psalm 141:10). "Selah" (Spurgeon says, "We may sit down at the pit's mouth and view with wonder the just retaliations of providence."[275]).

Homily

This is a Psalm composed by David when he fled from Saul in the cave. Adam Clarke says, "It is very likely that this Psalm was made to commemorate his escape from Saul in the cave of En-gedi, where Saul had entered without knowing that David was there, and David cut off the skirt of his garment."[276]

Snares (like used for catching various birds, fish and animals) of various shapes and forms have been strewn (metaphorically) in the way of the believer by the archenemy of the soul, seeking his demise. By their nature they are secretive and unexpected, for "surely in vain the net is spread in the sight of any bird" (Proverbs 1:17). The *snares* or *pits* are personalized to each, based upon their most susceptible temptation and weakest point. Though visibly it is impossible to see the traps until it's too late, the spiritual believer certainly may discern (spiritually see) their "location" and avoid captivity. See Proverbs 15:21; Proverbs 28:7; Hosea 14:9; Philippians 1:9–10; 1 John 4:1.

Experience also is an aid in escaping them. Learn from past experiences of vulnerability. Satan is sly and will reset the same type of trap again and again if it is thought to be effective. Scripture cautions—by admonition and by example—not to underestimate the enemy's power to bring a Christian down. If the adversary can destroy a Samson, a David, and a Demas, then all of us are certainly vulnerable (Judges 16:18–21; 2 Samuel 11:3–5; 2 Timothy 4:10). Paul cautions, "Let him that thinketh he standeth take heed lest he fall" (1 Corinthians 10:12). And Peter warns, "Be sober, be vigilant; because your adversary the devil, as a roaring lion, walketh about, seeking whom he may devour" (1 Peter 5:8). Avoid people, places, and pleasures that present a temptation (Ephesians 4:27).

> Through many dangers, toils and snares
> I have already come.
> 'Tis grace has brought me safe thus far,
> And grace will lead me home. ~ John Newton (1779)

Spurgeon, the great London pastor of the nineteenth century, offers great counsel regarding battling Satan, when he states, "Thou wast once a servant of Satan, and no king will willingly lose his subjects. Dost thou think that Satan will let thee alone? No, he will be always at thee, for he 'goeth about like a roaring lion, seeking whom he may devour.' Expect trouble, therefore, Christian, when thou lookest beneath thee. Then look around thee. Where art thou? Thou art in an enemy's country, a stranger and a sojourner. The world is not thy friend. If it be, then thou art not God's friend, for he who is the friend of the world is the enemy of God. Be assured that thou shalt find foe-men everywhere. When thou sleepest, think that thou art resting on the battlefield; when thou walkest, suspect an ambush in every hedge."[277]

> Amidst a thousand snares I stand
> Upheld and guarded by Thy hand;
> That hand unseen shall hold me still
> And lead me to Thy holy hill.[278]

David, in facing the relentless snares of King Saul, was able to say, "My heart is fixed, O God, my heart is fixed: I will sing and give praise. Awake up, my glory; awake, psaltery and harp: I myself will awake early. I will praise thee, O Lord, among the people: I will sing unto thee among the nations. For thy mercy is great unto the heavens, and thy truth unto the clouds" (Psalm 57:7–10). "Knit to God, a heart is firm. The Psalmist's was steadfast because it had taken refuge in God; and so, even before his rescue from his enemies came to pass, he was emancipated from the fear of them, and could lift this song of praise."[279] Every believer that knits his soul to the heart of God in trust, allegiance and devotion likewise will know victory over the enemy, prompting the song of praise. Even in times of stumbling into a snare, the heart that is stayed on Jehovah will find bountiful mercy that will lift him from the miry clay and set his feet upon a solid ROCK. See Psalm 40:1–3.

The Bottom Line: Spurgeon remarks, "What with pitfalls and snares, weak knees, weary feet, and subtle enemies, no child of God would stand fast for an hour, were it not for the faithful love [Christ] which will not suffer his foot to be moved."[280] "And what joyous confidence and what sweet rest in God! 'If I cannot see the brightness of Your face, the shadow of Your wings will be enough for me. Only let me get near You—only permit me humbly to trust You, and it will be enough for me "until these calamities pass."'"[281] See Psalm 57:1.

9. Corrupt Judicial Leaders   Psalm 58:1–5

"Do ye indeed speak righteousness, O congregation? do ye judge uprightly, O ye sons of men? Yea, in heart ye work wickedness; ye weigh

the violence of your hands in the earth. The wicked are estranged from the womb: they go astray as soon as they be born, speaking lies. Their poison is like the poison of a serpent: they are like the deaf adder that stoppeth her ear; Which will not hearken to the voice of charmers, charming never so wisely."—Psalm 58:1–5.

"Do ye indeed speak righteousness" (Tate says, "'Indeed, is the righteousness you should speak mute in your mouth?'—meaning that those addressed [judges] pronounce sentences in such ways as to negate the effectiveness of the justice they are supposed to establish."[282] Kirkpatrick says, "'To speak righteousness' means 'to pronounce just sentences.' Justice and uprightness are characteristics of God's judgement [Psalm 9:8], which ought to be reflected by all earthly judges."[283]).

"O congregation?" (Jamieson-Fausset-Brown says "literally, 'Oh, dumb'; the word used is never translated 'congregation.'"[284] [O dumb ones.] Rawlinson says, "It is an epithet applied to the judges of the people, and not to the congregation."[285] Barnes says, "The allusion is clearly to some public act of judging; to a judicial sentence; to magistrates and rulers; to people who 'should' give a righteous sentence; to those in authority who 'ought' to pronounce a just opinion on the conduct of others."[286]). "Do you judge uprightly" (Barnes says, "Do you judge right things? are your judgments in accordance with truth and justice?"[287]).

"O ye sons of men?" (Benson says, "So he calls them, to remind them that they also were men and must give an account to God for all their hard speeches and unrighteous decrees against him."[288] Rawlinson says, "Both questions are asked in bitter irony."[289]). Yea, "in heart ye work wickedness; ye weigh the violence of your hands in the earth" (Bratcher and Reyburn say, "Instead of being, as they should be, just judges of people, they are guilty of *wrongs* and *violence*; the latter could be taken in a legal sense as injustice, lawlessness, which the rulers [or judges] perpetuate through a corrupt administration of justice."[290] Corrupt, they alter the scales of justice, weighing matters wrongly and unjustly. See Ecclesiastes 10:16.).

"The wicked are estranged" (Alexander says "denoting the condition of estrangement, alienation, from God and from all goodness.

The wicked thus described are the whole class, of which his persecutors formed a part."[291]) "from the womb" (Alexander says, "from their birth, literally, from the belly."[292] Calvin says, "We all come into the world stained with sin, possessed, as Adam's posterity, of a nature essentially depraved, and incapable, in ourselves, of aiming at anything which is good; but there is a secret restraint upon most men, which prevents them from going all lengths in iniquity."[293] Dickson says, "Men's wicked actions prove the wickedness of their natures."[294]).

"They go astray as soon as they be born, speaking lies" (Rawlinson says, "What the Psalmist means is that those who ultimately become heinous sinners, for the most part show, even from their early childhood, a strong tendency towards evil. He implies that with others the case is different. Though there may be in them a corruption of nature (Psalm 51:5), yet, on the whole, they have good dispositions, and present a contrast to the ungodly ones whom he is describing."[295]).

"Their poison is like the poison of a serpent" (Barnes says "their malignity; their bad spirit; that which they utter or throw out of their mouth. The reference here is to what they speak or utter [Psalm 58:3], and the idea is, that it is penetrating and deadly."[296] Plumer says "'poison', elsewhere rendered also 'rage', 'wrath,' 'fury,' 'anger'; see on Psalm 6:1, where it is rendered 'hot displeasure.' Here it means venom."[297] *Serpent* is generic for any *poisonous* snake.[298]).

"They are like the deaf adder that stoppeth her ear" (Barnes says *charmers* "means properly 'whisperers, mutterers,' and it refers here to those who made use of spells or incantations—sorcerers or magicians."[299] The adder was thought to be deaf for its difficulty to be charmed by snake charmers. It was as if they *shut their ears* stubbornly to the charmers, refusing to hear. Spurgeon says, "Many serpents have been conquered by the charmer's art, but men such as the Psalmist had to deal with, no art could tame or restrain; therefore, he likens them to a serpent less susceptible than others to the charmer's music, and says that they refused to hear reason, as the adder shuts her ear to those incantations which fascinate other reptiles. Man, in his natural corruption, appears to have all the ill points of a serpent without its excellences."[300] Death was in the fangs of the poisonous snake; likewise with the corrupt Judges.).

43

"Which will not hearken to the voice of charmers, charming never so wisely." (Barnes says "making use of the most cunning or skillful of their incantations and charms. The meaning is that the utmost skill of enchantment will be unsuccessful. They are beyond the reach of any such arts. So with the people referred to by David. They were malignant and venomous, and nothing would disarm them of their malignity and destroy their venom."[301]).

Homily

"Corruption masquerading as justice was the psalmist's concern."[302] It appears from the text that King Saul called a council together to judge David in absentia for treason against the throne. The judges desiring to gain the favor of the king pronounced David guilty unjustly. Psalm 58 is David's response to the miscarriage of justice toward him. He calls the judges "dumb"; "wicked"; "sons of men" (they were as he, mere man); "poisoners" (like the poison of a deadly viper, their words were venomous); and "unjust"(they tipped the scales of justice in favor of Saul wrongfully). The judges were so wicked that they were *deaf* to the presentation of evidential proof of David's innocence. David assures them of their coming judgement by Him that sits on the eternal throne (Psalm 58:6–9).

"Judges have often been false to their trust. They have prostituted their power to selfish ends."[303] Solomon was sorely vexed over the wickedness in the judicial system. He said, "I also noticed that under the sun there is evil in the courtroom. Yes, even the courts of law are corrupt!" (Ecclesiastes 3:16 NLT). Corruption extended beyond King Saul to the judicial court, causing a miscarriage of justice with regard to David. It is a sad day for any country when the judiciary acts unjustly, criminally and prejudicially toward the accused. It appears that such corruption has infiltrated our nation's highest judicial branch of government. Regardless of political affiliation, all agree that strenuous measures ought to be undertaken to rectify the problem if it is indeed found to exist. Every man, regardless of social class, deserves *fairness at the hands* of those that judge him. And that may be assured only if the corrupt judges are reprimanded and removed from the bench.

Agesilaus, the Spartan king, in most respects was inflexibly just but not so with regard to friends. A short letter to Hydreius the Carian cites proof of this: "If Nicias is innocent, acquit him; if he is not innocent, acquit him on my account; however, be sure to acquit him."[304]

In contrast the righteous judge with truth, honor and integrity. "Mercy and truth preserve the king: and his throne is upholden by mercy" (Proverbs 20:28). The righteous reject bribes to alter decisions or the law. "A wicked man taketh a gift out of the bosom to pervert the ways of judgment" (Proverbs 17:23). They expose and punish the wicked. "Partiality in judging is not good. Whoever says to the wicked, "You are in the right," will be cursed by peoples, abhorred by nations, but those who rebuke the wicked will have delight, and a good blessing will come upon them" (Proverbs 24:23–25 ESV). The righteous restrain from appetites and activity which interfere with judging honorably. "It is not for kings, O Lemuel, it is not for kings to drink wine; nor for princes strong drink: Lest they drink, and forget the law, and pervert the judgment of any of the afflicted" (Proverbs 31:4–5). "Open thy mouth for the dumb in the cause of all such as are appointed to destruction. Open thy mouth, judge righteously, and plead the cause of the poor and needy" (Proverbs 31:8–9). See Deuteronomy 1:16.

The Bottom Line: James Garfield, in July, 1877, said "Now more than ever the people are responsible for the character of their Congress. If that body be ignorant, reckless, and corrupt, it is because the people tolerate ignorance, recklessness, and corruption."[305] The words yet ring true.

10. God Is Able to Deliver You   Psalm 59:1–4

"Deliver me from mine enemies, O my God: defend me from them that rise up against me. Deliver me from the workers of iniquity, and save me from bloody men. For, lo, they lie in wait for my soul: the mighty are gathered against me; not for my transgression, nor for my sin, O LORD. They run and prepare themselves without my fault: awake to help me, and behold."—Psalm 59:1–4.

"Deliver me from mine enemies" (here refers specifically to Saul's armed soldiers that surrounded David's house. Rawlinson says, "He has enemies, both domestic and foreign. In his early youth Saul becomes his enemy out of jealousy; then most of Saul's courtiers espouse their master's quarrel. He has enemies at the court of Achish; enemies in his family, even among his sons, as Absalom; enemies among his counsellors, as Ahithophel; foreign enemies on all sides of him—Philistines, Edomites, Moabites, Ammonites, Amalekites, Syrians, Mesopotamians, etc. Against all of them he invokes God's aid, and by God's aid he triumphs over all."[306]).

"O my God: defend me from them that rise up against me." (Jennings and Lowe say *defend* "means 'Set me high out of the reach of.'"[307] Barnes says, "The idea is that of placing him, as it were, on a tower, or on an eminence which would be inaccessible."[308]). Deliver me from the "workers of iniquity" (Saul and the men he assigned the murderous task.[309]). AND save me from "bloody men" (Saul's men commissioned to kill him; those whose task was to shed his blood.).

For, lo, "they lie in wait for my soul" (Saul's men lay in wait to ambush David. Harman says, "The people have planned their attacks with military precision, and they are busy stirring up strife against the psalmist."[310]) "the *mighty* are gathered against me" (Barnes says "strong men; hostile men; cruel men. Saul would employ on this occasion not the weak, the cowardly, the faint-hearted, but men of courage and strength; men who were unscrupulous in their character; men who would not be likely to be moved by entreaty or turned from their purpose by compassion."[311]).

"Not for my transgression, nor for my sin, O Lord." (Spurgeon says, "He appeals to Jehovah that he had done no ill. His only fault was that he was too valiant and too gracious, and was, besides, the chosen of the Lord; therefore the envious king could not rest till he had washed his hands in the blood of his too popular rival."[312]). "They run and prepare themselves" (Plumer says *prepare* "signifies to set things in order, or make arrangements."[313] The soldiers are to go in haste, taking whatever provisions necessary to accomplish the mission.[314]).

"Without my fault" (David was conscience of his innocence. He had not harmed Saul nor broken any of his laws.[315]). "Awake" (Spurgeon says, "When others go to sleep, keep thou watch, O God....Only look at thy servant's sad condition and thy hand will be sure to deliver me. We see how thorough was the Psalmist's faith in the mercy of his Lord, for he is satisfied that if the Lord do but look on his case it will move his active compassion."[316] Harman says, "The call to God to 'arise' is a standard expression in the Psalter."[317]). "To help me" ("It is a prayer that God would meet him, or come to him, and aid him."[318]). "AND, behold." (Rawlinson says, i.e., "see how things are—how innocent I am; how unjust and cruel are my enemies!"[319]).

Homily

Psalms 51, 52, 54, 56, 57 and 58 cited historical occurrences in David's life. Psalm 59 does likewise but by looking back to David's first confrontation with Saul. The Psalm is entitled, "When Saul sent, and they watched the house to kill him (David)." Spurgeon summarizes the Psalm, "They were all round the house with the warrant of authority, and a force equal to carrying it out. He was to be taken dead or alive and carried to the slaughter. No prowess could avail him to break the cordon [Oxford dictionary says 'a line or circle of police, soldiers, or guards preventing access to or from an area or building.'] of armed men, neither could any eloquence stay the hand of his bloody persecutor. He was taken like a bird in a net, and no friend was near to set him free. Unbelief would have suggested that prayer was a waste of breath, but not so thinks the good man, for he makes it his sole resort. He cries for deliverance and leaves ways and means with his God."[320] See Psalm 59:10.

The story unfolds in 1 Samuel 19:11–18. Saul sends ample soldiers to David's house at night to "watch him" (to make sure he doesn't escape) and to slay him the next morning. David's wife, Michal, somehow learns of the plot, saying, "If thou save not thy life to night, to morrow thou shalt be slain" (1 Samuel 19:11). "Though his enemies were even at hand to destroy him, yet he assures himself that God had ways to deliver him."[321] And He does. David listened and heeded Michal's counsel, escaping through a window (1 Samuel 19:12). Men, this proves that it is always good to listen to your wife!

The lesson is clear. God has the power to deliver from whatever or whoever the "enemy" may be that assails. With David, exhibit undeterred faith in God and confront the enemy saying, "Because of his strength will I wait upon thee: for God is my defense" (Psalm 59:9). Like David, pray, "Deliver me," and then start looking for the "open window" of escape that God always provides. See Psalm 107:41.

'Tis the grandest theme through the ages rung;
'Tis the grandest theme for a mortal tongue;
'Tis the grandest theme that the world e'er sung:
Our God is able to deliver thee.

He is able to deliver thee;
He is able to deliver thee.
Though by sin oppressed,
Go to Him for rest.
Our God is able to deliver thee. ~ W. A. Ogden (1887)

The Bottom Line: Alexander Maclaren says, "Trust [God] as what He is, and trust Him because of what He is, and see to it that your faith lays hold on the living God Himself and on nothing besides."[322] Spurgeon says, "*For God is my defense*, my high place, my fortress, the place of my resort in the time of my danger. If the foe be too strong for me to cope with him, I will retreat into my castle, where he cannot reach me."[323]

11. Rally around the Banner   Psalm 60:4

"Thou hast given a banner to them that fear thee, that it may be displayed because of the truth. Selah."—Psalm 60:4.

Thou hast "given a banner to them that fear thee" (Clarke says "a sign, something that was capable of being fixed on a pole."[324] Spurgeon says, "He gave them an ensign, which would be both a rallying point for their hosts, a proof that He had sent them to fight, and a guarantee of victory."[325] Barnes says, "The word rendered 'banner' means properly anything elevated or lifted up, and hence, a standard, a flag, a sign, or a signal. It may refer to a standard reared on lofty mountains or high places during an invasion of a country, to point out to the people a place of rendezvous or a rallying place [Isaiah 5:26; Isaiah 11:12; Isaiah 18:3] or it may refer to a standard or ensign borne by an army; or it may refer to the flag of a ship [Ezekiel 27:7; Isaiah 33:23]. Here it doubtless refers to the flag, the banner, the standard of an army; and the idea is that God had committed such a standard to his people that they might go forth as soldiers in his cause. They were enlisted in his service, and were fighting his battles."[326]

Plumer says, "the word [banner] occurs about twenty times; applied to a ship it means her sail; applied to Korah and his company, a sign, i. e., a signal warning to others [Numbers 26:10]; in Numbers 21:8–9, a pole; in all other cases, banner, ensign, or standard. What was the banner God had given them? In Exodus 17:15, we have Jehovah Nissi, the Lord my banner. It would make good sense to say that the Lord had given Himself, and so had become the banner of His people.'[327]).

That it may be "displayed because of the truth" (Barnes says "in the cause of truth; or, in the defense of justice and right. It was not to be displayed for vain parade or ostentation; it was not to be unfolded in an unrighteous or unjust cause; it was not to be waved for the mere purpose of carrying desolation, or of securing victory; it was that a righteous cause might be vindicated, and that the honor of God might be promoted."[328]). "Selah" (Spurgeon says, "There is so much in the fact of a banner being given to the hosts of Israel, so much of hope, of duty, of comfort, that a pause is fitly introduced. The sense justifies it, and the more joyful strain of the music necessitates it."[329] Jennings and Lowe say, "The Selah at the end of v. 4 may refer to the musical rather than to the logical divisions of the Psalm....In that God has by helping the southern army raised a standard which is to serve for the protection of His saints, David passes from prayer to thanksgiving (v. 6), not however without a final ejaculatory prayer: 'Save with Thy right hand, and answer me.'"[330]).

Homily

Psalm 60 presents another historical account of David's life cited in the Psalms. The lengthy but informative title—the longest in the Psalter—details an event in his life while he was king of Israel. It states of

David "when he strove [battled] with Aram-naharaim and with Aram-zobah [the united forces of the Arameans], when Joab returned [He and Abishai had been fighting elsewhere.] and smote of Edom in the valley of salt twelve thousand [a decisive victory for Israel]." The historical account is recorded in 2 Samuel 8:13 wherein the number slain was said to be 18,000. William S. Plumer says, "The discrepancy may be explained by supposing that the title contains the numbers slain by one division of the army, or that the twelve thousand were slain in the battle, and the residue in the flight."[331] Though David is credited with the victory (2 Samuel 8:13), the title ascribes it to Joab. Spurgeon states a possible solution to what appears to be a discrepancy. He says that in the Roman and Grecian history a victory in battle may be ascribed to anyone that is part of its supervision.[332] Allan Harman is in agreement with Spurgeon.[333]

To summarize, while King David was away from Jerusalem fighting along the Euphrates River, the Edomites attacked the city. Psalm 60 cites something of their success. David dispatches Joab, a chief commander, to battle the Edomites. He did so victoriously, as the title states. Upon David's return, he finished the conquest, destroying the Edomite strongholds (2 Samuel 8:14).[334] J. M. Boice says, "That sequence of events might explain why Joab is credited with killing twelve thousand Edomites in Psalm 60, while David is credited with striking down eighteen thousand Edomites in 2 Samuel 8:13."[335] Thus the Psalm is written following the major disaster by the Edomites in the land.

Thou hast given a banner [Jesus] to them that fear thee. The church has been given a banner or ensign to be a rallying point for all believers to unitedly fight against the foes of unrighteousness and evil until they are subdued to the Lordship of Christ Jesus. God's faithfulness to keep His promises is our banner.

That it may be displayed because of the truth. Spurgeon comments, "Our right to contend for God, and our reason for expecting success, are found in the fact that the faith has been once committed to the saints, and that by the Lord himself....Banners are for the breeze, the sun, the battle. Israel might well come forth boldly, for a sacred standard was borne aloft before them. To publish the Gospel is a sacred duty; to be ashamed of it a deadly sin. The truth of God was involved in the triumph of David's armies—he had promised them victory; and so in the proclamation of the Gospel we need feel no hesitancy, for as surely as God is true He will give success to His own Word. For the truth's sake, and because the true God is on our side, let us in these modern days of warfare emulate the warriors of Israel and unfurl our banners to the breeze with confident joy."[336]

Isaiah declares that Jesus Christ is the banner of the redeemed. "On that day the root of Jesse [a descendant of Jesse; referring to Jesus] will stand as a banner for the peoples. The nations will look to him for guidance, and his resting place will be glorious" (Isaiah 11:10 CSB). Jesus is a banner to those that "fear Him" (acknowledge and submit to Him). He is the One around whom the saved rally in unity, courage, and obedience that He might receive the glory and honor deserved among all men, and that all men might bow their knee unto Him in subjection, acclaiming Him as King of kings and Lord of lords. Matthew Henry remarks, "His love is the banner over them; in His name and strength they wage war with the powers of darkness, and under Him the church becomes terrible as an army with banners."[337]

See Song of Solomon 2:4.

Jesus is the proclaimed truth of God (John 14:6 and Romans 15:8), the believer's banner and pledge of conquest. Fighting battles under His command insures victory not because of the righteousness or goodness of believers, but as John Gill says "because of *his own truth and faithfulness in the performance of his promises* made concerning the displaying of this banner."[338] To know that as a believer we battle the enemy under the banner of the cross in the name and strength of Jesus Christ infuses courage, comradery and comfort. The cross is the believer's rallying point, not political or social issues. Jesus, our banner, said "And I, if I be lifted up from the earth, will draw all men unto me" (John 12:32). Lift the banner high; wave it constantly till the whole world knows Him who is "the way, the truth, and the life." See John 14:6 and Isaiah 49:22.

Stand up! Stand up for Jesus,
   Ye soldiers of the cross!
Lift high His royal banner;
   It must not suffer loss.

From vict'ry unto vict'ry
>   His army shall He lead,
Till every foe is vanquished
>   And Christ is Lord indeed. ~ George Duffield (1818–1888)

The Gospel's enemies, seeing the *Banner,* attack it and those that serve under it. But it cannot be demolished or defeated. Spurgeon, in the sermon *Our Banner,* says, "You remember that when divine justice came forth against Christ on Calvary, it made five tears in the great banner, and those five wounds, all glorious, are still in that banner! Since that day, many a shot has sought to riddle it, but not one has been able to touch it! Borne aloft, first by one hand and then by another, the mighty God of Jacob being the strength of the standard-bearers, that banner has bidden defiance to the leaguered hosts of the world, the flesh and the Devil! And never has it been trailed in the mire, and never once carried in jeering triumph by the adversary! Blessed are the tears in the banner, for they are the symbol of our victory! Those five wounds in the person of the Savior are the gates of Heaven to us! But, thank God, there are no more wounds to be endured—the person of our Lord is safe forever. 'A bone of Him shall not be broken.' His Gospel, too, is an unwounded Gospel, and His mystical body is uninjured. Yes, the Gospel is unharmed after all the strife of ages. The infidel threatens to rend the Gospel to pieces, but it is as glorious as ever! Modern skepticism has sought to pull it thread from thread, but has not been able so much as to rend a fragment of it!"[339]

There's a royal banner given for display
>   To the soldiers of the King;
As an ensign fair we lift it up today,
>   While as ransomed ones we sing.

Marching on, marching on,
>   For Christ count ev'rything but loss!
And to crown Him King, toil and sing
>   'Neath the banner of the cross! ~ D. W. Whittle (1884)

The Bottom Line: "He is Jehovah-nissi, 'the Lord my Banner,' whom it is our joy to follow, and around whom it is our delight to rally."[340]

12. Lead Me to the Rock That Is Higher Than I   Psalm 61:2–4

"Truly my soul waiteth upon God: from him cometh my salvation. He only is my rock and my salvation; he is my defence; I shall not be greatly moved. How long will ye imagine mischief against a man? ye shall be slain all of you: as a bowing wall shall ye be, and as a tottering fence. They only consult to cast him down from his excellency: they delight in lies: they bless with their mouth, but they curse inwardly. Selah."—Psalm 61:2-4.

"From the end of the earth" (David was forced into exile or banishment from his homeland and throne by Absalom, beyond the Jordan River. See 2 Samuel 17:22. Jennings and Lowe say, "i.e., probably from the land on the eastern coast of Jordan."[341]) "Will I cry unto thee, when my heart is overwhelmed" (Rawlinson says *overwhelmed* means, "when my heart fainteth."[342] The word means to cover as with a garment, i.e., David's soul is enveloped with darkness and calamity.[343] Jennings and Lowe say, "'shrink into oneself,' as we say, on account of sorrow, or any overwhelming emotion."[344] Spurgeon says about David's crying out to God that "[i]t was a wise resolution, for had he ceased to pray, he would have become the victim of despair; there is an end to a man when he makes an end to prayer. Observe that David had never dreamed of seeking any other God; he did not imagine the dominion of Jehovah to be local: he was at the end of the Promised Land, but he knew himself to be still in the territory of the great King; to Him only does he address his petitions."[345] Hengstenberg says, "The Psalmist grounds his prayer not only on what God has been, but on what he always is to him."[346] Henry says, "That which separates us from our other comforts should drive us so much the nearer to God, the fountain of all comfort."[347]).

"Lead me to the rock that is higher than I." (Poole says "convey me into some high and secure fortress, which I could not reach without thy succor [help; assistance], and where mine enemies cannot come at me."[348] Gill says, "Christ is meant, the Rock of Israel, the Rock of our salvation, and our refuge. He is higher than David, and all the kings of the earth; higher than the angels in Heaven, and than the heavens themselves [Hebrews 7:26]; and who by His height is able to protect and defend His people from all their enemies; and by the shade He casts to refresh and comfort them; and by the sufficiency in Him to supply all their wants; for He is as a rock impregnable."[349]).

For Thou hast been a "shelter for me, and a strong tower from the enemy." (God in the past had been his refuge, place of safety from trouble, and he is sure He will be again.).

I will "abide in thy tabernacle forever" (Barnes says, "This expresses the confident assurance that he would be restored to his home, and to the privileges of public worship."[350] Benson says, "David speaks of abiding in God's tabernacle forever, because it was a type and figure of Heaven [Hebrews 9:8, 24]. And those that dwell in His tabernacle, as it is a house of duty, during the short time of their abode on earth, shall dwell in that tabernacle which is a house of glory during an endless eternity."[351]).

"I will trust in the covert of thy wings." (The NET Bible Notes say, "The metaphor compares God to a protective mother bird."[352] See Psalm 17:8, Psalm 36:7; Psalm 57:1; Psalm 63:7; Psalm 91:4.) "Selah" (Jennings and Lowe say, "With *Selah* the Psalmist seems to pass on to a substantial proof that the confidence he has expressed in the preceding verse is not ill-grounded."[353]).

Homily

"The Davidic authorship of this Psalm seems to us undeniable. Its phraseology and figures of speech are just such as we find in other Davidic compositions, and in particular its language coincides with that of Psalms 42, 43 and 84 written at the time when he was driven out of the kingdom by Absalom."[354] David knew from past experiences with God that He was dependable and trustworthy to help in the hour of need. Therefore in exile in a distant land far from home, family and friends with his heart deeply crushed by what Absalom had done, he cries out to God for comfort, strength and help. See 2 Samuel 15:13–18. "In his weakness he calls out, and desires to find a sure place of refuge with his God."[355]

Like David, you may be in exile far away from family and friends, overwhelmed with grief, hurt and trouble. But remember God is wherever you are. There is no locale on earth where He is not and He stands ready to respond to your prayer for help. He will *lead you to the rock that is higher than you.*

Attend unto my prayer. J. W. Reeve states, "For our encouragement, how very numerous are the instances recorded in the Word of God of definite prayers on the part of God's saints, and definite answers on the part of God! No fewer than eighty-eight distinct prayers of men of God, and eighty-eight distinct answers from the Lord, are recorded in the Old Testament; and no fewer than forty-eight instances of the same kind occur in the New Testament."[356]

From the end of the earth will I cry unto thee. Prayer is always present. There is not a place on earth (loneliness, isolation from friends and their ability or willingness to help) or season of life (regardless of its difficulty, sorrow, sickness or trouble) to which God's "help" does not extend. See Psalm 139:8–13. David "overwhelmed" by trouble in faith ("will I cry") asked that he might be *led to that Rock,* God (the Lord Jesus Christ). Spurgeon says not only do we need the Rock, but guidance to it by the Holy Spirit. It is the Holy Spirit that illumines man's darkness, showing him sin and his need for salvation in Jesus Christ, the Solid Rock and the Rock of Ages. In Spurgeon's day it was not unusual for ships to wreck off the northern coast of England, causing the loss of many lives because the rocks were inaccessible. He tells of a man who resided atop one such cliff who chiseled steps into it from the beach upward to a place of safety. Drowning mariners using the steps were able to get to a higher rock, that otherwise was too high for them, thus climbing to save their lives. A time came when the steps were worn away by the storms and a chain railing was erected to help the drowning ones be rescued. Spurgeon says, "The illustration is self-interpreting. Our experience leads us to understand this verse right well, for the time was with us when we were in such amazement of soul by reason of sin, that although we knew the Lord Jesus to be a sure salvation for sinners, yet we could not come at Him, by reason of our many doubts and forebodings. A Savior would have been of no use to us if the Holy Spirit had not gently led us to Him, and enabled us to rest upon Him. To this day we often feel that we not only want a rock, but to be led to it."[357] The Holy Spirit is to man what the chiseled steps and chain railing was to the drowning mariners. He leads man to Jesus Christ by conviction of sin and divine illumination of truth. See John 16:8, 13; 1 Corinthians 2:10; 1 Corinthians 12:3.

All that flee to the Rock have found shelter and refuge in the *covert of His wings.*

In the shadow of His wings
There is peace, sweet peace,
Peace that passeth understanding,
Peace, sweet peace that knows no ending.

In the shadow of His wings
There is peace, sweet peace,
In the shadow of His wings
There is peace (sweet peace). ~ J. B. Atchinson (1890)

Joseph Parker stated, "David cried from the end of the land! We have cried from the same extremity. By processes too subtle for us to comprehend, God has often caused our misfortunes to become our blessings. In the midst of the psalmist's trouble there rises an aspiration— 'lead me to the rock that is higher than I.' The self-helplessness expressed in this prayer moves our entire sympathy. 'Lead me'—what a blind man who had wandered from the accustomed path would say; 'lead me'— what a lame man would say who had fallen by reason of his great weakness; 'lead me'—what a terrified man would say who had to pass along the edge of a bottomless abyss. It is in such extremities that men best know themselves. David wished to be led to the rock; he wished to stand firmly, to stand above the flood line, to have rest after so great disquietude. Then there is a rock higher than we? We have heard of Jesus Christ by this strange name; we have heard of Him as the Rock of ages; we have heard of Him as the Rock in the wilderness; we have heard of Him as the Stone rejected of the builders but elected of God to the chief place."[358]

From the ends of the earth (From the ends of the earth)
From the depth of the sea (From the depth of the sea)
From the height of the heaven (From the height of the heaven)
Your name we praise. ~ Hillsong United

Lead me to the rock that is higher than I. Spurgeon wrote, "The thought of JESUS CHRIST, WHO IS THE ROCK THAT IS HIGHER THAN WE ARE. Here is a man who is a great sinner. 'Ah!' he says, 'I am indeed a great sinner; my iniquities reach so high that they have ascended above the very stars; they have gone before me to the judgment seat of God, and they are clamouring for my destruction.' Well, sinner, come thou here, and measure this Rock. Thou art very high, it is true; but this Rock is higher than thou art. Here comes another forward; he is not a man full of doubts and fears, but he is a man of hopeful spirit. 'Oh!' says he, 'I have many sins, but I hope that the Lord Jesus Christ will take them all away. I have many wants, but I hope that He will supply them. I shall have many temptations, but I hope that He will ward them off. I shall have many difficulties, but I hope He will carry me through them.' Ah, man, I like to see thee have a good long measuring rod, when it is made of hope. Hope is a tall companion; he wades right through the sea, and is not drowned; you cannot kill him, do what you may. Hope is one of the last blessings God gives us, and one that abides last with us. If a man is foodless, and without covering, still he hopes to see better days by and by. Now, sinner, thy hopes, I would have thee to see, are very tall, and very high; but remember, this Rock is higher than any of thy hopes. 'Well,' cries another, 'from what I have heard, and what I have read in God's Word, I am expecting very great things of Christ when I shall see Him as He is. Oh, sir, if He be better than the communion of His saints can make Him, if He be sweeter than all His most eloquent preachers can speak of Him, if He be so delightful that those who know Him best cannot tell His beauties, what a precious—what a glorious—what an inconceivable Christ He must be!' Ah, I am glad thou art measuring Christ by thine expectation. But let me tell thee, high as thy expectations are, He is higher than thou art. Expect what thou mayest; but when thou seest Him, thou wilt say with the Queen of Sheba, 'The half was not told me.' Now, as some of you will be exercised with troubles, remember that the Rock is higher than you are; and when your troubles reach you, if you are not high enough to escape them, climb up to the Rock Christ, for there is no trouble that can reach you when you get there."[359]

The Bottom Line: With David, ask the Lord "to lead you to the Rock that is higher than yourself." Without being "led" to Him, we will never get to Him. As the chiseled steps and chain railing on the cliff led mariners to a place of safety, just so the Holy Spirit is willing and able to lead you to Jesus Christ, the Rock of Salvation. In times of crisis and trouble, flee to "the strong tower" (impregnable tower[360]) of Almighty God to be kept safe from the enemy. See Psalm 61:3.

13. Silence before God   Psalm 62:5

"My soul, wait thou only upon God; for my expectation is from him."—Psalm 62:5.

My soul, "wait thou only upon God" (To *wait* is to be patiently silent before the Lord; *only* or alone indicates confident trust in the Lord to act.[361] Spurgeon says, "Be still silent, O my soul! submit thyself completely, trust immovably, wait patiently."[362] Barnes says, "The meaning is, that he would commit the whole cause to God, and that his soul would thus be calm and without apprehension."[363] Plumer says, "The meaning is, Bow to the sovereign will of God; in silence submit to Him, hoping in His mercy, and not despairing of His aid, but being subject to Him in a spirit of patience."[364] Harman says to "find rest" in God.[365]).

For "my expectation is from him" (In verse 1 David uses *salvation* instead of *expectation,* of which Bratcher and Reyburn say, "*Help* translates the Hebrew verb 'to save,' which is used some forty-seven times in Psalms. It means to rescue; save; deliver from illness, physical peril, enemies, or death—anything that threatens the well-being or life of the one who prays. It is the verb from which the noun 'savior' is formed, as is the proper name [*Joshua,* which in its Greek form becomes Jesus]."[366] *Expectation,* says Gill, means "my hope."[367] David's hope wasn't from within himself or outside in man but in God totally. God alone was the foundation for his hope and confidence.).

Homily

The title gives authorship to David. Though uncertain, it appears David composed the Psalm during the rebellion of his son Absalom, at which time he had to flee from Jerusalem.[368] Psalm 62:4 seems to allude to Absalom's flattery to steal the people's allegiance from King David and the use of lies to ultimately dethrone him. His life in danger, he looks *only* unto the Lord as his "salvation" (Psalm 62:1); "rock" (Psalm 62:2); "defense" (Psalm 62:6); "strength" (Psalm 62:7); and "refuge" (Psalm 62:7). David is confident that God will grant the help warranted (Psalm 62:8). Matthew Henry paraphrases Psalm 62:2b, "'If God is my strength and mighty deliverer, *I shall not be greatly moved* (that is, I shall not be undone and ruined); I may be shocked, but I shall not be sunk.' Or, 'I shall not be much disturbed and disquieted in my own breast. I may be put into some fright, but I shall not be afraid with any amazement, nor so as to be put out of the possession of my own soul. I may be perplexed, but not in despair' [2 Corinthians 4:8]."[369] Matthew Henry concludes, "This hope in God will be an anchor of the soul, sure and steadfast."[370] "It is only by constant self-exhortation that the calmness of Psalm 62:1 can be maintained, especially when the recollection of his enemies' double-faced behavior stirs his indignation."[371] "He [David] was so assaulted as to be like a leaning wall and a rickety fence [terms applied to the psalmist, not to the assailants]. Yet he experienced inward calm and strength even while sorely mistreated."[372] Any address or prayer to God is absent in the psalm. It however does mention several attributes of God (strength, savior, defender, refuge).

In times of crisis and calamity "wait thou only upon God: for my expectation is from him." This is what to do when you don't know what to do. Patiently trust, rely upon the Lord to intervene as He deems best to grant help in the hour of dire need, refusing in panic to look to others for resolution. In faith expect Him to come to your rescue. Spurgeon says, "We expect from God because we believe in him. Expectation is the child of prayer and faith, and is owned of the Lord as an acceptable grace. We should desire nothing but what would be right for God to give, then our expectation would be all from God; and concerning truly good things we should not look to second causes, but to the Lord alone, and so again our expectation would be all from Him. The vain expectations of worldly people come not;...our expectations are on the way, and in due season will arrive to satisfy our hopes. Happy is the man who feels that all he has, all he wants, and all he expects are to be found in his God."[373]

Alexander McLaren, in his exposition of Psalm 62:1 and Psalm 62:5, exhorts the believer to make a vigorous effort to be still and silent before the Lord. He writes, "That vigorous effort is expressed here by the very form of the phrase ['Wait thou only upon God']. The same word which began the first clause begins the second also. As in the former it represented for us, with an emphatic 'Truly,' the struggle through which the Psalmist had reached the height of his blessed experience, so here it represents in like manner the earnestness of the self-exhortation which he addresses to himself. He calls forth all his powers to the conflict, which is needed even by the man who has attained to that height of communion, if he would remain where he has climbed. And for us, brethren, who shrink from taking these former words upon our lips, how much greater the need to use our most strenuous efforts to quiet our souls. If the summit reached can only be held by earnest endeavor, how much more is needed to struggle up to it from the valleys below! The silence of the soul before God is no mere passiveness. It requires the intensest energy of all our being to keep all our being still and waiting upon Him. So put all your strength into the task, and be sure that your soul is never so intensely alive as when in deepest abnegation it waits hushed before God. Trust no past emotions. Do not wonder if they should fade even when they are brightest. Do not let their evanescence tempt you to doubt their reality. But always when our hearts are fullest of His love, and our spirits stilled with the sweetest sense of His solemn presence, stir yourselves up to keep firm hold of the else passing gleam, and in your consciousness let these two words live in perpetual alternation: 'Truly my soul waiteth upon God. My soul! wait thou only upon God.'"[374]

> Be still, my soul; the Lord is on thy side.
>> Bear patiently the cross of grief or pain.
> Leave to thy God to order and provide;
>> In every change He faithful will remain.
> Be still, my soul; thy best, thy heavenly, Friend
> Through thorny ways leads to a joyful end.
>
> Be still, my soul; thy God doth undertake
>> To guide the future as He has the past.
> Thy hope, thy confidence, let nothing shake;
>> All now mysterious shall be bright at last.
> Be still, my soul; the waves and winds still know
> His voice who ruled them while He dwelt below.

Be still, my soul, though dearest friends depart
    And all is darkened in the vale of tears;
Then shalt thou better know His love, His heart,
    Who comes to soothe thy sorrows and thy fears.
Be still, my soul; thy Jesus can repay
From His own fulness all He takes away.

Be still, my soul; the hour is hastening on
    When we shall be forever with the Lord;
When disappointment, grief, and fear are gone,
    Sorrow forgot, love's purest joys restored.
Be still, my soul; when change and tears are past,
All safe and blessed we shall meet at last.
        ~ Catharine Amalia Dorothea von Schlegel (1752)

The Lord is our only expectation (hope, comfort). W. S. Plumer states, "When we find Him, we need seek no further. He is all-sufficient. The more He is tried, the more He is found to be the very friend we need."[375] Spurgeon stated, "Most people want something to see, something tangible to the senses, to be the object of their confidence, but David rests only in God."[376] Oswald Chambers wrote, "Has God trusted you with His silence—a silence that has great meaning? God's silences are actually His answers....If we only take as answers those that are visible to our senses, we are in a very elementary condition of grace."[377]

Rest in the Lord; wait patiently for Him. See Psalm 37:7. Martin Luther states, "In Hebrew, 'Be silent to God and let Him mold thee.' Keep still and He will mold thee to the right shape."[378]

The Bottom Line: The absence of quietude (silence) communion with the Lord is the robber of man's peace and hope. Take time to be "still" and "know that I am the Lord." Refuse to allow the noises around or within you to drown out the precious words of the Lord that say, "*My peace I give unto you: not as the world giveth, give I unto you. Let not your heart be troubled, neither let it be afraid*" (John 14:27). Spurgeon said, "My Lord never fails to honour His promises; and when we bring them to His throne, He never sends them back unanswered. Therefore I will wait only at His door, for He ever opens it with the hand of munificent grace. At this hour I will try Him anew. But we have 'expectations' beyond this life. We shall die soon; and then our 'expectation is from Him.' Do we not expect that when we lie upon the bed of sickness He will send angels to carry us to His bosom?"[379] With David, say to your soul, "My soul, wait thou only upon God; for my expectation (both presently and eternally) is from him." Trust Him to do what is expedient and best, even if it means vetoing personal desires and plans.

14. Following Hard after God   Psalm 63:8

"My soul followeth hard after thee: thy right hand upholdeth me."—Psalm 63:8.

My soul "followeth hard" (Barnes says "means properly to cleave to; to adhere; to be glued to; to stick fast."[380] Poole says, "i.e., pursueth thee eagerly, diligently, and resolvedly, and as it were step by step, when thou seemest to run away from me; which is the emphasis of this Hebrew word."[381]).

"After thee" (Not after that which God might do for him, but God Himself.) "Thy right hand upholdeth me" (Barnes says, "God upheld him with all his strength. The meaning is, that God sustained him in life; defended him in danger; kept him from the power of his enemies."[382]). Allan Harman says in the Psalm at large, "The repetition of 'I' and 'my' points to the personal nature of the appeals, while the use of 'you' or 'your' directs attention to his source of help and salvation."[383]).

Homily

The title states the Psalm was composed when David was in the wilderness of Judah, that is, in the *forest of Hareth* (1 Samuel 22:5) or in *the wilderness of Ziph* (1 Samuel 23:15).[384] Gordon Franz states, "King David was in a very inhospitable environment with disastrous circumstances beyond his control when he composed Psalm 63. His son, Prince Absalom, instigated a revolt against him. King David fled eastward from Jerusalem through the Judean Desert, most likely at the end of the summer (2 Samuel 16:1). David escaped to the Levitical city of Mahanaim, in the friendlier region of Gilead on the other side of the Jordan River (2 Samauel 17:24)."[385] Albert Barnes likewise wrote, "David was repeatedly driven into that wilderness in the time of Saul; and the general structure of the psalm would accord well with any one of those occasions; but the mention of the 'king' in Psalm 63:11, as undoubtedly meaning David, makes it necessary to refer the composition of the psalm to a later period in his life, since the title 'king' was not given to him in the time of Saul. The psalm, therefore, was doubtless composed in the time of Absalom—the period when David was driven away by the rebellion, and compelled to seek a refuge in that wilderness. It belongs, if this view is correct, to the same period in the life of David as Psalm 42:1–11; Psalm 43:1–5; Psalm 61:1–8; and probably some others."[386]

It's not for the "creature comforts" that David sighs but the manifested presence of the Lord. All about him seemed to be a spiritual desert, a land where the *living water* that alone satisfies thirst was absent. His lips are parched, soul famished, for lack of it and he cries out in desperation, "My soul thirsteth for thee: my flesh longeth for thee in a dry and thirsty land, where no water is" (Psalm 63:1). David uses a similar metaphor in Psalm 42:1–2. It's imperative that in the wildernesses of spiritual drought you resolve to do as David did and say, "My soul followeth hard after thee" (Psalm 63:8).

My soul followeth hard after thee. Albert Barnes says, "The idea here is that of adhering to, or cleaving to; and the meaning is, that the Psalmist adhered firmly to God, as pieces of wood glued together adhere to each other; that he, as it were, stuck fast to Him; that he would not leave Him or be separated from Him. The language represents the feelings of true piety in adhering firmly and constantly to God, whatever there may be that tends to separate us from Him."[387] But Barnes observes, "The adhesion of bodies by glue is a striking but not an adequate representation of the firmness with which the soul adheres to God. Portions of matter held together by glue may be separated; the soul of the true believer never can be separated from God."[388] Matthew Henry remarks, "To press hard after God is to follow Him closely, as those that are afraid of losing the sight of Him, and to follow Him swiftly, as those that long to be with Him."[389] W. S. Plumer says "commonly rendered cleaveth, or sticketh."[390] Hengstenberg says, "Cleaves to Him, like a bur to a coat."[391] Adam Clarke says, "My soul cleaves, or is glued after Thee."[392] Waterland says, "My soul hath kept close—hath adhered to Thee."[393] See Genesis 2:24; 34:3; Joshua 23:8 and Psalm 119:31.

A. W. Tozer states, "To have found God and still to pursue Him is the soul's paradox of love, scorned indeed by the too-easily-satisfied religionist, but justified in happy experience by the children of the burning heart....Come near to the holy men and women of the past and you will soon feel the heat of their desire after God. They mourned for Him, they prayed and wrestled and sought for Him day and night, in season and out, and when they had found Him the finding was all the sweeter for the long seeking. Moses used the fact that he knew God as an argument for knowing Him better. 'Now, therefore, I pray thee, if I have found grace in thy sight, show me now thy way, that I may know thee, that I may find grace in thy sight'; and from there he rose to make the daring request, 'I beseech thee, show me thy glory.' God was frankly pleased by this display of ardor, and the next day called Moses into the mount, and there in solemn procession made all His glory pass before him. David's life was a torrent of spiritual desire, and his Psalms ring with the cry of the seeker and the glad shout of the finder. Paul confessed the mainspring of his life to be his burning desire after Christ. 'That I may know Him' was the goal of his heart, and to this he sacrificed everything. 'Yea doubtless, and I count all things but loss for the excellency of the knowledge of Christ Jesus my Lord: for whom I have suffered the loss of all things, and do count them but refuse, that I may win Christ.'"[394]

To follow hard after God (to run, thirst after Him) pictures to me Phillip in pursuit of the Ethiopian's chariot. He refused to give up the pursuit until finally he "joined himself to the chariot" (i.e., glued himself to it). See Acts 8:29–30. Maintain hot pursuit of God in holy communion and conduct. Glue thyself (cleave unto) to His chariot of intimate fellowship, worship and devotion. And then even in the wildernesses of desolation, despair and defeat, like David, you will be able to say, "Thy right hand upholdeth me" (Psalm 63:8). That is, the almighty power and strength of God sustains. "When thou passest through the waters, I will be with thee; and through the rivers, they shall not overflow thee: when thou walkest through the fire, thou shalt not be burned; neither shall the flame kindle upon thee. For I am the LORD thy God" (Isaiah 43:2). There is no hope for any man to live uprightly outside of the strength of Almighty God. Man is but as a filthy rag, but with God he can do wonders.[395] See Isaiah 64:6 and Hebrews 11:33–38. Arnd comments, "God holds heaven and earth with his hand, he will therefore be able both to hold up and to bear such a little atom of dust as thou art."[396]

Note that it was "when the Philistines heard that they had anointed David king over Israel, all the Philistines came up to seek David" (2 Samuel 5:17). Afraid of King David's following of the Israelites, arch enemies (Philistines) mustered up their entire army to pursue and crush him. See 1 Samuel 29:1. A. F. Kirkpatrick concurs, "The Philistines were alarmed by the union of the Israelites under a king of proved vigour, who had inaugurated his reign by a brilliant military achievement."[397] It is often the case that when a opportunity to do good for the Lord arises and we initiate it, that Satan opens the battlements of Hell to blast mercilessly.[398]

The Bottom Line: Matthew Henry wrote, "To press hard after God is to follow Him closely, as those that are afraid of losing the sight of Him, and to follow Him swiftly, as those that long to be with Him. This David did."[399] A. W. Tozer says, "I want deliberately to encourage this mighty longing after God. The lack of it has brought us to our present low estate. The stiff and wooden quality about our religious lives is a result of our lack of holy desire. Complacency is a deadly foe of all spiritual growth. Acute desire must be present or there will be no manifestation of Christ to His people. He waits to be wanted. Too bad that with many of us He waits so long, so very long, in vain."[400] Gregory of Nazianzus (c. 330–389) expressed it well: "God thirsts to be thirsted for." He longs to be longed for by His people.

15. Poisonous Arrows   Psalm 64:3–7

"Who whet their tongue like a sword, and bend their bows to shoot their arrows, even bitter words: That they may shoot in secret at the perfect: suddenly do they shoot at him, and fear not. They encourage themselves in an evil matter: they commune of laying snares privily; they

say, Who shall see them? They search out iniquities; they accomplish a diligent search: both the inward thought of every one of them, and the heart, is deep. But God shall shoot at them with an arrow; suddenly shall they be wounded."—Psalm 64:3–7.

"Who" (David's enemies, perhaps during the time of Absalom's revolt or Saul's persecution. He had many, for often they are mentioned in his Psalms.) "whet their tongue" (Plumer says the Hebrew tense is "have whetted, implying that they have done it for some time, and are doing it still."[401] Barnes says, "Who sharpen their tongue; that is, they utter words that will cut deep, or penetrate the soul. The idea is that of slander or reproach."[402]).

"Like a sword" (Spurgeon says, "As warriors grind their swords, to give them an edge which will cut deep and wound desperately, so do the unscrupulous invent falsehoods calculated to inflict pain, to stab the reputation, to kill the honor of the righteous."[403]). AND "bend their bows to shoot their arrows" (Jamieson-Fausset-Brown Bible says "literally, 'tread,' or, 'prepared.' The allusion is to the mode of bending a bow by treading on it."[404]).

Even "bitter words" (Clarke says, "Their defamatory sayings are here represented as deadly as poisoned arrows."[405] Dahood says "with poisonous substance [they] tip their arrows." SPCL uses a good simile: "They shoot their poisonous words like arrows."[406] The same word for bitter or bitterness is found in 1 Samuel 15:32; 2 Samuel 2:26; Proverbs 5:4 and Ecclesiastes 7:26.).

That they may "shoot in secret" (ambushes of the enemy from which they shoot poisonous arrows) "at the perfect" (Kirkpatrick says "the upright, blameless man."[407] Rawlinson says, "David does not scruple to call himself 'perfect,' using the word in the sense in which it is used of Job [Job 1:1; 2:3]."[408]) "suddenly do they shoot at him" (Barnes says, "At an unexpected time, and from an unlooked-for quarter."[409] The arrows shot are those of lies and slander.[410] Spurgeon says, "They give their unsuspecting victim no chance of defending himself; they pounce on him like a wild beast leaping on its prey. They lay their plans so warily that they fear no detection."[411] Hengstenberg says "'suddenly' is 'while he is thinking there is no harm.'"[412] Dilday and Kennedy say, "Shooting an arrow was the figure employed both for the assault of the evil men and for their overthrow (vv. 4, 7)."[413]).

"And fear not" (Bratcher and Reyburn say "means that they are not afraid that anyone will see them or accuse them of wrongdoing."[414] These slanderous enemies fear not man or God.). They "encourage themselves in an evil matter" (Ellicott says, "Literally, '*they strengthen for themselves* an evil thing,' which evidently means that they take their measures carefully, and are prepared to carry them out resolutely."[415] Kirkpatrick says, "They make strong for themselves an evil scheme, sparing no pains to make their plot successful."[416]).

"They commune of laying snares privily" (Rawlinson says, "The ungodly continually set traps for the righteous, who are so simple that they often fall into them. We do not know the exact proceedings of his enemies against David at the time, the narrative of 2 Samuel 15 being so brief; but it was probably by some trickery that David was induced to quit the stronghold of Jerusalem, and so yield the seat of government, and many other advantages, to his rival."[417] Ellicott says, "Better, they calculate how they may lay snares privily. The conspirators carefully and in secret go over every detail of their plot."[418]); they say, "Who shall see them?" (Kirkpatrick says, "More exactly the Hebrew means, Who will see to them? They have persuaded themselves that there is no God who will take any account of their proceedings."[419]). Bratcher and Reyburn say, "These wicked people think that no one, including God, sees what they are doing."[420]).

"They search out iniquities" (Barnes says, "The original word [denotes] the act of exploring—as when one searches for treasure, or for anything that is hidden or lost—implying a deep and close attention of the mind to the subject. So here they examined every plan, or every way which was suggested to them, by which they could hope to accomplish their purpose."[421]).

"They accomplish a diligent search: both the inward thought of every one of them, and the heart, is deep."(Kirkpatrick says, "We have perfected [say they] a consummate plan."[422] Clarke says, "The word [translated *search*], which is used three times, as a noun and a verb, in this sentence, signifies to strip off the clothes. 'They investigate iniquities;

---

they perfectly investigate an investigation.' Most energetically translated by the old Psalter: 'They ransacked wickednesses.' To ransack signifies to search every corner, to examine things part by part, to turn over every leaf, to leave no hole or cranny unexplored. But the word *investigate fully* expresses the meaning of the term, as it comes...from *in,* taken privately, and *vestire,* to clothe, stripping the man bare, that he may be exposed to all shame, and be the more easily wounded."[423] Barnes says, "*Is deep*—a deep-laid scheme; a plan that indicates profound thought; a purpose that is the result of consummate sagacity [*Cambridge Dictionary* says 'having or showing understanding and the ability to make good judgments']. This is the language of the author of the Psalm. He admitted that there had been great talent and skill in the formation of the plan. Hence, it was that he cried so earnestly to God."[424] Plumer says, "They search out iniquities, or wickednesses, or unrighteousness, i. e., methods of accomplishing their wicked purposes. And they rack their brain to find out something more nefarious ['morally bad', *Cambridge Dictionary*] and fatal than ever, and so they accomplish a diligent search."[425]).

"But God shall shoot at them with an arrow; suddenly shall they be wounded" (David says the enemy may shoot poisonous arrows at him but God will shoot back. That is, in the same way they persecute David God will punish them [shoot arrows at them].[426] *Suddenly*, quickly and unexpectingly will they incur wounding in retribution from God. Barnes says, "The blows which they thought to give to others would come on themselves, and this would occur at an unexpected moment."[427] Calvin says, "The poison concocted in their secret counsels, and which they revealed with their tongues, would prove to have a deadly effect upon themselves."[428] Clarke says, "This, if the Psalm refers to the times of David, seems to be prophetic of Saul's death. The archers pressed upon him, and sorely wounded him with their arrows [1 Samuel 31:3]."[429]).

Homily

Jennings and Lowe state, "There is every reason to accept the Title of Authorship, 'to David,' as authentic. The Psalm opens in the same way as other Davidic petitions [Psalms 4, 5, 17]; it complains, as do so many Davidic Psalms, of a secret conspiracy of the hostile party; we have common Davidic comparisons, viz., that of slander and cruel words to sharp weapons, and that of the malicious scheme to a carefully concealed snare."[430] David composed the Psalm when Gad the prophet told him, "Stay not in Masrob for King Saul seeks thy life." Others say it was written during his persecution by Saul or the rebellion of Absalom.[431] The Psalm depicts the sinister plot of the wicked to assassinate the good character and reputation of the righteous, and the retributive hand of God in response. In essence the Psalm details how David's enemies seek to defame him (to cause his demise in popularity; follow-ship) through poisonous arrows of lies and slander shot at him from the most unexpected places at the most unexpected times from the most unexpected people suddenly.

All believers, especially those that walk uprightly, standing uncompromisingly for the truth, are candidates for slander. To have poisonous and destructive arrows shot at you from all directions without warning and suddenly is fearful. In such times pray with David, "Preserve my life from fear of the enemy. Hide me from the secret counsel of the wicked; from the insurrection of the workers of iniquity" (Psalm 64:1–2). As I write, the similarity between David and the current President of the United States, Donald Trump, is clear with regard to the enemy's relentless assault on his character through *multitudes of poisonous arrows*. The venomous arrows which are shot from the bows of friends and colleagues but primarily the media are designed to lessen his popularity to bring a quick demise to his presidency (as with David). By God's grace the arrows to date have been retarded, failing in their purpose.

Whet their tongue as a sword. W. S. Plumer remarks, "Comparing words to swords is frequent in the Psalms [Psalms 55:21; 57:4; 59:7]. When words are made as sharp as possible by wit and malice, they have a frightful keenness of penetration."[432] Poisonous arrows (lies, slander, defamatory remarks, and disparaging innuendos) sadly unseat judicial leaders and ministerial staff. Spurgeon is correct in saying, "A lie will go round the world while truth is pulling its boots on."[433]

Dwight L. Moody said, "Slander has been called 'tongue murder.' Slanderers are compared to flies that always settle on sores, but do not touch a man's good parts. If the archangel Gabriel should come down to earth and mix in human affairs, I believe his character would be assailed inside of forty-eight hours. Slander called Christ a gluttonous man and a winebibber. He claimed to be the Truth, but instead of worshipping Him, men took Him and crucified Him."[434] And if the wicked assailed the good name of Christ, surely they will assail that of His disciples. "We should form the habit of letting all slander and gossip go in one ear and out the other instead of letting it go out our mouths."[435] The listening to and spreading of slanderous remarks makes one a coconspirator with the talebearer in the destruction he precipitates. "Do not be ready," declares C. H. Spurgeon, "to receive such reports; there is as much wickedness in believing a lie as in telling it, if we are always ready to believe it. There would be no slanderers if there were no receivers and believers of slander."[436] Solomon underscores the point: "Whoever goes about slandering reveals secrets; therefore do not associate with a simple babbler" (Proverbs 20:19 ESV), and, "Where no wood is, there the fire goeth out: so where there is no talebearer, the strife ceaseth" (Proverbs 26:20). Simply stated, don't stoke or fuel the slanderer's fire, but attempt to smother it. Peter the Great said, "It is easy to splash mud, but I would rather help a man to keep his coat clean." [437]

John MacArthur recounts the news of slander that ended tragically. "They were a happy little family living in a small town in North Dakota, even though the young mother had not been entirely well since the birth of her second baby....[E]ach evening the neighbors were aware of a warmth in their hearts when they would see the husband and father being met at the gate by his wife and two little children. There was laughter in the evening, too, and when the weather was nice, Father and the children would romp together on the back lawn while Mother looked on with happy smiles.

"Then one day a village gossip started a story saying that [the father] was being unfaithful to his wife, a story entirely without foundation. But it eventually came to the ears of the young wife and it was more than she could bear.

"Reason left its throne and that night when her husband came home there was no one to meet him at the gate, no laughter in the house, no fragrant aroma coming from the kitchen—only coldness and something that chilled his heart with fear.

"And down in the basement he found the three of them hanging from a beam. Sick and in despair the young mother had first taken the lives of her two children and then her own.

"In the days that followed, the truth of what had happened came out—a gossip's tongue [had wrought] a terrible tragedy."[438]

The young wife is representative of myriads of people over the centuries (perhaps like you) whose lives were turned upside down all due to the maliciousness of someone spreading an untruth (intentionally or unintentionally) about them or about one they greatly loved or admired. Though vindication may come, irreparable damage is often already done. The scars of slander forever linger.

In times of slander, handle it gracefully, looking to God, as did David, for strength to endure, protection and vindication. Leave retribution in the hands of God, knowing that what the wicked "dish out" on you will in time be dished out upon them (Psalm 64:7). Chuck Swindoll remarks, ""LEAN HARD! Stop and think. Job did precisely that. While speaking the truth, he left the defense of his own character in the Lord's hands. He was firm and deliberate, but he remained in control. I repeat, I understand what it's like to be unjustly maligned. I have been accused of things, and that rumor has kept me awake. It has made my stomach churn. It has taken away my appetite. I have determined not to pay any attention to it, yet found that I was unable to turn it off in my mind. Not until I decided to leave things in the Lord's hands and rest in His sovereign control, did I find inner peace. Without exception (Please hear this!) without exception, not until I deliberately stepped back and leaned hard on my God, did my mind begin to relax, my emotions settle down, and my inner peace return. I say again, the truth will win out. And God will be glorified."[439] Amen and Amen.

The Bottom Line: Spurgeon summarizes, "Our God is very pitiful, and He will surely rescue His people from so desperate a destruction. It will be well for us here to remember that this is a description of the danger to which the Psalmist was exposed from slanderous tongues. Verily this is not an overdrawn picture, for the wounds of a sword will heal, but the wounds of the tongue cut deeper than the flesh, and are not soon cured. *Slander leaves a slur, even if it be wholly disproved.* Common fame, although notoriously a common liar, has very many believers. Once let an ill word get into men's mouths, and it is not easy to get it fully out again."[440]

16. God Heareth Prayer   Psalm 65:2

"O thou that hearest prayer, unto thee shall all flesh come."— Psalm 65:2.

O "thou"(Barnes says "who hast revealed thyself as a God hearing prayer—one of the leading characteristics of whose nature it is that thou dost hear prayer."[441]) that "hearest prayer" (Rawlinson says "a necessary and inalienable attribute of God. Calvin rightly observes on the passage: 'God can no more divest himself of his attribute of hearing prayer than of being.'"[442] Poole says "delightest to hear and answer the prayers of Thy people in Zion; which he justly mentions as one of the chiefest of God's favors and privileges vouchsafed to His church.'[443]).

"Unto thee shall all flesh come" (Not just the nation of Israel and the Jews but all peoples of all lands. Barnes says, "That is, all people—for the word is here used evidently to denote mankind. The idea is, that there is no other resource for man, no other help, no other refuge, but the God that hears prayer."[444]).

Homily

A Psalm of David. W. S. Plumer wrote, "Some think it was composed for the feast of tabernacles, and some for the passover, or for spring. It was evidently composed when some mercy had awakened the spirit of gratitude, and the mind was led to take an extended view of God's goodness. This is often the case."[445]

God has the reputation for hearing prayer. It "is His inalienable attribute, His 'nature and property,' to hear and answer prayer."[446] Spurgeon states, "God not only has heard, but is now hearing prayer, and always must hear prayer, since He is an immutable being and never changes in His attributes. What a delightful title for the God and Father of our Lord Jesus Christ! Every right and sincere prayer is as surely heard as it is offered."[447] John Gill says God hears prayer "so as to answer it sooner or later, in one way or another, and always in the fittest time, and in the best way; so as to fulfil the requests and supply the wants of men, so far as may be for their good, and God's glory; which is a proof of the omnipresence, omniscience, and all sufficiency of God; who can hear the prayers of His people in all places at the same time, and knows all their persons and wants, and what is most proper for them, and can and does supply all their needs, and causes all grace to abound towards them."[448] Max Lucado remarked, "Our prayers may be awkward. Our attempts may be feeble. But since the power of prayer is in the One who hears it and not in the one who says it, our prayers do make a difference."[449]

Unto thee shall all flesh come. All "flesh" (mankind) is sinful, weak and frail, in desperate need for divine help, forgiveness and salvation. In that, human means cannot satisfy, secure or save. The door unto the throne of Him who alone can, stands open for every man's use. Albert Barnes says, "No other being can meet his actual needs; and those needs are to be met only in connection with prayer. All people are permitted to come thus to God; all have need of His favor; all must perish unless, in answer to prayer, He interposes and saves the soul."[450] The "ears" of Holy God are accessible to prayer through the Cross of Jesus Christ, man's Mediator to God [I Timothy 2:5]. Hebrews says, "Having therefore, brethren, boldness to enter into the holiest by the blood of Jesus" [Hebrews 10:19]. The first prayer from the sinner's lips that God hears is the same as that of the Publican: "God be merciful to me a sinner" (Luke 18:13). It is the atoning blood of Jesus Christ for sin in man's life that enables prayer to be heard and answered. Spurgeon says, "To come to God is the life of true religion; we come weeping in conversion, hoping in supplication, rejoicing in praise, and delighting in service....[E]ach one who tries the true God is encouraged by his own success to persuade others also, and so the kingdom of God comes to men, and men come to it."[451]

"First comes forgiveness by expiation, for such is the meaning of 'covering' [purge away (Psalm 65:3)]. Then the cleansed soul has 'access with confidence'; then approaching, it happily dwells a guest in the house and is supplied with that which satisfies all desires."[452]

By terrible things in righteousness wilt thou answer us. God not only hears prayer but answers it in wondrous ways. Spurgeon observes,

"The direct allusion here is, no doubt, to the Lord's overthrow of the enemies of His people to strike terror into both friends and foes. We do not always know what we are asking for when we pray; when the answer comes, it is possible that we may be terrified by it. We seek sanctification, and trial will be the reply; we ask for more faith, and persecution scatters us. Nevertheless, it is good to ask on, for nothing which the Lord grants in His love can do us any harm. Terrible things will turn out to be blessed things after all, when they come in answer to prayer."[453]

Who art the confidence of all the ends of the earth, and of them that are afar off upon the sea. Albert Barnes says, "The word *confidence* as used here means that God is the source of trust, or, that all proper reliance, by all people, in all parts of the earth and on the sea, must be in Him; that is, that there is no other on whom people can properly rely. It does not mean that all people actually repose such confidence in Him, which would not be true—but that He is the only true source of confidence."[454] See Ephesians 3:11–12.

"So we can say with confidence, 'The Lord is my helper, so I will have no fear. What can mere people do to me?'" ~ Hebrews 13:6 NLT.

Calvin states, "The answer of our prayers is secured by the fact that in rejecting them God would in a certain sense deny his own nature."[455] Dickson said, "The hearing and granting of prayer are the Lord's property, and his usual practice, and his pleasure, and his nature, and his glory."[456] "Delays are not refusals; many a prayer is registered, and underneath it the words: 'My time is not yet come.' God has a set time as well as a set purpose, and He who orders the bounds of our habitation orders also the time of our deliverance."[457] George W. Truett wrote, "Let us pray more! Prayer is the first agency we are to employ for the promotion of any spiritual undertaking. Prayer links us with God. 'Without me, ye can do nothing.' 'I can do all things through Christ who strengtheneth me.' Prayer breaks down difficulties. It opens fast closed doors. It calls forth workers: 'Pray ye, therefore, the Lord of the harvest, that he will send forth laborers into his harvest.' It releases energies for the spread of Christ's kingdom and truth, beyond anything any of us can ever measure. It brings victory in hours of crisis. It gives power to the preached gospel."[458]

> Prayer links us with God. Prayer breaks down difficulties. It opens fast closed doors. It calls forth workers into His harvest. It brings victory in hours of crisis. It gives power to the preached gospel.
> George W. Truett

The Bottom Line: God heareth the prayers of His redeemed children readily and speedily. "Shall not our praises balance our prayers? If the Lord gives goodness, shall not we give gratitude?"[459] See Psalm 65:11. He stands ready to hear the prayers for help of any man who by faith comes to Him through the Lord Jesus Christ. It is the Christian's joyous duty to publicize this wondrous news to the ends of the earth.

17. Bearing Testimony for the Lord   Psalm 66:16–17

"Come and hear, all ye that fear God, and I will declare what he hath done for my soul. I cried unto him with my mouth, and he was extolled with my tongue."—Psalm 66:16-17.

"Come and hear, all ye that fear God" (The Psalmist invites all true worshippers of God [they that reverence Him] to hear his testimony of the goodness of God toward him.) AND I will "declare what he hath done" (The Psalmist had been set free from "bondage" [as Israel had in whole] and wants to communicate that glorious news to the community of faith.) "for my soul" (Barnes says, "The words 'for my soul' are equivalent to 'for me.' Literally, 'for my life.'"[460]).

He was extolled with "my tongue" (Harman says, "The idiom 'under the tongue' may be similar to the English one 'on the tip of the tongue.'"[461] The psalmist received a speedy reply from God and immediately rendedred praise unto Him for it.[462]

Homily

Both the authorship and date of the Psalm's composition are uncertain. J. A. Alexander remarks, "The resemblance to the forty-sixth Psalm has led some to suppose that this psalm was occasioned by the same event."[463] Jennings and Lowe suggest, "Some of these features however are to be found in Psalms which apparently celebrate the

75

overthrow of Sennacherib (Psalm 47, 76), and it is not unlikely that this Psalm, like its predecessor, belongs to the time when Israel saw its territory wholly cleared of the Assyrian invader."[464] Allan Harman wrote, "No precise historical setting can be given for Psalm 66. It seems to be a song of thanksgiving after some victory by the nation, such as when Sennacherib of Assyria was defeated (2 Kings 19:35–36)."[465] The bottom line is, scholars can only speculate as to its occasion.

Come and hear. Matthew Henry stated, "Note, God's people should communicate their experiences to each other. We should take all occasions to tell one another of the great and kind things which God has done for us, especially which he has done for our souls, the spiritual blessings with which he has blessed us in heavenly things; these we should be most affected with ourselves, and therefore with these we should be desirous to affect others."[466] Scott remarked, "Besides the general example of gratitude for our mercies, which we publicly exhibit, we should more particularly declare to those who fear God, what he has done for our souls, and how he has heard and answered our prayers; they alone are capable of understanding our experience, and they will be edified and encouraged by it, and will join with us in prayer and praise, and this will turn to our mutual comfort, and to the glory of God."[467]

I will declare what he hath done for my soul. Allan Harman states, "The same lips that prayed were ready to praise."[468] Albert Barnes says, "The phrase would embrace all that God had done by his gracious intervention in delivering the people from bondage. The language here is such as may be used by anyone who is converted to God, in reference

(a) to all that God has done to redeem the soul;
(b) to all that he has done to pardon its guilt;
(c) to all that he has done to give it peace and joy;
(d) to all that he has done to enable it to overcome sin;
(e) to all that he has done to give it comfort in the prospect of death;
(f) to all that he has done to impart the hope of heaven.

The principle here is one which it is right to apply to all such cases. It is right and proper for a converted sinner to call on others to hear what God has done for him."[469]

I love to tell the story;
'Twill be my theme in glory
To tell the old, old story
of Jesus and His love. ~ Katherine Hankey (1834–1911)

Spurgeon advises, "Testimonies ought to be borne by all experienced Christians, in order that the younger and feebler sort may be encouraged by the recital to put their trust in the Lord. To declare human doings is needless; they are too trivial, and, besides, have trumpeters enough. Let each speak for himself; secondhand experience lacks the flavor of first-hand interest. Let no mock modesty restrain the grateful believer from speaking of himself, or rather of God's dealing to himself, for it is justly due to God; neither let him shun the individual use of the first person, which is most correct in detailing the Lord's ways of love."[470] "Those to whose souls God has been gracious desire to tell of what God has done for them—not for the sake of ostentation or pride, still less from hypocrisy, but from irrepressible gratitude to God and with the view of honoring God, to whom they are so much indebted; also that they may do good to those to whom they tell of what God has done. It does do them good, for practical and experimental statements are well suited to help others in the heavenward way. And the telling does good to his own soul likewise. He receives sympathy, awakens delight, so that he and they to whom he speaks are comforted, and rejoice together."[471]

One of the most effective methods of witnessing is the use of one's salvation testimony. A personal testimony should include five specific points that comfortably, concisely and simply may be shared in three to five minutes. The Apostle Paul's testimony to Agrippa serves as its worthy pattern. See Acts 26:3–29.

(1) My life before meeting Christ (Acts 26:3–11)
(2) How I came to realize my need of Christ (Acts 26:12–14)
(3) What I did to become a Christian (Acts 26:15–18)
(4) My life since I became a Christian (Acts 26:19–23)
(5) Appeal: Would you be willing to do as I did and receive Jesus Christ into your life as Lord and Savior? (Acts 26:27–29)

Jacques Lefevre, evangelist of the Swiss Reformation, prayed, "When will Christ be all in all? When will the only study, the only consolation, the only desire of all be to know the Gospel, to cause it to advance everywhere, and to be firmly persuaded, as our ancestors of this primitive church, dyed by the blood of martyrs, who understood that knowing nothing except the Gospel is to know everything."[472]

He turned the sea into dry land. See Psalm 66:6. Macduff declared, "Oh, remember this: There is never a time when we may not hope in God. Whatever our necessities, however great our difficulties, and though to all appearance help is impossible, yet our business is to hope in God, and it will be found that it is not in vain. In the Lord's own time help will come."[473]

Presently your feet may be traveling the river bed of the Red Sea with its mighty huge walls of water on both sides in flight from the troublesome Egyptians, but God will give deliverance. In the journal of life you will proclaim, "He turned the sea into dry land: they went through the flood on foot: there did we rejoice in him" (Psalm 66:6).

The Bottom Line: There are two primary types of testimonial audiences, the Christian community and the unsaved (In congregational gatherings they are usually combined.). The Psalmist in Psalm 66:16 addresses the former. But both ought to be and must be embraced. It is important to fine tune or adapt the testimony for the proper audience for maximum results.

To share with an unsaved audience a testimony about how God blesses tithing, though good, would not strike the spark in the soul needed to quicken to repentance and salvation. Francis Ridley Havergal wrote, "Every year I live—in fact, nearly every day—I seem to see more how all the peace, happiness and power of the Christian life hinges on one thing. That one thing is taking God at His Word, believing He really means exactly what He says, and accepting the very words that reveal His goodness and grace without substituting other words or changing the precise moods and tenses He has seen fit to use."[474]

18. Sin Hinders Prayer   Psalm 66:18

"If I regard iniquity in my heart, the Lord will not hear me."— Psalm 66:18.

If I "regard" (Harman says, "If a person looks with satisfaction on his sin [the Hebrew text says 'if I had looked on'], then God will not hear him."[475] To cherish sin in the heart.) "iniquity" (Swanson says "evil, wickedness, iniquity, i.e., an act (of many kinds) which is morally evil and corrupt, and damaging to one's relationship to God and others, according to a standard [1 Samuel 15:23]."[476]) "in my heart" (Barnes says "if I have cherished it [sin] in my soul, if I have gloated over past sins, if I am purposing to commit sin again, if I am not willing to abandon all sin and to be holy."[477]). "The Lord will not hear me" (Barnes says, "That is, He will not regard and answer my prayer. The idea is, that in order that prayer may be heard, there must be a purpose to forsake all forms of sin."[478]).

Homily

There is much praying by many with no effect due to unconfessed sin in the heart. To them prayer really is a "waste" of time, all because of unwillingness to unblock the channel for its access to the throne of God through confession and repentance. *If I regard iniquity in my heart.* Matthew Henry wrote, "That is 'If I have favourable thoughts of it, if I love it, indulge it, and allow myself in it, if I treat it as a friend and bid it welcome, make provision for it and am loth to part with it, if I roll it under my tongue as a sweet morsel, though it be but a heart sin that is thus countenanced and made much of, if I delight in it after the inward man, God will not hear my prayer, will not accept it, nor be pleased with it, nor can I expect an answer of peace to it.' Note, iniquity, regarded in the heart, will certainly spoil the comfort and success of prayer; for the sacrifice of the wicked is an abomination to the Lord."[479] Adam Clarke says, "If I have seen iniquity in my heart—if I have known it was there, and encouraged it; if I pretended to be what I was not; if I loved iniquity, while I professed to pray and be sorry for my sin—the Lord Adonai, my Prop, Stay, and Supporter, would not have heard; and I should have been left without help or support."[480] George Horne further gives elucidation: "The prayer which is 'heard,' is the prayer of the penitent, heartily grieved and wearied with sin, hating, and longing to be delivered from it. For God heareth not hypocrites, who, while they outwardly disavow, yet inwardly 'regard' and cherish 'iniquity'; from which every one who nameth the name of Christ ought to depart."[481] Oswald Chambers wrote, "It is no use praying unless we are living as children of God. Then, Jesus says— 'Everyone that asketh receiveth.'"[482] See Matthew 5:24 and John 15:7.

Verily God hath heard me. See Psalm 66:19. Obviously the Psalmist had engaged in confession, for his prayers had been heard. Adam Clarke says "a sure proof that my prayer was upright, and my heart honest, before him."[483] W. S. Plumer remarked, "The issue showed that God approved the Psalmist's character and conduct."[484] J. A. Alexander states, "The doubt subjected in the foregoing verse had been removed in his case by the application of the test there mentioned. God had already heard his prayer and thereby borne witness that he was not guilty of the duplicity in question."[485]

The first step in prayer is confession of sin. Only upon its removal by divine cleansing through the blood of the Lord Jesus Christ can prayer avail. See 1 John 1:9; 3:21–22 and John 9:31.

The Bottom Line: Spurgeon writes, "Nothing hinders prayer like iniquity harbored in the heart; as with Cain, so with us, sin lies at the door and blocks the passage. If you refuse to hear God's commands, he will surely refuse to hear your prayers."[486]

19. Praying for the World   Psalm 67:1–3

"God be merciful unto us, and bless us; and cause his face to shine upon us; Selah. That thy way may be known upon earth, thy saving health among all nations. Let the people praise thee, O God; let all the people praise thee."—Psalm 67:1-3.

The words are in part a repetition of the priestly benediction in Numbers 6:24–26.

"God" (God and God alone is man's source of underserved mercy.) "be merciful unto us" (the lovingkindness and grace of God to pardon sin. Spurgeon says, "Mercy is a foundational attribute in our salvation. The best saints and the worst sinners may unite in this petition."[487]).

AND "bless us" (Tate says, "The blessing of God consists in his ongoing presence in life, his sustaining of the well-being of the world, and his providing family [Psalm 128], food [Psalm 132:15], dew [Psalm 133:3], rain [Hosea 6:3], etc. A. A. Anderson remarks, 'In a sense God's blessing was not an independent force, but rather the active help of God himself, so that one could not have the blessing without the giver.'"[488] Tate says, "The presence of God comes with his blessing."[489]).

AND "cause his face to shine upon us" (Bratcher and Reyburn say "it means to look on someone with favor, mercy, kindness."[490] Tate says, "The shining forth of the face of God among his people is a metaphor for his goodwill and blessing [Psalms 4:6; 31:16; 44:3; 80:3, 7, 19; 89:15; 119:135]. A shining, bright face reveals a person of good disposition and is a sign of inward pleasure."[491] See Proverbs 16:15. In contrast, the opposite is also true; God's hidden face reveals dismay [Psalms 10:1; 30:7; 44:24; 104:29; Deuteronomy 31:18].[492]).

"That thy way" (Alexander says "Thy way, i.e., Thy mode of dealing with Thy people, referring more particularly here to providential favors, the knowledge of which he hopes to see extended to all nations, as a means to the promotion of still higher ends."[493] The *way* of salvation. Jesus said, "I am the way, the truth, and the life: no man cometh unto the Father, but by me" [John 14:6].) "may be known upon earth" (Tate says, "'Knowing' is not restricted to mental cognition; it includes experiential knowing and action."[494]).

"Thy saving health among all nations." (Clarke says "'thy salvation.' The great work which is performed in God's way, in destroying the power, pardoning the guilt, cleansing from the infection, of all sin; and filling the soul with holiness, with the mind that was in Christ. Let all nations—the whole Gentile world, know that way, and this salvation!"[495])

"Let the people praise thee, O God; let all the people praise thee" (Clarke, keeping with the thought of the prophetic nature of the Psalm, says, "When this is done, the people—the Gentiles, will praise thee; all will give thanks to God for His unspeakable gift."[496] Others take it to mean the same, as do Spurgeon, Henry and Gill.).

Homily

David is the author of the Psalm. Adam Clarke remarked, "It is supposed to have been written at the return from the Babylonish captivity, and to foretell the conversion of the Gentiles to the Christian religion."[497] "This Psalm is founded upon the promise given in Leviticus 26:3, 'If ye walk in my statutes, and keep my commandments, and do them; then will I give you rain in due season, and the land shall yield her increase…and I will give peace in the land…and ye shall chase your enemies, and they shall fall before you.'…Psalm 45 described the corn and the fruits as ripening to harvest. Psalm 67 is a prayer and thanksgiving after the harvest, about the time of the feast of Tabernacles."[498]

Spurgeon says, "This Psalm contains a prayer for the church of Israel, as also for the Gentile world, whose conversion he prophetically describes."[499] Matthew Henry summarizes the Psalm: "A prayer for the enlargement of Christ's kingdom. All our happiness comes from God's mercy; therefore the first thing prayed for is, God be merciful to us, to us sinners, and pardon our sins. Pardon is conveyed by God's blessing, and secured in that. If we, by faith, walk with God, we may hope that His face will shine on us. The Psalmist passes on to a prayer for the conversion of the Gentiles, which shows that the Old Testament saints desired that their advantages might also be enjoyed by others."[500]

> Prayer is the mighty engine that is to move the missionary work.
> A.B. Simpson

The believer's prayer is likewise not simply to be "bless me" but "bless us." It ought to extend to all the peoples and nations of the world that they may know intelligently and experientially the wondrous grace and mercy of God manifested through His Son, the Lord Jesus Christ, in salvation. D. James Kennedy said, "So often we pray narrowly, attending only to our own needs. Instead, we should pray broadly for everyone. We should pray for the lost that they might be saved and for the saved that they might win the lost."[501] J. C. Ryle urges, "We should try to bear in our hearts the whole world, the heathen."[502] Billy Graham said, "To get nations back on their feet, we must first get down on our knees."[503] A. B. Simpson says, "Prayer is the mighty engine that is to move the missionary work."[504]

Ask of me and I shall give thee the heathen for thine inheritance. See Psalm 2:8. Though the words were directed to Jesus from God, certainly they have application for the believer. God told Jesus that upon His asking, He would give Him a great ingathering from the heathen world. The heathen would be "broken down by Messiah's power, broken down before God in repentance and brought to accept and to own Him as the righteous Lord and Savior."[505] See Psalm 2:9. H. A. Ironside said, "I never come to a missionary meeting but I feel as though there ought to be written right across the entire platform, 'Ask of me, and I shall give Thee the heathen for Thine inheritance and the uttermost parts of the earth for Thy possession.'"[506]

Believers ought not only to pray for the unreached nations and peoples but especially for laborers to be sent out to them. Jesus said, "Pray ye therefore the Lord of the harvest, that he will send forth laborers into his harvest" (Matthew 9:38). Only God can call forth the laborers. Therefore, prayers and petitions for them is not to be made of convention or denominational headquarters or anyone else but Him. Jesus clearly said that harvest helpers are not to be solicited by man but divinely summoned, not recruited "in" but prayed "out" through prayer. See the author's book *Evangelistic Praying: Intercession for Laborers and the Lost.*

William Feather remarked, "After saying our prayers, we ought to do something to make them come true."[507]

The Bottom Line: Andrew Murray wrote, "Without prayer, even though there may be increased interest in missions, more work for them, better success in organization and greater finances, the real growth of the spiritual life and of the love of Christ in the people may be very small."[508]

20. God's Care for the Orphan and Widow   Psalm 68:5

"A father of the fatherless, and a judge of the widows, is God in his holy habitation."—Psalm 68:5.

"A father of the fatherless" (God watches over the orphan as the warden watches over one in his ward. Hengstenberg says, 'Orphans and widows are expressions designed to individualize the miserable.'[509]). AND a "judge of the widows" (Alexander says "judge, vindicator, patron, one who does them justice."[510]

Barnes says, "That is, He will see justice done them; he will save them from oppression and wrong."[511] Kirkpatrick says, "The orphan and the widow are typical examples of the friendless and unprotected who are under God's special guardianship [Psalm 10:14; Psalm 146:9; Hosea 14:3]."[512] Plumer says, "*Father and Judge* seem to bear the general sense of defender, protector, vindicator; the first best expresses the pity and tenderness of God; the latter, His authority and ability to protect."[513]).

Is God in his "holy habitation"? (Rawlinson says, "The heavenly and not the earthly dwelling-place—whether tabernacle or temple—seems to be intended. God from His holy seat in the highest Heaven pours down His grace and mercy, His defense and protection, on all those who specially need His aid."[514]).

Homily

A Psalm of David. "Accordingly it is generally supposed by those who accept the traditional account of the authorship to have originated in some Davidic victory, which had been aided by the presence of the Ark in the field of battle, or the celebration of which had been attended with religious solemnities....According to Böttcher, Tholuck, and Hengstenberg, it is that over the Syrians and Ammonites [2 Samuel 11 and 12]."[515] It is noteworthy that fifteen words the psalmist uses are not found elsewhere in the Old Testament.[516]

Matthew Poole wrote, "By the spirit of prophecy David looked through and beyond the present actions and types unto the great mysteries of Christ's resurrection and ascension into Heaven, and of the special privileges of the Christian church, and of the calling of the Gentiles unto God."[517] W. S. Plumer said, "This Psalm certainly contains Gospel truths."[518] Martin Luther wrote, "It is a signal prophecy concerning Christ."[519]

Albert Barnes remarks of Psalm 68:5: "This is one of the most tender appellations [*Merriam-Webster,* "an identifying name or title"] that could be given to God, and conveys one of the most striking descriptions that can be given of His character. We see His greatness, His majesty, His power, in the worlds that He has made—in the storm, the tempest, the rolling ocean; but it is in such expressions as this that we learn, what we most desire to know, and what we cannot elsewhere learn, that He is a Father; that He is to be loved as well as feared. Nothing suggests more strikingly a state of helplessness and dependence than the condition of orphan children and widows; nothing, therefore, conveys a more affecting description of the character of God—of His condescension and kindness—than to say that He will take the place of the parent in the one case, and be a protector in the other."[520]

God cares for the orphan and opposes all who deal with them mischievously (Deuteronomy 10:18; Psalm 10:14, 17–18; 68:5; 82:3; 146:9). He is their defender against injustice. He is their protector, watching over them lest they are taken advantage of in some way or mistreated. He is the Almighty God and "His omnipotence is engaged and employed for their protection, and their proudest and most powerful oppressors will not only find themselves an unequal match for this, but will find that it is at their peril to contend with it."[521] The text also assures the widow that God cares for and watches over her with protection. David underscores the truth: "The LORD watches over the sojourners; he upholds the widow and the fatherless, but the way of the wicked he brings to ruin" (Psalm 146:9 ESV). Our gracious and compassionate Lord draws a circle of fire about the confines of the widow, keeping injurious intruders out. The widow can assuredly depend upon the Lord for help (Jeremiah 49:11). None who seek to take advantage of a defenseless widow (unjust dealings, robbery, and deceit) will escape God's fury; he will be brought to "ruin." See Luke 20:47. Scott said, "God's condescension is equal to His majesty: He always patronizes the afflicted and oppressed; and poor sinners, helpless and exposed more than any destitute orphans, are readily admitted among His sons and daughters, and share all the blessings of that high relation."[522] Arnd comments, "Great potentates in the world respect the noblest and the richest in the land, the men who may adorn their court and strengthen their authority. But the highest glory of God is to compassionate the miserable."[523]

Matthew Henry summarizes the text, "He is a Father of the fatherless, to pity them, to bless them, to teach them, to provide for them, to portion them. He will preserve them alive (Jeremiah 49:11), and with Him they shall find mercy (Hosea 14:3). They have liberty to call Him Father, and to plead their relation to Him as their guardian (Psalm 146:9; Psalm 10:14, 18). He is a judge or patron of the widows, to give them counsel and to redress their grievances, to own them and plead their cause (Proverbs 22:23). He has an ear open to all their complaints and a hand open to all their wants."[524]

But the text may also be applied spiritually to those that have been abandoned by friends, deserted by parents, or those that have left father and mother for the "sake of the call."[525] All they that are like *fatherless ones* in their helpless estate may apply the promise personally.

The Bottom Line: God is the protector and provider of the orphan and widow, sometimes through supernatural means (the widow at Zarephath [1 Kings 17:8–16]), while in others through ordinary people like you and me (Mordecai's adoption of Esther [Esther 2:7]). James states pure and undefiled religion is "to visit and help and care for the orphans and widows in their affliction and need, and to keep oneself unspotted and uncontaminated from the world" (James 1:27 AMPC). A mark of spirituality is the care one gives to widows and orphans.

21. Messianic Prophecy—a Clear Picture of Jesus Christ

Psalm 69:4, 8–9, 21–23, 25

"They that hate me without a cause are more than the hairs of mine head: they that would destroy me, being mine enemies wrongfully, are mighty: then I restored that which I took not away."

"I am become a stranger unto my brethren, and an alien unto my mother's children. For the zeal of thine house hath eaten me up; and the reproaches of them that reproached thee are fallen upon me."

"They gave me also gall for my meat; and in my thirst they gave me vinegar to drink. Let their table become a snare before them: and that

which should have been for their welfare, let it become a trap. Let their eyes be darkened, that they see not; and make their loins continually to shake."

"Let their habitation be desolate; and let none dwell in their tents."—Psalm 69:4, 8–9, 21–23, 25.

"They hated me without a cause" (These words are directly quoted by Jesus in John 15:25 referring to His enemies.) are "more than the hairs of mine head" (Gill says, "They were a multitude that came to take Him in the garden; and it was the multitude that the priests and Pharisees instigated to ask for the release of Barabbas, and the crucifixion of Jesus; and a vast number of people followed Him to the cross, and insulted Him on it; the Gentiles and the people of Israel were gathered together against Him."[526]).

They "that would destroy me, being mine enemies wrongfully, are mighty" (Gill says "the great men of the earth, kings and princes, as Herod and Pontius Pilate, and also the infernal principalities and powers, who were concerned in contriving those lies [about Jesus], and putting them into the minds of men; for Satan is the father of lies and falsehood."[527]) then "I restored that which I took not away" (Jesus restored the glory of God that was taken away by man's sin, satisfied justice that He never violated, fulfilled the law that He never broke, made divine atonement [satisfaction] for sins that He never committed, restored righteousness that He never took away.[528]).

"I am become a stranger unto my brethren, and an alien unto my mother's children." (Henry says, "This was fulfilled in Christ, whose brethren did not believe on Him [John 7:5], who came to His own and His own received Him not [John 1:11], and who was forsaken by His disciples."[529] Even His mother's son [His half-brother] James rejected Him until His resurrection [1 Corinthians 15:7]. John 7:5 says, "For neither did his brethren believe in him."). "For the zeal of thine house hath eaten me up" (The words are directly quoted about Jesus in John 2:17 in reference to the cleansing of the Temple. Spurgeon says, "His burning ardor, like the flame of a candle, fed on His strength and consumed it. Some men are eaten up with lechery, others with covetousness, and a third class with pride, but the master passion with our great leader was the glory of God, jealousy for His name, and love to the divine family."[530]).

AND "the reproaches of them that reproached thee are fallen upon me" (The words are quoted by Paul in reference to Jesus in Romans 15:3. Man's antagonism and hostility toward God was also manifested toward His Son.) "They gave me also gall for my meat; and in my thirst they gave me vinegar to drink" (Benson says, "Instead of affording Me [Jesus] that pity and comfort which My condition required, they barbarously added to My affliction. These words were only metaphorically fulfilled in David, but were properly and literally accomplished in Christ; the description of whose sufferings, it seems, was principally intended here by the Holy Ghost, who therefore directed David's pen to these words."[531] *Gall* was offered to Jesus upon the Cross, but He refused to drink it [Matthew 27:34]. Barnes says, "It may not be possible to determine precisely what is denoted here by the word, but it undoubtedly refers to some poisonous, bitter, deadly, stupefying substance given to a sufferer, 'instead' of that which would be wholesome food, or suited to sustain life."[532] Likewise Jesus was given *vinegar* [John 19:29–30] which was sour wine, unfit to drink.). To summarize, Psalm 69:21 was literally fulfilled as we find in Matthew 27:34; Matthew 27:48; Mark 15:23; Mark 15:36; Luke 23:36 and John 19:28–30.).

"Let their table become a snare before them: and that which should have been for their welfare, let it become a trap. Let their eyes be darkened, that they see not" (Directly quoted by Paul in Romans 11:9–10. It refers to the rejecters of Christ. *Table.* Vincent says "representing material prosperity: feasting in wicked security; some explain of the Jews' presumptuous confidence in the law."[533] Wesley says "in that prophetic imprecation, which is applicable to them, as well as to Judas. A recompense—of their preceding wickedness. So sin is punished by sin; and thus the Gospel, which should have fed and strengthened their souls, is become a means of destroying them."[534] "Learn here, that to the obstinate and obdurate [*Merriam-Webster* says 'stubbornly persistent in wrongdoing'] enemies of God, the best things become baneful, and through their own corruption become the instruments and means of their own destruction. Let their table be made a snare, a trap, and a stumbling-block."[535]).

"Let their habitation be desolate; and let none dwell in their tents." (Quoted by Peter in Acts 1:20. Gill says, "What the Psalmist says of the enemies of the Messiah in general, is applied by the apostle to Judas in particular. In the Hebrew text, [Psalms 69:25] the words are in the plural number, 'let their habitation be desolate, and let none dwell in their tents'; and refer to all the enemies of Christ, the chief priests, elders of the people, Scribes and Pharisees, who covenanted with Judas to give him so much money to betray Christ into their hands; and who delivered him to the Roman governor, by whom, at their instigation, he was crucified; and particularly may well be thought to include Judas, who betrayed him to them; and therefore are very fitly interpreted of him: though not to be understood to the exclusion of the others, whose house was to be left desolate, and was left desolate, as our Lord predicted, [Matthew 23:38]."[536]).

Homily

The Psalm was composed by David and is Messianic. It is one of the most quoted Psalms in the New Testament: verse 4 (John 15:25); verse 9 (John 2:17); verse 21 (Matthew 27:34, 48); verses 22–24 (Romans 11:9–10); verse 24 (Revelation 16:1); verse 25 (Acts 1:20).[537] Arno C. Gaebelein says of Psalm 69, "What a precious Psalm it is! It begins with the cry of the one who bore our sins in His body, who suffered for our sake. It ends with the glorious results of His atoning work."[538] J. M. Boice says, "Seven of its thirty-six verses are directly quoted, and others furnish themes relating to Christ's work that are expanded in the Gospels."[539] Gaebelein, in noting the numerous references to Messiah in the Psalm and their literal fulfillment in Jesus, says, "No further evidence is needed that the Lord Jesus Christ in His suffering and rejection is here described."[540]

The purpose of messianic prophesies is to bear witness of the person and ministry of Jesus Christ. Though the virtuous life, atoning death and resurrection of Jesus to be man's Savior from the penalty and power of sin stands on its own, prophecy does validate it, providing doubters with added evidence to believe. Psalm 69 is one of the most obviously messianic Psalms, being quoted less in the New Testament than only Psalms 22 and 110.[541] In the honest pondering of its prophecies regarding the coming Messiah and their literal fulfillment hundreds of years later in Jesus Christ, one is brought with Peter to say to Him, "Thou art the Christ, the Son of the living God" (Mathew 16:16).

The Bottom Line: Prophesy protects from deception by counterfeit messiahs. Only the true Messiah (Christ) would fulfill its *forth-telling* about His life, works, family, rejection, miracles, death, resurrection, second-advent, etc. Prophesy authenticates the real Messiah. Prophesy instills confidence and faith in Jesus as the Messiah, the Savior of the world.

22. A Prayer for Comfort and Deliverance in Time of Need

Psalm 70:1–5

"Make haste, O God, to deliver me; make haste to help me, O LORD. Let them be ashamed and confounded that seek after my soul: let them be turned backward, and put to confusion, that desire my hurt. Let them be turned back for a reward of their shame that say, Aha, aha. Let all those that seek thee rejoice and be glad in thee: and let such as love thy salvation say continually, Let God be magnified. But I am poor and needy: make haste unto me, O God: thou art my help and my deliverer; O LORD, make no tarrying."—Psalm 70:1–5.

"Make haste" (This is the second Psalm that is repeated. Psalm 53:1–6 is repeated in Psalm 14:1–7 and Psalm 70 in Psalm 40:13–17. There is a difference between the two in the opening two words: *Make haste* rather than *Be pleased.* Spurgeon says Psalm 70 opens "more urgently with, 'Make haste'; or, as in the Hebrew, with an abrupt and broken cry, 'O God, to deliver me; O Lord, to help me hasten.'"[542] "O God" (Another difference between the two Psalms is that David uses *Elohim* [Psalm 70:1, the name "God"] instead of *Jehovah* [Psalm 40:13, the divine name "LORD"] at the first of the sentence for some unknown reason.[543] Outside these alterations, the remainder of the text is the same with slight variations. However, the changes are unimportant to understanding that which David is communicating.[544]).

"To deliver me" (rescue) "make haste to help me, O LORD" (Several times in the Psalm David cries out to God for quick, urgent help.) "Let them be ashamed and confounded that seek after my soul: let them be turned backward, and put to confusion, that desire my hurt." (Spurgeon says, "His enemies desired to put his faith to shame, and he eagerly intreats that they may be disappointed, and themselves covered with confusion."[545] *My soul* is translated *my life,* thus: "I ask that you defeat and confuse the people who try to kill me."[546] *Turned back* refers to the defeat of the Psalmist's enemies.[547] Spurgeon says, "When people labor to turn others back from the right road, it is God's retaliation to turn them back from the point they are aiming at."[548]).

"Let them be turned back for a reward of their shame that say, Aha, aha." (Let them become desolate ["turned back"]. Ross says, "Enemies tried to bring him to ruin [Psalm 35:4, 8; 38:12]. So his plea was urgent. He prayed that those who had shamed and disgraced him [Psalm 69:19] would themselves be in shame [Psalm 70:2–3; 71:13] and turned back in disgrace [Psalm 6:10; 40:14], no longer able to scorn him [Aha!])."[549] Spurgeon says, "How fond people are of taunts, and if they are meaningless *ahas* it matters nothing so long as they sting the victim. Rest assured, the enemies of Christ and his people will be paid in their own coin; they loved scoffing, and they will become a proverb forever."[550]). Let all those that seek thee rejoice and be glad in thee: and let "such as love thy salvation say continually" (May all that are thankful ["love thy salvation"] for the Lord's saving them evermore ["continually"] rejoice and be glad in Him.[551])

"Let God be magnified" (Merriam-Webster says "to cause to be held in greater esteem or respect."[552] Spurgeon says, "Those who have tasted divine grace, and are therefore wedded to it, are a somewhat more advanced race, and these will not only feel joy but will with holy constancy and perseverance tell abroad their joy, and call upon men to glorify God. The doxology, 'Let the LORD's name be magnified,' is infinitely more ennobling than the dog's bark of 'Aha, aha.'"[553] Henry says, "Let us then be assured that, if it be not our own fault, the joy of the Lord shall fill our minds and the high praises of the Lord shall fill our mouths. Those that seek God, if they seek Him early and seek Him diligently, shall rejoice and be glad in Him, for their seeking Him is an evidence of His good-will to them and an earnest of their finding Him [Psalm 105:3]. There is pleasure and joy even in seeking God, for it is one of the fundamental principles of religion that God is the rewarder of all those that diligently seek Him. Those that love God's salvation shall say with pleasure, with constant pleasure [for praising God, if we make it our continual work, will be our continual feast], *Let God be magnified*, as He will be, to eternity, in the salvation of His people."[554]).

"But I am poor and needy" (Poor and needy occurs in six Psalms: Psalm 37:14; Psalm 40:17; Psalm 70:5; Psalm 74:21; Psalm 86:1; Psalm 109:16, 22.[555] The Psalmist ever acknowledges his weakness and frailty unto the Lord in pleading for help.) "make haste unto me, O God: thou art my help and my deliverer; O Lord, make no tarrying" (David closes the Psalm as he began, begging God for immediate deliverance, rescue, salvation from his enemies. Here again *Jehovah* replaces *Elohim*.[556]).

Homily

The Psalm is entitled *A Psalm of David to bring to remembrance*. Craigie says, "The word is sometimes associated with the 'memorial offering' as described in Leviticus 2:2 and 24:7. But equally, the term might imply no more than it says, namely that the Psalm was for regular use by a sufferer in bringing his plight to God's remembrance."[557] The Psalm is a variation of Psalm 40:13–17.

Make haste to help me, O Lord. "Importunity prevails where indifference fails."[558] It is always proper and expedient to bring pressing concerns and troubles to God's "remembrance." Family and friends sometimes are unwilling or unable to help, but the Lord is always both willing and able to rally to our assistance. He is our *refuge* in the time of trouble and tribulation (Psalm 46:1–2); *strong tower* in the time of personal conflict (Psalm 61:3); *strong Rock* in times of weakness and frailty (Psalm 31:2); that *friend that sticketh closer than a brother* in times of horrendous grief, sorrow and loneliness (Proverbs 18:24); *the potter* who takes the broken pieces of one's life and molds them into something beautiful (Isaiah 64:8); *the vine* supplying nutriment to the branches, His children, that they may experience abundant life and bear much fruit for the kingdom of God (John 15:5); *the wonderful counsellor* to impart wisdom for handling life's problems and pains (Isaiah 9:6 and John 14:16); *the Good Shepherd* that lays down His life for His sheep that they might be saved (John 10:11); *the light of the world* illuminating the spiritual darkness, showing man the right path to travel (John 8:12); *the great emancipator* setting the prisoner free from the strongholds of sin and satanic bondage (John 8:36); *the bread of life* that satisfies the longing of the soul (John 6:35–51) and *the sympathizing Jesus* who "speaks the drooping heart to cheer."[559] See Matthew 9:12; Mark 1:41 and Isaiah 66:13.

Martin Luther wrote the renowned hymn "A Mighty Fortress" probably in the period of 1527–1528. It is one of the most translated hymns, being translated into over 200 languages. It erroneously is oft ascribed as the *Battle Hymn of the Reformation* written to celebrate the event by Luther; *The Festival of the Reformation* commemoration was not celebrated in Luther's lifetime. The hymn rather was written, it is believed, to be a hymn of comfort. Scholars suggest several things that led to its writing: a man that embraced Luther's teaching was martyred in August 1527; in the fall of 1527 a plague swept through Wittenberg; in December 1527 Luther wrote to a colleague saying, "We are all in good health except for Luther himself, who is physically well, but outwardly the whole world and inwardly the Devil and all his angels are making him suffer"; in January 1528 Luther wrote saying he was battling the worst time of temptation (the German word he used was *Anfechtung,* which refers to affliction, trial, suffering and temptation[560]) in his life; and in May 1528, following six months of wrestling with God in prayer to heal his baby daughter Elizabeth, she died.[561] In addition to all of these devastating trials, he constantly was burdened with the heavy abuses in the Roman church and the displeasure of many for his biblical stance.

Thus out of Luther's adversities and grief he wrote a hymn of comfort for all that experience troubles and trials.

> A mighty Fortress is our God,
> A Bulwark never failing;
> Our Helper He amid the flood
> Of mortal ills prevailing.

For still our ancient foe
Doth seek to work us woe;
His craft and power are great;
And, armed with cruel hate,
On earth is not his equal.

Did we in our own strength confide,
    Our striving would be losing;
Were not the right Man on our side,
    The Man of God's own choosing.
Dost ask who that may be?
Christ Jesus, it is He;
Lord Sabaoth His Name,
From age to age the same,
And He must win the battle.

And though this world, with devils filled,
    Should threaten to undo us,
We will not fear, for God hath willed
    His truth to triumph through us.
The Prince of Darkness grim,
We tremble not for him;
His rage we can endure,
For lo! his doom is sure.
One little word shall fell him.

That Word above all earthly powers,
    No thanks to them, abideth;
The Spirit and the gifts are ours
    Through Him who with us sideth.
Let goods and kindred go,
This mortal life also.
The body they may kill;
God's truth abideth still.
His Kingdom is forever. ~ Martin Luther (1483–1546)

James Hastings wrote, "What we need most is certainty of God, that we may hold fast our faith in Him. We shall still be beset by mystery, and the world's sorrow and our own pain will still remain a terrible problem, but we shall see enough to make us willing to believe and wait. We shall let every experience of trial and sorrow bring some lessons to withdraw our hearts from the love of the material. We shall learn to look upon the whole discipline of life as a means of sanctification, and in our highest moments we shall see it to be a terror to be left of God, and shall pray that the beautiful promise may be true for us: *As one whom his mother comforteth, so will I comfort you.* When we do, the last word to us is not tribulation, but joy. Even suffering only sets a seal on faith, like the kiss of God upon the brow. Faith sees far enough into the meaning of tribulation to see in it the sign of love; for it sees in it the Father's hand."[562] See Isaiah 66:13.

L. B. Cowman wrote, "Crowns are cast in crucibles, and the chains of character found at the feet of God are forged in earthly flames. No one wins the greatest victory until he has walked the winepress of woe. With deep furrows of anguish on His brow, the 'man of sorrows' (Isa. 53: 3) said, 'In this world you will have trouble' (John 16: 33). But immediately comes the psalm of promise, 'Take heart! I have overcome the world.'"[563]

The footprints are visible everywhere. The steps that lead to thrones are stained with spattered blood, and scars are the price for scepters. We will wrestle our crowns from the giants we conquer. It is no secret that grief has always fallen to people of greatness.

The Bottom Line: David's reminder to God to help in reality is his reminder to ask God to help (God needs no reminder of our need or frailty). Luther is right: "And though this world, with devils filled, should threaten to undo us, we will not fear, for God hath willed, His truth to triumph through us." Amen and Amen.

23. Resolutions on Growing Old with God   Psalm 71:9

"Cast me not off in the time of old age; forsake me not when my strength faileth."—Psalm 71:9.

"Cast me not off" (Bratcher and Reyburn say "the verb means 'throw off, reject.'"[564]) in the "time of old age" (The Psalmist is an old man as he writes [see Psalm 71:18]). "Forsake me not" (He pleads for God not to abandon him.) "when my strength faileth" (i.e., when he grows feeble and frail[565]).

Homily

Allen Harman states, "There is no heading to help set the Psalm in a particular historical setting, or to note any ascription of authorship."[566] J. A. Alexander wrote, "The psalm indeed contains a summary of the doctrine taught in this Book and in the Scriptures generally, as to the connection between happiness and goodness. It is well placed, therefore, as an introduction to the whole collection, and *although anonymous, was probably composed by David.* It is altogether worthy of this origin, and corresponds, in form and substance, to the next psalm, which is certainly by David."[567] C. H. Spurgeon is of the same persuasion.

"This psalm written by an old man, is especially suitable for an old man. It is numbered seventy-one; and it may suit those who have reached that age; but it is also appropriate to us all in prospect of the days of feebleness that will come to us, sooner or later, if we are spared to grow old."[568] Hengstenberg wrote, "There may be truth in the assumption that David here comforts the suffering righteous man in his old age with that same comfort wherewith he himself had been comforted in his old age."[569] Spurgeon says, "David was not tired of his Master, and his only fear was lest his Master should be tired of him. The Amalekite in the Bible history left his Egyptian servant to famish when he grew old and sick, but not so the Lord of saints; even to hoar hairs he bears and carries us. Alas for us, if we were abandoned by our God, as many a courtier has been by his prince! Old age robs us of personal beauty, and deprives us of strength for active service; but it does not lower us in the love and favor of God....*Forsake me not when my strength faileth*. Bear with me, and endure my infirmities. To be forsaken of God is the worst of all conceivable ills, and if the believer can be but clear of that grievous fear, he is happy: no saintly heart need be under any apprehension upon this point."[570]

Albert Barnes elucidates the text, "When old age comes with its infirmities, its weaknesses, its trials; when my strength fails me; when my eyes grow dim; when my knees totter; when my friends have died; when I am no longer able to labor for my support; when the buoyant feelings of earlier years are no more; when my old companions and associates are gone and I am left alone, Thou who didst watch over me in infancy; who didst guard me in childhood and youth; who hast defended me in manhood; who hast upheld me in the days of sickness, danger, bereavement, trouble—do Thou not leave me when, in advanced years, I have special need of thy care; when I have reason to apprehend that there may come upon me, in that season of my life, troubles that I have never known before; when I shall not have the strength, the buoyancy, the elasticity, the ardor...of other years to enable me to meet those troubles; and when I shall have none of the friends to cheer me whom I had in the earlier periods of my course. It is not unnatural or improper for a man who sees old age coming upon him to pray for special grace, and special strength, to enable him to meet what he cannot ward off."[571]

Here's my *Ten Resolutions on Growing Old with God*[572] based upon Psalm 71 that I heartily commend.

1) I will ditch the talk about my aches and pains and speak of God's greatness and goodness. God and man alike hate a grumbler, whiner and complainer. "My lips shall greatly rejoice when I sing unto thee; and my soul, which thou hast redeemed" (v. 23). *Avoid a grumbling tongue.* "And when the people complained, it displeased the LORD: and the LORD heard it" (Numbers 11:1). To God's displeasure, the Israelites complained and grumbled in the wilderness about His manner of provision for their needs. I certainly don't want that to be my disposition in old age. There are few things worse than hearing Christians grumble and complain, in light of all God has done and is doing for them. See Lamentations 3:39.

2) I will reminisce about God's goodness to me continuously. "My tongue also shall talk of thy righteousness all the day long" (v. 24). "Christians have many treasures," says C. H. Spurgeon, "to lock up in the cabinet of memory."[573] And in old age I intend to open the cabinet, recalling God's manifold goodness unto me throughout life. As I do, my heart certainly will swell with praise, shouting with the Psalmist, "I bless the holy name of God with all my heart. Yes, I will bless the Lord and not forget the glorious things he does for me. He forgives all my sins. He heals

me. He ransoms me from hell. He surrounds me with loving-kindness and tender mercies. He fills my life with good things! My youth is renewed like the eagle's" (Psalm 103:1–5 TLB)!

3) I will exhibit hope and trust in God as I did in my youth, stubbornly refusing to yield to despair or depression, despite frailty or infirmity or abode in a nursing home or hospital. "For thou art my hope, O Lord GOD: thou art my trust from my youth" (v. 5).

4) I will look to God, not man or unto my own self as a refuge in the time of difficulty, suffering, sorrow and sickness. "Be thou my strong habitation, whereunto I may continually resort:...for thou art my rock and my fortress [and] my strong refuge" (vv. 3, 7). Solomon states that God's name is like "a strong tower" that keeps us safe and secure from the enemy (Proverbs 18:10). A tower in biblical days provided protection for people in times of different types of emergencies. God's name is like that strong tower for the saved. In times of emergencies (all sorts of trouble or crisis or problems), when the believer calls on God's name, He will grant protection. This tower is so deep that no bomb can undermine it, so thick that no missile can penetrate it, so high that no ladder can scale it or arrow of Hell reach it (Psalm 27:5). I am resolved to run into this strong tower in the time of difficulty to find comfort, peace, help and hope. Mediation upon my Lord and His Word will be my constant discipline and delight. Spurgeon wrote, "Meditation puts the telescope to the eye, and enables us to see Jesus after a better sort than we could have seen him if we had lived in the days of His flesh. Would that our conversation were more in Heaven, and that we were more taken up with the person, the work, the beauty of our incarnate Lord. More meditation, and the beauty of the King would flash upon us with more resplendence. Beloved, it is very probable that we shall have such a sight of our glorious King as we never had before, when we come to die. Many saints in dying have looked up from amidst the stormy waters, and have seen Jesus walking on the waves of the sea, and heard Him say, 'It is I, be not afraid.' Ah, yes! when the tenement begins to shake, and the clay falls away, we see Christ through the rifts, and between the rafters the sunlight of Heaven comes streaming in. But if we want to see face to face the 'King in his beauty' we must go to Heaven for the sight, or the King must come here in person. Oh, that he would come on the wings of the wind!"[574]

5) I will pray more. "Incline thine ear unto me, and save me" (v. 2). Prayer is the never failing means whereby the believer is sustained physically, strengthened spiritually and renewed mentally. Thomas Watson said, "Prayer delights God's ear; it melts His heart and opens His hand. God cannot deny a praying soul."[575] In old age there is more time to pray and more for which to pray. With Andrew Murray I want "the place of secret prayer [to] become to me the most beloved spot on earth."[576]

6) I will not compromise the biblical convictions of my youth but will fully adhere unto them. "O God, thou hast taught me from my youth" (v. 17). Old age is not the time to backpedal on biblical principles and beliefs taught and embraced in younger years. Additionally, I resolve to spend more time in the Word, soaking in its spiritual nutrients which enhances life to its fullest.

7) Instead of wavering, I resolve to press on passionately and perseveringly in order to finish well. "O God, be not far from me: O my God, make haste for my help" (v. 12).

8) I will tell of the Lord more than ever. "My mouth shall shew forth thy righteousness and thy salvation all the day" (v.15). Instead of keeping silent in old age about Jesus, may He enable me to have many opportunities to win souls, whether the pulpit be a church or hospital, wheelchair or nursing home. I claim the promise of Psalm 92:14, which states, "Even in old age they will still produce fruit; they will remain vital and green" (NLT).

9) I will look for the silver lining of blessing in the woes of life I must experience, and render praise unto the Lord. "Thou, which hast shewed me great and sore troubles, shalt quicken me again" (v.20). I want to display faith in the fire, trusting God to be with me in its midst bringing glory to His name and using it for good in my life (Romans 8:28).

10) I will resist evolving into the *stereotypes* of old people and becoming like many who are elderly (grouchy, critical, complaining, negative, cantankerous, unproductive, self-centered or overly demand-ing). "Thou shalt increase my greatness, and comfort me on every side. I will also praise thee with the psaltery, even thy truth, O my God: unto thee will I sing with the harp, O thou Holy One of Israel. My lips shall

greatly rejoice when I sing unto thee; and my soul, which thou hast redeemed" (vv. 21–23).

In old age I want my countenance and conduct to reflect His presence in me. I am not a singer, but I want to join the Psalmist in being a singer in old age, praising God for manifold blessings, comfort and salvation. Sometimes joy begets singing; sometimes singing begets joy. Therefore whatever state I find myself in, I want to engage in singing unto the Lord. It is medicine to the soul.

The Bottom Line: Spurgeon remarks, "His comforts you will never be able to exhaust in all your life; but you will find that the bottle of your joys will be as full when you have been drinking seventy years, as it was when you first began."[577] As one who is seventy, I can attest wholeheartedly that Spurgeon is correct. Amen.

24. Of His Kingdom There Shall Be No End

Psalm 72:2, 4–5, 8, 10–11, 15, 17

"He shall judge thy people with righteousness, and thy poor with judgment."

"He shall judge the poor of the people, he shall save the children of the needy, and shall break in pieces the oppressor. They shall fear thee as long as the sun and moon endure, throughout all generations."

"He shall have dominion also from sea to sea, and from the river unto the ends of the earth."

"The kings of Tarshish and of the isles shall bring presents: the kings of Sheba and Seba shall offer gifts. Yea, all kings shall fall down before him: all nations shall serve him."

"And he shall live, and to him shall be given of the gold of Sheba: prayer also shall be made for him continually; and daily shall he be praised."

"His name shall endure for ever: his name shall be continued as long as the sun: and men shall be blessed in him: all nations shall call him blessed."—Psalm 72:2, 4–5, 8, 10–11, 15, 17.

"He" (reference to King Solomon but more specifically to the Messiah, King Jesus.) "shall judge thy people with righteousness" (It will be a government ruled justly and fairly.) AND thy "poor with judgment" (Barnes says, "It is one of the primary ideas in the character of a king that he is the fountain of justice, the maker of the laws, the dispenser of right to all his subjects."[578]) "He shall judge the poor of the people; he shall save the children of the needy, and shall break in pieces the oppressor." (See Isaiah 11:3–4 which applies to the Messiah and is similar. Spurgeon says, "Clothed with divine authority, he shall use it on the behalf of the favored nation, for whom He shall show Himself strong, that they be not misjudged, slandered, or in any way treated maliciously. His sentence shall put their accusers to silence, and award the saints their true position as the accepted of the Lord. What a consolation to feel that none can suffer wrong in Christ's kingdom."[579]).

"They shall fear [reverence] thee as long as the sun and moon endure, throughout all generations. He shall have dominion also from sea to sea, and from the river unto the ends of the earth." (Rawlinson says, "The righteous government of the king shall spread abroad the 'fear of God,' and establish pure religion in the land, while the world continues. Here the Psalm first becomes distinctly Messianic, passing on from the reigning monarch to the ideal king whom he typifies."[580] *Throughout all generations*. Spurgeon says, "Humanity shall not wear out the religion of the Incarnate God. No infidelity shall wither it away, nor superstition smother it; it shall rise immortal from what seemed its grave....As long as there are men on earth Christ shall have a throne among them....[S]ince he ascended to his throne...his dominion has not been overturned, though the mightiest of empires have gone like visions of the night."[581]).

"The kings of Tarshish and of the isles shall bring presents: the kings of Sheba and Seba shall offer gifts" (a prophesy that the Messiah would be brought gifts from men of the east. See Matthew 2:1, 11. Arabia is called the land of the east [Genesis 25:6] and the Arabians [people of Seba and Sheba, the Sabeans] are called men of the east [Judges 6:3]).[582] "Yea, all kings shall fall down before him: all nations shall serve him." (Rawlinson says, "This prophecy has not yet been fulfilled in the letter; but it may one day be exactly accomplished."[583] See Philippians 2:10–11.).

"And he shall live" (Barnes says "the life of the Messiah would be perpetual; that he would not be cut off as other sovereigns are; that there would be no change of dynasty; that he would be, as a king, the same—unchanging and unchanged—in all the generations of people, and in all the revolutions which occur on the earth."[584]) AND to him shall be given of "the gold of Sheba" (As tokens of gratitude for saving and protecting them, the redeemed will give Him costly offerings.[585]).

"Prayer also shall be made for him continually" (Barnes says "not for him personally, but for the success of his reign, for the extension of his kingdom. Prayer made for 'that' is made for 'him,' for he is identified with that."[586] Spurgeon says, "The verse may, however, be read as 'through him,' for it is by Christ as our Mediator that prayer enters Heaven and prevails."[587]).

AND "daily shall he be praised." (Gill says "ascribe blessing, honor, praise, and glory to Him; because of His perfections and excellences; because of redemption and salvation by Him; and on account of the various blessings of grace, and the daily supplies of it."[588] *Daily*. Barnes says "every day; constantly. It will not be only at stated and distant intervals—at set seasons, and on special occasions—but those who love Him will do it every day."[589]).

"His name shall endure forever" (Benson says, "Namely, the honor and renown of His eminent wisdom, and justice, and goodness."[590] Spurgeon says, "In its saving power, as the rallying point of believers, and as renowned and glorified, His name will remain forever the same."[591]). "His name shall be continued as long as the sun: and men shall be blessed in him: all nations shall call him blessed" (Benson says, "Perpetually; as a constant and inseparable companion of the sun; as long as the sun itself shall continue....To the end of time and to eternity, His name shall be celebrated; every tongue shall confess it, and every knee shall bow before it. And the happiness shall also be universal, complete, and everlasting; men shall be blessed in Him truly and for ever."[592]).

Homily

A Psalm composed for Solomon by David at the time he was enthroned as King of Israel. The title inscription for Psalm 72 reads, "A Psalm *for* Solomon." It is noteworthy that though Solomon wrote 1,005 songs, only one or perhaps two Psalms (Psalm 72 and Psalm 127) are attributed to him. It is, however, possible that he may have authored some of the psalms to which no author is named. B. H. Carroll agrees with Poole that the author is not Solomon but David.[593] Authorship simply is undeterminable, but it seems to lean toward David more than anyone else.

David "desired that the wisdom of God might be in him, that his reign might be a remembrance of the kingdom of the Messiah. It is the prayer of a father for his child; a dying blessing."[594] Albert Barnes says, "Though it is to be admitted that the Psalm was designed to refer ultimately to the Messiah, and to be descriptive of 'his' reign, yet there is no impropriety in supposing that the Psalmist believed the reign of Solomon would be, in some proper sense emblematic of that reign, and that it was his desire the reign of the one 'might,' as far as possible, resemble that of the other. There is no improbability; therefore, in supposing that the mind of the Psalmist might have been directed to both in the composition of the Psalm, and that while he used the language of prayer for the one, his eye was mainly directed to the characteristics of the other."[595] Spurgeon concurs, saying "that David, or at least the Holy Ghost, which dictated this Psalm, did look beyond Solomon, and unto the Messiah, of whom Solomon was an illustrious and unquestionable type, seems as manifest from divers passages of this Psalm, which do not agree to Solomon, nor to any other king but the Messiah, and from the confession of the Jewish doctors themselves, who so understand it. It must therefore be acknowledged, that, as many others are, this Psalm is also a mixed Psalm, belonging to Solomon in part...but unto Christ more clearly and fully."[596]

David, under the inspiration of the Holy Spirit, foresaw the rule and redemptive act of the Messiah, the Lord Jesus Christ, through the prophetic front window of the future. We view it through the back window of established history, seeing it wondrously fulfilled, saying with David, "Blessed be his glorious name for ever; and let the whole earth be filled with His glory; Amen and Amen" (Psalm 72:19).

The mercy and grace of Christ in securing our salvation and blessing us with benefits beyond compare prompts the giving of presents, prayers and praises unto Him (Psalm 72:17).

Presents. With the Wise Men, the redeemed worship Christ with their treasures, costly gifts worthy of a King [see Romans 15:16]—but above all in the presentation of the greatest gift of all, themselves [see Romans 12:1–2].

Prayers. Pray for *God's Person* to be reverenced: "Hallowed be thy name." Pray that God's name (it speaks of who God is) will be treated with respect and reverence. Pray that *God's Program* will be expanded: "Thy kingdom come." Pray that's God's rule will encompass the whole world and that there will be less and less sin and more and more people who love Jesus. Pray for family members, friends, and others to be saved. Pray that *God's Plan* will be accomplished: "Thy will be done." Pray that what God wants to do in, with, and through your life will be done. Pray that God's divine desire will be fulfilled with all people and nations. David prayed earnestly, and so must the believer. Alexander states, "Prayer in this verse is virtually a prediction, as the Psalmist only asks what he knows that God will give."[597]

Matthew Henrys says "how he even shuts up his life with this prayer (v. 20). This was the last Psalm that ever he penned, though not placed last in this collection; he penned it when he lay on his death-bed, and with this he breathes his last: 'Let God be glorified, let the kingdom of the Messiah be set up, and kept up, in the world, and I have enough, I desire no more. With this let the prayers of David the son of Jesse be ended. Even so, come, Lord Jesus, come quickly.'"[598] "May we spend our days, and end our lives, praying for the spread of His Gospel."[599] Can we pray anything less or more important.

Praises. "Daily he shall be praised." Not just upon rising in the morning or on Sunday or in time of special blessing but continuously "His praise shall be in my mouth." Albert Barnes says, "It is not necessary to say that this accords with the truth in reference to those who are the friends and followers of the Messiah—the Lord Jesus. Their lives are lives of praise and gratitude. From their dwellings daily praise ascends to Him; from their hearts praise is constant; praise uttered in the closet and in the family; praise breathed forth from the heart, whether on the farm, in the workshop, on a journey, or in the busy marts of commerce. The time will come when this shall be universal, when He who can take in at a glance the condition of the world will see it to be a world of praise, when

He who looks on all hearts at the same moment will see a world full of thankfulness."[600] See Psalm 34:1.

Note: *The prayers of David the son of Jesse are ended.* (See Psalm 72:20.) Adam Clarke wrote, "This was most probably the last Psalm he ever wrote. There may be several in the after part of this book which were written by him; but they were probably composed in a former period of his life, for this was the end of the poetic prayers of David the son of Jesse."[601] John Gill writes, "This psalm is thought by some to be the last that was written by David, though put in this place; and it is certain that the Psalms are not always placed in the order of time in which they were written: this being, as is supposed, made by him in his old age, when Solomon his son was appointed and set upon his throne by his order; on account of which he composed it, with a view to the Messiah, the antitype of Solomon."[602] Whatever it may mean, J. J. S. Perowne states, "It does not prove that all the Psalms of the first two Books were regarded as David's, or that he wrote none of those which in the later Books go by his name."[603]

The Bottom Line: Matthew Henry summarizes, "His Gospel has been, or shall be, preached to all nations. Though He needs not the services of any, yet He must be served with the best. Those that have the wealth of this world, must serve Christ with it, do good with it. Prayer shall be made through Him, or for His sake; whatever we ask of the Father, should be in His name. Praises shall be offered to Him: we are under the highest obligations to Him. Christ only shall be feared throughout all generations. To the end of time, and to eternity, His name shall be praised. All nations shall call HIM blessed."[604]

25. Narrow Escapes   Psalm 73:1–5; 17–19

"Truly God is good to Israel, even to such as are of a clean heart. But as for me, my feet were almost gone; my steps had well nigh slipped. For I was envious at the foolish, when I saw the prosperity of the wicked. For there are no bands in their death: but their strength is firm. They are not in trouble as other men; neither are they plagued like other men."

"Until I went into the sanctuary of God; then understood I their end. Surely thou didst set them in slippery places: thou castedst them down into destruction. How are they brought into desolation, as in a moment! they are utterly consumed with terrors."—Psalm 73:1–5, 17–19.

Truly "God is good to Israel" (The Psalmist begins with a strong declaration of faith: God is good to His people) even to such as are of a "clean heart" (Bratcher and Reyburn say, "To be pure in heart is not only to be free of hidden sins, but to be faithful in one's devotion to God's Law; it is to be single-minded in one's loyalty to Him.'[605]).

But as for me, "my feet were almost gone; my steps had well-nigh slipped" (spiritually, not physically. The Psalmist's faith and confidence in God was undermined by the false perception that the wicked prospered more than the righteous. It was like one walking upon a slippery floor or icy precipice—no stability or traction. Plumer says, "It expresses extreme sadness and dejection. The cause of this dreadful depression was that he was tempted to give up first truths of religion."[606]).

"For I was envious at the foolish, when I saw the prosperity of the wicked." (*Envious* translates as "jealous." *Prosperity* translates as "prosperity or success."[607] Clarke says, "I saw persons who worshipped not the true God, and others who were abandoned to all vices, in possession of every temporal comfort, while the godly were in straits, difficulties, and affliction. I began then to doubt whether there was a wise providence; and my mind became irritated."[608]).

"For there are no bands in their death: but their strength is firm." (Barnes says, "The word rendered 'bands' here means properly 'cords tightly drawn' [Isaiah 58:6]; then, pains, pangs, torments—'as if' one were twisted or tortured with pain, as a cord is closely twisted."[609] The Psalmist was upset that the wicked died in "peace" without terror of facing Almighty God. Spurgeon observes, "We usually expect that in death a difference will appear, and the wicked will become evidently in trouble. The notion is still prevalent that a quiet death means a happy hereafter. The Psalmist had observed that the very reverse is true. Careless persons become casehardened, and continue presumptuously secure, even to the last. Some are startled at the approach of judgment, but many more have received a strong delusion to believe a lie."[610]).

"They are not in trouble as other men; neither are they plagued like other men" (Barnes says, "They are exempt from the common burdens and troubles of humanity."[611] *Plagued*. Benson says, "They escape even common calamities."[612]). "Until I went into the sanctuary of God; then understood I their end." (The Psalmist's warped, confused thinking is resolved when he enters the Temple perhaps by the instruction received. Rawlinson says, "The Psalmist, in his perplexity, took his doubts into the sanctuary of God, and there, 'in the calmness of the sacred court' (Kay), reconsidered the hard problem."[613]).

"Surely thou didst set them in slippery places: thou castedst them down into destruction." (Benson says, "Their happiness hath no firm foundation; it is very unstable, like a man's standing on very slippery ground. Thou castedst them down into destruction—the same hand which raised them will soon cast them down into utter ruin. 'Worldly prosperity,' says Dr. Horne, 'is as the narrow and slippery summit of a mountain, on which, to answer the designs of His providence, God permits the wicked, during His pleasure, to take their station; till, at length, the fatal hour arrives, when, by a stroke unseen, they fall from thence, and are lost in the fathomless ocean of sorrow, torment, and despair.'"[614]).

"How are they brought into desolation, as in a moment!" (Rawlinson says, "There is something very striking in the suddenness with which the prosperity of a wicked man often collapses. Saul, Jezebel, Athaliah, Epiphanes, Herod Agrippa, are cases in point; likewise, Nero, Galerius, Julian."[615]) "they are utterly consumed with terrors" (Barnes says "iterally, 'they perish; they are destroyed by terrors'; that is, by terrible things, or by things suited to produce terror in the mind. The idea is not that they are destroyed by their own fears, but that things come upon them which are suited to overwhelm the soul, and that by those things they are utterly destroyed."[616]).

Homily

J. A. Alexander states, "There is not the slightest ground for doubting the correctness of the title, which ascribes the psalm to Asaph, the contemporary of David and his chief musician, and himself moreover an inspired psalmist."[617]

Asaph wrestles with why good things happen to bad people while bad things happen to good people. See Psalm 37. Obviously this inner faith struggle has been mirrored in God's people down through the ages. He thus writes to declare the error in such thinking to bring comfort and encouragement. J. A. Alexander wrote, "Asaph's was no affected scepticism; Asaph was a real doubter. In a certain sense he may be looked upon as the Thomas of the Old Testament, but the doubt of Thomas, as we all know, was about a fact and about a dogma which underlay that fact—the resurrection of Jesus Christ from the dead; the doubt of Asaph was about the moral truth of the government of God, for the cause of his doubt about the goodness of God was the inequality of human society, the fatal injustice as it appears to some in the distribution of the good things of this life. It was the base and mean character of many of those who are the most tremendous winners in what seems to be the ignoble lottery sometimes of a successful life."[618]

My feet were almost gone. See Psalm 73:2. The Psalmist experienced a narrow escape in his jealousy over the prosperity or success of the wicked. J. M. Boice writes, "In other words, his problem was that he compared their health, wealth, and prosperity with his lack of prosperity and was resentful that God would allow such a state to continue....[Our problem is thinking] that God is not treating us the way we think he should, that other people seem to be doing better than we are, that we have to struggle for a living while they coast along without any obvious trouble. Our problem is envy, and envy is criticizing God. It is sin."[619]

Until I went into the sanctuary of God. See Psalm 73:17. Asaph's means of resolving the doubt was in entering "into the sanctuary of God" for "then understood I their end." Jennings and Lowe state, "[T]here, in company with 'the generation of God's children,' joining with them in the worship of Jehovah, and hearing the words of the Law [doubtlessly also praying], he became convinced that in the end (whenever that might be), under the government of Perfect [righteousness], goodness must prevail, and wickedness must perish."[620]

There are many importance reasons to give attendance at God's house.

You ask me why I go to church;
I give my mind a careful search—
Because I need to breathe the air
Where there is an atmosphere of prayer.
I need the hymns that churches sing;
They set my faith and hope on wing.
They keep old truths and memory green,
Reveal the work of things unseen.
Because my boy is watching me
To know whatever he can see
That tells him what his father thinks.
And with his eager soul he drinks
The things I do in daily walks,
The things I say in daily talks.
If I with him the church will share,
My son will make his friendships there.
                           ~ *Baptist Messenger, September 23, 1943*

The wicked may appear to prosper over the righteous, but their feet are upon a slippery slope. Sudden and sure calamity and destruction will be their lot. See Psalm 73:19. Benson says, "Their happiness is like that of a dream, wherein a man seems highly pleased and transported with ravishing delights, but when he awakes he finds himself deceived and unsatisfied." See Psalm 73:20. Fuller wrote, "If the wicked flourish and thou suffer, be not discouraged. They are fatted for destruction; thou art dieted for health."[621]

Though troubles assail and danger affright,
Though friends should all fail and foes unite,
Yet one thing secures us, whatever betide:
The Scripture assures us the Lord will provide.
No strength of our own or goodness we claim;
Yet, since we have known the Saviour's great Name,
In this our strong tower for safety we hide:
The Lord is our power, the Lord will provide.
                           ~ John Newton (1725–1807)

Matthew Henry says, "There are storms that will try the firmest anchors."[622] What occasions put your soul in jeopardy, requiring a "narrow escape"? Perhaps it was association with improper people, undisciplined eyes with regard to the internet, flirting with a lustful appetite, impulsiveness to satisfy wants, being alone in an isolated place with a person not your spouse, hearing ungodly counsel, browsing deviant material, or that of the Psalmist. "We have grazed rocks on which others were broken; slipped on brinks over which others fell; singed our wings in flames by which others perished."[623] Oh, how you ought to contemplate your "narrow escapes" and shudder in fear for what may have occurred and thank God that it did not! Be continuously thankful for the mercies of God that enabled the "narrow escape," but simultaneously let it serve as warning to avoid such "slippery places" in the future. Presumptuous arrogance is dangerous and deadly. *A narrow escape yesterday is no guarantee for another*. See I Corinthians 10:12 and Romans 11:20. Be compassionate and exhibit loving sympathy toward him that slipped and fell upon that same slope you narrowly escaped.

Thy shoes shall be iron and brass; and as thy days, so shall thy strength be (Deuteronomy 33:25). Alexander Maclaren wrote, "Each of us may be sure that if God sends us on stony paths, He will provide us with strong shoes, and He will not send us out on any journey for which He does not equip us well."[624]

The Bottom line: "The pilot, steering his barque [sailing ship] safely into port, sometimes knows how, through lack of seamanship, he nearly made shipwreck. And the successful merchant remembers crises in his history when he found himself on the brink of ruin—when the last straw only was wanting to precipitate the catastrophe. And like narrow escapes occur in the spiritual life."[625]

26. Remember Thy Redeeming Purchase   Psalm 74:1–9

"O God, why hast thou cast us off for ever? why doth thine anger smoke against the sheep of thy pasture? Remember thy congregation, which thou hast purchased of old; the rod of thine inheritance, which thou

hast redeemed; this mount Zion, wherein thou hast dwelt. Lift up thy feet unto the perpetual desolations; even all that the enemy hath done wickedly in the sanctuary. Thine enemies roar in the midst of thy congregations; they set up their ensigns for signs. A man was famous according as he had lifted up axes upon the thick trees. But now they break down the carved work thereof at once with axes and hammers. They have cast fire into thy sanctuary, they have defiled by casting down the dwelling place of thy name to the ground. They said in their hearts, Let us destroy them together: they have burned up all the synagogues of God in the land. We see not our signs: there is no more any prophet: neither is there among us any that knoweth how long."—Psalm 74:1–9.

"O God, why hast thou cast us off forever?" (*Cast off* refers to something valueless that has been discarded, rejected.[626]) why doth "thine anger smoke" (Kirkpatrick says "a metaphor for the outward signs of the fire of wrath."[627]) against "the sheep of thy pasture?" (God's own people, those to whom He has promised protection and provision. See Psalm 95:7; Psalm 100:3 and John 10:14.).

"Remember thy congregation" (*Remember* in the sense of keep your people in mind, not in the sense of forgetfulness.[628] Barnes says, "The word rendered 'congregation' means properly an 'assembly,' a 'community,' and it is frequently applied to the Israelites, or the Jewish people."[629]) which "thou hast purchased of old; the rod of thine inheritance, which thou hast redeemed; this mount Zion, wherein thou hast dwelt" (Barnes says, "Thou hast 'purchased' them to thyself, or as thine own, by redeeming them from bondage [Egyptian], thus securing to thyself the right to them, as one does who redeems or purchases a thing."[630] In a spiritual sense this is what God has done for the believer through the riches of His grace in Christ Jesus. *The rod of thine inheritance*, the Israelites were the inherited "property" of God from olden times. Them He redeemed in their deliverance from Egyptian bondage.[631] *Mount Zion*—Jerusalem.).

"Lift up thy feet unto the perpetual desolations" (Ellicott says "a poetical expression. God is invoked to hasten to view the desolation of the Temple."[632] *Perpetual desolations* mean complete ruins or destruction.[633]) even all that the "enemy hath done wickedly in the sanctuary" (Rawlinson says, "The Babylonians had plundered the temple of all its treasures, breaking the precious Phoenician bronze work into pieces, and carrying off everything of value that was portable [2 Kings 25:13–17]. They had also 'burnt the house of the Lord' [v. 9], and 'broken down the walls of Jerusalem' [v. 10] and the walls of the temple to a large extent [v. 7]."[634]).

"Thine enemies roar in the midst of thy congregations" (Rawlinson says, "The temple did not pass into the enemy's hands without fighting and bloodshed; the battle cry of the assailants and their shouts of triumph when victorious resounded through it."[635]) "they set up their ensigns for signs" (Spurgeon says, "Idolatrous emblems used in war were set up over God's altar, as an insulting token of victory, and of contempt for the vanquished and their God."[636]).

"A man was famous according as he had lifted up axes upon the thick trees. But now they break down the carved work thereof at once with axes and hammers." (Formerly a man derived his skill and praise from cutting timber from the forest to erect elaborately carved work for the sanctuary, but now it is in demolishing the same.[637]).

They have "cast fire into thy sanctuary, they have defiled by casting down the dwelling place of thy name to the ground. They said in their hearts, Let us destroy them together: they have burned up all the synagogues of God in the land." (Benson says, "The Chaldeans first polluted, and then set fire to Solomon's temple, and burned that stately and costly fabric down to the ground."[638]).

"Burned up all the synagogues." (Benson says "all the public places wherein the Jews used to meet together to worship God every Sabbath day, as is mentioned Acts 13:27, and upon other occasions. That the Jews had such synagogues is manifest, both from these and other places of Scripture, and from the testimony of the Hebrew doctors, and other ancient and learned writers, who affirm it, and particularly of Jerusalem, in which they say there were above four hundred."[639] Poole says, "First they polluted it, and then they burnt it, and broke it in pieces."[640] See 2 Kings 25:9 and 2 Chronicles 36:19.).

We "see not our signs" (Kay says "divine ordinances, which were standing signs of God's presence—as the tabernacle, the sacrifices, the sabbaths."[641]) there is "no more any prophet" (Jamieson, Fausset and

Brown say, "To the bulk of the people, during the captivity, the occasional and local prophetical services of Jeremiah, Ezekiel, and Daniel would not make an exception to the clause, 'there is no more any prophet.'"[642]).

Neither is "there among us any that knoweth how long" (Rawlinson says, "Jeremiah's prophecy of the seventy years [Jeremiah 25:11–12] did not remove the doubt, since it was uncertain from what event the seventy years were to be counted. Jeremiah's prophecies, moreover, were not yet, in all probability, collected into a volume, and so may not have been known to the Psalmist."[643]).

Homily

The Psalm composed by Asaph (Allan Harmon suggests it was written by a later member of the sons of Asaph[644]) describes the Babylonian invasion and destruction of Jerusalem in 586 B.C. (2 Kings 24:10–25:12) or the Persecution of Antiochus Epiphanes in 167 B.C. and recounts the Exodus from Egyptian bondage. Commentators, for the main part, favor one or the other of the dates. Jennings and Lowe give great cause for the latter date based upon the destruction and calamity wrought upon the city.[645] A. F. Kirkpatrick however cites a stronger case for the former date: "On the whole, then, the view which seems most in accordance with the evidence is that these Psalms [Psalm 74 and 79] were written some fifteen or twenty years after the destruction of Jerusalem, about the same time as the Lamentations. The author might have been an eyewitness of the destruction of the Temple, which he describes so graphically, while at the same time the exile had lasted long enough to make it seem as though, in spite of Jeremiah's predictions of restoration, God had permanently rejected His people."[646] The essence of the Psalm is the believer's reconciliation of the destruction of Jerusalem and the Temple, and then the Babylonian captivity, with God's love and plan for Israel and Mount Zion.[647]

Remember thy congregation, which thou hast purchased. With the holy city, its sanctuaries and sacred vessels desecrated and consumed in fire to the roaring cheer of the Chaldeans, Asaph begs God to "remember" (think upon Thy people that You have so wondrously redeemed from the hand of Pharaoh's tyranny) and vindicate thy holy name (Psalm 74:10–11). Matthew Henry remarks, "God gave Egypt to ruin for their ransom, gave men for them, and people for their life (Isaiah 43:3, 4). 'Now, Lord, wilt Thou now abandon a people that cost Thee so dear, and has been so dear to Thee?' And, if the redemption of Israel out of Egypt was an encouragement to hope that He would not cast them off, much more reason have we to hope that God will not cast off any whom Christ has redeemed with His own blood; but the people of His purchase shall be forever the people of His praise."[648]

Paul presents the same argument, "He that spared not his own Son, but delivered him up for us all, how shall he not with him also freely give us all things?" (Romans 8:32). Spurgeon says, "What a mighty plea is redemption. From before the world's foundation the chosen were regarded as redeemed by the Lamb slain: shall ancient love die out, and the eternal purpose be frustrated? Can election fail and eternal love cease to flow? Impossible. The woes of Calvary, and the covenant of which they are the seal, are the security of the saints."[649] The divine purchase or transaction at Calvary "which thou hast purchased of old" (2,000 years ago) shall ever be enduring proof of God's everlasting love for His children despite troubles and trials at the hand of the "Chaldeans." Hear Paul convincingly say, "Who shall separate us from the love of Christ? shall tribulation, or distress, or persecution, or famine, or nakedness, or peril, or sword? As it is written, For thy sake we are killed all the day long; we are accounted as sheep for the slaughter. Nay, in all these things we are more than conquerors through him that loved us" (Romans 8:35–37). God's merciful and gracious purchase of Christians from the power and penalty of sin through the death of His Son Jesus upon the Cross is sure grounds for His help in their hour of need.

In the midst of conflict and trouble it is easy to think "the desolation is perpetual," never ending (Psalm 74:3), but remember, "in his favor is life: weeping may endure for a night, but joy cometh in the morning" (Psalm 30:5). The night will give way to light; the storm clouds to the bright rays of blue skies and bright sun. God will both grant His child rescue and deliverance and vindicate His name (Psalm 74:18, 22–23). The wicked will not escape the judgment of God for their reproaches upon His name and cause or upon the redeemed. Be assured, "the wicked shall not be unpunished: but the seed of the righteous shall be delivered" (Proverbs 11:21).

Your hand shall find out every foe
And as a fiery furnace glows
With raging heat and living coals
They will feel your wrath upon their souls.

~ Warrior (Sojourn Music)

The Bottom Line: In trials like those of Job or the Israelites, remember the mighty hand of God that in former days in salvation wrought your deliverance from the strong hand of Satan and sin. See Psalm 74:22–23. It took a miracle. If God did that, and He did, He surely will deliver you from whatever else assaults and assails in life. Of this, you have His impeachable word. "He that spared not his own Son, but delivered him up for us all, how shall he not with him also freely give us all things?" (Romans 8:32).

27. A Thanksgiving Prayer to the Uplifting God   Psalm 75:1

"Unto thee, O God, do we give thanks, unto thee do we give thanks: for that thy name is near thy wondrous works declare."—Psalm 75:1.

Unto "thee, O God, do we give thanks" (What precipitated the Psalm is unknown.) "unto thee do we give thanks" (The statement of gratitude is twice repeated for emphasis.[650] Spurgeon says, "Faith promises redoubled praise for greatly needed and signal deliverances."[651]). For that "thy name" (Plumer says, "God's name is here put either for God Himself, or for that by which He makes Himself known. Both senses are authorized."[652] Tate says, "Yahweh's name is of great significance [Exodus 3:13–15]. In the biblical world names meant more than designations of people; names conveyed their essential being [Genesis 32:27, Mark 5:9]. Consequently Yahweh's name reveals His character [Exodus 34:14; Jeremiah 33:2; Amos 5:8; 9:6] and is the focus of love [Psalm 69:36], fear [Psalm 61:5], and praise [Isaiah 26:10; Psalm 18:49; 1 Chronicles 16:10]."[653]).

"Is near" (Rawlinson says, "Thy providence and care are close to us."[654] Spurgeon says, "God is at hand to answer and do wonders;...ever in our darkest days [He] is most near."[655]) "thy wondrous works declare" (Barnes says, "The meaning seems to be, 'They,' that is, the people, 'declare thy wondrous works.' Thy marvelous doings constitute the foundation for praise—for the praise now offered."[656] Rawlinson says, "The 'wondrous works' are those of times past [Psalm 74:12–15], whereof the Psalmist anticipates a continuance or repetition."[657] Hengstenberg says, "One of God's wonders placed before the eyes gives reality also to all the others."[658]).

Homily

A Psalm composed by Asaph. J. A. Alexander wrote, "The immediate historical occasion we have no direct means of determining; but the one to which the Psalm itself seems most appropriate is the destruction of the Assyrian host in the reign of Hezekiah."[659] Allan Harman agrees, stating, "The most probable date is the Assyrian siege of 701 B.C."[660] Changes in speakers occur within the Psalm. In verse 1, Asaph speaks; in verses 2–5 God is the speaker; and then Asaph continues to speak in verses 6–10.

Martin Luther says, "This is a Psalm of consolation against all turbulent and hardened hypocrites, who boast of their church and their name, and despise all threatenings, and all exhortations; ever speaking like those arrogant hypocrites in Psalm 12. 'Who is Lord over us?'"[661] McCullough remarked that, "It is not clear whether the Psalmist is thinking of God's constant judgments in this present world, or of a final definitive judgment at the end of the age."[662] Both interpretations are valid, for all of God's judgments on earth (Sodom and Gomorrah; the Noahic Flood and numerous other "judgments") are "pledges" of the ultimate judgment at the end of the world.[663] Henry H. Halley summarized the teaching of this psalm as "the certain destruction of the wicked and certain triumph of the righteous in the day when the earth shall be dissolved."[664]

For that thy name is near thy wondrous works declare. God's name reveals His character. Jennings and Lowe remark, "i.e., we thank Thee, and thanks are indeed due; for Thou art verily accessible to our prayers, and Thy wonders on our behalf are spoken of throughout the world."[665] Allan Harman states, "Knowledge of God's past deeds on their behalf brings reassurance to the people in their present distress."[666]

Unto thee, O God, do we give thanks. The Psalm expresses praise and gratitude unto God, the "uplifting God." "For not from the east or from the west and not from the wilderness *comes lifting up*, But it is God who executes judgment, putting down one and lifting up another" (Psalm 75:6–7 ESV). "All the horns of the wicked I will cut off, but the horns of the righteous shall be lifted up" (Psalm 75:10 ESV). The circumstances of the Psalm's background are unknown. The occasion may have been the romping, *uplifting* victory over Sennacherib during Hezekiah's reign (2 Kings 19:35); the continuation of the Babylonian captivity (Psalm 74); David's *uplifting* (restoration to the throne) following Absalom's treasonous revolt (2 Samuel 19:9–11) or another historical event in which God *uplifted* Israel to victory in battle. Certainly David's *uplifting* in Psalm 40:1–2 comes to mind, wherein he says, "I waited patiently for the Lord. He turned to me and heard my cry. He *lifted me out* of the pit of destruction, out of the sticky mud. He stood me on a rock and made my feet steady" (NCV).

Every Christian has reason to praise God endlessly for his *uplifting* from the miry clay of sin's degradation, defilement and damnation. See Psalm 40 and 74.

> I was sinking deep in sin, far from the peaceful shore,
> Very deeply stained within, sinking to rise no more;
> But the Master of the sea heard my despairing cry,
> From the waters lifted me; now safe am I.
>
> Love lifted me! Love lifted me!
> When nothing else could help, Love lifted me.
> Love lifted me! Love lifted me!
> When nothing else could help, Love lifted me.
> ~ James Rowe (1912)

But also the believer ought to render gratitude and praise to the Lord for the many *uplifting's* since conversion—from bondage to freedom over a habitual and addictive sin, from sickness to health, from business collapse to prosperity, from failure to success, from despair to delight, from defeat to triumph, and from reproach to respect. Spurgeon says, "Never let us neglect thanksgiving, or we may fear that another time our prayers will remain unanswered. As the smiling flowers gratefully reflect in their lovely colors the various constituents of the solar ray, so should gratitude spring up in our hearts after the smiles of God's providence. Unto Thee do we give thanks. We should praise God again and again. Stinted gratitude is ingratitude. For infinite goodness there should be measureless thanks."[667]

> We should praise God again and again. Stinted gratitude is ingratitude. For infinite goodness there should be measureless thanks.
> Charles Spurgeon

William E. Sangster said, "God never gives a blessing just for the hour. Every special blessing is not only for the hour itself, but for the future. It is a pledge; it is as though God were to say, 'I'll do this for you now, then you will always know that you are the object of my love.' What a sad thing it is, therefore, that we forget so soon. That is why new dangers can startle you with fear and dismay. You have forgotten the past mercies. You would have been calm and confident in the presence of new trouble had you remembered vividly the old deliverance, had you kept it fresh in mind and been able to say, 'The God who delivered me then, didn't deliver me then to desert me now.'"[668]

Thy wondrous works declare. Indeed the Lord has done *wondrous works* in the life of all His children. Matthew Henry remarks, "There are many works which God does for His people that may truly be called wondrous works, out of the common course of providence and quite beyond our expectation. These wondrous works declare the nearness of His name; they show that He Himself is at hand, nigh to us in what we call upon Him for, and that He is about to do some great things for His people, in pursuance of His purpose and promise. When God's wondrous works declare the nearness of His name it is our duty to give Him thanks, again and again to give Him thanks."[669] J. I. Packer said, "We need to discover all over again that worship is natural to the Christian, as it was to the godly Israelites who wrote the Psalms, and that the habit of celebrating the greatness and graciousness of God yields an endless flow of thankfulness, joy, and zeal."[670]

> For all the blessings of the year,
> For all the friends we hold so dear,
> For peace on earth, both far and near,
> We thank Thee, Lord.
>
> For life and health, those common things
> Which every day and hour brings,
> For home, where our affection clings,
> We thank Thee, Lord.
>
> For love of Thine, which never tires,
> Which all our better thought inspires
> And warms our lives with heavenly fires,
> We thank Thee, Lord. ~ Albert H. Hutchinson (1909)

I will sing praises to the God of Jacob. See Psalm 75:9. The psalm ends as it begins, with praise. Allan Harman wrote, "It is surprising the number of times in the Psalter that God is called 'the God of Jacob' (20:1; 46:7; 75:9; 76:6; 81:1, 4; 84:8; 94:7; 114:7; 132:2, 5; 146:5). This is either to recall the special relationship between God and Jacob, or else a reminder that he is still the God of Jacob's descendants."[671]

The Bottom Line: "By him therefore let us offer the sacrifice of praise to God continually, that is, the fruit of our lips giving thanks to his name" (Hebrews 13:15). John Bunyan said, "A sensible thanksgiving for mercies received is a mighty prayer in the Spirit of God. It prevails with Him unspeakably."[672]

See Psalm 103:1–5. Hengstenberg remarked, "One of God's wonders placed before the eyes gives reality also to all the others."[673] Fuller wrote, "The more we meditate upon His astonishing love, His amazing sacrifice, the more we feel that if we had a thousand minds, hearts, souls, we would crown Him Lord of all."[674]

28. The Divine Warrior who Defends His People   Psalm 76:1–9

"In Judah is God known: his name is great in Israel. In Salem also is his tabernacle, and his dwelling place in Zion. There brake he the arrows of the bow, the shield, and the sword, and the battle. Selah. Thou art more glorious and excellent than the mountains of prey. The stouthearted are spoiled, they have slept their sleep: and none of the men of might have found their hands. At thy rebuke, O God of Jacob, both the chariot and horse are cast into a dead sleep. Thou, even thou, art to be feared: and who may stand in thy sight when once thou art angry? Thou didst cause judgment to be heard from heaven; the earth feared, and was still, When God arose to judgment, to save all the meek of the earth. Selah."—Psalm 76:1–9.

In "Judah" (Plumer says, "Judah was a powerful tribe and the seat of political power for the whole nation. God was known by the whole history of the Jewish nation, by the laws and statutes He gave His people, and by the judgments He executed."[675]) is "God known" (Kirkpatrick says, "By this recent deliverance He has once more 'made Himself known in her palaces as a sure refuge.'"[676] Benson says, "God's people do not worship an unknown god, as the Athenians did [Acts 17:23], but one who hath made Himself known, not only by His Word and ordinances, but also by the glorious effects of His wisdom and power, exerted on their behalf, and against their potent and malicious enemies."[677]).

His "name is great in Israel" (Bratcher and Reyburn say, "The name of God stands here especially for His fame as the triumphant victor over Israel's enemies."[678] Rawlinson says, "i.e., greatly honored and regarded, on account of what has happened."[679]). "In Salem" (Barnes says, "This was the ancient name for Jerusalem, and is evidently so used here. It continued to be given to the town until the time of David, when it was called 'Jerusalem.' The word properly means 'peace,'…[it] also is His tabernacle, and His dwelling place in Zion."[680] God chose Jerusalem as His royal city so that both Judah [the southern kingdom] and Israel [the northern kingdom] may be comforted with the assurance of the Divine Warrior's presence in their midst.[681]).

Also is "his tabernacle" (the tent of meeting where God was worshipped. It was the place He made His home.[682]) and "his dwelling place in Zion" (Barnes says, "That is, on Mount Zion—the portion of Jerusalem in which David built his own palace, and which he made the place of public worship. This remained so until the Temple was built on Mount Moriah."[683]).

"There" (The word seems to indicate that the battle with the invading army took place in the vicinity of Jerusalem. This makes possible it was the battle that resulted in the defeat of the Assyrian general Sennacherib in 701 B.C. [2 Kings 19:35].[684]) "brake he the arrows of the bow" (Barnes says "is literally, 'the lightnings of the bow,' the word rendered 'arrows' meaning properly 'flame'; and then, 'lightning.' The idea is that the arrows sped from the bow with the rapidity of lightning."[685] Tate leans to their being "incendiary arrows."[686] See Psalm 7:13.) "the shield, and the sword" (the weapons that God demolished of the enemy). AND "the battle" (Tate says, "In this context the weapons of war are clearly meant."[687]).

"Thou art more glorious and excellent than the mountains of prey." (Plumer says, "*Mountains* are the figurative representations of kingdoms, and *mountains of prey* are kingdoms that practice rapine ['the violent seizure of someone's property' (Oxford Dictionary)] and spoliation ['the action of ruining or destroying something' (Google Dictionary)]. The figure is drawn from mountains made terrible by being inhabited by powerful animals that live on prey. The Psalmist says that God is over and above all earthly dynasties, however exalted and terrible."[688] Spurgeon says, "Far more is Jehovah to be extolled than all the invading powers which sought to oppress His people, though they were for power and greatness comparable to mountains....[T]he Psalmist despised such renown, and declares that the Lord was far more illustrious. What are the honors of war but [boasts] of murder?...But the [Lord's] terrible deeds are done in justice for the defense of the weak and the deliverance of the enslaved. Mere power may be glorious, but it is not excellent. When we behold the mighty acts of the Lord, we see a perfect blending of the two qualities."[689]).

"The stouthearted are spoiled" (Poole says "*are spoiled* of all that glory and advantage which they either had already gotten, or further expected, from the success of their present expedition, which they promised to themselves. They became a prey to those upon whom they hoped to prey."[690] Rawlinson says, "['The stout heart of the King of Assyria'], is itself spoiled in turn."[691] Bratcher and Reyburn summarize, "The stout-hearted are the brave enemy soldiers; and their spoil are their weapons and armament, which were taken from them. [The] RSV [says] their spoil means the weapons and objects these defeated soldiers had plundered from others."[692]).

"They have slept their sleep" (metaphor for death) and "none of the men of might have found their hands" (Spurgeon says, "They cannot lift a finger, for the rigor of death has stiffened them. O God, thus shalt Thou fight for us, and in the hour of peril overthrow the enemies of Thy Gospel. Therefore in Thee will we trust and not be afraid."[693] Rawlinson says, "The mighty men, suddenly assaulted by the grim destroyer, Death, can make no resistance; they are paralyzed; they cannot even move a hand."[694]).

At thy rebuke, O God of Jacob, both "the chariot and horse are cast into a dead sleep" (The *chariot and horse* were the two main arms of the Assyrian military.[695] Benson says, "By a rebuking blast sent from Thee; both the chariot and horse are cast into a dead sleep—are rendered motionless and useless, like persons in a dead sleep. The horses were killed, as well as their riders, and the chariots were of no further service."[696] Alexander says, "'Put to sleep' is here used to translate a passive participle, denoting not a mere state or condition, but the violence by which it is produced. The sleep meant is of course the sleep of death."[697]).

"Thou, even thou, art to be feared" (Benson says, "Thy majesty is to be reverenced, Thy sovereignty to be submitted to, and Thy justice to be dreaded, by those that have offended Thee. Let all the world learn, by this event, to stand in awe of the great God."[698] Barnes says, "The particular 'reason' suggested here why God should be had in reverence, was the display of His power in overthrowing by a word the mighty hosts that had come against the holy city."[699]) AND "who may stand in thy sight when once thou art angry?" (A rhetorical question. Bratcher and Reyburn say, "No human being can withstand God's anger. All opposition ceases; all resistance disappears."[700]).

"Thou didst cause judgment to be heard from heaven" (Spurgeon says, "So complete an overthrow was evidently a judgment from Heaven; those who saw it not, yet heard the report of it, said, 'This is the finger of God.' Man will not hear God's voice if he can help it, but God takes care to cause it to be heard. The echoes of that judgment executed on the haughty Assyrian are heard still, and will ring on down all the ages, to the praise of divine justice."[701] Rawlinson says, "By the destruction of Sennacherib's host, God spoke, as it were, with a voice of thunder, to the whole earth. He delivered a 'judgment,' or a 'sentence' [Revised Version], which could not be ignored."[702]).

"The earth feared, and was still" (Barnes says, "The overthrow of these enemies of Thy people was a manifest judgment from Thee, and should be so regarded. *The earth feared*—The world itself seemed to hear the voice of God, and to stand in awe. *And was still*—It seemed to be profoundly attentive to what God said, and as if it reverently listened to His voice. It is not uncommon in the Scriptures to represent the earth—the hills, the mountains, the streams, the rivers, the plains—as conscious of the presence of God; as either rejoicing or trembling at His voice. Compare Psalm 65:12–13; Psalm 114:3–7; Habakkuk 3:8–11."[703]). "When God arose to judgment, to save all the meek of the earth" (Rawlinson says, "God's vengeances on the wicked are, in great measure, for the relief of the righteous. Sennacherib's discomfiture relieved 'the meek of the earth,' i.e., not only Israel, but many other downtrodden and oppressed nations. The Psalmist's sympathies are with all the victims of Assyrian ambition."[704]).

Homily

Asaph (a different man from the earlier cited Asaph) composes the Psalm to celebrate God's defeat of the Assyrian general Sennacherib in 701 B.C. (2 Kings 19:35). It serves as a staunch reminder that God is the Mighty Warrior who forever defends His people from the hand of the enemy. It takes but a word from His mouth to rout the strongest and fiercest armies. See Psalm 76:6; 2 Kings 19:34–35 and Psalm 33:6. It is a truth that if God be for us, who can possibly stand against us. See Romans 8:31.

Note several contrasts between the spiritual and the physical gleaned from the Psalm.

The enemy is not Sennacherib but one even mightier. Peter describes him as "your adversary the devil, [who] as a roaring lion, walketh about, seeking whom he may devour" (1 Peter 5:8). Albert Barnes says, "The lion here is not the crouching lion—the lion stealthfully creeping toward his foe—but it is the raging monarch of the woods, who by his terrible roar would intimidate all so that they might become an easy prey."[705] Matthew Poole adds that it's Satan's purpose to *devour* man, "not lightly hurt, but swallow up and utterly destroy, by himself or his instruments."[706] See John 10:10.

The battleground is not near Jerusalem but in our heart. As God made His *home* in Jerusalem near His people to assure them of His constant presence and protection (Psalm 76:2), He has done the same thing in the believer's heart (Galatians 2:20; John 15:4). The soul is the arena for spiritual warfare; thankfully the King reigns therein. Hallelujah! Continuously the enemy assaults the fortress of the soul, seeking its complete demise and the dethroning of the King (Jesus).

The battle is not against the weaponry of "flesh and blood [chariots and horses and flaming arrows and sharp swords], *but against principalities, against powers, against the rulers of the darkness of this world, against spiritual wickedness in high places"* (Ephesians 6:12). The archenemy of God and man, Satan, will be thwarted, driven back when the believer faces him dressed in the full armor of God while standing firm in the power of Christ (Ephesians 6:13). Though "stouthearted," brave, confident and arrogant, Satan and his demons shall be "spoiled" (rendered powerless, impotent by having their weapons stripped) by the mighty hand of God. See Colossians 2:15; 1 John 4:4 and Psalm 75:10. Morison comments, "Compared with the Eternal there is no object of legitimate fear in the universe. He can do whatsoever seemeth good to Him. Before Him no enemy can possibly stand, when once His wrath is kindled. Beneath His shadow the most inveterate and formidable foes cannot injure the objects of His unchanging love."[707]

The believer's conquest of and triumph over the enemy is exactly the same as was that of Israel. "At thy rebuke, O God of Jacob, both the chariot and horse are cast into a dead sleep" (Psalm 76:6). It is God's rebuke of Satan that grants triumph over him and his devices. In times of spiritual warfare, ask Him to speak that strong word against forces of evil. W. S. Plumer said, "The best appointed armies, the most magnificent warlike preparations under God's rebuke soon come to nought."[708] Matthew Henry wrote, "With what pleasure may we Christians apply all this [Psalm 76:1–9] to the advantages we enjoy by the Redeemer! It is through Him that God is known; it is in Him that God's name is great; to Him it is owing that God has a tabernacle and a dwelling-place in His church. He it was that vanquished the strong man armed, spoiled principalities and powers, and made a show of them openly."[709]

> Amidst a thousand snares I stand
> Upheld and guarded by thy hand;
> That hand unseen shall hold me still
> And lead me to thy holy hill.[710]

As with the nation Israel, may we often celebrate the triumphs of God on our behalf.

> Swift to its close ebbs out life's little day.
> Earth's joys grow dim; its glories pass away.
> Change and decay in all around I see;
> O Thou who changest not, abide with me.
>
> I fear no foe, with Thee at hand to bless;
> Ills have no weight and tears no bitterness.
> Where is death's sting? Where, grave, thy victory?
> I triumph still, if Thou abide with me.
> ~ Henry Francis Lyte (1847)

Surely the wrath of man shall praise thee. See Psalm 76:10. Dilday and Kennedy say, "The probable meaning is that in the divine purpose even violent acts will be overruled for ultimate good. That is, the resultant judgment will lead the wicked to recognize God and inspire the righteous to praise him."[711]

The Bottom Line: Spurgeon says, "What with pitfalls and snares, weak knees, weary feet, and subtle enemies, no child of God would stand fast for an hour, were it not for the faithful love [Christ] which will not suffer his foot to be moved."[712]

29. The Dark Night of the Soul   Psalm 77:1–3

"I cried unto God with my voice, even unto God with my voice; and he gave ear unto me. In the day of my trouble I sought the Lord: my sore ran in the night, and ceased not: my soul refused to be comforted. I remembered God, and was troubled: I complained, and my spirit was overwhelmed. Selah."—Psalm 77:1–3.

I "cried unto God with my voice, even unto God with my voice" (Asaph prays audibly, not merely mentally.[713] The repetition indicates the intensity of the appeal.[714] Spurgeon says, "He used his voice also, for though vocal utterance is not necessary to the life of prayer, it often seems forced upon us by the energy of our desires."[715] Plumer says, "The meaning is, prayed very earnestly and fervently."[716]). AND "he gave ear unto me" (Gill says, "His prayer was not without success; God is a God [who is] hearing and answering prayer, according to His promise [Psalm 50:15]."[717] Spurgeon says, "Importunity prevailed. The gate opened to the steady knock. It will be so with us in our hour of trial; the God of grace will hear us in due season."[718]).

In the "day of my trouble I sought the Lord" (Barnes says, "This trouble may have been either mental or bodily; that is, it may have arisen from some form of disease, or it may have been that which sprang from difficulties in regard to the divine character, government, and dealings."[719] Gill says trouble "which sometimes arises from themselves, the strength of their corruptions, the weakness of their graces, their backwardness to duties, or poor performance of them; sometimes from others, from the profaneness or persecutions of the men of the world, from the heretical notions or wicked lives of professors; sometimes from the temptations of Satan, and at other times from the Lord himself more immediately, by His withdrawing His presence from them, or by laying His afflicting hand upon them; but, let the trouble come from what quarter it may, it is always right to seek the Lord."[720]).

My "sore ran in the night, and ceased not" (Spurgeon and others count this portion of the verse wrongly translated. Barnes translates it correctly in saying, "The idea is, that his hand was stretched out in earnest supplication, and that this continued in the night when these troubles came most upon him. See Psalm 77:4, 6."[721] Clarke says, "The literal meaning of [the words], which we translate *my sore ran,* is *my hand was stretched out,* i.e., in prayer."[722]). "My soul refused to be comforted" (Barnes says, "My heart was so melancholy and downcast; my spirits were so crushed; my mind was so dark; I had become so morbid, that I loved to cherish these thoughts. I chose to dwell on them. They had obtained possession of me, and I could not let them go. There was nothing that my own mind could suggest, there was nothing that occurred to me that would relieve the difficulty or restore peace to my soul. These sad and gloomy thoughts filled all my soul, and left no room for thoughts of consolation and peace."[723]).

"I remembered God, and was troubled" (Benson says, "Yea, the thoughts of God, and of His infinite power, wisdom, truth, and goodness, which used to be very sweet and consolatory to me, were now causes of terror and trouble, because these divine attributes appeared to be all engaged against me; and God Himself, my only friend, now seemed to be very angry with me, and to have become mine enemy."[724]). "I complained, and my spirit was overwhelmed" (*Complained.* Barnes says, "Or rather, I 'mused' or 'meditated.' The word used here does not necessarily mean to complain. It is sometimes used in that sense, but its proper and common signification is to meditate."[725] *Overwhelmed.* The meditation or musing only added to his misery.). Upon remembering the goodness of the Lord, the Psalmist's spirit was revived and peace restored [Psalm 77:10–15].).

Homily

Scott favors the Psalm's authorship by Asaph, a contemporary of David.[726] Luther states, "This Psalm sets forth to us God and the ways of God: that is, how he works, and what he does, in his church and in the saints."[727] Calvin wrote, "Whoever was the penman of this Psalm, the

Holy Spirit seems, by his mouth, to have dictated a common form of prayer for the church in her afflictions, that even under the most cruel persecutions the faithful might not fail to address their prayers to heaven."[728] Jennings and Lowe wrote, "The affliction is obviously personal, not national. The writer is unknown, and the only clue to the date of his composition lies in its connection with the 'prayer' of Habakkuk (Habakkuk 3)."[729] Harmon sees nothing within the Psalm to connect it with a historical event or date.[730]

Walter Brueggemann writes, "Brevard S. Childs is no doubt right in seeing that the Psalms as a canonical book is finally an act of hope. But the hope is rooted precisely in the midst of loss and darkness, where God is surprisingly present."[731] Matthew Henry says, "Drooping saints that are of a sorrowful spirit may here as in a glass [mirror] see their own faces."[732] Life is difficult. It always will be difficult. Part and parcel of life are certain heartaches, sorrows, failures, disappointments and frustrations from which none are exempt. While I was a college student, a chapel speaker said something I have never forgotten, something I hope you will etch upon the walls of your mind. He simply said, "There's a tolerable solution for every intolerable problem you face." I have proved that statement to be true time and again. Life is hard but God is good. He promises to walk through every storm, sorrow, bitter disappointment, lonely moment and failure with you. He can do anything but fail you. Therefore fear not that which happens to or around you, relying upon Him who will not "fail thee nor forsake thee" (Deut. 31:6). Days of emotional and physical upheaval will come, but they will PASS. The darkness eventually must give way to the light. God promises to still the boisterous winds and waves beating upon the vessel of your life, saying, "Peace be still." Don't panic. Wait on Him. Trust in Him. Soon the raging sea will become as glass and tranquility will reign again. "In his favor is life: weeping may endure for a night, but joy cometh in the morning" (Psalm 30:5).

James Montgomery Boice writes, "What is the dark night of the soul? It is a state of intense spiritual anguish in which the struggling, despairing believer feels he is abandoned by God."[733] Adrian Rogers reminds us, "If you will read biographies of great Christians, almost all of them will talk about something they call the dark night of the soul. I mean, they're serving God; they're loving God; and then, things come—

perplexities. They can't understand."[734] Warren Wiersbe remarks, "At times even the most dedicated Christian feels 'in the dark' and wonders why God seems so far away. During the Boxer Rebellion, the China Inland Mission suffered greatly; and its founder, J. Hudson Taylor, said to a friend, 'I cannot read; I cannot think; I cannot even pray; but I can trust.' It was a dark time, but God eventually gave light."[735] I too know such a dark time; mine though was precipitated by the deceit and betrayal of "close friends."

In experiencing the "Dark Night of the Soul" ("my spirit was overwhelmed" [Psalm 77:3]), like the Psalmist, immediately resort to God, pleading His gracious intervention, even if He seems distant or hidden. See Psalm 77:1–2. Matthew Henry says, "Days of trouble must be days of prayer, days of inward trouble especially, when God seems to have withdrawn from us; we must seek Him and seek till we find Him. In the day of his trouble he did not seek for the diversion of business or recreation, to shake off his trouble that way, but he sought God, and His favor and grace. Those that are under trouble of mind must not think to drink it away, or laugh it away, but must pray it away."[736] Calvin said, "However much we may experience of fretting, sorrow, and disquietude, we must persevere in calling upon God even in the midst of all these impediments."[737]

Cry unto God. The Lord hears audible and mental praying ("he gave ear unto me" [Psalm 77:1]) but the former at times is immensely therapeutic, enabling one to vent the pent up agony, anger and pain. It also retains focus in praying. *My hand in the nighttime was stretched out unto the Lord ceaselessly* (Psalm 77:2). The praying was incessant importunity. Albert Barnes says "in his painful meditations in the night watches—in thinking on God and His ways, as he lay upon his bed, he stretched out his hand in fervent prayer to God."[738] Keep knocking on Heaven's door until it opens. See Luke 11:8 and Matthew 7:8. *Will the Lord cast off forever? And will he be favorable no more?* Asaph makes inquiry to himself of the goodness of the Lord (Psalm 77:7–9) asking rhetorical questions whose answers were a loud no. It is unknown whether the inquiries were "most of questioning or doubting."[739] John Gill observes, "*Unbelief* in the Psalmist said, the Lord will cast 'me', or 'His people,' off, for either or both may be understood; which so appears when God hides His face, or does not immediately arise to help; or suffers the enemy to prevail, and difficulties and discouragements to obtain and continue; but *Faith* says, He will not cast off His people, whom He foreknew, from having a share in His affections, from being interested in His covenant, from His sight, and being the objects of His care, from enjoying the privileges of His house and family, or so as to perish eternally."[740]

> Verbalize the doubts and then allow faith to answer based upon the God of history, the Bible and the mercies of God experienced by others and yourself.

In times when most deeply distraught, when the heart is bleeding profusely (Psalm 77:2), sleep is evasive (Psalm 77:4) and comfort is not to be found after talking to God, talk to yourself. Verbalize the doubts and then allow faith to answer based upon the God of history, the Bible and the mercies of God experienced by others and yourself. *I will remember the works of the Lord: surely I will remember thy wonders of old* (Psalm 77:11). Remember God's former mercies unto you (Psalm 77:10–15). Spurgeon says, "Fly back, my soul, away from present turmoil, to the grandeurs of history, the sublime deeds of Jehovah, the Lord of Hosts; for He is the same and is ready even now to defend His servants as in days of yore. Surely I will remember Thy wonders of old. Whatever else may glide into oblivion, the marvelous works of the Lord in the ancient days must not be suffered to be forgotten....When faith has its seven years of famine, memory like Joseph in Egypt opens her granaries."[741] "The remembrance of the works of God will be a powerful remedy against distrust of His promise and goodness; for He is God, and changes not."[742]

W. A. Criswell remarked, "Whether in the yesteryear gone by, or whether in the today, or whether in the tomorrow He is always the same in His person,...in His offices, [and]...in His presence....What a comfort to know that though I may change, He will not. What a comfort to know that though my life fades away, He abides forever. What a solace and what a comfort to know that though my feet may tremble, the Rock on which I stand is never moved. And what a blessedness to realize that the salvation He has offered to me is like Christ Himself, unchanging, abiding forever and forever."[743] See Malachi 3:6 and Hebrews 13:8.

When darkness seems to hide His face,
I rest on His unchanging grace. ~ Edward Mote (1797–1874)

God our maker giveth songs in the night. See Job 35:10. James Hastings wrote, "When, then, our text [Job 35:10] speaks of God, 'who giveth songs in the night,' it evidently means that it belongs to Him to put songs of praise and joy into the Christian's heart in seasons of sorrow and trial. It belongs to God, and to God alone, to give such songs. A thoughtless world seeks its happiness in that which is outward—in worldly pleasure, in earthly aims, and in the creature. So long as the outward path is smooth, pleasures succeeding each other, and keeping the mind in a perpetual state of excitement—so long as success crowns those earthly aims, and either money or fame increases—so long the world has its songs. But let a change come over the scene. Let these pleasures fail, its schemes end in disappointment, and its all is gone. The world may sing in its day—its short and uncertain day. But it knows not, and can never learn, songs in the night. It cannot even understand them. The most it can do is to keep silence. But the Christian's noblest and most elevated songs are not those which he sings in the day, but those which rise up in the night-season of sorrow—songs sung with tearful eyes and a heaving heart."[744] Charles Simeon says, "Take this for your pattern, Brethren. You may be brought into trials, which may seem to menace your very existence; but, however the storm may rage, your Saviour is embarked in the vessel with you; yea, and is also sitting at the helm. Only reflect on His conflicts, victories, and triumphs; and you will see the way that is marked out for you; and as He fought and overcame, and is set down upon His Father's throne, so shall you also overcome, and enjoy the full recompence of your trials upon your Father's throne for ever and ever."[745]

What a journey the Psalmist transverses from gloom and doom (Psalm 77:1–6) to hope and peace (Psalm 77:13–20). The Psalm opens with disappointment, dismay and doubt but rallies to encouragement, trust and joy—and in doing so serves as a picture of God's faithfulness to His child that is overwhelmed with grief, sorrow, and trouble. The testimony of myriads of believers is, "I called to the LORD in my distress, and I cried to my God for help. From his temple he heard my voice, and my cry to him reached his ears" (Psalm 18:6 CSB).

131

J. C. Ryle said a check "without a signature at the bottom is nothing but a worthless piece of paper. The stroke of a pen confers on it all its value. The prayer of a poor child of Adam is a feeble thing in itself, but once endorsed by the hand of the Lord Jesus, it availeth much."[746]

My soul refused to be comforted. Spurgeon wrote, "When you hear the Gospel and refuse to be comforted by it, there is a wrong done to the minister of God. He sympathizes with you, he desires to comfort you, and it troubles him when he puts before you the cup of salvation, and you refuse to take it (see Psalm 116:12–13)....But worse than that, you wrong God's Gospel....You put it away as though it were a thing of nought. You wrong this precious Bible. It is full of consoling promises, and you read it, and you seem to say, 'It is all chaff.'...Oh, but the Bible does not deserve to have such a slur cast upon it. You do wrong to the dear friends who try to comfort you....Above all, you do wrong to your God, to Jesus, and to His Holy Spirit. The crucifixion of Christ is repeated by your rejection of Christ."[747] Up and be done with such refusal and avail yourself at once of the healing medicine in the person of the Lord Jesus Christ.

Andrew Bonar declared, "There is a day coming when we shall, with Christ our Head, sing of the Church's safe guidance to her rest, in such strains as these, remembering how often by the way we were ready to ask, 'Has God forgotten to be gracious?' We are taught by the harp of Asaph, in moments of despondency, to 'remember the days of old,' and assure ourselves that the God of Israel liveth—the God of the Passover night, the God of the Red Sea, the God of the Pillar cloud, the God of Sinai, the God of the wilderness, the God of Jordan—the God, too, we may add, of Calvary, and the God of Bethany, who shall lead us as he led Israel, even when earth shakes again, till that day when he comes to cast some light on 'his way that was in the sea, and his paths that were in the great waters, and his footsteps' that were a mystery."[748]

The Bottom Line: John of the Cross said, "In the dark night of the soul, bright flows the river of God."[749] C. S. Lewis says, "God whispers to us in our pleasures, speaks to us in our conscience, but *shouts* in our pain."[750] Tholuck commented, "They are real men of prayer with whom, when answers fail to be forthcoming, the thirst for prayer gets not weakened, but inflamed with great ardor."[751] Brueggemann remarks, "The reason the darkness may be faced and lived in is that even in the darkness, there is One to address. The One to address is in the darkness but is not simply a part of the darkness (John 1:1–5). Because this One has promised to be in the darkness with us, we find the darkness strangely transformed."[752] Alexander Maclaren states, "There can be no faith so feeble that Christ does not respond."[753]

30. The Theological Schoolhouse for Children   Psalm 78:1–4

"Give ear, O my people, to my law: incline your ears to the words of my mouth. I will open my mouth in a parable: I will utter dark sayings of old: Which we have heard and known, and our fathers have told us. We will not hide them from their children, shewing to the generation to come the praises of the LORD, and his strength, and his wonderful works that he hath done."—Psalm 78:1–4.

"Give ear, O my people" (The Psalmist calls for special attention of the Israelites to what is about to be spoken.[754]) to "my law" (Rawlinson says, *"Hat-torah*—torah with the article—is 'the Law'; but torah alone is any teaching or instruction."[755]): incline your ears to the words of my mouth. I will "open my mouth" (expound truth) in a "parable" (Bratcher and Reyburn say "translates *mashal* 'proverb, saying.'"[756] Clarke says, "Or, I will give you instruction by numerous examples."[757] Jesus spoke in parables, an obvious indirect messianic prophecy that He fulfilled. See Matthew 13:34–35. Calvin says "grave and striking sentences, such as adages, or proverbs, or apothegms."[758]).

I will utter "dark sayings of old" (translates "riddles."[759] Asaph's use of *parable* and *dark sayings* means that he will expound instruction by means of proverbs [parables, wise sayings].[760] Kirkpatrick says the dark sayings were "lessons drawn from the history of ancient times, from the Exodus, when Israel was 'born' as a nation, onward."[761] *Dark sayings.* Barnes says, "The idea here is, that the point was intricate or obscure; it was not well understood, and he purposed 'to lay it open,' and to make it plain."[762]).

Which "we have heard and known, and our fathers have told us" (Spurgeon says, "The receipt of truth from the lips of others laid the instructed believer under solemn obligation to pass on the truth to the next generation. Blessed be God, we have now the less mutable testimony of written revelation, but this by no means lessens our obligation to instruct our children in divine truth by word of mouth. Ministers and Sabbath-school teachers were never meant to be substitutes for mothers' tears and fathers' prayers."[763]).

"We will not hide them from their children" (Rawlinson says, "They shall still be handed down in the same way. We of this generation will still continue the practice of handing down, by word of mouth, to the next generation, how God has dealt with Israel. Asaph's Psalms were written, it must be remembered, to be recited in the services of the sanctuary."[764] See 2 Chronicles 29:30. Spurgeon says, "Our negligent silence must not deprive our own and our father's offspring of the precious truth of God."[765]).

Shewing to the generation to come "the praises of the Lord, and his strength, and his wonderful works that he hath done" (Bratcher and Reyburn say "'the praises,' in the sense of 'praiseworthy deeds.'"[766] And his strength and his "wonderful works" (Bratcher and Reyburn say it is a term that "occurs quite often in Psalms to refer to the extraordinary acts of Yahweh on behalf of the people of Israel."[767]).

Homily

Asaph composes the Psalm probably several years after Solomon was enthroned king of Israel. See Psalm 78:69. It details historical events that occurred until David's death, not any afterward, and refers to the Temple Solomon built. See Psalm 78:72. Rawlinson says, "The abrupt conclusion when David's time is reached indicates that the writer cannot carry the lessons of history any further."[768] The Psalmist scorns especially Ephraim for breaking away from Judah and forsaking the worship of God. "They kept not thecovenant of God, and refused to walk in his law" (Psalm 78:10). J. M. Boice explains Asaph's reference to Ephraim. "We are reminded [at the conclusion of the Psalm] that God rejected Ephraim as the tribe out of which the great and enduring kingship of David should come, choosing Judah instead (vv. 67–68), and that God even 'abandoned the tabernacle of Shiloh,' which was in Ephraim's territory, and replaced it by Mount Zion (vv. 60, 68). In the early days of this history, at the time of the invasion and conquest of Canaan, Ephraim was the largest and most prominent of the twelve tribes. By the time of the writing of Psalm 78, Judah had eclipsed her. This is important for what Asaph wants to say. For what he is recalling to our minds is that sin brings judgment and that unbelief has consequences."[769]

Ephraim's major problem (but also that of all the people) was that they "forgat his works, and his wonders that he had showed them" (Psalm 78:11)—the dividing of the Red Sea when pursued by Pharaoh's army, enabling them to pass on dry land (Psalm 78:13); the pillar of fire by night and the cloud by day by which God guided their safe travel (Psalm 78:14); the water from the rocks that quenched their thirst (Psalm 78:15–16) and the manna and quail provided for their food (Psalm 78:25–29). Asaph says, "For all this they sinned still, and believed not for his wondrous works" (Psalm 78:32). They murmured, complained, and doubted God's ability to care for them (Psalm 78:17, 18, 22). God punished them. Ephraim serves as a parable, a teachable lesson to remind man that God will punish sin.

Ephraim (and all Israel) repents, but it turns out to be insincere (counterfeit), for "Nevertheless they did flatter him with their mouth, and they lied unto him with their tongues. For their heart was not right with him" (Psalm 78:35–37). God however did not deal with them as they deserved but showed compassion and forgiveness (Psalm 78:38–39). Grateful we are that He deals with us in like manner, not according to justice but grace and mercy. See Ephesians 2:4–5.

Though blessed immeasurably time and again, how prone man is to 'forget His works' and stumble into spiritual doubt and hypocrisy. And sadly some men are "Ephraimites"; those in whom "religious privilege cannot restrain [an evil heart of unbelief]; miracles cannot convince it; nor mercies persuade it; nor awful judgments permanently change it."[770] To summarize, God detests worship that flows from lying lips; shows disdain for Him; disobeys His instructions; is indifferent to His will, unfaithful to His allegiance, dismissive of His wondrous goodness; and is hypocritical in repentance. Such is nauseating to Him.

The second theme of the Psalm has to do with parental instruction. The Psalm instructs Israel to remember and pass down to their children the history of God's wondrous works and unfailing compassion among their forefathers primarily in the Exodus deliverance and wilderness wandering. Likewise they were to teach them about the unfaithfulness and murmuring that occurred during that time that sorely grieved and displeased the Lord. Every generation has the innate obligation and responsibility assigned to it by the Lord to pass on to the next the teaching of the Lord (Holy Scripture) and His mighty acts among His people ("His wonderful works"). The church is ever only one generation away from becoming extinct. This indicates so well why Moses instructed parents to instill God's truth and teachings upon the walls of their children's heart. See Deuteronomy 6:5–9. Spurgeon elucidates, "The first lesson for a child should be concerning his mother's God. Teach him what you will, if he learn not the fear of the Lord he will perish for lack of knowledge....Around the fireside fathers should repeat not only the Bible records, but the deeds of the martyrs and reformers, and moreover the dealings of the Lord with themselves both in providence and grace. [Children should be] taught cheerfully by word of mouth by their own mothers and fathers, as well as by the printed pages of what they too often regard as dull, dry task books."[771]

Every home that has children is to have *a school for their spiritual instruction and training*. Deuteronomy 6:5 states, "And thou shalt teach them diligently unto thy children, and shalt talk of them when thou sittest *in thine house.*" Timothy's house had a schoolhouse. Paul said of him "And that from a child thou hast known the holy scriptures, which are able to make thee wise unto salvation through faith which is in Christ Jesus" (2 Timothy 3:15). Timothy's mother, Eunice, and Grandmother, Lois, taught him to know and love Jesus. Samuel's house was a schoolhouse. Hannah's faith and godliness were instilled in young Samuel. John and Charles Wesley's house was a schoolhouse. Their mother, Susannah, devoted several hours a week with them (each alone) regarding spiritual things. Someone has said, "The Methodist Church began at Susannah Wesley's knee, when she rocked Charles in a cradle and held John on her lap while she patiently taught him to read, 'In the beginning God created the heaven and the earth.'" Homes like Timothy's, Samuel's and John and Charles Wesley's produce godly men and women who enhance the kingdom of God.

Expound the Word continuously within the home to your children (teach doctrines, attributes of God, commandments). Ingrain in them sound biblical principles to govern all of life (the author's book *Life Lessons from Proverbs* is an excellent resource). Teach them right from wrong. Clarify Christian beliefs and values. Instill good and honorable habits. Instruct them about prayer, daily devotions, Scripture memory, and church attendance. Warn them about the dangers of wrong companions, dishonesty, disobedience to God, and immorality. Encourage them to witness to friends and serve the Lord regardless of cost or consequence. Intermingle along the journey the wonderful works God has performed for His people and church and you personally. J. M. Boice comments, "One thing we are to abhor as Christian parents is "values-neutral" education. Our culture wants it. In fact, it fights for it. But then we get a world in which the young avoid hard work, laugh at honesty, steal, and in some cases kill with no apparent conscience. We should not be surprised. We should struggle to make sure that our children are taught morality grounded in the character of God and supported by the life and power of our Savior Jesus Christ."[772] We must teach this in our homes. If necessary we must teach it in our own schools—when the country's schools begin to destroy what we believe and hold dear."

Colton wrote, "Falsehood is often rocked by truth; but she soon outgrows her cradle and discards her nurse."[773] Children are born with falsehood, the Adamic nature to turn away from God. Parents are to rock them in the cradle of truth in hopes of thwarting that nature from dominating and ruining their life. Often it simply boils down to how well parents *rock the cradle* that determines which prevails.

The Bottom Line: God is nauseated over hypocrisy, and promises to punish the sin. He says, "I know thy works, that thou art neither cold nor hot: I would thou wert cold or hot. So then because thou art lukewarm, and neither cold nor hot, I will spue thee out of my mouth" (Revelation 3:15–16). Secondly, Christian parents are mandated to bring their children up in the discipline (training) and instruction of the Lord (Ephesians 6:4). Dilday and Kennedy state, "Religious instruction is indispensable. Each oncoming generation must be taught to recognize

God's hand in life and history. Each youth must be led to distinguish between a changing society and moral values that do not change."[774]

31. Troubled by Old Sins   Psalm 79:8–9

"O remember not against us former iniquities: let thy tender mercies speedily prevent us: for we are brought very low. Help us, O God of our salvation, for the glory of thy name: and deliver us, and purge away our sins, for thy name's sake."—Psalm 79:8–9.

"Remember not" (To recollect, recall. Plumer says, "Time may obliterate our remembrance of sin, but with God it never grows out of date."[775]) against us "former" (The sins of our ancestors. Pre-exilic sins that angered God.[776] An example is seen in Manasseh [2 Kings 24:3].) "iniquities" (Swanson says, "1. sin, wickedness, iniquity, i.e., wrongdoing, with a focus of liability or guilt for this wrong incurred [Exodus 34:7]; 2. guilt, i.e., a judicial state of being liable for a wrong done, and so receive a punishment or judicial sentence [1 Samuel 20:8]."[777]).

Let thy "tender mercies" (compassion) "speedily" (hasty, swiftly, quickly) "prevent us" (Perowne says, "COME TO MEET. God's mercy must anticipate, come to meet man's necessity."[778]): for we are brought "very low" (Coppes says "to hang down"[779], a state of distress and despair). Help us, O God of "our salvation" (Brown and Briggs say "deliverance, rescue, salvation."[780]) for the "glory" (honor and reputation) "of thy name" (Strong says "Carries the idea of 'conspicuous position, an appellation [as in God justifying His name of fame and reputation], as a mark or memorial of individuality; by implied honor, authority, character.'"[781]).

AND "deliver us" (to recover, rescue, save), AND "purge away our sins" (Not only had their ancestors sinned prior to the exile, but they had also during the exile. Strong says, "to cover; appease, make [an] atonement, cleanse, disannul, forgive, be merciful, pacify, pardon, purge [away], put off, [make] reconcile [-liation]."[782]) "for thy name's sake" (reputation, honor).

Homily

A Psalm composed by Asaph regarding the Babylonian conquest of Jerusalem under Nebuchadnezzar (586 B.C.). The Temple and city were savagely destroyed (Psalm 79:1), bodies were strewn in the streets, left unburied, for the Babylonians would not bury them and the Jews could not (vv. 2–3); and the sacred city had been defiled by heathens with their sacrilegious acts (v. 1). Rawlinson says, "The Babylonians defiled the temple by breaking into it, seizing its treasures and ornaments (Jeremiah 52:17–23), and finally setting fire to it (v. 13)."[783] Psalm 137 depicts the people's woeful estate: "By the rivers of Babylon, there we sat down, yea, we wept, when we remembered Zion. We hanged our harps upon the willows in the midst thereof. For there they that carried us away captive required of us a song; and they that wasted us required of us mirth, saying, Sing us one of the songs of Zion. How shall we sing the LORD'S song in a strange land?" (vv. 1–4). In this state of utter despair and drooping physically and spiritually, Asaph, in behalf of the people, cries out to God for rescue, restoration (Psalm 79:8–9, 11) and vindication (vv. 6–7, 12).

Remember not our old sins. Spurgeon states, "Generations lay up stores of transgressions to be visited upon their successors; hence this urgent prayer."[784] Asaph prays that God would not hold the people accountable for the sins of their forefathers. Scripture indicates that God visits upon a generation the sins of the former generations. See Exodus 20:5 34:7; Leviticus 20:5; 26:39–40; Numbers 14:18, 33. Of this truth all are able witnesses. The foundational sin of old that has plagued man in every generation and will continuously was committed by Adam and Eve in the garden. "Wherefore, as by one man sin entered into the world, and death by sin; and so death passed upon all men, for that all have sinned" (Romans 5:12). The sin of rebellious disobedience to God by our first parents gave birth to the seed of utter corruption and poisonous depravity in every man of every generation, producing with it the present and eternal judgment of God. See Romans 6:23.

Let thy tender mercies speedily meet our need. The Psalmist begs the Lord not to "chastise or punish them for them [old sins], but that He would pardon them; for forgiveness of sin is sometimes expressed by a nonremembrance of it (Isaiah 43:25), or that He would not 'remember unto' them; that is, put them in mind of them, lay them home and heavy upon their consciences, charge them with the guilt of them, and demand satisfaction for them; which is causing them to possess the sins of their youth, or former ones (Job 13:26)."[785] Well might the believer utter such a plea, for often he is shackled and held captive to old sins that ought to be buried in the grave of God's forgiveness and forgetfulness. It is not for want of assurances that man yet is haunted by old sins, for Holy Scripture says that upon confession, God will "cast all their sins into the depths of the sea" (Micah 7:19); "cast all my sins behind [His] back" (Isaiah 38:17); and "as far as the east is from the west, so far hath he removed our transgressions from us" (Psalm 103:12). Man wrongly often equates lack of forgetfulness of old sins with lack of forgiveness.

For we are brought very low. Being held prisoner to old sins that God has long forgotten and forgiven serves only to create unwarranted guilt and grief. Say unto the Lord with the Psalmist, "Let the sighing of the prisoner come before thee; according to the greatness of thy power preserve" (Psalm 79:11). Cry out, "Help us, O God of our salvation, for the glory of thy name: and deliver us, and purge away our sins, for thy name's sake" (v. 9). "O Lord, purge away, remove from me my sin of holding onto my old sins as if they have not been graciously and mercifully forgiven by You. Speedily deliver me from toting around 'dead bones' that only bring dishonor to You and despair to me."

To summarize, there are two kinds of guilt mentioned in the Bible. The first is that produced by the Holy Spirit when a wrong has been committed (John 16:8). Upon our expressing godly sorrow unto God over the sin (confession) and resolve not to engage in the act again (repentance), the sin is forgiven (2 Corinthians 7: 10).

> Don't go rummaging through the cemetery of past sins that long have been forgiven and buried.

The second kind is false guilt (accusations, condemnation) that originates with Satan. Satan will seek to sabotage God's promise to forgive every sinful act. He seeks to steal our peace and happiness and to cause us to feel dirty and unworthy (shameful), by feeding the mind the lie that God did not forgive when we asked, or that we must pay more for the wrong committed to satisfy God. The key to victory over haunting, hurting guilt is in recognizing its source (Satan, the father of lies) and steadfastly, stoutly rejecting giving any place to it (John 8:44). Don't go rummaging through the cemetery of past sins that long have been forgiven and buried (Ephesians 4:27). A. W. Tozer stated, "Are you still afraid of your past sins? God knows that sin is a terrible thing—and the Devil knows it, too. So he follows us around and as long as we will permit it, he will taunt us about our past sins. As for myself, I have learned to talk back to him on this score. I say, 'Yes, Devil, sin is terrible—but I remind you that I got it from you! And I remind you, Devil, that everything good— forgiveness and cleansing and blessing—everything that is good I have freely received from Jesus Christ.'"[786] Tozer continues, "Why do we claim on one hand that our sins are gone and on the other act just as though they are not gone? Brethren, we have been declared, "Not Guilty!" by the highest court in all the universe....Now, on the basis of grace as taught in the Word of God, when God forgives a man, He trusts him as though he had never sinned."[787]

There however is a *healthy remembrance of old sins*. Even Paul urges the believer to recall them. "Know ye not that the unrighteous shall not inherit the kingdom of God? Be not deceived: neither fornicators, nor idolaters, nor adulterers, nor effeminate, nor abusers of themselves with mankind, Nor thieves, nor covetous, nor drunkards, nor revilers, nor extortioners, shall inherit the kingdom of God. And such were some of you: but ye are washed, but ye are sanctified, but ye are justified in the name of the Lord Jesus, and by the Spirit of our God" (1 Corinthians 6:11).

Remembering old sins is humbling and self-abasing, prompting cautionary conduct lest they be committed again.

Remembering old sins is humbling and self-abasing, prompting cautionary conduct lest they be committed again. This truth was dramatized by a father that took his son into the garage and drove a nail into the wall. He said, "Son, pull the nail out with this hammer." The boy used the claw end of the hammer to extract the nail. The father then said, "Now, pull out the nail hole." *Nail holes* are able reminders of weaknesses and vulnerabilities. Ray Steadman comments, "Once we have given way to temptation it will forevermore remain an area of weakness where we can easily give way again. It does not matter how long we live; it will remain an area of weakness. We can fall again, and more easily than we did the first time....We are capable of being again whatever we once were, whenever we fall back into the flesh. Sin leaves a permanently weak place in the wall, and we will forevermore have to fight a particularly difficult battle at that point. It does not mean that we have to fail or give way again."[788] *Nail holes* are preventatives to committing the same sins again.

> My sin, oh, the bliss of this glorious thought!
> My sin, not in part but the whole,
> Is nailed to the cross, and I bear it no more.
> Praise the Lord, praise the Lord, O my soul!
>
> ~ Horatio G. Spafford (1873)

The Bottom Line: Old sins have power to taunt and bring despair although they are dead in the grave. Make sure they have been placed under the covering of the blood of Jesus Christ for pardon (1 John 1:7) and then declare them forever erased. Refuse to allow skeletons of yesterday to harm and wreak havoc in life today.

32. Biblical Repentance   Psalm 80:3, 17

"Turn us again, O God, and cause thy face to shine; and we shall be saved."

"Let thy hand be upon the man of thy right hand, upon the son of man whom thou madest strong for thyself."—Psalm 80:3, 17.

"Turn us again" (Benson says, "He means, either to our former quiet and flourishing state; or, to thyself, from whom Ephraim and Manasseh, with the rest of the ten tribes, have apostatized."[789]) O God (Elohim).

AND "cause thy face to shine" (Bratcher and Reyburn say "means to look on someone with favor, mercy, kindness."[790] Gill says, "Grant Thy gracious presence, lift up the light of Thy countenance; favor with the manifestations of Thyself, the enjoyment of Thee, and communion with Thee through Christ; indulge us with the discoveries of Thy love, the joys

of salvation, the comforts of the Spirit, and larger measures of grace."[791]).
AND "we shall be saved" (restored, delivered, rescued).

"Let Thy hand be upon the Man of Thy right hand, upon the Son of Man, whom Thou madest strong for Thyself" (v. 17). Nichols says, "This is very remarkable, for the reference could only be to the One who so often spoke of Himself as the Son of Man, our blessed Lord. Rejected here, Heaven has received Him, and the Father has said: 'Sit on My right hand, until I make Thine enemies Thy footstool.'"[792]

Homily

Though composed by Asaph, the historical event related to it is counted uncertain by many. Boice however believes, "Since Psalm 80 focuses on the northern kingdom—it calls God the 'Shepherd of Israel' and speaks of Ephraim and Manasseh, two of the major northern tribes—and since it asks for Israel's deliverance, it is best seen as a plea for the deliverance of the northern kingdom sometime before its fall to the Assyrian armies in 721 B.C."[793] MacArthur agrees,[794] as do Rawlinson[795] and Clarke.[796] Dodd summarizes the Psalm saying, "There are evidently four parts in this Psalm; all of which conclude with this verse [Psalm 80:3], or with one varying very little from it. In the first, the Psalmist entreats God to assist them, as He formerly did their forefathers. In the second, he beseeches Him to have compassion upon their miserable condition. In the third, not to forsake those now for whom He had already done so much; and in the fourth, concludes with a prayer for their king, and a promise of future obedience, as a grateful return for God's favors."[797] Allan Harman states, "A psalm such as this confirms that in spite of the division of the kingdom into Israel (the ten northern tribes) and Judah (Judah and Benjamin), God had a concern for both."[798] In fact God sent messengers like Hosea and Amos, assuring Israel He had not abandoned them but had continuing concern for the northern tribes.[799]

Psalm 80:3 encapsulates biblical repentance. *Turn us*. It begins with acknowledgement and confession of sin and the total inability to rectify it with God. See Jeremiah 13:23 and Ephesians 2:8–9. Matthew Henry states, "They are conscious to themselves that they have gone astray from God and their duty, and have turned aside into sinful ways, and that it was this that provoked God to hide His face from them and to give them up into the hand of their enemies; and therefore they desire to begin their work at the right end: 'Lord, turn us to thee in a way of repentance and reformation.'"[800] Scott states, "We can neither expect the comforts of His love, nor the protection of His powerful arm, except we are partakers of His converting grace."[801] W. S. Plumer says, "It is madness for carnal men to expect God to treat them as dear children."[802]

> Repentance is more than just sorrow for the past; repentance is a change of mind and heart, a new life of denying self and serving the Savior as King in self's place.
> J. I. Packer

Turn (restore) *us again, O God.* It appeals to God who alone changes the leopard's spots restoring the soul to its purity, holiness and walk of devotion. "No conversion to God [is] but by his own grace; we must frame our doings to turn to him."[803] See Hosea 5:4 and Ephesians 2:8–9. *Turn.* The word strikingly depicts repentance, for a person must be willing to change the course of woeful conduct for it to be actualized. A. T. Robertson says the word *repent* means "Change your mind and your life. Turn right about and do it now."[804] Broadus used to say that "repent" was the most mistranslated word in the Bible, for its English equivalent means to be sorry, which falls far short of its Greek meaning. Repentance occurs only when a change in life (with regard to sin) takes place. It's not simply being sorry for doing that which is wrong. J. I. Packer said, "Repentance is more than just sorrow for the past; repentance is a change of mind and heart, a new life of denying self and serving the Savior as King in self's place."[805]

B. H. Carroll pleads: "O sinner, sinner, if you would know the things that make for you great peace; if you will, today, make one earnest, straightforward, honest effort to come to the Son of God for light, I pledge you my honor you will find it. Will you come? Sinner, turn; why will you die? Separate yourselves from the throng that shuts you in. MOVE! The law of motion is the law of life. Stir up your minds. Stagnation is death. Rouse your energies and exert your powers to overcome the inertia of long rest in sin. Break away from restraints. Throw off the stupor of irresolution. Convert inaction into movement. It is thy salvation; seek it. It is thy promise; claim it. It is thy door of escape; knock, knock, now; knock loudly and escape for thy life. 'Whosoever shall call upon the name of the Lord shall be saved.'"[806]

Cause thy face to shine. "Causing the face to shine (v. 4b) is a sign of favor and good will (Numbers 6:25)."[807] Repentance next cries out for divine mercy and compassion—the loving-kindness and favor of God (sorely needed but totally undeserved) to cover the sin in the cleansing blood of Jesus Christ (1 John 1:7). *And we shall be saved* (restored). M. E. Tate wrote, "'Restoration' is not just a readjustment of the material situation in Israel. 'Restore' applies simultaneously to external welfare and what takes place in the human soul (*metabasis* and *metanoia*). This is a cry for 're-creation' in a comprehensive sense."[808] Repentance involves *faith* in God's promise to restore, deliver or save (1 John 1:9). John Calvin said, "Can true repentance exist without faith? By no means. But although they cannot be separated, they ought to be distinguished."[809] The Psalmist was certainly confident that if God would but favor the people, they would be delivered from their present despair and captivity to their former prosperous and spiritual estate. Spurgeon says, "All that is wanted for salvation is the Lord's favor. No matter how fierce the foe or dire the captivity, the shining face of God ensures both victory and liberty. This verse is a very useful prayer, since we too often turn aside."[810]

Neither you nor I have prayed our last time for forgiveness and restoration to fellowship with the Lord. Thankfully each time in our soul distress over sin that we genuinely engage in repentance, crying, *Turn us again, O God,* He immediately comes to our rescue with bountiful mercies and compassion and is faithful *once again* to grant restortation or renewal. Hallelujah! See Psalm 80:14–18.

As sheep of His pasture (Psalm 80:1), heirs of His salvation (v. 3) and branches in His vine (vv. 14–15), the child of God is promised and assured of help in the hour of need. As Shepherd, He is our constant guide and companion, granting safety and security from all harm. As Savior, He is our rescuer, deliverer and restorer from the power and penalty of sin. As the True Vine, He is the source of our spiritual vitality, strength, victory over sin, nourishment and fruitfulness.

The Bottom Line: Jeremy Taylor remarks, "It is the greatest and dearest blessing that ever God gave to men, that they may repent; and therefore to deny or to delay it is to refuse health when brought by the skill of the physician—to refuse liberty offered to us by our gracious Lord."[811]

33. The Superficiality of Worship   Psalm 81:1–7

"Sing aloud unto God our strength: make a joyful noise unto the God of Jacob. Take a psalm, and bring hither the timbrel, the pleasant harp with the psaltery. Blow up the trumpet in the new moon, in the time appointed, on our solemn feast day. For this was a statute for Israel, and a law of the God of Jacob. This he ordained in Joseph for a testimony, when he went out through the land of Egypt: where I heard a language that I understood not. I removed his shoulder from the burden: his hands were delivered from the pots. Thou calledst in trouble, and I delivered thee; I answered thee in the secret place of thunder: I proved thee at the waters of Meribah. Selah."—Psalm 81:1–7.

"Sing aloud unto God" (Rawlinson says, "'Loud' singing is regarded as indicative of earnestness and sincerity. See 2 Chronicles 20:19; Nehemiah 12:42; Psalm 33:3; 98:4."[812] Praises rightfully flow from a soul set free from Satan's captivity. Asaph was saying it's time for celebratory worship with regard to God's past deliverances for Israel from the hand of oppressors.) "Our strength" (Bratcher and Reyburn say "means 'our defender' or 'our protector.'"[813] Spurgeon says, "The Lord was the strength of His people in delivering them out of Egypt with a high hand, and also in sustaining them in the wilderness, placing them in Canaan, preserving them from their foes, and giving them victory. To whom do men give honor but to those upon whom they rely; therefore, let us sing aloud unto our God, who is our strength and our song.'[814]).

Make a "joyful noise" (Rawlinson says, "The word translated 'make a joyful noise' is especially used of the blare of trumpets."[815]) unto the God of Jacob. "Take a psalm" (Barnes says "literally, 'lift up a psalm'; perhaps, as we should say, 'Raise the tune.' Or, it may mean, take an ode, a hymn, a psalm, composed for the occasion, and accompany it with the instruments of music which are specified."[816]).

AND bring hither the "timbrel, the pleasant harp with the psaltery" (Kirkpatrick says, "The timbrel, or tabret, was a tambourine or hand drum; the psaltery, like the harp, a stringed instrument."[817] Rawlinson says, "The instruments ordinarily used in the service of the sanctuary were harps, psalteries, and cymbals [1 Chronicles 15:16; 16:5; 25:6; 2 Chronicles 5:12; 29:25 and Nehemiah 12:27]. Here the timbrel seems to take the place of the cymbal."[818] Tate says, "The 'timbrel' was carried and beaten by hand, originally perhaps shaken with pieces of bronze between two membranes."[819]).

"Blow up the trumpet in the new moon, in the time appointed, on our solemn feast day" (*Trumpet*. Tate says, "The 'horn' is not the silver trumpets blown at each new moon according to Numbers 10:10. The *shophar* was made from the horn of an animal, usually a ram [Joshua 6:4–13]. The first reference to the *shophar* is in Exodus 19:16, and there are many others after that verse."[820] Bratcher and Reyburn say the horn used here was not to play a musical tune but to announce the start of the festival.[821] *New moon*. Kirkpatrick says, "If the month referred to is Tisri, [October] *our feast* must be the *Feast of Tabernacles*, which began at the full moon on the 15th of that month. It was often called simply "the feast" [1 Kings 8:2], and was regarded as the most joyous of all the feasts. The trumpet blowing at the beginning of the month is regarded as pointing forward to it, and it was repeated on the day itself.'[822]).

For this was a "statute for Israel and a law of the God of Jacob" (It was the law of the land, a solemn decree of the Lord. Benson says, "God hath appointed and commanded this solemn feast to be announced and observed in this manner.'"[823] See Exodus 12:3. *God of Jacob*. Kirkpatrick says, "The title...carries our thoughts back beyond the Exodus to the providential dealings of Jehovah with the great ancestor of the nation."[824] Tate says, "The festival is a celebration rooted in the events of the exodus from Egypt and the wilderness [vv. 7–8]."[825]).

"This he ordained in Joseph for a testimony" (Poole says, "*In Joseph*; among the posterity of Joseph, to wit, the people of Israel, as is evident both from the foregoing verse, where they are called Israel, and from the following words in this verse, where they are described by their coming out of Egypt, which was common to all the tribes of Israel, who are sometimes called by the name of Joseph, of which see on Psalm 80:1."[826] Jennings and Lowe say, "With the title 'Joseph' is linked a history of unswerving faithfulness amidst afflictions, appropriate to the present occasion of trial, when the people were tempted to 'go back from God.' And, accordingly, from that history is borrowed the imagery of the Psalm."[827]).

"When he went out through the land of Egypt: where I heard a language that I understood not" (Poole says, "The Egyptian language, which at first was very ungrateful and unknown to the Israelites [Genesis 42:23] and probably continued so for some considerable time, because they were much separated both in place and conversation from the Egyptians, through Joseph's pious and prudent design. This exposition is confirmed from Psalm 114:1, where this very thing is mentioned as an aggravation of their misery; and from other places of Scripture, where this is spoken of as a curse and plague, to be with a people of strange language, as Deuteronomy 28:49 and Jeremiah 5:15."[828]).

"I removed his shoulder from the burden: his hands were delivered from the pots" (Barnes says "the burden which the people of Israel were called to bear in Egypt. The reference is undoubtedly to their burdens in making bricks and conveying them to the place where they were to be used; and perhaps also to the fact that they were required to carry stone in building houses and towns for the Egyptians [compare Exodus 1:11–14; Exodus 5:4–17]. The meaning is that he had saved them from these burdens, to wit, by delivering them from their hard bondage."[829]).

"Thou calledst in trouble, and I delivered thee; I answered thee in the secret place of thunder" (Poole says it refers to what happened in the Exodus at the Red Sea [Exodus 14:10–12]; *place of thunder* to the dark and cloudy pillar, whence God thundered and fought against the Egyptians.[830] Others suggest that it refers to Sinai but they were out of *trouble* at that time.). "I proved thee at the waters of Meribah" (Barnes says "as in Hebrew, strife. This was at Mount Horeb [Exodus 17:5–7]. The trial—the proof—consisted in His bringing water from the rock, showing that He was God—that He was their God."[831] Kirkpatrick says, "The name

Meribah or Strife was a reminder of repeated unbelief and ingratitude (Exodus 17:7; Numbers 20:13; Psalm 78:20); of the long 'controversy' (Micah 6:2) of a long-suffering God with an obstinate people."[832]).

"Selah" (Rawlinson says, "The 'selah' after these words marks a pause, during which the people addressed might reflect on the manifold mercies which God had vouchsafed to them in Egypt, in the wilderness, and elsewhere."[833]

Homily

The title ascribes the Psalm to Asaph. Adam Clarke states, "It is pretty generally agreed that it was either written for or used at the celebration of the Feast of Trumpets (see Leviticus 23:24), which was held on the first day of the month Tisri, which was the beginning of the Jewish year; and on that day it is still used in the Jewish worship."[834]

The Feast of Tabernacles was to be celebrated on the new moon of October each year as a memorial of God's goodness to the nation of Israel with regard to the Exodus. Psalm 81 is a call to such observance. "One can almost hear the tumult of joyful sounds, in which the roar of the multitude, the high-pitched notes of singers, the deeper clash of timbrels, the twanging of stringed instruments, and the hoarse blare of rams' horns, mingle in concordant discord, grateful to Eastern ears, however unmusical to ours."[835]

Worship God in sincerity. Not just sincerity but sincerity founded in the truth. See Colossians 3:16. Looking in from without at that congregation of worshippers it would appear all is 'well with their soul with God.' But God declares all is not well (Psalm 81:8–16). J. M. Boice says, "What a strange anomaly: a happy, joyfully worshiping congregation and a neglected and offended God. Strange? Yes, but all too characteristic of religious people."[836] Religious people often worship God with their lips while their heart is far away from Him. See Matthew 15:8. It is such worship God counts nauseating and unacceptable.

Worship God in spirit. Jesus underscored acceptable worship ("true worshippers") in saying to the woman at Jacob's Well, "God is a Spirit: and they that worship him must worship him in spirit and in truth" (John 4:24). Any other sort of worship is futile. Barnes comments, "The word 'spirit' here stands opposed to rites and ceremonies and to the pomp of external worship. It refers to the 'mind,' the 'soul,' the 'heart.' They shall worship God with a sincere 'mind'; with the simple offering of gratitude and prayer; with a desire to glorify Him, and without external pomp and splendor. Spiritual worship is that where the heart is offered to God, and where we do not depend on external forms for acceptance."[837] Ellicott says, "Place, and time, and words, and postures, and sounds, and all things from without, are important only in so far as they aid in abstraction from the sensible world, and in elevation of the spirit within. The moment they distract, they hinder true worship."[838] Benson says "in our spirit, or inwardly in our minds and hearts, adoring His majesty, revering His power, humbled before His purity, confiding in His mercy, praising Him for His benefits, loving Him for His unspeakable love to us; being subject to His sway, obedient to His will, resigned under His dispensations, devoted to His glory, and aspiring after a closer union with Him, and a more full conformity to Him. And all this through the illuminating, quickening, and comforting influences of his Spirit; without which our worship is but a shadow without substance, a form without power, a body without a soul: the lifeless image of worship, without truth and reality: nay, a mere lie."[839] A. W. Tozer said, "Worship is no longer worship when it reflects the culture around us more than the Christ within us."[840]

> Worship is no longer worship when it reflects the culture around us more than the Christ within us.
> A. W. Tozer

Worship God in song. "Sing aloud...make a joyful sound unto the Lord." Spurgeon says, "Sing, in tune and measure, so that the public praise may be in harmony; sing with joyful notes, and sounds melodious. *Aloud.* For the heartiest praise is due to our good Lord. His acts of love to us speak more loudly than any of our words of gratitude can do. No dullness should ever stupefy our Psalmody, or halfheartedness cause it to limp along. Sing aloud, ye debtors to sovereign grace, your hearts are profoundly grateful: let your voices express your thankfulness."[841] W. S. Plumer says, "God's worship should not only be secret, but also social and public; and His public worship should be audible and intelligible, not tame, nor boisterous, but triumphant."[842]

> We sing the mighty power of God
> That made the mountains rise,
> That spread the flowing seas abroad
> And built the lofty skies.
> We sing the wisdom that ordained
> The sun to rule the day;
> The moon shines full at His command,
> And all the stars obey. ~ Isaac Watts (1715)

James Hastings states, "Music is the language of the unseen and eternal; and song is the accord of the heart with this, the utterance of eternity. Of course there are evil songs, which show that the heart of the singer is in accord with the dark nether world of evil; but good and holy songs show that the heart of the singer has caught the strains and chords of the bright, blessed world of God and the holy angels."[843]

> All creatures of our God and King,
> Lift up your voice and with us sing,
> Alleluia! Alleluia!
> Thou burning sun with golden beam,
> Thou silver moon with softer gleam,
> Oh, praise Him! Oh, praise Him!
> Alleluia! Alleluia! Alleluia!
>
> Thou rushing wind that art so strong,
> Ye clouds that sail in heav'n along,
> Oh, praise Him! Alleluia!
> Thou rising moon, in praise rejoice;
> Ye light of evening, find a voice.
> Oh, praise Him! Oh, praise Him!
> Alleluia! Alleluia! Alleluia! ~ St. Francis of Assisi (1225)

Scott observes, "All the worship which we can render is far beneath His glorious excellences and our immense obligations to Him, especially in our redemption from wrath and sin."[844]

The Bottom Line: A. W. Tozer frankly declared, "The church that can't worship must be entertained. And men who can't lead a church to worship must provide the entertainment."[845] Matthew Henry said, "We must be warm and affectionate in praising God, that we must with a hearty goodwill show forth His praise, as those that are not ashamed to own our dependence on Him and obligations to Him."[846] Hillsong sings, "If the sum of all our praises still falls shy, then we'll sing again a hundred billion times." Such ought to be the heart's desire of all the saints. Amen and Amen.

34. The "What Might Have Beens"   Psalm 81:13–16

"Oh that my people had hearkened unto me, and Israel had walked in my ways! I should soon have subdued their enemies, and turned my hand against their adversaries. The haters of the LORD should have submitted themselves unto him: but their time should have endured for ever. He should have fed them also with the finest of the wheat: and with honey out of the rock should I have satisfied thee."—Psalm 81:13–16.

"Oh that my people" (Israel) had "hearkened unto me" (listened), and Israel had "walked in my ways" (Plumer says, "To walk in God's ways is habitually to obey him."[847] J. A. Alexander says, "To listen to God's teaching and commands implies a docile and obedient spirit. To walk in his ways is to act as he approves and has required."[848] God's commandments, the Law.) I should "soon have subdued their enemies" (Barnes says, "The word rendered subdued means to bow down; to be curved or bent; and the idea is, that he would have caused them to bow down, to wit, by submission before them."[849]).

AND "turned my hand against their adversaries" (Alexander says, "The phrase itself denotes mere action; the idea of hostile or destructive action is suggested by the context."[850] Barnes says, "The act of turning the hand against one is significant of putting him away—repelling him—disowning him—as when we would thrust one away from us with aversion."[851]).

152

"The haters of the Lord" (Barnes says, "The enemies of the Lord, often represented as those who hate Him—hatred being always in fact or in form connected with an unwillingness to submit to God. It is hatred of His law; hatred of His government; hatred of His plans; hatred of His character. See Romans 1:30; John 7:7; John 15:18, 23–25."[852]) "should have submitted themselves unto him: but their time should have endured forever" (Plumer says, "*Submitted*, the verb literally signifies lied, deceived, dealt falsely, dissembled, yielded feigned obedience."[853] Barnes says, "The meaning is, that they would have been so subdued as to acknowledge His authority or supremacy, while it is, at the same time, implied that this would have been forced and not cordial."[854]).

"He should have fed them also with the finest of the wheat: and with honey out of the rock should I have satisfied thee" (Benson says, "He would have made their country exceedingly fruitful and productive, especially of wheat and other grain, in the highest perfection."[855] Barnes says, "Palestine abounded with bees, and honey was a favorite article of food."[856]).

Homily

A Psalm of Asaph. God reminisces over what might have been for Israel had they only hearkened unto His voice. See Psalm 81:13–16. In obeying God, Israel would have experienced victory rather than defeat (Psalm 81:14), much instead of little (Psalm 81:16) and the best instead of the worst (Psalm 81:16).

> For of all sad words of tongue or pen,
> The saddest are these: "It might have been."[857]
> ~ John Greenleaf Whittier

Albert Barnes says, "This passage is designed mainly to show what would have been the consequences if the Hebrew people had been obedient to the commands of God (Psalm 81:14–16). At the same time, however, it expresses what was the earnest desire—the wish—the preference of God, namely, that they had been obedient, and had enjoyed His favor. This is in accordance with all the statements, all the commands, all the invitations, all the warnings, in the Bible."[858] Jamieson-Fausset-Brown says, "Obedience would have secured all promised blessings and the subjection of foes."[859] Instead, Israel forfeited them due to serving strange gods (Psalm 81:9), giving a deaf ear to the Lord's commands (Psalm 81:11a) and walking according to their own advice and guidance (Psalm 81:11b). Had they obeyed, they could have looked back with rejoicing, but instead they had to remember with regret.

Psalm 81:13–16 perhaps is the saddest lamentation in the Psalms, for God is seen mourning and grieving over what had happened to Israel in contrast to that which might have been had they only obeyed. The declarations of God's compassion and love here for obstinate sinners rings out as well in other portions of Scripture. Through Moses He said, "O that there were such an heart in them, that they would fear me, and keep all my commandments always, that it might be well with them, and with their children for ever!" (Deuteronomy 5:29). Jesus, in beholding the city of Jerusalem, wept over it, saying, "If thou *hadst known*...in this thy day the things which belong unto thy peace" (Luke 19:42). And hear the wailing words of Jesus once again saying, "O Jerusalem, Jerusalem, thou that killest the prophets, and stonest them which are sent unto thee, how often would I have gathered thy children together, even as a hen gathereth her chickens under her wings, and ye would not!" (Matthew 23:37). Benson says, "All these, and such like passages, manifest the tender mercies of God, and show that He is not only careful to provide for mankind the means of salvation, but that He grieves, speaking after the manner of men, and mourns, with paternal affection, over them, when their frowardness and obstinacy disappoint the efforts of His love."

Spurgeon says, "The condescending love of God expresses itself in painful regrets for Israel's sin and punishment....He would have smitten them once, and then have dealt them a return blow with the back of His hand [Psalm 81:14]. *See what we lose by sin*. Our enemies...could never overthrow us if we did not first overthrow ourselves. Sin strips a man of his armor, and leaves him naked to his enemies. Our doubts and fears would long ago have been slain if we had been more faithful to our God. Ten thousand evils which afflict us now would have been driven far from us if we had been more jealous of holiness in our walk and conversation. We ought to consider not only what sin takes from our present stock, but what it prevents our gaining: reflections will soon show us that sin always costs us dear. If we depart from God, our inward corruptions are sure to make a rebellion. Satan will assail us, the world will worry us, doubts will annoy us, and all through our own fault."[860]

> If we are obsessed by God, nothing else can get into our lives—not concerns, nor tribulation, nor worries.
> Oswald Chambers

Matthew Henry says, "There is enough in God to fill our treasures (Proverbs 8:21), to *replenish* every hungry soul (Jeremiah 31:25), to supply all our wants, to answer all our desires, and to make us completely happy."[861] But the treasures are conditional upon man's obedience and submission to Him. Often we are the means of our own undoing and deprivation of God's best plans and intentions.

Alexander Maclaren states, "There is no worse fate for a man than to be allowed to do as he chooses. The 'ditch,' sooner or later, receives the man who lets his active powers, which are in themselves blind, be led by his understanding, which he has himself blinded by forbidding it to look to the One Light of Life."[862] Oswald Chambers wrote, "If we are obsessed by God, nothing else can get into our lives—not concerns, nor tribulation, nor worries. And now we understand why our Lord so emphasized *the sin of worrying.* How can we dare to be so absolutely unbelieving when God totally surrounds us? To be obsessed by God is to have an effective barricade against all the assaults of the enemy. 'He himself shall dwell in prosperity' (Psalm 25:13 NKJV). God will cause us to 'dwell in prosperity,' keeping us at ease, even in the midst of tribulation, misunderstanding, and slander, if our 'life is hidden with Christ in God' (Colossians 3:3 NLT). We rob ourselves of the miraculous, revealed truth of this abiding companionship with God. 'God is our refuge' (Psalm 46:1). Nothing can break through His shelter of protection."[863]

Ponder what might have been had you walked in the way of God. 'He should have fed *you* with the finest of the wheat: and with the honey out of the rock *would I* have satisfied thee' (Psalm 81:16). The "what might have been's" of yesterday are forever gone, never to return. Learn from the past, determining not to make its same mistakes and sins, resulting in forfeiture of God's blessings.

Open thy mouth wide, and I will fill it. See Psalm 81:10. With limitless provision in answer to his prayers, the believer is to "come boldly unto the throne of grace, that we may obtain mercy, and find grace to help in time of need" (Hebrews 4:16). Whatever lack that is experienced, let us 'make our requests known unto Him' (Philippians 4:6), for God will not 'withhold any good thing from those who walk uprightly' (Psalm 84:11b). To all that walk unrightly (regardless of place [social status] or race or face) is declared, "Open thy mouth wide, and I will fill it." All that is necessary to make a withdrawal from Heaven's Bank is to request it. Sadly it is often true as James writes, 'we have not, [simply] because we ask not' (James 4:2).

> What more can He say than to you He hath said,
> To you who for refuge to Jesus have fled?
> ~ from "How Firm a Foundation"

"He that spared not his own Son, but delivered him up for us all, how shall he not with him also freely give us all things?"—Romans 8:32.

Charles Simeon exhorts, "Only reflect on what he has done, and how impossible it was any fallen creature should dare to ask SUCH things at God's hands, and you need not fear to enlarge your petitions, to the utmost extent of language to express, or of imagination to conceive.... Only spread your wants before Him freely, and you shall find that 'He is able to do for you exceeding abundantly above all that you can ask or even think.'...Go to him, then, and 'pray to him with all prayer and supplication in the Spirit'; yea, 'pray without ceasing' and 'give him no rest' till He has answered your requests."[864]

> In living obediently and righteously unto the Lord and praying to and trusting Him, you will know *the what ares*, not *the what might have beens* in every facet of life as it pertains to that which is the "good, acceptable and perfect will of God that concerneth thee."

In living obediently and righteously unto the Lord and praying to and trusting Him, you will know *the what ares*, not the *what might have beens* in every facet of life as it pertains to that which is the 'good, acceptable and perfect will of God' that concerneth thee. See Romans 12:2.

156

The Bottom Line: Matthew Henry wrote, "People are not religious, because they will not be so. God is not the Author of their sin; He leaves them to the lusts of their own hearts, and the counsels of their own heads; if they do not well, the blame must be upon themselves. The Lord is unwilling that any should perish. What enemies sinners are to themselves! It is sin that makes our troubles long, and our salvation slow."[865] See 2 Peter 3:9. To the measure in which the "mouth" is opened (exhibition of faith and confidence in God's desire and willingness to hear and answer prayer) is it made "full." The law that governs financial giving also applies to faithful (in contrast to faith-less) praying. "He which soweth sparingly shall reap also sparingly; and he which soweth bountifully shall reap also bountifully" (2 Corinthians 9:6).

35. The Judge's Prayer   Psalm 82

"God standeth in the congregation of the mighty; he judgeth among the gods. How long will ye judge unjustly, and accept the persons of the wicked? Selah. Defend the poor and fatherless: do justice to the afflicted and needy. Deliver the poor and needy: rid them out of the hand of the wicked. They know not, neither will they understand; they walk on in darkness: all the foundations of the earth are out of course. I have said, Ye are gods; and all of you are children of the most High. But ye shall die like men, and fall like one of the princes. Arise, O God, judge the earth: for thou shalt inherit all nations."—Psalm 82.

"God standeth" (He stands as the supreme Judge of the world.) in the "congregation of the mighty" (Barnes says "refers to magistrates considered as a body or class of people; as those who have assemblages or meetings, with special reference to their duties as magistrates."[866] He judgeth among the "gods" (i.e. judges.[867] Criswell says, "The reference to 'gods' is best understood here and in v. 6 as an allusion to the corrupt and unjust judges of Israel [Exodus 21:6; 22:8, 9]. Human rulers who administer justice are looked upon in Scripture as being divinely appointed and responsible before God [Deuteronomy 1:17; Romans 13:1–7]."[868]).

"How long will ye judge unjustly" (Benson says, "The Psalmist speaks to them in God's name, and reproves them for their continued unrighteousness in their public administrations."[869]). AND "accept the persons of the wicked?" (Rawlinson says, "Accepting men's persons is favoring them unduly on account of their position or outward circumstances. It was strictly forbidden in the Mosaic Law [see Deuteronomy 16:19; Leviticus 19:15]."[870] Benson says "by overlooking the merits of the cause, and giving sentence according to your respect or affection to the person. It appears from Isaiah 1:23, that the courts of justice were very corrupt in Hezekiah's reign, at which time probably this Psalm was written."[871]).

"Defend the poor and fatherless: do justice to the afflicted and needy." (The judges are told to make sure that the poor and the orphan, those who have no natural protector, are treated justly and right; to pronounce just judgment upon them. God is not advising that they render verdicts in their favor because they are poor or an orphan.) "Deliver" (Gill says "from his adversary and oppressor, who is mightier than he, and draws him to the judgment seat; when it is not in his power to defend himself against him, and get out of his hands, unless a righteous judge will show a regard to him and his cause."[872]) the poor and needy: rid them out of the "hand of the wicked" (Rescue them from their oppressors.).

"They know not, neither will they understand" (Barnes says, "They not merely judged unjustly, and were not merely partial in the administration of justice [Psalm 82:2], but they did not desire to understand their duty, and the true principles on which justice should be administered. They were at no pains to inform themselves, either in regard to those principles, or in regard to the facts in particular cases."[873]).

"They walk on in darkness" (The unjust judges were not only ignorant of the facts in the case but also of the Law by which they were to render verdicts.[874]) "all the foundations of the earth are out of course" (Gill says, "By the perversion of justice, towns, cities, commonwealths, kingdoms, and states are thrown into the utmost disorder and confusion."[875]).

"I have said" (Kirkpatrick says, "It is by God's appointment that they have been invested with divine authority to execute judgement in His name."[876] See Romans 13:1.) "Ye are gods" (the unjust judges and magistrates which the Psalm addresses) AND "all of you are children of the most High" (Benson says "representing My person, and bearing both My name and lively characters of My majesty and authority, as children bear the name and image of their parents."[877]).

But "ye shall die like men, and fall like one of the princes" (Rawlinson says, "Even the fact of your being representatives of God, shall not save you from condign punishment. Ye shall be punished with death, as other wicked men are punished [Psalm 73:18]."[878]). "Arise, O God, judge the earth" (Spurgeon says, "Come, thou Judge of all mankind, put the bad judges to Thy bar and end their corruption and baseness. Here is the world's true hope of rescue from the fangs of tyranny."[879]).

For "thou shalt inherit all nations" (*Inherit.* The NET Bible Notes say "here means 'to own; to possess.'"[880] Barnes says, "That is, the whole earth belonged to God, and the administration of its affairs pertained to Him. As those had failed who had been appointed under Him to the office of judges—as they had not been faithful to their trust—as no confidence could be reposed in them—the Psalmist calls upon God to interfere, either by appointing other magistrates; or by leading those who were in office to just views of their duty; or by His own direct judgments, punishing the wicked, and rewarding the righteous, by the interpositions of His providence."[881]).

Homily

A Psalm of Asaph. The date of the Psalm is uncertain. John Gill states, "This Psalm was written for the use of persons in power, for the instruction of kings and princes, judges and civil magistrates."[882] "Officials are accountable ultimately to God for their public trust, for their opportunity to promote the betterment of people."[883] Jennings and Lowe wrote, "This Psalm is addressed to certain national magistrates, in whose hands the administration of justice had become a tool for partiality and peculation."[884] The "setting" is the courtroom where God sits on the bench as Judge.

Ye are gods. Human judges (see John 10:34–38) serve as God's representatives to govern without partiality or favoritism in full consideration of all the facts with judicial prudence (Psalm 82:3). The Psalmist tells us why the august title of "gods" is applied to such persons in power—namely, because to them "the word of God came."[885] "They were recipents of a Divine Word, constituting them in their office, and, in so far as they discharged its duties, their decrees were God's Word ministered by them."[886] Such judgeship not only ensures equality in fairness for all verdicts rendered but deters corruption in society at large. The Psalmist as God's spokesman reminds corrupt judges that though in a position of honor and prestige, they are not "the untouchables," that God will strike them with swift and severe punishment (Psalm 82:7). Judges must remember above all else that theirs is a "sacred office" that is to be governed by the Holy and Just God.

How long will ye judge unjustly and accept the persons of the wicked? Matthew Henry said, "It is bad to rob any man, but most absurd to rob the poor, whom we should relieve; to squeeze those with our power whom we should water with our bounty; to oppress the afflicted, and so add affliction to them; to give judgment against them, and so to patronize those who do rob them, which is as bad as if we robbed them ourselves. Rich men will not suffer themselves to be wronged; poor men cannot help themselves, and, therefore, we ought to be the more careful not to wrong them."[887] Allan Harmon wrote, "Just as God was the one who rescued and delivered, so the judges are commanded to imitate Him and to free the needy from the power of the wicked."[888]

> Even they can claim from you as judge no more than justice, but if you give them no more than justice,...at least be sure that you give them that to the full.
> Charles Spurgeon

Do justice to the afflicted and needy. See Psalm 82:3. Judges or magistrates are specifically ordered by the Lord to look out for the welfare of the weak and helpless (the orphan, poor, oppressed). Matthew Henry says, "These are clients whom there is nothing to be got by, no pay for serving them, no interest by obliging them; yet these are those whom judges and magistrates must concern themselves for, whose comfort they must consult and whose cause they must espouse."[889] "Do justice," that is, do what is right but don't bend the rules for them. Spurgeon says, "Even they can claim from you as judge no more than justice,...but if you give them no more than justice, at least be sure that you give them that to the full."[890] George Horne comments, "A charge is here given (Psalm 82:3–4), by the Spirit of God, to all magistrates, much like that which king Jehoshaphat gave to his judges; 2 Chronicles 19:6, 7: "Take heed what ye do: for ye judge not for man, but for the LORD, who is with you in the judgment. Wherefore now let the fear of the LORD be upon you; take heed and do it: for there is no iniquity with the LORD our God, nor respect of persons, nor taking of gifts."[891]

All the foundations...are out of course. See Psalm 82:5b. Corrupt judges cause chaos. W. S. Plumer wrote, "Bad rulers are a frightful scourge."[892] Hengstenberg states, "Everything is ruined by them—they ruin everything."[893] Morison said, "How terrible is the state of any nation, in which wicked men are the principal parties raised to posts of honor, and in which the ungodly are protected, and the excellent of the earth are trampled in the dust (Psalm 12:8)."[894] The Expositor's Bible Commentary states, "And, since they who were set to be God's representatives on earth, and to show some gleam of His justice and compassion, were ministers of injustice and vicegerents [Oxford Dictionary: "a person exercising delegated power on behalf of a sovereign or ruler"] of evil, fostering what they should have crushed, and crushing whom they should have fostered, the foundations of society were shaken, and, unless these were swept away, it would be dissolved into chaos. Therefore the sentence must fall, as it does in Psalm 82:6–7. The grant of dignity is withdrawn. They are stripped of their honors, as a soldier of his uniform before he is driven from his corps. *The judge's robe, which they have smirched*, is plucked off their shoulders, and they stand as common men."[895]

But ye shall die like men. George Horne states, "All magistrates act in His name, and by virtue of His commission. He is invisibly present at their assemblies, and superintends their proceedings. He receives appeals from their wrongful decisions; He will one day rehear all causes at His own tribunal, and reverse every iniquitous sentence, before the great congregation of men and angels."[896] Calvin frankly says, "The dignty with which judges are invested can form no excuse or plea why they should escape the punishment which their wickedness deserves."[897]

The Judge's Prayer
May the Almighty grant that the cause of truth, justice, and humanity shall in no wise suffer at my hands.
President Abraham Lincoln

Upon Abraham Lincoln's securing the Republican Party's presiential nomination, Joshua Giddings sent a letter of congratulations in which he urged him to "avoid corrupting influences." Lincoln, on May 21, 1860, responded, saying, "I am not wanting in the purpose, though I may fail in the strength, to maintain my freedom from bad influences. Your letter comes to my aid in this point most opportunely." Lincoln then closed the letter with words that form a prayer for all judges. "May the Almighty grant that the cause of truth, justice, and humanity shall in no wise suffer at my hands."[898] *The Judge's Prayer* ought to be emblazoned upon the heart of every judge and inscribed upon the wall of their offices.

They know not, neither will they understand: they walk in darkness. See Psalm 82:5a. Dishonorable judges lack heavenly wisdom in rendering verdicts. In fact, God says these judges refuse to "understand," therefore they walk in the darkness of ignorance of His governing rules (unable to discern between what is morally right and wrong). Judges (God's representatives on the bench) ought to pray as Solomon for divine wisdom (1 Kings 3:9) that they may not only walk in the light but allow that light to be manifest in their judgeship. John says, "This is the message we have heard from him and proclaim to you, that God is light, and in him is no darkness at all. If we say we have fellowship with him while we walk in darkness, we lie and do not practice the truth. But if we walk in the light, as he is in the light, we have fellowship with one another, and the blood of Jesus his Son cleanses us from all sin" (1 John1:5–7 ESV).

The Bottom Line: Extend gratitude to judges and magistrates for serving our Lord honorably and rightly. Pray they will not become tainted by corrupting influences and always have courage to do what is right, regardless of political pressure or personal cost. Matthew Henry comments, "There are two words with which we may comfort ourselves and one another, in reference to the mismanagement of power among men: one is, *Hallelujah, the Lord God omnipotent reigneth*; the other is, *Surely I come quickly.*"[899]

36. When God Is Silent   Psalm 83:1

"*Keep not thou silence, O God: hold not thy peace, and be not still, O God.*"—Psalm 83:1.

"Keep not thou silence, O God" (Henry says, "The Psalmist here begs of God to appear on the behalf of His injured threatened people. *Keep not thou silence,* O God! but give judgment for us against those that do us an apparent wrong."[900] Plumer says, "The prayer is that God would not allow wickedness to go on unchecked."[901] Alexander says, "This is a general introductory petition, that God would not remain inactive and indifferent to the dangers which environed His own people."[902] Harman says, "The actual expression 'Do not keep silent' only occurs here and in Isaiah 62:7."[903]). "Hold not thy peace" (Benson says, "Be not deaf to our prayers and to the blasphemies of Thine and our enemies."[904]).

AND "be not still, O God" (Jamieson, Fausset and Brown say "literally, 'not quiet,' as opposed to action."[905]). Rawlinson summarizes, "A crisis has come which calls for the Divine interference. If his people are to be saved, God must no longer sit still. Compare the frequent calls on God to 'arise' (Psalm 3:7; Psalm 7:6; Psalm 44:26; Psalm 68:1)."[906]

Homily

The Psalm concludes the writings of Asaph. Israel was under siege by a huge confederacy seeking its destruction. See Psalm 83:4. Nations included in the attack were Edom, the Ishmaelites, Moab, the Hagarenes, Gebal, Ammon, Amalek, Philistia, and Tyre (Psalm 83:6–7). Assyria supported the effort (Psalm 83:8). The actual timeline for the invasion is unknown, but many scholars place it during the reign of Jehoshaphat. See 2 Chronicles 20. Jennings and Lowe are among the view's dissenters, saying, "We are...of the opinion that, while the Southeastern invasion in the time of Jehoshaphat is in many respects similar to the invasion here described, our want of information renders it impossible to assert positively that it is this danger which [evokes] the Psalmist's prayer. We find no difficulty in this conclusion; for there is no reason to imagine that we have in the historical books of the Old Testament either an exact or an exhaustive account of all the invasions to which the sacred nation was exposed."[907] A. F. Kirkpatrick concludes the discussion of the Psalm's historical occasion in saying, "On the whole, the invasion recorded in 2 Chronicles 20 offers the closest parallel and the best illustration, and the Psalm may have been written with reference to it."[908]

Threatened with extermination by a mighty coalition of armies, the nation of Israel begs God not to remain silent but intervene victoriously in their behalf. Spurgeon stated, "We may regard this Psalm as a prophecy of what will happen to the enemies of God's people, though it reads like a prayer or wish of the writer. God's enemies are making a noise, and the psalmist's prayer is that the Lord himself would speak and answer them."[909]

A New Testament story of God's silence is John 11:1–6. The sisters of Lazarus (Mary and Martha) notified Jesus that Lazarus was sick (John 11:3). Benson explains, "Observing his sickness was of a dangerous kind, and therefore being full of concern for him, knowing where Jesus was, [they] thought proper to send him word of it; for they firmly expected that He, who had cured so many strangers, would willingly come and give health to one whom He so tenderly loved."[910] *He whom thou lovest is sick.* See John 11:3b. Trench says, "Those whom Christ loves are no more exempt than others from their share of earthly trouble and anguish: rather are they bound over to it more surely."[911] Albert Barnes remarks, "In sickness we should implore the aid and presence of Jesus. He only can restore us and our friends; He only can perform for us the office of a friend when all other friends fail; and He only can cheer us with the hope of a blessed resurrection."[912] *Yet he abode two days still in the same place.* See John 11:6. But Jesus was silent in response to the letter. The silence in that Bethany home must have been both perplexing and disturbingly painful. Especially when Lazarus died (John 11:14).

This sickness is that the Son of God might be glorified thereby. See John 11:4b. Our Lord in His silences has gracious intentions of which we are not aware, as was the case with the two sisters. "His lingering so long after their message came, did not proceed from want of concern for His friends, but happened according to the counsels of His own wisdom. For the length of time that Lazarus lay in the grave put His death beyond all possibility of doubt, and removed every suspicion of a fraud, and so afforded Jesus a fit opportunity of displaying the love He bare to Lazarus, as well as His own almighty power, in His unquestionable resurrection from the dead. It is true, the sisters were thus kept a while in painful anxiety, on account of their brother's life, and in the conclusion were pierced with the sorrow of seeing him die. Yet they would think themselves abundantly recompensed by the evidence accruing to the Gospel from this astonishing miracle, as well as by the inexpressible surprise of joy which they felt, when they received their brother again from the dead."[913] His silences are purposed for His glory and our highest good.

He cried with a loud voice, Lazarus come forth. See John 11:43. Alexander Maclaren comments, "The 'loud voice' was as needless as the rolling away of the stone. It was but the sign of Christ's will acting. And the acting of His will, without any other cause, produces physical effects. Lazarus was far away from that rock cave. But, wherever he was, he could hear, and he must obey. So, with graveclothes entangling his feet, and a napkin about his livid face, he came stumbling out into the light that dazed his eyes, closed for four dark days, and stood silent and motionless in that awestruck crowd. One Person there was not awestruck. Christ's calm voice, that had just reverberated through the regions of the dead, spoke the simple command, 'Loose him, and let him go.' To Him it was no wonder that He should give back a life. For the Christ who wept is the Christ whose voice all that are in the graves shall hear, and shall come forth."[914]

> Lord, we don't understand
> Why you waited so long;
> But His way is God's way,
> Not yours or mine.
> And isn't it great,
> When he's four days late,
> He's still on time. ~ Karen Peck & New River

Many of the Jews, which came to Mary, and had seen the things that Jesus did, believed on him. See John 11:45. Benson says they believed on Jesus as the Messiah. "Indeed, so incontestable a proof of His power and authority left them no room to doubt of His character. They knew that no impostor could perform any miracle; and so great a one as the resurrection of a person who had been in the grave four days was a miracle worthy of the Messiah himself."[915] The reason for Jesus' earlier silence is here revealed. See Isaiah 54:7–8.

Oswald Chambers observes, "His silence is the sign that He is bringing you into an even more wonderful understanding of Himself. Are you mourning before God because you have not had an audible response? When you cannot hear God, you will find that He has trusted you in the most intimate way possible—with absolute silence, not a silence of despair, but one of pleasure, because He saw that you could withstand an even bigger revelation. If God has given you a silence, then praise Him—He is bringing you into the mainstream of His purposes. The actual evidence of the answer in time is simply a matter of God's sovereignty. Time is nothing to God."[916]

Keep not silent, O God. Spurgeon said, "One word of Thine can deliver Thy people; therefore, O Lord, break Thy quiet and let Thy voice be heard. Hold not Thy peace, and be not still, O God. Here the appeal is to El, the Mighty One. He is intreated to act and speak, because His nation suffers and is in great jeopardy....The psalmist...asks not for "a leader bold and brave," or for any form of human force, but casts his burden upon the Lord, being well assured that His eternal power and Godhead could meet every difficulty."[917]

The Bottom Line: Trust God in the silences. "God's speaking is His acting; for with Him saying and doing are the same thing."[918]

37. One Day in Your House Is Better Than...   Psalm 84:10

"For a day in thy courts is better than a thousand. I had rather be a doorkeeper in the house of my God, than to dwell in the tents of wickedness."—Psalm 84:10.

"For a day in thy courts" (That is in the house of God. "The Tabernacle certainly had only one court: the arrangement of the Davidic tent-temple, however, is indeed unknown to us, and according to reliable traces it may be well assumed that it was more gorgeous and more spacious than the old Tabernacle, which remained in Gibeon."[919]) "is better" (The Psalmist testifies that to be in God's house in worship far exceeds any earthly pleasure of any sort anywhere.) "than a thousand elsewhere" (*Thousand elsewhere* [elsewhere is implied]. Henry says, "Better than a thousand, he does not say days; you may supply it with years, with ages, if you will, and yet David will set his hand to it."[920]). I had rather be a "doorkeeper in the house of my God" (Rawlinson says this 'was exactly what the Korahite Levites were [1 Chronicles 9:19; 26:1, 12–19].).

Than to dwell in the tents of wickedness. As their ancestor, Korah, had done [Numbers 16:26].[921] Kirkpatrick says "the sense clearly is, 'I had rather perform the humblest service at the temple of Him who tolerates no evil [Psalm 5:4] than be entertained as a guest where wickedness makes its home.'"[922] Henry says, "Let us account one day in God's courts better than a thousand spent elsewhere; and deem the meanest place in His service preferable to the highest earthly preferment."[923] Barnes gives a slightly different take, saying, "The verb used here is derived from a noun signifying sill or threshold, and it would seem to mean here to stand on the threshold; to be at the door or the entrance, even without the privilege of entering the house: I would prefer that humble place to a residence within the abodes of the wicked. The verb here used occurs nowhere else in the Scriptures. The exact idea is not, as would seem from our translation, to keep the door, as in the capacity of a sexton or servant, but that of occupying the sill—the threshold—the privilege of standing there, and looking in, even if he was not permitted to enter. It would be an honor and a privilege to be anywhere about the place of public worship, rather than to be the occupant of a dwelling-place of sin."[924]).

"House of my God" (Spurgeon says, "If Jehovah be our God, His house, His altars, His doorstep, all become precious to us."[925]) "than to dwell in the tents of wickedness" (Gill says "meaning not houses built by wicked men, or with money ill got; but where wicked men dwelt, and who were so bad as to be called wickedness itself; perhaps the Psalmist might have in his mind the tents of Kedar, where he had sometimes been [Psalm

120:5]. Now to live in the meanest place in the house of God, to wait at the door as a porter, to lie there as a beggar, to sit upon the threshold, and much more to go often over it, or be that itself, was abundantly preferable than to dwell 'an age' in the house of princes and great men, being wicked; than to live in the most pompous manner, at ease and in plenty, enjoying all the good things of life that heart can wish for. One hour's communion with God in His house is better than all this."[926] Spurgeon says, "The lowest station in connection with the Lord's house is better than the highest position among the godless."[927]).

Homily

Charles Haddon Spurgeon says of Psalm 84, "This sacred ode is one of the choicest of the collection; it has a mild radiance about it, entitling it to be called the Pearl of Psalms. If the twenty-third be the most popular, the one-hundred-third the most joyful, the one-hundred-nineteenth the most deeply experimental, the fifty-first the most plaintive, this is one of the most sweet of the Psalms of peace."[928]

I agree with Spurgeon that the Psalm has a "Davidic" ring to it, though its author is uncertain. Jennings and Lowe equally believe the Psalm was composed by David: "We are convinced that Psalm 42 is to be assigned to David; and, bearing in mind how frequently the title 'Anointed,' here claimed by the writer, is applied in the Psalms to David, we are led to infer that it is he who is the author of Psalm 84. The circumstances of David's banishment during Absalom's insurrection are such as might well evoke Psalm 42; those of his restoration are equally applicable to Psalm 84."[929] The Psalm's title is addressed "A Psalm for the sons of Korah." The reference to the king in verse 9 indicates the Psalm was written possibly before the exile.

In I Chronicles 24 it states that the tribe of the Levites (which included the sons of Korah) was assigned various places of service in the Lord's house. The sons of Korah (the Korahites) were assigned the role as "gatekeepers" or "doorkeepers." This knowledge throws much insight into the understanding of Psalm 84:10. Though their task might have seemed to be menial in the Lord's service, it was one filled with indescribable and incomparable joy. Even the "least" of services for the Lord (as man may count it, certainly not God) far exceeds the pleasure of the "greatest" of worldly positions. Even just being at the "door" of the house of God (the threshold of its entrance) far exceeds any joy the world affords. The Psalmist identifies with the Korahites' love and devotion to God and His house, declaring, "For a day in thy courts is better than a thousand. I had rather be a doorkeeper in the house of my God, than to dwell in the tents of wickedness" (Psalm 84:10).

My soul longeth, yea, even fainteth for the courts of the Lord. David pined for the "courts of the Lord" that he might experience sweet communion with the Lord. W. S. Plumer remarks, "This verse more than any other shows that the Psalmist was now in some way deprived of the privileges of the sanctuary, either in the time of Saul, or in the rebellion of Absalom."[930] All the regenerate of the Lord, as David, "longeth" for communion with and worship unto the Lord in His house. *Yea, the sparrow hath found an house and the swallow a nest for herself, even thy altars.* See Psalm 84:3. Jennings and Lowe say, "It need scarcely be said that this is a metaphorical expression of the sense of protection and peace, with which the Psalmist and his companions in exile approach again the sanctuary. In Psalm 11, written during persecution, David speaks of those who advised him to flee "as a bird" to the mountains. Similarly here, when restored to tranquillity, he compares himself to a bird, which, after flying from place to place, has at last found a nook where its brood may be left in security."[931]

For a day in thy courts is better than a thousand. Albert Barnes says, "Better—happier—more profitable—more to be desired—than a thousand days spent elsewhere. That is, I should find more happiness— more true joy—in one day spent in the house of God, in His worship, in the exercises of true religion—more that will be satisfactory to the soul, and that will be dwelt on with pleasure in the memory when life is coming to a close—than I could in a thousand days spent in any other manner."[932] Spurgeon comments, "Under the most favorable circumstances in which earth's pleasures can be enjoyed, they are not comparable by so much as one in a thousand to the delights of the service of God. To feel His love, to rejoice in the person of the anointed Savior, to survey the promises and feel the power of the Holy Ghost in applying precious truth to the soul, is a joy which worldlings cannot understand, but which true believers are ravished with. Even a glimpse at the love of God is better than ages spent in the pleasures of sense."[933]

I had rather be a doorkeeper in the house of my God. "In Mount Zion God himself dwells: there He holds His court: there He sits upon His throne; thither all His servants come to behold His glory, to worship at His footstool, and to receive the tokens of His gracious favour. There, though invisible, are assembled all the hosts of Heaven; so that the humble worshipper, when coming thither, is justly said to have 'come unto Mount Zion, and unto the city of the living God, the heavenly Jerusalem, and to an innumerable company of angels, to the general assembly and church of the first-born that are written in heaven, and to God the Judge of all, and to Jesus the Mediator of the new covenant, and to the blood of sprinkling, that speaketh better things than the blood of Abel.'"[934]

Than to dwell in the tents of the wicked. "To bear burdens and open doors for the Lord is more honor than to reign among the wicked."[935]

Certainly Timothy Dwight (1880) in *I Love Thy Kingdom, Lord* captures the Christian's love and devotion to the church of God.

> I love Thy kingdom, Lord,
>> The place of Thine abode,
> The church our blest Redeemer saved
>> With His own precious blood.
>
> I love Thy church, O God;
>> Her walls before Thee stand,
> Dear as the apple of Thine eye
>> And graven on Thy hand.
>
> For her my tears shall fall;
>> For her my prayers ascend;
> To her my cares and toils be giv'n,
>> Till toils and cares shall end.
>
> Beyond my highest joy
>> I prize her heav'nly ways,

Her sweet communion, solemn vows,
Her hymns of love and praise.

Sure as Thy truth shall last,
To Zion shall be giv'n
The brightest glories earth can yield,
And brighter bliss of Heav'n.

> Many believe it is possible to be a "good Christian" without joining (or even attending) a local church, but God would strongly disagree.
> Rick Warren

It's paradoxical to be a "Christian" and not hunger and thirst for the privilege to attend God's house in worship on a regular basis. Surely the redeemed attest with David, "I was glad when they said unto me, Let us go into the house of the LORD" (Psalm 122:1). Worship is something believers *get* to do, not *have* to do! Rick Warren said "Many believe it is possible to be a "good Christian" without joining (or even attending) a local church, but God would strongly disagree."[936] Charles Simeon wrote, "As for those who only occasionally visit the house of God, merely for form sake or to perform a duty, it cannot be expected that they should derive much benefit to their souls. But those who, in the habit of their minds, 'dwell,' as it were, 'in God's courts,' will find their souls exceedingly elated and comforted. They will acquire, yea, and speedily too attain, a disposition of mind that is little understood by the world at large, a spirit of praise and thanksgiving, not unlike to that which animates the hosts above."[937] Preachers preach (as they should) that believers are commanded to church faithfulness and detail its glorious and wondrous benefits (which are innumerable). But to David the bottom line to attend the house of God was to bask in the presence of God. This passion was prompted by a deep-seated love for Him. Man will do for "love's sake" what he will not for any other reason, regardless of pressure or preaching. Paul realized this truth in asking Philemon for the forgiveness of Onesimus, his runaway slave. He said, "Yet for love's sake I rather beseech thee" to 'forgive him and treat him even as you would me' (Philemon 1:9, 12). Philemon replied favorably. The account shows the truth applies not just to the church but to relationships as well.

Ultimately we treat the church and others based upon the intensity of our love.

They go from strength to strength. See Psalm 84:7. Jennings and Lowe state, "Observe that the course of these believers is expressed under the figure of a pilgrimage. The metaphor is familiar enough to us; to the Jew, bound by the Law to go up to Jerusalem at the occurrence of the three great Feasts, it was doubly significant."[938] Matthew Henry says, "*They go from strength to strength*; their company increases by the accession of more out of every town they pass through, till they become very numerous....Or the particular persons, instead of being fatigued with the tediousness of their journey and the difficulties they met with, the nearer they came to Jerusalem the more lively and cheerful they were, and so went on stronger and stronger (Job 17:9). Thus it is promised that those that wait on the Lord shall renew their strength (Isaiah 40:31). Even where they are weak, there they are strong. They go from *virtue to virtue* (so some); it is the same word that is used for the virtuous woman. Those that press forward in their Christian course shall find God adding grace to their graces (John 1:16). They shall be changed from glory to glory (2 Corinthians 3:18), from one degree of glorious grace to another, till, at length, every one of them appears before God in Zion, to give glory to Him and receive blessings from Him. Note, those who grow in grace shall, at last, be perfect in glory."[939] Spurgeon wrote, ""That is, they [Christians] grow stronger and stronger. Usually, if we are walking, we go from strength to weakness; we start fresh and in good order for our journey, but by-and-by the road is rough, and the sun is hot, we sit down by the wayside, and then again painfully pursue our weary way. But the Christian pilgrim having obtained fresh supplies of grace, is as vigorous after years of toilsome travel and struggle as when he first set out."[940]

> Between a king on his throne and a beggar on the dunghill there is no disparity at all, when compared with that between a creature and his Creator.
> Charles Simeon

Charles Simeon states, "Now, conceive of a poor man admitted only to 'the threshold' of this holy place, and compare his state with that of the most distinguished favourite of an earthly monarch; and say, whether the honor conferred on him be not infinitely higher than any which earthly courtiers can possess? In truth, the matter admits not of comparison. Between a king on his throne and a beggar on the dunghill there is no disparity at all, when compared with that between a creature and his Creator; so that in this respect the Psalmist had just ground for his preference: for in proportion as 'God humbles himself, when he beholds the things which are on earth,' is that man exalted, who becomes the object of His condescension and grace."[941] At the foot of the Cross the ground is level as in the Church of the Living Christ. Here, if in no other realm, all men stand as equals in the presence of God. All are welcome. All enter and are accepted not based on position, power or wealth but the precious redeeming blood of the Lord Jesus Christ. See James 2:1–7.

> At the foot of the Cross the ground is level as in the Church of the Living Christ. Here, if in no other realm, all men stand as equals in the presence of God. All are welcome.

The Bottom Line: The question thus is how much do you really love Jesus? Its answer correlates with your faithfulness to the church and the degree of delight and joy experienced in its attendance and service (unless providentially hindered). The devout believer grows stronger and stronger in spiritual knowledge, virtue and grace, despite an aging and decaying body.

38. Heart-Cry for Revival

Psalm 85:6–9

"*Wilt thou not revive us again: that thy people may rejoice in thee? Shew us thy mercy, O LORD, and grant us thy salvation. I will hear what God the LORD will speak: for he will speak peace unto his people, and to his saints: but let them not turn again to folly. Surely his salvation is nigh them that fear him; that glory may dwell in our land.*"—Psalm 85:6–9.

"Wilt thou not" (Kirkpatrick says, "*Thou* is emphatic. Thou Who alone canst; Thou Who art pledged to it by Thy word."[942]) "revive us again" (Barnes says, "The word rendered 'revive' means 'to live; to cause to live'; and the idea is that of recovering them from their condition as a state of death; that is, restoring them as if they were dead."[943]) The

Concise Oxford English Dictionary) says "restore to or regain life, consciousness, or strength."[944]).

That ("thy people may rejoice in thee" (Swanson says "bring joy, gladden, make merry, bring happiness."[945] Rawlinson says, "The 'revival' and 'rejoicing' came in Nehemiah's time, when the dedication of the wall of Jerusalem was kept 'with gladness, both with thanksgiving, and with singing, with cymbals, psalteries, and with harps' [Nehemiah 12:27]."[946] Criswell says, "Literally, 'You alone' is emphatic and underscores the biblical premise that any genuine restoration of the national and spiritual life of a country has its origin in God."[947]).

"Shew us" (Vine, Unger and White say "to see, observe, perceive, get acquainted with, gain understanding, examine, look after (see to), choose, discover."[948]) "thy mercy, O Lord" (Vine, Unger and White say, "loving-kindness; steadfast love; grace; mercy; faithfulness; goodness; devotion."[949]) AND "grant us thy salvation" (Swanson says deliverance, salvation, safety, victory, "i.e., protection that produces freedom from a present danger"[950]).

I will "hear what God the Lord will speak" ("to hear, listen to, obey."[951] Benson says "diligently observe; what God the Lord will speak— Either by His prophets and other messengers, or by His providence, for that also hath a voice: I will hear what answer God will give to these my prayers. And the Psalmist, by declaring what he would do, teaches all the Israelites what they ought to do; namely, attentively to hearken to the voice of God, in whatever way He should be pleased to speak to them, and to receive His gracious declarations and promises in faith and expectation, and His holy precepts and dispensations in obedience and submission: and especially that they should wait to know what answer God would return to their prayers."[952]).

"For he will speak peace unto his people" (Vine, Unger and White say, "*shalom* 'peace; completeness; welfare; health.'"[953]) "to his saints" (Swanson says, "the godly, i.e., the ones faithful to God as a group (1 Samuel 2:9; Psalm 4:3); Holy One, i.e., a special one dedicated and faithful (Psalm 16:10)"[954]). BUT "let them not turn again to folly" (Barnes says "a solemn admonition to all who have been afflicted, and who have been restored, that they return not to their former course of life....The way which they had formerly pursued was folly. It was not mere sin, but there was in it the element of foolishness as well as wickedness."[955] And there was the danger of relapse.).

"Surely" (certainly, assuredly) "his salvation is nigh" (Deliverance, rescue is right at hand.) them that "fear him" (Kirkpatrick says, "Those who answer to their calling as 'saints.'"[956] It is to show reverence for Holy God by honoring and obeying Him.) "that glory may dwell in our land" (Benson says, "That we may once again see glorious days in our land; may recover our ancient glory, the tokens of God's presence with us, the most eminent of which we have now utterly lost."[957] Kirkpatrick says, "'Glory' is the manifest Presence of Jehovah, which Ezekiel saw departing from the doomed city [10:18], but returning to it in the glorious restoration [43:4 ff.]. 'Dwell' is the word specially used of the abiding of God among His people, from which later the Hebrews derived the term Shekinah for the Presence of God in the Tabernacle and Temple [Exodus 40:34–35; 2 Chronicles 7:1–3]. Comp. Zechariah 2:10–11; Zechariah 8:3. The promise of the words was to be fulfilled in the Incarnation [John 1:14]."[958] And it was.).

Homily

J. A. Alexander states, "There is nothing in the title, or the psalm itself, to determine its date or confine its application to any particular historical occasion. It seems to be appropriate to every case in which the fulfilment of the promise (Leviticus 26:3–13) was suspended or withheld."[959] It may have been composed following the Babylonian captivity. See Psalm 85:1. The Psalmist renders praise and thanksgiving to God for Israel's rescue from captivity (Psalm 85:1–3); prays for His continued unfailing love, Israel's restraint from a return to sinful disobedience, their continued restoration (revival), the joy of the Lord to be again in the hearts of His people and His glory to be manifested (Psalm 85:7–9).

The Psalm is the believer's *heart-cry for revival* personally and nationally. Spiritual declension exists among the saints (the faithful ones of God), calling for incessant prayer that God will bring revival and restoration to His people. James Stewart said, "A church that needs to be revived is a church that is living below the norm of the New Testament pattern....It is a tragic fact that the vast majority of Christians today are living a sub-normal Christian life....The church will never become normal until she sees revival."[960] "A church," writes Spurgeon, "should be a camp of soldiers, not an hospital of invalids. But there is exceedingly much difference between what ought be and what is, and consequently many of God's people are in so sad a state that the very fittest prayer for them is for revival. Some Christians are, spiritually, but barely alive."[961]

> A church should be a camp of soldiers, not an hospital of invalids.
> Charles Spurgeon

What is revival? Charles Finney says, "Revival is the renewal of the first love of Christians, resulting in the conversion of sinners to God. It presupposes that the church is backslidden, and revival means conviction of sin and searching of hearts among God's people. Revival is nothing less than a new beginning of obedience to God, a breaking of heart and getting down in the dust before Him with deep humility and forsaking of sin. A revival breaks the power of the world and of sin over Christians. The charm of the world is broken, and the power of sin is overcome. Truths to which our hearts are unresponsive suddenly become living. Whereas mind and conscience may assent to truth, when revival comes, obedience to the truth is the one thing that matters."[962]

Revive us again. See Psalm 85:6. Albert Barnes says, "The image is that of returning spring after the death of winter, or the young grass when the rain descends after a long drought, and when everything seemed to be dead. So of the people referred to in the Psalm; everything among them was like such a winter, when there is neither leaf, nor flower, nor grass, nor fruit; or like such a drought, when desolation is seen everywhere; or like the grave, where the dead repose. The image of spring, after a long and dreary winter, is one also which will properly describe the condition of the church when the influences of the Spirit have been long withheld, and when, under the visitations of grace, religion seems to live again among the people of God."[963]

Where does revival begin? Revival begins with the man in the pulpit confessing, weeping and casting himself down before the house of God (see Ezra 10:1), then spreads to those in the pew (see Ezra 10:12) declaring, "We have trespassed against our God." *Prayer is the essential.* Spurgeon remarked, "Christian men should never speak of 'getting up a' revival.' Where are you going to get it up from? I do not know any place from which you can get it up. We must bring revival down if it is to be worth having. We must enquire of the Lord to do it for us. Too often the temptation is to enquire for an eminent revivalist or ask whether a great preacher could be induced to come. Now I do not object to inviting soul-winning preachers or to any other plans of usefulness, *but our main business is to enquire of the Lord*, for after all, He alone can give the increase."[964] T. L. Cuyler said, "In my own ministerial experience the spiritual operations known as 'revivals' generally began in a prayer-meeting....A cold prayer-meeting inevitably makes a frigid church. Hang your thermometer up in the prayer-meeting. Watch the first indication of the Spirit."[965]

ILLU.:

James Burns says of the Welsh revival (1904) that it "sprang up in a time when the church was poorly attended and sinful indulgences abounded everywhere. *Suddenly in response to prayer*, God's hand swept across the nation resulting in renewed spiritual interest. People crowded into the churches in the three services it held every day (10 a.m.–12 midnight). The services consisted mostly of singing, testimonies and prayer and some preaching. Saints were revived, infidels were saved, hundreds of drunks, thieves and thugs were born again, and multitudes of the socially and most respected prominent were converted. Additionally, debts were settled, theaters and pubs went out of business, and the mules in the mines couldn't work due to the new vocabulary of the converted workers."[966] On September 23, 1857, due to failure in visitation attempts to restore the backslidden, Jeremy Lanphier rented a building to conduct a lunch-time prayer meeting. Only six people showed. Relentlessly he continued to host the prayer meeting. On the third week, the forty in attendance requested him to host it daily. The stock market crash (October 10, 1857) served to prompt more attendees. Within six months the number that attended the prayer time was 10,000 in New York City. The prayer revival was reported in the news media which sparked revivals all over the country and into Ireland, Scotland, Wales, England, Europe, South Africa, India, Australia, and the Pacific islands. It was from that small prayer lunch prayer time on Fulton Street that the Third Great Awakening sprung. Upon its conclusion some 50,000 New Yorkers were saved, and every week for two years across the country

50,000 conversions were said to have occurred. This was the last great American revival.[967]

May the saints pray, "Do it again, Lord. Do it again." Both the Welsh revival and the Third Great Awakening were born in the chambers of prayer (as were all that have occurred). *I will hear what the Lord shall speak.* See Psalm 85:8. That which God says in answer to my prayers will I obey and adhere to. In praying for revival it is pivotal that *all* the Lord says in response be immediately and completely heeded.

At the heart of revival praying is saying to the Lord, *Show thy marvelous lovingkindness* (Psalm 17:7). Spurgeon's sermon on the text cites: 1) "Your sin is very great, dear friend. I cannot exaggerate it, because your own sense of its greatness far surpasses any descriptions I could give. You feel that, if God were to pardon you, it would be a marvelous thing. If He were, in one moment, to take all your guilt away, and to send you home completely forgiven, it would be a marvelous thing. Yes, it would, it would; but I beg you to pray this prayer, 'Lord, show forth Your marvelous lovingkindness in me.'" 2) "Lord, reveal Your marvelous lovingkindness to me, so as to give me high joys and ecstasies of delight." 3) "And, when we have done that, I think we may put up this prayer for ourselves, as to our own usefulness. You want to do good, dear brother—dear sister. Well, then, pray to God, 'Show me Your marvelous lovingkindness, O Lord! Use even such a feeble creature as I am. Let Heaven, and earth, and Hell itself, see that You can save souls by poor ignorant men as well as by inspired apostles and learned doctors.'" 4) "May God be pleased to send us as many conversions as we had at the first—yes, and I shall add, and ten times as many! And if ever there have been revivals in the church of God that have been really marvelous, brothers and sisters, let us take up the cry, 'Lord, show Your marvelous lovingkindness again. Send us another Whitefield, and another Wesley, if such will be the kind of men that will bless the world. Send us another Luther, another Calvin, another Zwingli, if such are the men that will bless the world. Lord, send us another Augustine, or another Jerome, if such are the men by whom You will bless the world. But, in some way or other, Lord, show us Your marvelous lovingkindness.'"[968] Let us pray constantly and fervently, "Lord, show thy marvelous lovingkindness as in days of old." See Psalm 89:49.

What does revival bring? *That thy people may rejoice in thee.* Broken fellowship results in loss of joy. Spurgeon says, "Those who were revived would rejoice not only in the new life but in the Lord who was the author of it. Joy in the Lord is the ripest fruit of grace; all revivals and renewals lead up to it. By our possession of it we may estimate our spiritual condition....A genuine revival without joy in the Lord is as impossible as spring without flowers, or daydawn without light."[969] Revival restores the believer to rightness with God and holiness of walk which spurs Spirit-sent rapturous joy.

> Revive us again; fill each heart with thy love.
> May each soul be rekindled with fire from above.
> ~ W. P. Mackay (1863)

Spurgeon offers a word of challenge to the minister. "When a minister obtains this revival he preaches very differently from his former manner. It is very hard work to preach when the head aches and when the body is languid, but it is a much harder task when the soul is unfeeling and lifeless. *It is sad, sad work—painfully, dolorously, horribly sad, but saddest of all if we do not feel it to be sad, if we can go on preaching and remain careless concerning the truths we preach, indifferent as to whether men are saved or lost!* May God deliver every minister from abiding in such a state! Can there be a more wretched object than a man who preaches in God's name truths which he does not feel, and which he is conscious have never impressed his own heart? To be a mere sign-post, pointing out the road but never moving in it, is a lot against which every true heart may plead night and day."[970]

The Bottom Line: Jesus warns about being overtaken by "the cares of this world" (Mark 4:19). These may be good things pushed to the extreme or actual "lusts" producing spiritual stagnation and impotency. Oswald Chambers cautions, "It is incredible what enormous power there is in simple things to distract our attention away from God. Refuse to be swamped by 'the cares of this world.'"[971] See Hebrews 12:1. Curtis Hutson said, "There is nothing better than old-fashioned revivals where the half-asleep Christians wake up....An old-fashioned revival where people get excited about the things of God—there is nothing better!"[972] "Lord it is from Thee revival must come. Hear my prayer of confessional repentance and restore me unto Thy sweet fellowship and holiness in walk. Kindle the flame of revival in my soul that will burn out the 'dew and dross of sin,' allowing Your rule within me again and then spread that flame to others through me. Amen."

39. Good News for the Sinner   Psalm 86:5

"For thou, Lord, art good, and ready to forgive; and plenteous in mercy unto all them that call upon thee."—Psalm 86:5.

For "thou, Lord" (Aitken says, "The word 'Lord' is not, as a mere English reader might suppose, the same word as that which is rendered 'Lord' in the first verse. That is 'Jehovah.' This means just what our English word 'lord' means: it conveys the general idea of authority and dominion."[973]) "art good" (Gill says, "Essentially and independently good, from whom every good and perfect gift comes; good in Himself, and good to others; good to all, in a providential way; and good to His own special people in a way of grace: this is asserted by Christ [Matthew 19:17]"[974]).

AND "ready to forgive" (Gill says "there is forgiveness with Him, and it is to be had without difficulty; He has largely provided for it; He is forward unto it, He freely giving it; it is according to the riches of His grace; He does abundantly pardon; no sooner is it asked but it is had; this David knew by experience [Psalm 32:5]"[975]).

AND "plenteous" (Various translators say, "extensive, great, abundant, enough.") "in mercy" (The loyal, unfailing loving-kindness of God.) "unto all them" (To everyone regardless of their sin.) "that call upon thee" (Gesenius and Tregelles say "to cry out, to call."[976] All that cry out to the Lord Jesus for forgiveness of sin and salvation [see Acts 20:21 and Romans 10:9–13] will receive it).

Homily

The Psalms are divided into five books:
Book 1 (Psalms 1–41)
Book 2 (Psalms 42–72)
Book 3 (Psalms 73–89)

Book 4 (Psalms 90–106)
Book 5 (Psalms 107–150).

This is the only Psalm in Book III attributed definitively to David, and it is largely made up of quotations from other parts of the Psalter.[977] The thrust of the Psalm is that God is "Good at giving and forgiving; supplying us with His good, and removing our evil."[978] Dilday and Kennedy state, "The exact nature of the psalmist's crisis is not told. But he considered the circumstances extremely serious. The 'day of trouble' involved those who hated him (v. 17) and affliction which brought him to the brink of death (lowest hell, v. 13)."[979]

Psalm 86:5 certainly is "Good News" for the sinner. It encapsulates the gist of saving grace as presented in the New Testament.

1) It implies that which man needs most has been procured through the work of Jesus Christ upon the cross. Man's sin (disobedience to God and His commandments) brought separation (temporal and eternal) between God and himself. In Scripture this separation (consequence of sin) is called "death." Paul exclaims, "Wherefore, as by one man sin entered into the world, and death by sin; and so death passed upon all men, for that all have sinned" (Romans 5:12).

2) It states that man does not have the ability to reconcile himself to God. Were such possible, David never would have prayed, "Be merciful unto me," a sinner (Psalm 86:3).

Nothing can for sin atone,
Nothing but the blood of Jesus;
Naught of good that I have done,
Nothing but the blood of Jesus. ~ Robert Lowry (1876)

3) It states that which man is unable to do for himself, God has provided. *For thou, Lord, art good and ready to forgive.* The leopard cannot change his spot; neither the sinner his perilous condition. See Jeremiah 13:23. "But," says Paul, though this is true, "God commendeth his love toward us, in that, while we were yet sinners, Christ died for us" (Romans 5:8). God, through the death of His Son upon the cross, did for man what he could not do for himself. Out of His unfailing love and

compassion, God made a way by which man may be delivered from the "miry pit" of sinful degradation and condemnation, unto life abundant and eternal. See John 3:16.

4) *Unto all them that call upon thee.* Further the Good News of the Gospel states that the provision of forgiveness is not for a select few but for "all." It is a "whosoever will may come" provision. See Romans 10:13 and Revelation 22:17. Frederick William Faber (1862) wrote "There's a wideness in God's mercy, like the wideness of the sea." And that wideness includes you.

5) *Plenteous in mercy.* There is no danger of God's loving-kindness being exhausted, regardless of the many that may receive it. Spurgeon says, "God does not dispense his mercy from a slender store...so impoverished as to give out altogether, but...His goodness flows [abundantly]."[980] I like the old revival hymn that reminds us of the vastness of the supply of God's mercy to forgive, which says,

> There's room at the cross for you.
> Though millions have come, there's still room for one;
> Yes, there's room at the cross for you. ~ Ira F. Stanphill (1946)

6) *Ready to forgive.* It states that God's mercy to forgive and save is immediately available. Matthew Henry comments, "He is a sin-pardoning God; not only He can forgive, but He is ready to forgive, more ready to forgive than we are to repent."[981]

7) *That call upon thee.* Though God's gracious and complete cleansing of sin is available for all, it is only imparted unto them that cry unto Him for it. See John 6:37. "He is a prayer-hearing God; He is plenteous in mercy, very full, and very free, both rich and liberal unto all those that call upon Him; He has wherewithal to supply all their needs and is openhanded in granting that supply."[982]

The Bottom Line: Everyone needs God's mercy for forgiveness of sin. Without it man is eternally damned without hope. Though undeserved and unmerited, it is readily available in Jesus. See Ephesians 2:4. It is attained by asking the Lord, as did the publican in the Temple who said, "God be merciful to me a sinner" (Luke 18:13). John Bunyan well said, "A returning penitent, though formerly bad as the worst of men, may by grace become as good as the best."[983]

40. A Psalm for Times of Trouble   Psalm 86:7, 17

"In the day of my trouble I will call upon thee: for thou wilt answer me....because thou, LORD, hast holpen me, and comforted me."—Psalm 86:7, 17.

In the "day of my trouble" (Barnes says, "That is, I do it now; I have done it; I will do it. The language implies a habit, or a steady purpose of mind, that in all times of trouble he would make God his refuge."[984] *Trouble.* Rawlinson says, "The nature of the trouble is not distinctly stated; but it appears to have been caused by domestic rather than foreign enemies."[985] The Teachers Bible Commentary says, "More than renewed help and protection were asked. The Psalmist entreated God to answer his prayer in such a conspicuous way as to impress the godless."[986] See Psalm 86:17).

"I will call upon thee" (To cry out or summon, invoke. See Psalm 86:5. David cried unto Him that alone could and would hear and respond.) "for thou wilt answer me" (Barnes says, "This also implies a fixed and steady assurance of mind, applicable not only to this case, but to all similar cases."[987]). Because thou, LORD, hast "helped me" (Gesenius and Tregelles say "to help, aid. The primary idea lies in girding, surrounding, hence defending."[988]).

AND "comforted me" (Gesenius and Tregelles say, "to signify, to declare grief or pity."[989] To lament or grieve because of the misery of others.[990] Spurgeon says, "God does nothing by halves; those whom He helps He also consoles, and so makes them not merely safe but joyful."[991] Gill says, "He comforted him by helping him against his enemies, and out of his troubles; and, by doing both, showed him a token for good, and filled his enemies with shame and confusion."[992]).

Homily

The title ascribes the Psalm to David. John Gill summarizes Psalm 86:7: "David had his troubles, both inward and outward, before and after he came to the throne, in private and public life; and every good man has his troubles; and there are some particular times or days of trouble; which trouble arises from different causes; sometimes from themselves, their corruptions, the weakness of their grace, and the poor performance of their duties; sometimes from others; from the persecutions of the men of the world; from the wicked lives of profane sinners, and especially professors of religion, and from the spread of false doctrine; sometimes from Satan and his temptations; and sometimes from the more immediate hand of God in afflictions, and from the hidings of His face: these troubles do not last always; they are but for a day, for a particular time; and such a season is a fit one for prayer, and the Lord invites and encourages His people to call upon Him in prayer when this is the case, Psalm 50:15."[993]

Among the gods there is none other like unto thee. See Psalm 86:8. David attests that Jehovah was incomparable to any other "god." This is not to be understood that he believed in the existence of other gods, for he clearly rejects that belief in Psalm 86:10. It was his way of saying that the "gods" of other nations were false gods.[994] God is incomparable, totally unique in character and works. See Exodus 15:11; Deuteronomy 3:24; Isaiah 40:18. God's divine attributes distinguish and set Him completely apart from any other. He is the "incomparable One." W. S. Plumer states, "The reason why God never wrought a miracle to convince an atheist of the divine existence is that the works of creation and providence are as wondrous as any miracle (v. 8). If men will not believe the former, neither would they the latter."[995]

Jehovah God is incomparable to the "gods" of the world. God is *Omnipotent*. He is all-powerful. God can do anything He wants to do, and no man or nation can stop Him. C. H. Spurgeon stated, "God's power is like Himself, self-existent, self-sustained. He is Himself the great central source and originator of all power." God is *Omniscient*. He is all-knowing. There is nothing of which God is unaware. Has it ever occurred to you that nothing has ever occurred to God? God is *Omnipresent*. He is present everywhere at the same time. God is *immutable*. He remains ever the same. "Jesus Christ the same yesterday, and to day, and for ever" (Hebrews 13:8). God is *love*. God loves man and desires him to be saved (John 3:16). This love of God is uninfluenced by anything man has done or may do and is never ending. "We love him, because he first loved us" (1 John 4:19) God is *holy* and *righteous,* incapable of doing wrong or failing to do as He declares (Isaiah 6:3). God in His holiness is intolerant of sin, hating what it does to the person who commits it and the impact it has upon others and the world. God is *merciful* ever ready to forgive the sinner, reconciling him unto Himself (2 Corinthians 5:18–19; Ephesians 2:4). God is *creator, owner* and *sustainer* of all that exists (Colossians 1:16–17).

For thou art great. See Psalm 86:10.There is no hell on earth so deep but that God's grace (God's lovingkindness and favor to help in the hour of need) can go deeper still and no sorrow of heart so deep but that God's grace can go deeper still. Where heartache and despair abound, God's grace abounds more. Out of the fullness of Christ Jesus we have and continue to have "grace for grace" (John 1:16). No matter how awesome, grand or superlative you think God's grace to be, it yet is that much greater. James underscores my point in saying, "He gives a greater grace" (James 4:6 NASB). Grace is greater than our sin but equally greater than our trouble or sorrow.

> He's bigger than all the giants of pain and unbelief;
> God is bigger than any mountain that I can or cannot see.
> He's bigger than any discouragement, bigger than anything;
> My God is bigger than any mountain that I can or cannot see.[996]

The words of Jesus to the Apostle Paul are true for all believers: "My grace is enough for you, for my power is made perfect in weakness" (2 Corinthians 12:9 NET). Paul said in 2 Corinthians 3:5, "Our sufficiency is from God" (ESV). God's grace is enough, yea more than enough, to bear you up in the hour of severest trouble or deepest sorrow if but to Him you call.

I will call upon thee, for thou wilt answer me. Spurgeon says, "A pious resolve backed by a judicious reason. It is useless to cry to those who cannot or will not hear. Our experience confirms us in the belief that Jehovah the living God really does aid those who call upon him, and therefore we pray because we really find it to be a practical and effectual means of obtaining help from God in the hour of need. There can be no reason for praying if there be no expectation of the Lord's answering."[997] Albert Barnes states, "He [David] had firm confidence in God at all times; an unwavering belief that God is a hearer of prayer."[998] See His promises to answer prayer in Psalm 50:15; Jeremiah 33:3; Matthew 7:7–1, 21:22 and John 15:7.

For thou Lord hast helped me and comforted me. See Psalm 86:17b. Spurgeon's theme in much of his preaching and writing upon the subject of prayer was that believers should pray with arguments in order to make their case scripturally. Certainly this practice is more for our benefit than that of God's. If we are unable to cite clear reasons as to why God should answer our prayers, then they perhaps are wrong or in need of revising.[999] J. M. Boice says, "David buttresses his prayers with sound arguments."[1000] David's plea (argument) for help and comfort is based upon what God has done for him in the past in response to praying. The "Psalmist can ask great things when he is well assured that he who has given much grace can give more grace."[1001] Like David, the believer's assurance that prayer is not futile is based upon faith in the promises of God in Holy Scripture (for He cannot lie [Hebrews 6:18]) and personal experiences along with that of myriads of others. Further, David argues that in God's answering of his prayer, He will be glorified among the heathen. See Psalm 86:17a. No greater argument or reason for God to hear our prayer is there than that He be honored, exalted and revealed as the true God through its answer. See Psalm 115:1.

J. I. Packer remarked, "I am graven on the palms of His hands. I am never out of His mind. All my knowledge of Him depends on His sustained initiative in knowing me. I know Him, because He first knew me and continues to know me. He knows me as a friend, One who loves me; and there is no moment when His eye is off me or His attention distracted from me, and no moment, therefore, when His care falters. This is momentous knowledge. There is unspeakable comfort—the sort of comfort that energizes, be it said, not enervates—in knowing that God is constantly taking knowledge of me in love and watching over me for my good."[1002]

Are you weary; are you heavyhearted?
Tell it to Jesus; tell it to Jesus.

Are you grieving over joys departed?
Tell it to Jesus alone. ~ Edmund Lorenz (1876)

Spurgeon comments, "There are too many thorns in this nest [world] for us to abide comfortably in it. This world is under the curse, so it still brings forth thorns and thistles, and in the sweat of our brows do we eat our bread until we return to the earth out of which man was at first taken. Were this world really to be our home, it would be a terrible fate for us....[I]t would be sad, indeed, for us to know that we had continually to dwell where the shadow of the curse always lingers and where we have only the shadow of the cross to sustain us under it. But faith comes into this unpromising field and believes she shall see the goodness of the Lord even here!...She knows that she will see more of her God in the land beyond the flood, but still *she believes to see the goodness of the Lord even in this land of the living which is so distracted and disturbed with sorrows, cares and trials and tribulations.*"[1003] See Psalm 27:13.

"'I had never known,' said Martin Luther's wife, 'what such and such things meant, in such and such psalms, such complaints and workings of spirit; I had never understood the practice of Christian duties, had not God brought me under some affliction.' It is very true that God's rod is as the schoolmaster's pointer to the child, pointing out the letter, that he may the better take notice of it; thus He pointeth out to us many good lessons which we should never otherwise have learned."[1004]

The Bottom Line: In times of trouble and grief resort to God who promises to help and comfort. David says God is "great and doest wondrous things: thou art God alone" (Psalm 86:10). He waits to do *wondrous things* for you. You are not meant to bear heavy burdens alone. "Casting all your care upon him; for he careth for you" (I Peter 5:7). God says to place the troubles, trials and tribulations of life upon His shoulders. "Tell them to Jesus alone."

41. The New Jerusalem, the City of God (Heaven)   Psalm 87:3

"Glorious things are spoken of thee, O city of God. Selah."—Psalm 87:3.

"Glorious things are spoken of thee" (Plumer says "Glorious histories, glorious predictions, glorious songs, glorious doctrines, glorious laws, glorious ordinances of worship, glorious promises and privileges were rehearsed and freely spoken of in Jerusalem of old, as they also are in the true church, the mother of us all. Compare Psalms 48:2–3; 50:2; Isaiah 2:2; 60:1–22; Jeremiah 3:17; Hebrews 12:22; Revelation 21, 22."[1005] Alexander says, "Glorious or honourable things, in the way of prophecy and promise, the fulfilment of which is here implied."[1006]). "O city of God" (Spurgeon says, "This is true of Jerusalem. It is yet more true of the church. We may glory in her without being braggarts; she has a luster which none can rival. Never let thy praises cease, O bride of Christ, in whom the Lord himself has placed His delight, calling you by that pearl of names, Hephzibah—'for my delight is in her.' The years to come will unveil your beauties to the astonished eyes of all peoples."[1007]).

Homily

W. S. Plumer states, "Scott dates this Psalm 1045 B.C.; Clarke, about 536 B.C. Some think it was written by David. This is the more probable opinion. Others ascribe it to one of the sons of Korah, whose name is not given. Others think we have no clue whatever to the authorship."[1008] Martin Luther said, "This is a prophecy concerning the kingdom of Christ and the church, in times to come."[1009] Tholuck states, "A glorious Psalm, its theme is the great hope of the conversion of the world to the sanctuary of Zion."[1010] A. F. Kirkpatrick wrote, "It is a prophecy in Old Testament language of 'the Jerusalem that is above, which is our mother' (Galatians 4:26). It looks forward to the time when the Gentiles shall no longer be 'alienated from the commonwealth of Israel' but 'fellow citizens with the saints, and of the household of God' (Ephesians 2:12, 19). We must not indeed read the full Christian idea of the new birth into the words 'This one was born there,' for primarily they refer to nations not to individuals; yet we may see in them a foreshadowing of the truth that a new birth is requisite for entrance into the kingdom of God (John 3:3 ff.)."[1011] Vance Havner stated, "What man needs is not a boost from below but a birth from above."

What man needs is not a boost from below but a birth from above.
Vance Havner

The city of God referenced by the Psalmist was the city of God of which glorious, wondrous things were spoken by the prophets and the Holy Spirit. George Horne says, "Pleasant for situation, and magnificent in its buildings, it was the delight of nations, the joy of the whole earth; there was the royal residence of the kings of Judah; there were the temple, and the ark, and the glory, and the king of Heaven dwelling in the midst of her: her streets were honored with the footsteps of the Redeemer of men; there He preached and wrought His miracles, lived, died, and rose again; thither He sent down His Spirit, and there He first laid the foundation of His church."[1012] Matthew Henry writes, "Let us not be ashamed of the [gospel] church of Christ in its meanest condition, nor of any that belong to it, nor disown our relation to it, though it be turned ever so much to our reproach, since such glorious things are spoken of it, and not one iota or tittle of what is said shall fall to the ground."[1013]

The Lord loveth the gates of Zion more than all the dwellings of Jacob. See Psalm 87:2. Why? It is in Zion or the church (public assembling of believers to worship) that God meets with His people. See Matthew 18:20. Spurgeon comments, "The love of God is greatest to His own elect nation. God delights in the prayers and praises of Christian families and individuals, but He has a special eye to the assemblies of the faithful. The great festivals, when the crowds surrounded the temple gates, were fair in the Lord's eyes, and this should lead each separate believer to identify with the church of God; where the Lord reveals His love the most, there should each believer most delight to be found."[1014] It is in Zion that God's truth is heard. It is Zion that is called the "house of prayer." See Matthew 21:13. It is in Zion where sinners are saved. Charles Simeon wrote, "Under the Christian dispensation He [God] has honoured His church, dwelling in it; as He has said, "I am with you alway, even to the end of the world." There He reveals His glory, even "all the glory of the godhead, in the face of Jesus Christ." There He makes known all the riches of His grace and love. There He communes with His people who present their supplications before Him, "drawing nigh to them, whilst they draw nigh to him;" and giving them answers of peace; not indeed visibly, as by the Urim and Thummim of old, but really, and satisfactorily to their souls. In a word, though unknown in every other place under Heaven, "He is known in her palaces as a refuge."[1015]

189

When God counts up the people, He shall say this man was born there. See Psalm 87:6. The greatest work on earth has its foundation in the church of Jesus Christ, evangelism of the sinner and edification of the saint. The relevancy of any church hinges upon the answer to two questions: "Are souls born there?" and "Are saints edified there?" It is Zion that is a foreshadow of the New Jerusalem. See John 14:1–3. The saint ought to love the "gates of Zion" even as the Lord does. See Psalm 122:1. The soul that has been loosed from the shackles of sin and the blindness of Satan unto a lively hope in Christ Jesus through the preaching of the Word in the church may say with grave confidence, "I was born there."

Glorious things are spoken of thee, O city of God. "Two glories are linked with it: His foundation and those who belong to it."[1016] John Newton (1725–1807) wrote the hymn "Glorious Things of Thee Are Spoken, Zion City of our God" based on this Psalm.

> Saviour, if of Zion's city
>   I, through grace, a member am,
> Let the world deride or pity,
>   I will glory in Thy name.
> Fading is the worldling's pleasure,
>   All his boasted pomp and show;
> Solid joys and lasting treasure
>   None but Zion's children know.

But as glorious as the old Jerusalem (Zion) was, it fails to compare in the least to the splendor and majestic beauty of the New Jerusalem (Heaven). John, in his vision on the Isle of Patmos, said, "And I John saw the holy city, new Jerusalem, coming down from God out of heaven, prepared as a bride adorned for her husband" (Revelation 21:2). Albert Barnes explains this aspect of John's vision: "Here it [New Jerusalem] refers to the residence of the redeemed, the heavenly world, of which Jerusalem was the type and symbol. It is here represented as 'coming down from God out of heaven.' This, of course, does not mean that this great city was 'literally' to descend upon the earth, and to occupy any one part of the renovated world; but it is a symbolical or figurative representation, designed to show that the abode of the righteous will be splendid and glorious."[1017] The text probably means that the redeemed of God that make up the New Jerusalem will descend with Christ (the second coming), where they will be met by living believers.[1018]

The New Jerusalem is a *place of Reception* by Jesus. Jesus, not an angel, will meet and greet the believer at Heaven's door (John 14:3).

It is a *place of Reunion* with saints. The saint will fellowship with not only redeemed parents, children, grandparents, and friends known, but also with the host of the redeemed unknown, like the prophets, disciples, patriarchs, missionaries and evangelists. C. H. Spurgeon stated, "It is sweet to die in the Lord: it is a covenant-blessing to sleep in Jesus. Death is no longer banishment, it is a return from exile, a going home to the many mansions where the loved ones already dwell"[1019] (1 Corinthians 13:12).

It is a *place of Release*. It is "Hallelujah Square" because everybody is healthy and happy, having been freed from the grip of pain, sickness, crippling illness, suffering, and the constant pull of Satan toward sin (Revelation 21:4).

It is a *place of Rest*. It has been said a person enters this world crying and goes out sighing. The saint gets tired and worn with the demands of livelihood and battling the foes of darkness, but 'a day of rest' (Hebrews 4:9) is coming for the redeemed when he "will lay down his sword down by the riverside and study war no more." A Christian works, knowing soon the labor will end with eternal rest in the Father's presence.

It is a *place of Rejoicing* (Revelation 5:11–12). In Heaven, the saint's joy will overflow into a song of praise and adoration to the King for making salvation possible. On earth, mankind is plagued with troubles and disappointments that rob us of joy and peace, but this is not so in Heaven. Paul Little declared, "Heaven will not be the boring experience of strumming a harp on a cloud, as some facetiously characterize it. It will be the most dynamic, expanding, exhilarating experience conceivable. Our problem now is that, with our finite minds, we cannot imagine it."[1020]

The New Jerusalem is a *place of Reward*. See Revelation 22:12. The Bible states at least five rewards the believer may receive. See

Revelation 2:10; 1 Thessalonians 2:19; 2 Timothy 4:8; 1 Peter 5:1–4 and 1 Corinthian 9:24–27.

It is a *place of Responsibility.* Heaven is a place not only of worship but also of work. Christians will serve God in various ways for all eternity. See Revelation 22:3.

And its beauty is beyond description. John describes the New Jerusalem in Revelation 21:10–23.

> And once again the scene was changed;
> > New earth there seemed to be.
> I saw the Holy City
> > Beside the tideless sea.
>
> The light of God was on its streets;
> > The gates were open wide,
> And all who would might enter,
> > And no one was denied.
>
> No need of moon or stars by night,
> > Or sun to shine by day;
> It was the new Jerusalem
> > That would not pass away.
>
> Jerusalem! Jerusalem!
> > Sing for the night is o'er!
> Hosanna in the highest!
> > Hosanna for evermore! ~ William Blake (1804)

The Bottom Line: As rapturous as the joy presently is for the believer to be a member of the gospel church, it is incomparable to that which awaits in the New Jerusalem. Only those whose names are written down in the Lamb's book of life will be granted entrance. See Revelation 21:27 and Psalm 87:6. C. S. Lewis wrote, "If you read history, you will find that the Christians who did most for the present world were precisely those who thought most of the next. It is since Christians have largely ceased to think of the other world that they have become so ineffective in this."[1021]

42. The Saddest Psalm   Psalm 88:1–9

"*O LORD God of my salvation, I have cried day and night before thee: Let my prayer come before thee: incline thine ear unto my cry; For my soul is full of troubles: and my life draweth nigh unto the grave. I am counted with them that go down into the pit: I am as a man that hath no strength: Free among the dead, like the slain that lie in the grave, whom thou rememberest no more: and they are cut off from thy hand. Thou hast laid me in the lowest pit, in darkness, in the deeps. Thy wrath lieth hard upon me, and thou hast afflicted me with all thy waves. Selah. Thou hast put away mine acquaintance far from me; thou hast made me an abomination unto them: I am shut up, and I cannot come forth. Mine eye mourneth by reason of affliction: LORD, I have called daily upon thee, I have stretched out my hands unto thee.*"—Psalm 88:1–9.

"O Lord God of my salvation" (Luther says, "O God, my Savior." Gill says "the author both of temporal and spiritual salvation [see Psalm 18:46]. From the experience the Psalmist had had of the Lord's working salvation for him in times past, he is encouraged to hope that He would appear for him and help him out of his present distress; his faith was not so low, but that amidst all his darkness and dejection he could look upon the Lord as his God, and the God of salvation to him."[1022]).

"I have cried day and night before thee" (Kay says "literally, 'by day have I cried—by night before Thee'; a trembling, gasping utterance."[1023] Holladay and Kohler say "cry of wailing, call for help."[1024] The Psalmist is not referring to his regular prayer life but rather to this specific time of trouble and trial.) Let "my prayer come before thee: incline thine ear unto my cry" (Barnes says "as if there were something which hindered it, or which had obstructed the way to the throne of grace; as if God repelled it from him, and turned away His ear, and would not hear."[1025] He prays that God might *hear* his cry for help; bend His ear to listen.).

"For my soul is full of troubles" (*Full* refers to "have had enough"; "plenty"; "to have in access." *Troubles*. Swanson says "distress, misery, calamity, ruin, misfortune, i.e., a state of hardship in some circumstance [Exodus 32:14];...misery, suffering, i.e., a feeling or attitude of anxiety or distress."[1026]).

AND "my life draweth nigh" (Coppes, Harris, Archer and Waltke say, "The root [of the word 'draweth' in the Hebrew] denotes that which pertains when one thing [or person] physically contacts another."[1027]) "unto the grave" (Barnes says, "Hebrew, to Sheol....It may mean here either the grave, or the abode of the dead. He was about to die. Unless he found relief he must go down to the abodes of the dead."[1028] Spurgeon says, "All his life was going, spiritual, mental, bodily."[1029]).

I am "counted with them that go down into the pit" (Spurgeon says, "My weakness is so great that both by myself and others I am considered as good as dead. If those about me have not ordered my coffin they have at least conversed about my sepulcher, discussed my estate, and reckoned their share of it."[1030] The NLT says, "I am as good as dead."). I am as a man that hath no "strength" (Swanson says "context favors 'strength,' with a reference to a state of death in which one has no physical abilities."[1031]).

"Free among the dead, like the slain that lie in the grave" (Bratcher and Reyburn say, "The Psalmist compares himself to a lifeless corpse left unburied (verse 5a); he is like a dead man already buried (verse 5b)."[1032] Barnes says, "The idea is that he was to all appearance near the grave, and that there was no hope of his recovery. It is not here, however, the idea of release or emancipation which was mainly before his mind, or any idea of consolation as from that, but it is the idea of death—of hopeless disease that must end in death."[1033]) "whom thou rememberest no more" (Bratcher and Reyburn say *rememberest* (forgotten) "means ignored, disregarded, overlooked."[1034]).

AND they are cut off from thy hand" (Kirkpatrick says "severed from Thy gracious help and protection."[1035] Barnes says, "The Hebrew is literally 'from Thy hand,' but still the idea is that it was by the agency of God. They had been cut down, and were forgotten—as if God regarded them no more; [to] molder in the grave—in that deep, dark, cold, silent, repulsive abode, as if even God had forgotten [them]."[1036]).

"Thou hast laid me in the lowest pit, in darkness, in the deeps" (The NLT says, "You have thrown me." Landes says "to set, stand, place; to ordain, cause to occur."[1037] Rawlinson says, "The affliction whereof the Psalmist complains has come direct from the hand of God. It is some severe stroke of illness which has brought him to his last gasp. The 'lowest pit' is here metaphorical—the deepest depth of calamity."[1038] He is in a state of *darkness* where the light of God's favor doth not shine and in the *deeps* helpless as the waters are overflowing or drowning him.[1039]).

"Thy wrath" (anger, rage, fury) "lieth hard upon me"(Barnes says, "Presses me down; burdens me."[1040]). AND thou hast "afflicted me with all thy waves" (Barnes says "literally, 'thy breakers'; that is, with expressions of wrath like the waves of the sea, which foam and break on the shore. Nothing could be a more striking image of wrath. Those 'breakers' seem to be so furious and angry, they rush along with so much impetuosity, they are so mighty, they dash with such fury on the shore, that it seems as if nothing could stand before them."[1041]).

Thou hast put away "mine acquaintance far from me" (Kirkpatrick says, "Like Job he is deserted even by his familiar friends (not merely acquaintance, as AV), and this is due to the act of God, Who has smitten him with a sickness which makes them loathe even the sight of him. [Psalm 31:11; Job 19:13 ff., v. 19]. He seems to describe himself as a leper like Job."[1042]) thou hast made me an "abomination unto them" (Swanson says "detestable thing, abomination, repulsion, i.e., an object which is loathsome and abhorrent."[1043]).

"I am shut up, and I cannot come forth" (Barnes says "as in prison; to wit, by disease, as when one is confined to his house."[1044] To keep back, keep in detention, be restrained.[1045]) "Mine eye mourneth by reason of affliction" (Swanson says to "have a grieving appearance, have a sad look, languish of my eye, have sorrow, languish."[1046] The Psalmist weeps profusely. Kirkpatrick says, "The sunken, lacklustre eye is the sure sign of suffering. [Psalm 6:7; Psalm 31:9; Job 17:7.]"[1047]). Lord, I have "called daily upon thee" (Though without response the Psalmist states he did not give up in praying (begging, crying out) for help and deliverance.) I have "stretched out my hands unto thee" (Spurgeon says, "As a little child stretches out its hands to its mother while it cries."[1048]).

Homily

Authorship is unknown. W. S. Plumer states, "Those who insist on this Psalm having a historic occasion are much divided in view."[1049]

H. C. Leupold wrote, "It is the gloomiest Psalm found in the Scriptures. The Psalmist is as deeply in trouble when he has concluded his prayer as he was when he began it."[1050] J. J. Stewart Perowne said, "This is the darkest, saddest Psalm in all the Psalter. It is one wail of sorrow from beginning to end."[1051] Jennings and Lowe state, "The Psalm itself is of the most cheerless character....The subject is a personal affliction of an intolerable nature; sickness, embittered by the desertion of friends, above all by a consciousness of God's displeasure. The hopelessness of the Psalmist is manifested more and more as the Psalm advances, as if the disclosure of his sorrows did but increase his sense of their poignancy."[1052] Matthew Henry remarks, "This Psalm is a lamentation, one of the most melancholy of all the Psalms; and it does not conclude, as usually the melancholy Psalms do, with the least intimation of comfort or joy, but, from first to last, it is mourning and woe."[1053] J. M. Boice writes, "It is good that we have a Psalm like this, but it is also good that we have only one. It reminds us that life is filled with trouble, even to the point of despair, even for mature believers."[1054] Spurgeon said, "It was only a cry, a cry as of an animal in pain or, at best, the cry of a child....I think this is the darkest of all the psalms; it has hardly a spot of light in it. The only bright words are in the first verse. The rest of the psalm is dark and dreary."[1055] Spurgeon states the reason the psalm should be read is that we may in times of despondency trace the footprints of another person who has been there before us.[1056]

Despite the horrendous troubling and hopeless despair of the Psalmist, he yet looks to the Lord for help ("God of my salvation", v. 1). It is uncertain as to the cause of the difficulty. It may have been a loathsome sickness or disease such as leprosy. Tholuck states, "It is very probable that the particular affliction is purposely concealed from us, as in the case of Paul's thorn in the flesh, that the language of the composition may be appropriated by many."[1057] See 2 Corinthians 12:6–8. Rawlinson states, "It may be suspected that the Psalmist's affliction was of a kind which made him 'unclean.'"[1058] Whatever the trouble, it certainly was bad enough to cause the Psalmist to feel that God had abandoned him (Psalm 88:5), friends (even the best) and acquaintances had deserted him (Psalm 88:8), that the anger of God continuously as ocean "waves" beat upon him (Psalm 88:7), and that there was no way out ("I am shut up, and I cannot come forth," Psalm 88:8). Derek Kidner certainly is correct in saying, "This is the saddest prayer in the Psalter."[1059] Outside of the very first verse the entire Psalm is nothing but gloom and doom and hopelessness and helplessness. Unlike other Psalms with similar complaint and despair, this one ends where it begins—in utter darkness. The Psalmist experiences "the dark night of the soul" without resolution. See Psalm 88:18.

The Psalm reminds the believer that he is not exempt from the severest of trials medically, materialistically, emotionally or religiously. It encourages us that in such times of providential visitation, satanic attack or chastisement of the Lord, we should relentlessly cry out unto the God of our salvation for deliverance and comfort, as the Psalmist did. See Psalm 88:2, 9. Spurgeon says, "His distress had not blown out the sparks of his prayer, but quickened them till they burned perpetually like a furnace at full blast."[1060] Thus must be ours be when afflicted. *Incline thine ear to my cry.* See Psalm 88:2. The Psalmist's circumstance but reminds us of that regarding Job. Both were righteous, yet both severely suffered. J. M. Boice writes, "We know from the beginning and ending of Job that God had a purpose in Job's suffering. It was to demonstrate before Satan, the demons, and the watching angels that a man will serve God for love's sake quite apart from what God may do for him materially. But the point of Job is that this great patriarch did not himself know what was going on. And neither apparently did the Psalmist."[1061] John Bunyan was a minister in the 1600s who was incarcerated in Bedford Prison for twelve years. In that Bedford jail through the tears of incarceration was perhaps the greatest piece of Christian literature (outside the Bible) birthed, *The Pilgrim's Progress.*[1062]

God certainly purposed this great book to be written through the suffering of Bunyan (though he was clueless as to the literay masterpiece for the Christian faith it would prove to be). Oftimes it's not until the suffering or sorrow is over that its purpose is fully known, but we yet in such great trials should specifically ask of the Lord, "What is Thy purpose in this sickness, suffering, sorrow, loss or trouble? Reveal unto me that which Thou would have me to learn and do, my Lord and my Savior." Wherein God allows trouble in whatever form to visit, it is designed with good purpose. It may be sent in love to discipline us, to teach us, to strengthen us, to purify us or simply draw us closer to

Himself. It may be sent that through it testimony may be rendered that brings glory and honor to Him. Regardless of the trouble or purpose, continuously pray in humility, "Thy will be done."

Keep the right theological view. In the "dark night of the soul," man is prone to interpret what is happening from a wrong perspective. He is apt to look at it through darkly shaded lenses. *Whom thou rememberest no more.* See Psalm 88:5. The Psalmist was wrong. God never abandons or forsakes His own children. Most of his other references to God likewise are wrong, having been spoken from a disillusioned and bewildered imagination. *Like the slain that lie in the grave.* See Psalm 88:5. The Psalmist again utters untruth, stating that death results in hopelessness, that it is merely a "pit" in which man is thrust where there is nothing but darkness and despair. Though death bears a sting, it is swallowed up in victory for the child of God. See 1 Corinthians 15:55.

In concluding this homily, I quote again from Derek Kidner: "With darkness as its final word, what is the role of this Psalm in Scripture? For the beginning of an answer we may note the following:

1. "Its witness to the possibility of unrelieved suffering as a believer's lot. The happy ending of most Psalms of this kind is seen to be a bonus, not a due....

2. "The Psalm adds its voice to the 'groaning in travail' which forbids us to accept the present order as final." Kidner says that Psalm 88 is "a sharp reminder that 'we wait for adoption as sons, the redemption of our bodies' (Romans 8:22f).

3. "This author, like Job, does not give up. He completes his prayer, still in the dark and totally unrewarded. The taunt, 'Does Job fear God for naught?' is answered yet again.

4. "The author's name allows us, with hindsight, to see that his rejection was only apparent....His existence was no mistake; there was a divine plan bigger than he knew, and a place in it reserved most carefully for him."[1063]

The Bottom Line: The light obviously does come to the Psalmist's darkness but not at the time of the Psalm's composition, for God hears and answers the prayer of the saints. Pray on, believer, though you have prayed relentlessly for God's light to dissipate the darkness without answer, for it yet will happen in His timing. "But the God of all grace, who hath called us unto his eternal glory by Christ Jesus, after that ye have suffered a while, make you perfect, stablish, strengthen, settle you" (1 Peter 5:10).

43. We Have Heard the Joyful Sound   Psalm 89:15–16

"Blessed is the people that know the joyful sound: they shall walk, O LORD, in the light of thy countenance. In thy name shall they rejoice all the day: and in thy righteousness shall they be exalted."—Psalm 89:15–16.

"Blessed" (happy) is the "people" (the righteous, saved) that "know" (*Vine's Complete Expository Dictionary of Old and New Testament Words* says "to know, regard, recognize, pay attention to, be acquainted with."[1064]) "the joyful sound" (Swanson says "shouts of joyful acclaim; i.e., loud, shouting sound, likely with some meaningful words of acclaim [Ezra 3:11–13a; Job 8:21; 33:26; Psalm 27:6; 33:3; 47:6; 89:16]. Note: in context usually *means* joyful words."[1065] Harman says, "God's self-revelation of Himself (His 'name') becomes a ground of unceasing joy for His people, and the demonstration of His saving power an object of their praise."[1066]). They "shall walk, O Lord, in the light of thy counte-ance" (Spurgeon says, "For them it is joy enough that Jehovah is favorable to them; all day long this contents them and enables them with vigor to pursue their pilgrimage."[1067]).

"In thy name" (Poole says "in the knowledge and remembrance of Thy name, i.e., of Thy infinite power and goodness, revealed and imparted to them."[1068] Gill says "that know the joyful sound, and walk in the light of God's countenance, as they have reason to do; these will 'rejoice' in the Lord Himself, for His 'name' is Himself; in the perfections of His nature, as displayed in redemption and salvation by Christ; in Him as the God of all grace, as their covenant God and Father in Christ, and the God of their salvation; and they will rejoice in Christ, in His name, in which is salvation, and therefore precious; in His person, blood, righteousness, sacrifice, and fitness; and that 'all the day' long, continually; there is always reason, ground, and matter for rejoicing in Christ, though it is sometimes interrupted by sin, temptation, and desertion."[1069]).

Shall "they rejoice all the day" (Swanson says "be glad, be joyful, i.e., be in a state of an attitude or feeling of favorable circumstance [Psalm 9:14]; note: this joy may be expressed in song, shouts, or even joyous shrieks and calls."[1070] Henry says, "Those that rejoice in Christ Jesus, and make God their exceeding joy, have enough to counterbalance their grievances and silence their griefs; and therefore their joy is full (1 John 1:4) and constant; it is their duty to rejoice evermore."[1071]).

AND in "thy righteousness shall they be exalted" (Spurgeon says, "By the Lord's righteous dealings the saints are uplifted in due time, however great the oppression and the depression from which they may have suffered. If God were unjust, or regarded us as being without righteousness, we must be filled with misery; but as neither of these things are so, we are exalted indeed."[1072] Gill says the believer has been exalted "from a low estate of sin and misery to an high estate of grace and glory; from a state of condemnation and death to a state of justification of life; from being beggars on the dunghill, to sit among princes, and to inherit the throne of glory; such as are clothed with the righteousness of the Son of God are exalted to great honor, as to be admitted into the presence of the King of kings in raiment of needlework, to stand at His right hand in gold of Ophir, and to live and reign with Him for evermore in His kingdom and glory."[1073]).

Homily

The title ascribes the Psalm to *Ethan the Ezrahite*. W. S. Plumer wrote, "That this Psalm is Messianic is generally admitted, is proven by its contents, and by its being so quoted in the New Testament."[1074] A. F. Kirkpatrick speculates, "The Psalm was probably written during the exile. It can hardly be earlier than the destruction of Jerusalem and the downfall of the Davidic kingdom, and on the other hand there is nothing to indicate that it is later than the return from Babylon."[1075]

Alexander Maclaren is right in saying, "The Psalmist, when he says, 'Blessed is the people that know the joyful sound,' has no reference, as we ordinarily take him to have, to the preaching of the Gospel, but to the trumpet blasts that proclaimed the present God and throbbed with the gladness of the waiting worshippers. So that this exclamation is equivalent to 'Oh! how blessed are the people who are sure that they have God with them!' and who, being sure, bow before Him in loving worship."[1076] But in this homily I do want to make a spiritual application of it to the Gospel, for that is certainly, for those who hear and receive it, *the joyful sound of God unto salvation.*

The people that know the joyful sound. J. A. Alexander stated, "The unusual expression in the first clause seems to mean those who know how and have occasion to rejoice in the experience of God's favor. The last noun in Hebrew denotes any loud expression of exultation, either by voice or instrument."[1077] Matthew Henry says, "The Gospel is indeed a joyful sound, a sound of victory, of liberty, of communion with God, and the sound of abundance of rain; blessed are the people that hear it, and know it, and bid it welcome."[1078]

It is man's joyful sound in that it proclaims God's undeserved love for the world. God loves the world and wishes the salvation of all people regardless of face or race. "Wonder of wonders, that Jesus loves me." He never intended for man to go to Hell. It was designed for the Devil and the fallen angels.

It is man's joyful sound in that it proclaims the forgiveness of sins. Man is inapt to whitewash a single sin from his destitute and depraved soul which is the cause for separation from God presently and eternally. But what man is unable to do, God has done in his stead. Paul says, "But God commendeth his love toward us, in that, while we were yet sinners, Christ died for us" (Romans 5:8), and, "In whom we have redemption through his blood, even the forgiveness of sins" (Colossians 1:14).

It is man's joyful sound in that it proclaims a divine change. Man needs not only cleansing but changing from the inside out. And Christ enables the sanctification that produces that change. Regarding the change, the Lord declared, "Then will I sprinkle clean water upon you, and ye shall be clean: from all your filthiness, and from all your idols, will I cleanse you. A new heart also will I give you, and a new spirit will I put within you: and I will take away the stony heart out of your flesh, and I will give you an heart of flesh. And I will put my spirit within you, and cause you to walk in my statutes, and ye shall keep my judgments, and do them" (Ezekiel 36:25–27). Salvation changes man's attitudes and actions. Man's outward garments reflect the inner, the new nature birthed in salvation. Paul emphatically said, "Therefore if any man be in Christ, he is a new creature: old things are passed away; behold, all things are become new" (2 Corinthians 5:17).

> It's different now, since Jesus saved my soul.
> It's different now, since by His blood I'm whole.
> Satan had to flee, when Jesus rescued me;
> And now it's different, O-o-oh, so different now! ~ David Beatty

It is man's joyful sound in that God not only saves but sustains the soul that trusts in Him. The Lord promises to ever abide with His children in life's journey. In the days filled with laughter and sunshine and in those filled with dark clouds and gloom, He remains ever faithful. See Psalm 88.

> The soul that on Jesus hath leaned for repose,
> I will not, I will not desert to his foes;
> That soul, though all Hell should endeavor to shake,
> I'll never, no, never, no, never forsake! ~ John Rippon (1787)

It is man's joyful sound in that it proclaims life after death. Death no longer holds the final word about man's estate for Jesus conquered its power when He was raised from the dead. He that embraces the "joyful sound" of salvation is assured of a home in Heaven when life comes to an end. See 1 Corinthians 15:55.

Many are ignorant of the "joyful sound" unto salvation, and therefore it is the duty of all that have been saved to share it until the whole world knows. See Psalm 107:2

> We have heard the joyful sound:
>   Jesus saves! Jesus saves!
> Spread the tidings all around:
>   Jesus saves! Jesus saves!

Bear the news to every land;
    Climb the steeps and cross the waves.
Onward!—'tis our Lord's command:
    Jesus saves! Jesus saves! ~ Priscilla Owens (1829–1907)

The Blessed People (Psalm 89:15–18).[1079]
What they *Know*. "The joyful sound."
Where they *Walk*. "In the light of Thy countenance."
In what they *Rejoice*. "In Thy Name all the day."
How they are *Exalted*. "In Thy righteousness."
The Secret of their *Strength*. "Thou art."
The Sphere of their *Life*. "In Thy favor."
Their *Security*. "The Lord our Shield."

The Bottom Line: In light of all that the Gospel proclaims, it is no wonder that it is called "the joyful sound." All that hear it and receive it do shout with ecstasy, for they have found the pearl of great price! Calvin declared, "They [the redeemed] not only enjoy His benefits, but also confiding in His favor, they pass the whole course of their life in mental peace and tranquility."[1080] To confess to know the "joyful sound" and yet exhibit no joy or benefit in it is to be deceived as to one's true spiritual estate. See 2 Corinthians 5:17.

44. The Brevity and Uncertainty of Life   Psalm 90:4–12

"For a thousand years in thy sight are but as yesterday when it is past, and as a watch in the night. Thou carriest them away as with a flood; they are as a sleep: in the morning they are like grass which groweth up. In the morning it flourisheth, and groweth up; in the evening it is cut down, and withereth. For we are consumed by thine anger, and by thy wrath are we troubled. Thou hast set our iniquities before thee, our secret sins in the light of thy countenance. For all our days are passed away in thy wrath: we spend our years as a tale that is told. The days of our years are threescore years and ten; and if by reason of strength they be fourscore years, yet is their strength labour and sorrow; for it is soon cut off, and we fly away. Who knoweth the power of thine anger? even

according to thy fear, so is thy wrath. So teach us to number our days, that we may apply our hearts unto wisdom."—Psalm 90:4–12.

For a "thousand years" (The complete cycle of the seasons.) "in thy sight" (Barnes says in the Hebrew, "'In thy eyes'; that is, it so appears to Thee—or, a thousand years so seem to Thee, however long they may appear to man. The utmost length to which the life of man has reached—in the case of Methuselah—was nearly a thousand years [Genesis 5:27]; and the idea here is that the longest human life, even if it should be lengthened out to a thousand years, would be in the sight of God, or in comparison with His years, but as a single day."[1081]) are but as yesterday when it is past" (Kirkpatrick says, "Thou art eternal, for lapse of time makes no difference to Thee."[1082]).

AND "as a watch in the night" (There were three *watches* during the night in ancient times for protection by guards. These watches were relieved at intervals. Moses is saying that man's life is like a division of the night with regard to its brevity and a thousand years when it is past to God is like a small portion of a twenty-four hour day. The three night-watches are cited in Lamentations 2:19, the first; Judges 7:19, the middle and in Exodus 14:24; 1 Samuel 11:11, the third.[1083]).

"Thou carriest them away as with a flood" (Thomas says "to pour forth in floods, flood away:—away like a flood, poured, swept them away."[1084]) "they are as a sleep" (Gesenius and Tregelles say "(1) sleep, Proverbs 6:4; Ecclesiastes 8:16. (2) a dream, Psalm 90:5."[1085] The days of man's life are as a dream that disappears.) in the morning they are like "grass which groweth up" (Holladay and Köhler say to "sprout, bloom, produce blossoms."[1086]).

In the morning it "flourisheth, and groweth up" (Spurgeon says, "As grass is green in the morning and hay at night, so people are changed from health to corruption in a few hours....In the morning it flourisheth, and groweth up....The grass has a golden hour, as man in his youth has a heyday of flowery glory."[1087]) in the evening "it is cut down, and withereth" (Swanson says "wither away, i.e., be in a dried up state, inferring a loss of biological life [Job 14:2; 18:16; Psalm 37:2], wither [Psalm 90:6]"[1088]).

For we are "consumed by thine anger" (Vine, Unger and White say wrath means "wrath; heat; rage; anger."[1089] Kirkpatrick says, "This is the Psalmist's reason for reminding God of the frailty of human life. We—Israel—have been consumed through Thine anger, and through Thy wrath have we been dismayed. He speaks of it not as a general truth but as an actual experience."[1090] Spurgeon says, "This mortality is not accidental, neither was it inevitable in the original of our nature, but sin has provoked the Lord to anger, and therefore thus we die."[1091] Thou hast "set" (to place, to ordain, to cause to occur[1092]).

"By thy wrath are we troubled" (Spurgeon makes a needed clarification in saying "terror-stricken. A sense of divine anger confounded them, so that they lived as people who knew that they were doomed. This is true of us in a measure, but not altogether, for now that immortality and life are brought to light by the Gospel, death has changed its aspect, and, to believers in Jesus, it is no more a judicial execution. Anger and wrath are the sting of death, and in these, believers have no share; love and mercy now conduct us to Glory by way of the tomb. It is not seemly to read these words at a Christian's funeral without words of explanation and a distinct endeavor to show how little they belong to believers in Jesus. To apply an ode written by the leader of the legal dispensation under circumstances of particular judgment, in reference to a people under penal censure, to those who fall asleep in Jesus seems to be the height of blundering. We may learn much from it, but we ought not to misapply it by taking to ourselves, as the beloved of the Lord, that which was chiefly true of those to whom God had sworn in his wrath that they should not enter into His rest. When, however, a soul is under conviction of sin, the language of this Psalm is highly appropriate to his case, and will naturally suggest itself to the distracted mind. No fire consumes like God's anger, and no anguish so troubles the heart as His wrath."[1093]).

Our "iniquities before thee" (Swanson says "sin, wickedness, iniquity, i.e., wrongdoing, with a focus of liability or guilt for this wrong incurred [Exodus 34:7]; 2. guilt, i.e., a judicial state of being liable for a wrong done, and so receive a punishment or judicial sentence [1 Samuel 20:8]."[1094] our "secret" (Harris, Arche and Waltke say "be hidden, concealed, secret."[1095]) "sin" (The word bears the same meaning as iniquities—wrongdoing and guilt; justified punishment.) in the light of Thy countenance.

"For all our days are passed away in thy wrath" (Swanson says "wrath, anger, fury, rage, i.e., a state of intense displeasure, implying outbursts as actions of anger."[1096]) we spend our years as a "tale that is told" (Barnes says, "It means here, evidently, thought; that is, life passes away as rapidly as thought."[1097] Kirkpatrick says, "Literally, we consume our years as a sigh: they are past as quickly as a sigh, itself the expression of sorrow and weariness."[1098]).

"The days of our years are threescore years and ten" (Carroll says, "There is a teaching in this Psalm not found elsewhere in the Bible. It is in verse 10 and relates to the allotted time for man to live."[1099] Barnes says "not as life originally was, but as it has been narrowed down to about that period; or, this is the ordinary limit of life. This passage proves that the Psalm was written when the life of man had been shortened, and had been reduced to about what it is at present; for this description will apply to man now. It is probable that human life was gradually diminished until it became fixed at the limit which now bounds it, and which is to remain as the great law in regard to its duration upon the earth."[1100]).

AND if by "reason of strength" (Basically the meaning is good health, vigor, unusual strength; a body that has been spared physical decline by maintaining the laws of good health.[1101]) they be fourscore years, yet is "their strength" (Poole says "their strongest and most vigorous old age. Or, their excellency, or pride; that old age which is their glory, and in which men do commonly glory."[1102]) "labor" (Gesenius and Tregelles say "(1) heavy, wearisome labor [Ecclesiastes 1:3; 2:11]; used figuratively of the mind [Psalm 73:16]. (2) the produce of labor [Psalm 105:44; Ecclesiastes 2:19]. (3) weariness, trouble, vexation."[1103]).

AND "sorrow" (Swanson says "evil, wickedness, iniquity, i.e., an act (of many kinds) which is morally evil and corrupt, and damaging to one's relationship to God and others, according to a standard [1 Samuel 15:23]; note: calamity, trouble, misfortune, suffering, i.e., an unfavorable circumstance which causes hardship."[1104]).

For it is soon "cut off" (Gesenius and Tregelles say "to pass through, to pass over, or away, 'for it [human life] soon passes away, and we fly away.'"[1105] Barnes says "that life is soon passed over, and that we flee away, as if driven by the wind; as if impelled or urged forward as chaff or any light substance is by a gale."[1106] AND "we fly away" (Alexander says, "It is applied to the driving of the quails by a strong wind over the camp of Israel [Numbers 11:31]. It may here agree with God Himself, or with a subject undefined, one drives (us), which is tantamount to saying, *we are driven. Fast*, literally (in) *haste or hastily*. And, as a necessary consequence *we fly* before the propellent power."[1107]).

"Who knoweth" (Vine, Unger and White say "to know, regard, recognize, pay attention to, be acquainted with."[1108]) the "power of thine anger?" (Benson says, "The greatness, and force, and dreadful effects of Thine anger, conceived against the sons of men, and in particular against Thine own people, for their sins? Few or none sufficiently apprehend it, or steadfastly believe it, or duly consider it, or are rightly affected with it: all which particulars are comprehended under this word *knoweth*."[1109]).

Even according "to thy fear, so is thy wrath" (Poole says, "According to that fear or dread which sinful men have of a just and holy God. These fears of the Deity are not vain bugbears and the effects of ignorance and folly or superstition, as heathens and atheists have sometimes said, but are just and built upon solid grounds and justified by the terrible effects of Thy wrath upon mankind."[1110] Ellicott says, "It is only the persons who have that fearful and bowed apprehension of His Majesty, and that sacred dread of all offence to Him, which is called the "fear of God." And this is not inconsistent with a child-like trust and love, and a peaceful security ["Of whom, then, shall I be afraid?"]. On the other hand, those who scoff against religion often become the victims of wild and base terror."[1111]).

"So teach us to number our days" (Benson says, "By thy Spirit and grace, as Thou hast already taught us by Thy Word; to number our days— to consider the shortness and miseries of this life, and the certainty and nearness of death, and the causes and consequences thereof."[1112]) that we may "apply our hearts unto wisdom" (Barnes says "by taking a just account of life, that we may bring to it a heart truly wise, or act wisely in view of these facts. The prayer is that God would enable us to form such an estimate of life, that we shall be truly wise, that we may be able to act 'as if' we saw the whole of life, or as we should do if we saw its end."[1113]

Harman says, "Wisdom in the Old Testament is not just theoretical knowledge and understanding, but rather the ability to apply that God-given knowledge to the practical affairs of life."[1114]).

Homily

Psalm 90 was composed by Moses, and therefore it's the oldest in the psalter. Its historical setting may have been the events of Numbers 20 (the death of Moses' sister, Miriam [v. 1], Moses' disobedience in striking the rock instead of speaking to it [vv. 8, 11], Moses' inability to enter Canaan [v. 12], and the death of Moses' brother, Aaron [v. 28]. Such happenings certainly would have spurred thoughts of death and life's brevity.

Moses likens man's lifetime to seven things.

(1 Moses says that man's years upon the earth are from God's perspective merely a small *speck* of a day, for a "thousand years" in His sight are but as a day (See Psalm 90:4).

(2 He states they are like the changing of the guards at specific intervals during the night watches. Man's years upon this earth are not even equal to an entire night in its length, only one small portion of it (Psalm 90:4).

(3 Moses says that the years of man's life are like unto a dream in that they quickly disappear (Psalm 90:5).

(4 He says that man's life is like a blade of grass that in the morning "grows up" into full blossom, only then to wither and die in the evening (Psalm 90:6). Calvin remarks, "It makes little difference as to the sense of the text, whether we make grass or each man the nominative to the verbs."[1115] In Psalm 90:4 he said that man's life span was like the length of *one watch* in the night. Here he says it doesn't even last for an entire day.

(5 Moses says that man's life span is like "a tale that is told" (Psalm 90:9). That is, it's like a sigh or groan. Albert Barnes comments that a tale that is told is merely a passing thought. He says, "It has no permanency. It makes no impression. Thought is no sooner come than it is gone. So rapid, so fleeting, so unsubstantial is life."[1116]

(6 Moses states man's life is like a mighty gale force wind that blows it away quickly (Psalm 90:9). It's like chaff or straw the wind blows away. Here now but swept away quickly.

(7 He says that man's life is like a bird that "flies away" (Psalm 90:10). From the moment of our very birth we swiftly fly toward death.[1117]

Moses' emphasis on the brevity of life was intended to get the Israelites then and believers today to "apply our hearts unto wisdom" (Psalm 90:12); that is, to redeem the time (the days of life) by using it in keeping with God's Word and will that it may be lived, however brief it may be, happily and profitably unto His glory and honor. See Ephesians 5:16–17. To do this man must pray for divine "wisdom." J. I. Packer in *Knowing God* indicates that "wisdom" in Scripture always means knowledge of the course of action that will please God and secure life.[1118] Benson says "that we may heartily devote ourselves to the study and practice of true wisdom; meaning, undoubtedly, that wisdom which alone is such in the sense of the Holy Scriptures; namely, the fearing God and keeping His commandments, or true, genuine godliness and righteousness; that so, by making a right use of this short, uncertain space of time allotted us here, we may prepare for another state, a state of happiness hereafter. For Moses could not intend hereby to give the Israelites any hopes that, by applying their hearts unto wisdom, they might procure a revocation of that peremptory [irreversible, binding, absolute] sentence of death passed upon all that generation; nor to suggest that other men might, by so doing, prevent their death; both which he very well knew to be impossible; but he intended to persuade the Israelites and others to prepare themselves for death, and for their great account after death, and, as they could not continue long in this life, and must expect much misery while they did continue in it, to make sure of the happiness of another."[1119]

Teach us to number our days. Man is so apt to discount the frailty of life, thus its unexpected, sudden ending. Death is no respecter of persons. It visits without forewarning or welcome the young and the old. It behooves us to heed Moses' advice to *number our days.* Don't take any one of them for granted or live any one of them without thought it may be the last. Live in the day at hand to its fullest by the wisdom of God as if tomorrow will not come. Such counsel is good but difficult to apply. This is why Moses prayed to the Lord that He would teach the Israelites and himself to do it ("Teach us to number our days"). Believers are to pray likewise. Matthew Henry writes, "It is an excellent art rightly to number our days, so as not to be out in our calculation, as he was who counted upon many years to come when, that night, his soul was required of him. We must live under a constant apprehension of the shortness and uncertainty of life and the near approach of death and eternity."[1120] See Luke 12:20.

Isaac Watts (1674–1748) paraphrased the Psalm:

> O God, our help in ages past,
>   Our hope for years to come,
> Our shelter from the stormy blast,
>   And our eternal home.

The Bottom Line: Horace said, "The brief sum of life forbids us the hope of enduring long." James says, "Yet you do not know [the least thing] about what may happen in your life tomorrow. [What is secure in your life?] You are merely a vapor [like a puff of smoke or a wisp of steam from a cooking pot] that is visible for a little while and then vanishes [into thin air]" (James 4:14 AMP). Arnd said, "When thou seest a garden in blossom, it is as if God took a flower in His hand and said, Behold, this is what thou art, and thy whole life."[1121]

45. The Seven I Will's of God (Psalm 91:14–16)

"Because he hath set his love upon me, therefore will I deliver him: I will set him on high, because he hath known my name. He shall call upon me, and I will answer him: I will be with him in trouble; I will deliver him, and honour him. With long life will I satisfy him, and shew him my salvation."—Psalm 91:14–16.

[God speaking] Because "he" (the child of God) hath "set his love upon me" (Gesenius and Tregelles say "to cleave to any one, i.e. to be

210

attached with very great love."[1122] Barnes says, "The Hebrew word expresses the strongest attachment, and is equivalent to our expression—"to fall in love." It refers here to the fact that God is the object of supreme affection on the part of His people; and it also here implies, that this springs from their hearts; that they have seen such beauty in His character, and have such strong desire for Him, that their hearts go out in warm affection toward him."[1123])

Therefore "will I deliver him" (The *Theological Wordbook of the Old Testament* says "escape, save, deliver."[1124] Spurgeon says, "Not because he deserves to be thus kept, but because with all his imperfections he does love his God; therefore not the angels of God only, but the God of angels himself will come to his rescue in all perilous times....It is love—love set upon God—which is the distinguishing mark of those whom the Lord secures from ill."[1125] Poole says, "I will abundantly recompense his love with my favor and blessing."[1126]).

"I will set him on high" (Holladay and Köhler say "be too high, fortified; have high success; inaccessible; be safe [Proverbs 18:10]; protect [Psalm 20:2]; make great against; be protected [Proverbs 29:25]"[1127]). Because "He hath known my name" (Vine, Unger and White say, "Essentially means: (1) to know by observing and reflecting [thinking], and (2) to know by experiencing. The first sense appears in Genesis 8:11, where Noah 'knew' the waters had abated as a result of seeing the freshly picked olive leaf in the dove's mouth; he 'knew' it after observing and thinking about what he had seen. He did not actually see or experience the abatement himself. In contrast to this knowing through reflection is the knowing which comes through experience with the senses, by investigation and proving, by reflection and consideration [firsthand knowing]."[1128] Gill says to know God's name is to "know" "Himself, His being, and perfections; His Son, the Angel of His presence, in whom His name, nature, and perfections are; and His name as proclaimed in Him, a God gracious and merciful; and this not merely notionally, but experimentally, and affectionately and fiducially; for such, that truly know Him, love Him, and trust in Him; and these exalt Him, and so are exalted and set on high by Him"[1129]).

"He shall call upon me" (Swanson says to "call, summon, i.e., call person, to come into one's presence."[1130]). AND "I will answer him" (The

Lord promises to respond to the believer's prayer. See Jeremiah 33:3). "I will be with him in trouble" (Swanson says "distress, calamity, anguish, i.e., a state of very unfavorable circumstance, with a focus on the emotional pain and distress of the situation."[1131] Spurgeon says, "Heirs of heaven are conscious of a special divine presence in times of severe trial. God is always near in sympathy and in power to help His tried ones."[1132]). "I will deliver him" (God will rescue in time of difficulty or trouble. See Psalm 91:14.).

AND "honor him" (Vine, Unger and White say "to be heavy, weighty, burdensome,…honored, glorious. This word…*Kabed* occurs more than 150 times in the Hebrew Bible. The verb's first occurrence is in Genesis 13:2 in the sense of "being rich": "And Abram was very rich." This usage vividly illustrates the basic implications of the word. Whenever *kabed* is used, it reflects the idea of 'weightiness,' or that which is added to something else. Thus, to be 'very rich' means that Abram was heavily 'weighted down' with wealth. This idea also explains how the word can be used to indicate the state of 'being honored' or 'glorious,' for honor and glory are additional qualities that are added to a person or thing."[1133] To summarize, God weighs His children down with great honor as Abraham was with great wealth. He honors with His constant friendship; love, help and manifold blessings that are incomparable and immeasurable now and then later, by allowing us to be named among the redeemed to live in His eternal Home forever with Him.).

"With long life will I satisfy him" (Spurgeon says, "The man described in this Psalm fills out the measure of his days, and whether he dies young or old he is quite satisfied with life, and is content to leave it."[1134] Poole says *with long life* means "either in this world, when it is expedient for my service, and for His benefit; or, at least, in the next world, where he shall live to eternity in the blissful sight and enjoyment of God in glory."[1135] Rawlinson says, "Length of days is always viewed in the Old Testament as a blessing, and a special reward for obedience [Exodus 20:12; Deuteronomy 5:16; 2 Kings 20:6; 2 Chronicles 1:11; Psalm 21:4; Proverbs 3:2, 16, etc.]. It is only in the New Testament that we learn how much "better" it is "to depart, and be with Christ" [Philippians 1:23]"[1136]).

AND "show him my salvation" (Clarke says, "'I will make him see [or contemplate] in my salvation.' He shall discover infinite lengths, breadths, depths, and heights, in My salvation. He shall feel boundless desires, and shall discover that I have provided boundless gratifications for them. He shall dwell in My glory, and throughout eternity increase in his resemblance to and enjoyment of Me. Thus shall it be done to the man whom the Lord delighteth to honor; and He delights to honor that man who places his love on Him. In a word, he shall have a long life in this world, and an eternity of blessedness in the world to come."[1137]).

Homily

The author of Psalm 91 is unknown. Of it Simon de Muis has said, "It is one of the most excellent works of this kind which has ever appeared. It is impossible to imagine anything more solid, more beautiful, more profound, or more ornamented. Could the Latin or any modern language express thoroughly all the beauties and elegancies as well of the words as of the sentences, it would not be difficult to persuade the reader that we have no poem, either in Greek or Latin, comparable to this Hebrew ode."[1138] It is a Messanic Psalm that Satan used in part in Jesus' wilderness temptations. See Matthew 4:6. Charles Simeon states, "The declarations concerning him [the Christian] in this Psalm may certainly be interpreted as relating to the Messiah, because when a passage out of it was applied to Christ, he did not deny its reference to Himself, but shewed with what limitations the passage was to be understood. That it refers also to the church cannot admit of doubt. Throughout the whole of it the character and blessedness of God's people are delineated, but with peculiar force and beauty in the concluding verses."[1139]

He hath set his love upon me. See Psalm 91:14. Jennings and Lowe state, "Oftentimes in the book of Psalms is the voice of the Almighty suddenly introduced as confirming and sealing the words of the Psalmist. Thus in Psalm 50:14–15, 'Pay unto the Lord thy vows,' says the Psalmist in tones of solemn exhortation; 'and call upon Me in the time of trouble, and I will deliver thee' is the reassuring response of the Almighty. So here, lost in his reverie and giving himself wholly up to the sweet consciousness of God's presence and continual protection, the Psalmist hears as it were a voice behind him saying (not to him, but of him), 'Because he hath loved Me, therefore will I deliver him...and shew him My salvation.'"[1140]

7 PROMISES

To the person that cleaves to the Lord with deep affection and devotion, He extends six promises. Matthew Henry elucidates, "They are such as have set their love upon Him; and those who rightly know Him will love Him, will place their love upon Him as the only adequate object of it, will let out their love towards Him with pleasure and enlargement, and will fix their love upon Him with a resolution never to remove it to any rival."[1141] It depicts not a casual acquaintance but one of the strongest affectionate and devoted attachments. In the New Testament sense it speaks of the "born-again" believer who counts "all things but loss for the excellency of the knowledge of Christ Jesus my Lord" (Philippians 3:8). Alexander Maclaren says to *set his love upon me* "implies the binding or knitting oneself to anything. Now, though love be the true cement by which men are bound to God, as it is the only real bond which binds men to one another, yet the word itself covers a somewhat wider area than is covered by the notion of love. It is not my love only that I am to fasten upon God, but my whole self that I am to bind to Him. God delights in us when we cling to Him."[1142] The promises therefore are not for everyone but for them that "know Him" intimately and walk with Him obediently and devotedly (as imperfectly as that might be). Keep in mind the promises are undeserved and unmerited even by the choicest of saints. They are not given by man's desert but God's delight.

1. *I will deliver him.* The first "I will" of God to them that "set his love upon Him" is the promise of rescue in the time of trouble, calamity or difficulty. In the next verse He reaffirms His promise to provide a means of escape or rescue to His children in their times of calamity or crisis. "From the snare of the fowler." See Psalm 91:3. Spurgeon comments, "God delivers His people from the snare of the fowler in two senses: from, and out of. First, He delivers them from the snare—does not let them enter it; and secondly, if they should be caught therein, He delivers them out of it. The first promise is the most precious to some; the second is the best to others."[1143]

2. *I will set him on high.* God promises to place the saint in a place that is inaccessible to the enemy. David said, "The name of the LORD is a strong tower: the righteous runneth into it, and is safe" (Proverbs 18:10).

3. *I will answer him.* What wondrous joy and peace it is to know that God actually bends His ear toward us when we pray to hear and fulfill our requests. Sorrow of sorrow's it would be if God's ear was deaf to our cry.

4. *I will be with him in trouble.* "Trouble" refers to times of distress, especially distress caused by emotional pain or anxiety. Spurgeon says, "'I am with him in trouble.' Heirs of Heaven are conscious of a special divine presence in times of severe trial. God is always near in sympathy and in power to help His tried ones."[1144] God will be with us in trouble to prevent our sinking under its burden.[1145] Charles Simeon wrote, "The people of God are exposed to troubles no less than others. But they are supported under them by the presence of their God. As the Son of Man walked with the Hebrew youths in the furnace, so will He with all His afflicted people; nor shall a hair of their head be singed."[1146]

> The people of God are exposed to troubles no less than others. But they are supported under them by the presence of their God.
> Charles Simeon

5. *I will honor him.* Matthew Henry says, "Those are truly honorable whom God puts honor upon by taking them into covenant and communion with Himself and designing them for His kingdom and glory."[1147] *Honor* bears the meaning of something weighted down, as one might be with riches of gold and silver. God has weighted down His children with a great honor that far exceeds the weight and value of silver and gold. John Gill remarked, "The Lord will honor such that know Him, and love Him: all His saints are honored by Him, by taking them into His family, and giving them a name better than that of sons and daughters of the greatest potentate; by clothing them with the righteousness of His Son; by adorning them with the graces of His Spirit; by granting them communion and fellowship with Himself, and by bringing them to His kingdom and glory."[1148] How can it be that the sovereign God would choose to so honor redeemed sinners such as you and me? See Isaiah 63:9 and 1 Samuel 2:30.

6. *I will satisfy him with long life.* God promises to give the saints a full and meaningful life. Matthew Henry says, "They shall live long enough: they shall be continued in this world till they have done the work

they were sent into this world for and are ready for Heaven, and that is long enough. Who would wish to live a day longer than God has some work to do, either by him or upon him?"[1149] See Deuteronomy 32:46–47.

I will show him my salvation. The promise extends beyond this life and the grave. Matthew Henry remarks, "It is more probably that the word refers to the better country, that is, the heavenly, which the patriarchs desired and sought: He will show him that, bring him to that blessed state, the felicity of which consists so much in seeing that face to face which we here see through a glass darkly; and, in the meantime, He will give him a prospect of it. All these promises, some think, point primarily at Christ and had their accomplishment in His resurrection and exaltation."[1150] What a thought, what a promise to know one day we will see Jesus face to face and ever be with Him in the glorious abode of Heaven. This He has promised. Hallelujah! See John 14:1–3. "He has Pisgah views of the promised land even here; and as soon as he has finished his appointed course, God will shew him his full salvation, causing him to behold all its glory and enjoy all its blessedness. Then shall be given to him a life which will fully satisfy his most enlarged desires. God will say to him, in the presence of the whole assembled universe, 'Come thou servant, whom I have decreed to "set on high," see the kingdom that was prepared for thee from eternity; take possession of it as thine own, and inherit it for ever.'"[1151]

> Standing on the promises that cannot fail,
> When the howling storms of doubt and fear assail,
> By the living Word of God I shall prevail,
> Standing on the promises of God. ~ Russell Kelso Carter (1886)

The Bottom Line: What comfort, assurance, peace and hope the "I will's of God" are to His children in times of calamity and trouble. Rest upon them. Rely upon them. All the various troubles and trials Psalm 91 references are ineffective against Him that "sets his love upon Him." Salter wrote, "Every promise is built upon four pillars: God's justice or holiness, which will not suffer Him to deceive; His grace or goodness, which will not suffer Him to forget; His truth, which will not suffer Him to change; and His power, which makes Him able to accomplish."[1152]

46. Palm Tree Christians   Psalm 92:12–15

"The righteous shall flourish like the palm tree: he shall grow like a cedar in Lebanon. Those that be planted in the house of the LORD shall flourish in the courts of our God. They shall still bring forth fruit in old age; they shall be fat and flourishing; To shew that the LORD is upright: he is my rock, and there is no unrighteousness in him."—Psalm 92:12–15.

The "righteous" (The upright, just.) shall "flourish like the palm tree" (Barnes says "that is, the beauty, the erectness, the stateliness, the growth of the palm tree—all this is an emblem of the condition, the prosperity, the happiness of a righteous man. The wicked shall be cut down, but the righteous shall flourish. This image—the comparison of a righteous man to a flourishing, majestic, green, and beautiful tree—is not uncommon in the Scriptures."[1153]).

He shall "grow" (Swanson says "be prosperous, i.e., be in a state of abundance and excess"[1154]) like "a cedar in Lebanon" (Poole says the cedar "spreads itself wide, and grows very high and strong, and is very durable, and in some sort incorruptible."[1155] Barnes says, "The idea in the passage...is, that the righteous will flourish like the most luxuriant and majestic trees of the forest; they may be compared with the most grand and beautiful objects in nature."[1156]).

Those that be "planted" (Holladay and Kohler say "plant, transplant."[1157] See Psalm 1:3.) "in the house of the Lord" (Gill says, "Such are they that are planted out of the wilderness of the world, and into Christ, and are rooted in Him, and are planted together in the likeness of His death and resurrection; have the graces of the Spirit of God implanted in them, have received the ingrafted word; and, in consequence of all this, are grafted into the olive tree, the church; or have a place and name there, better than that of sons and daughters, where they are as plants grown up in their youth; and which is here meant by 'the house of the Lord,' in allusion to the tabernacle, or temple, which had the figure of palm trees on the walls of it."[1158] Benson says "in the house of our God" means "in His church, of which all righteous persons are real and living members: those whom God, by His gracious providence and Holy Spirit, hath planted and fixed there."[1159] Some apply it to actual plants that are transplanted into the house of God. Psalm 92:14 seems to indicate the view of Gill and Barnes as correct.).

"Shall flourish in the courts of our God" (Benson says, "Like the trees just mentioned, they shall retain their pleasant verdure, extend their cooling shade, refresh many by their sweet and nourishing fruit, or support and adorn them by their useful qualities, and increase continually in grace and goodness."[1160]).

They shall "still bring forth fruit in old age; they shall be fat and flourishing" (Poole says, "When their natural strength decayeth, it shall be renewed; their last days shall be their best days, wherein as they shall grow in grace, so they shall increase in comfort and blessedness."[1161] Gill says, "Being thus planted and watered, they shall not only bring forth the fruits of righteousness, but shall continue, and go on to do so, and even when they are grown old; contrary to all other trees, which, when old, cease bearing fruit; but so do not the righteous; grace is often in the greatest vigor when nature is decayed; witness Abraham, Job, David, Zachariah, and Elisabeth, and good old Simeon, who went to the grave like shocks of corn, fully ripe: they shall be fat and flourishing; or 'green,' full of sap and moisture, abound with green leaves and precious fruit; or, in other words, abound in grace, and be fruitful in every good work."[1162]).

"To shew that the Lord is upright" (Rawlinson says, "The happy and flourishing old age of the righteous is a strong indication of God's faithfulness and truth, showing, as it does, that He keeps His promises, and never forsakes those that put their trust in Him."[1163] Spurgeon says, "Every aged Christian is a letter of commendation to the immutable fidelity of Jehovah."[1164]) he is "my rock" (The Lord is the provider of stability and security for the child of God. At least 20 times in the Psalms God is referred to as a Rock.[1165]).

AND there is "no unrighteousness in him" (Brown, Driver and Briggs say "injustice, unrighteousness, wrong."[1166] Spurgeon says, "He has tried us, but He has never allowed us to be tempted above what we are able to bear; He has delayed our reward, but He has never been unrighteous to forget our work of faith and labor of love. He is a friend without fault, a helper without fail. Whatever He may do with us, He is always in the right."[1167]).

Homily

With regard to authorship, Scott said, "In all probability David composed it."[1168] W. S. Plumer states, "Nor can we assign to it any historic occasion. It is probable it had none."[1169] Jennings and Lowe wrote, "It is obvious that in early times the terms 'Thy doing,' and 'the work of Thine hands,' were regarded as referring, not to recent mercies, but to the wonders of Creation. The Psalmist's joy was supposed to be roused by the contemplation of the great six days' work of Jehovah; herein he finds the doings which are 'great,' the designs which are 'very deep' (v. 5)."[1170] The Psalm's title indicates it was used on the Sabbath. The Jewish Mishnah states it was sung by the Levites in the temple.

Additionally Psalm 92 is saying that the righteous will prosper, the wicked perish. See Psalm 92:7, 12. "The Psalmist has just witnessed the downfall of adversaries who lay in wait for him; he has had convincing proof that wickedness, however seemingly triumphant, must eventually bring shame and degradation."[1171] To make the point poignantly clear, the Psalmist relates the righteous to the Palm tree. He says the wicked will be destroyed while "the righteous shall flourish like the palm tree" (Psalm 92:12). Note ten traits of the palm tree that spiritually characterize the Christian.

The palm tree grows straight. The Christian, despite the storms of conflict and calamity, remains *straight,* unbending in faith and practice. Like the three Hebrew children, he refuses to compromise even in the face of death. See Daniel 3:16–18. He exhibits a life of separation from the world, therefore is not twisted or warped mentally and spiritually, theologically or morally. See 2 Corinthians 6:17.

The palm tree bears fruit in old age. "They shall still bring forth fruit in old age; they shall be fat and flourishing" (Psalm 92:14). Matthew Henry says, "It is promised that they shall bring forth fruit in old age. Other trees, when they are old, leave off bearing, but in God's trees the strength of grace does not fail with the strength of nature. The last days of the saints are sometimes their best days, and their last work is their best work."[1172] The saint's bearing fruit in old age and flourishing in the graces of the Lord "show that the Lord is upright" and a sure "Rock" to the unbelieving world. See Psalm 92:15. Spurgeon said, "This mercy to the aged proves the faithfulness of their God, and leads them to show that the LORD is upright, by their cheerful testimony to His ceaseless goodness. We do not serve a Master who will run back from His promise."[1173]

The palm tree is a symbol of victory. It was the custom of the Romans to give a palm branch to symbolize triumph to victors in games and wars. In preparation for Jesus' arrival in Jerusalem (en route to the cross) the people covered the road that He was to travel with palm branches. See John 12:12–13. It is the custom of some believers to wear segments of the palm tree on Easter in celebration of our Lord's victory over death and the grave. In Revelation 7:9 the saints that overcame the enemy in the Great Tribulation praised the Lord upon the throne "clothed with white robes, and palms in their hand." The Christian life is that of victory over the world and death, in Christ Jesus. See Romans 8:37.

The palm tree cannot be grafted. Any effort to graft a palm tree results in its death. Though the Christian has been grafted into the family of God by the new birth (into the spiritual body of Christ) he cannot be ungrafted to be grafted into the domain of another master. It is impossible for him to be severed from the body of Christ. See Romans 11:24; John 10:28; 15:2 and Matthew 6:24.

The palm tree provides shade. Albert Barnes says, "Strictly speaking, the palm has no branches, but at the summit from forty to eighty twigs or leaf-stalks spring forth. These are referred to in Nehemiah 8:15. The leaves are set around the trunk in circles of about six. The lower row is of great length, and the vast leaves bend themselves in a curve toward the earth; as the circles ascend, the leaves are shorter."[1174] The palm tree provides a cooling, refreshing shade from the intense heat of the sun. Especially is this true in third world countries where modern air-conditioning is unknown, unavailable or unaffordable. Likewise the Christian provides a cooling and refreshing shade for the weary, worn, and wounded of the world.

The palm tree grows tall. The tallest palm tree is 197 feet tall and grows in Colombia (Colombia's national tree). Christians grow tall spiritually for they are nourished by the reading of God's Word and the discipline of communion with God in prayer. *Stunted* and *stumbling*

Christians suffer from malnutrition. The Christian is not to be a spiritual bonsai (small trees in containers that mimic the shape and scale of regular trees, deliberately kept from growing).

The palm tree is remarkably useful. Palm trees supply food (acai fruit, coconut, dates, betel nuts and oil) for wildlife and man. Its date seeds can be ground into a coffee substitute, its trunk and sturdy midribs of the leaves to make crates and furniture and roof-tops, its leaves woven into baskets, and its cluster stalks into rope or used as fuel. Additionally the sap of the palm tree is drinkable and can be boiled down to make palm-sugar candy. Its bud tips may be made into an edible salad.[1175] It is said that the tree also has medicinal value. The Christian life likewise is helpful and useful to others in supplying needs (by its bountiful fruit produced by the Holy Spirit in them) and as medicinal in Jesus' name to their hurts and sorrows. "They shall be fat and flourishing." Charles Simeon says, "For every season in the year they have appropriate fruit: and even to 'old age,' when other trees decay, these retain their vigour and fertility. There may, indeed, be a difference in the fruits produced by them at the different periods of life; that of youth being more beauteous to the eye; and that of age, more pleasant to the taste, as savouring less of crudity, and as being more richly flavoured through the influence of many ripening suns."[1176]

The palm tree is extremely durable. The palm tree is hurricane resistant, remaining upright in the fiercest of storms.[1177] The "Palm tree Christian" anchored to the solid Rock remains steadfast, immovable always abounding in the work of Christ. See 1 Corinthians 15:58.

The palm tree is an evergreen. Regardless of the season, the palm tree supplied with life-giving *sap* remains perennially green, unaffected by external conditions. Christians are constantly fed with life-giving *sap* by Christ which enables them to remain changeless despite the seasons of sorrow or joy; little or much; failure or success; and conflict or peace. See Philippians 4:12–13.

The palm tree has deep taproots. Palm trees, even in the driest and hottest of climates, are sustained by deep taproots that search out water. The believer's taproot is the Lord Jesus Christ who supplies life with the "living water" from a "well" that never will go dry. See Psalm 1:3 and John 4:14.

Flourish in the courts of the Lord. Albert Barnes says "the 'courts' of the house of God were properly the areas or open spaces around the tabernacle or the temple, but the word came also to denote the tabernacle or the temple itself, or to designate a place where God was worshipped."[1178] What an honor it was to the palm tree to be planted in the holy "church" yard and to be cultivated by the godly. Christian *palms* have the awesome honor and joy to be planted in His church, close to His presence and among His people. As palms in the courtyard of the "church," the believer is assured of caring cultivation and constant protection.

The Bottom Line: Vast dissimilarity to the healthy palm tree (spiritually) may indicate the failure to be rooted in Christ Jesus in the first place. If this be true of you, then you need to be rooted up and transplanted into the family of God through regeneration (the new birth). See Jude 12 and John 3:3.

47. Christ Reigns Supreme   Psalm 93

"The LORD reigneth, he is clothed with majesty; the LORD is clothed with strength, wherewith he hath girded himself: the world also is stablished, that it cannot be moved. Thy throne is established of old: thou art from everlasting. The floods have lifted up, O LORD, the floods have lifted up their voice; the floods lift up their waves. The LORD on high is mightier than the noise of many waters, yea, than the mighty waves of the sea. Thy testimonies are very sure: holiness becometh thine house, O LORD, for ever."—Psalm 93.

"The Lord reigneth" (Benson says, "He is the king and governor, not only of Israel, but of the whole world, as the last clause of the verse expounds it; and accordingly He will, in His due time, set up His empire over all nations, in the hands of His Son the Messiah. It was the Psalmist's glory and confidence that, though the nations boasted of the power and splendor of their kings, and trusted to their military preparations, yet the

Lord, the great Jehovah, the God of Israel, still reigned."[1179] Jennings and Lowe say, "his is the key-note of the Psalm before us, as of Psalms 97 and 99. Jehovah is depicted as if lately endued with the attributes of majesty and might, simply in accordance with the human view of the matter; what is meant is that mankind are now for the first time to be conscious of His possession of these attributes. The world is established by the accession of its lawful monarch; hitherto anarchy and confusion have raged unchecked, but now shall come a reign of peace and justice, such as is described in Isaiah 11....Observe that in this Psalm, and in the fellow Psalms 96–99, the great future appearance of Jehovah is treated as if an event that has already occurred.").

He is "clothed with majesty" (Swanson says "majesty, glory, splendor, i.e., having high status or rank [Isaiah 12:5; 26:10]."[1180]) the Lord is clothed with "strength" (power) wherewith he hath "girded himself" (Ward says, "The girding with strength refers to the girding in order to strengthen the loins, arms, knees, etc. When a Hindu is about to set off on a journey, to lift a burden, or to do something that requires exertion, he binds firmly his loose upper garment round his loins."[1181] Barnes says, "There is an allusion here to the mode of dress among the Orientals—the custom of girding the loins when one labored, or walked, or ran."[1182]).

"The world also is stablished, that it cannot be moved" (Spurgeon says, "Because Jehovah reigns, terrestrial things for a while are stable. We could not be sure of anything if we were not sure that He has dominion. When He withdraws His manifest presence from among men, all things are out of order; blasphemers rave, persecutors rage, the profane grow bold, and the licentious increase in wantonness; but when the divine power and glory are again manifested, order is restored, and the poor distracted world is at peace again. Society would be the football of the basest of mankind if God did not establish it, and even the globe itself would fly through space, like thistle-down across the common, if the Lord did not hold it in its appointed orbit. That there is any stability, either in the world or in the church, is the Lord's doings, and He is to be adored for it."[1183]).

"Thy throne is established" (Landes says "to be established, steadfast, sure; to be permanent, endure"[1184]) "of old" (Rawlinson says,

"Though God from time to time comes forward, as it were, and asserts His sovereignty, yet it is no new rule that He sets up. He has always been the King both of Heaven and earth. Thou art from everlasting. Not merely from 'of old,' but from all eternity."[1185] "thou art from everlasting" (Swanson says "forever, eternity, i.e., pertaining to an unlimited duration of time."[1186]).

"The floods have lifted up, O Lord, the floods have lifted up their voice" (Kirkpatrick says "lit., the rivers, rising up and threatening to inundate the land and sweep everything before them, are emblems of the great world powers threatening to overspread the world. Thus Assyria is compared by Isaiah to the Euphrates, 'the river' par excellence (Isaiah 8:7–8); Egypt by Jeremiah to the Nile (Jeremiah 46:7–8). Similarly the sea with its mighty breakers thundering against the shore as though it would engulf the solid land is an emblem of the heathen world menacing the kingdom of God, but all in vain. For the sea as an emblem of hostile powers, Psalm 46:3; Psalm 89:9; Isaiah 17:12–13."[1187]).

"The floods lift up their waves" (Barnes says, "They spend their strength; they break, and retire as if to recover their force, and then they renew their attack with the same result. But their power is limited. The rocky shore is unmoved. The earth abides. God is over all. His throne is unshaken. No violence of the elements can affect that; and, under His dominion, all is secure."[1188]). "The Lord on high is mightier than the noise of many waters, yea, than the mighty waves of the sea" (Poole says, "The King of Heaven is too strong for all earthly potentates, and will subdue them under His feet."[1189]).

Thy "testimonies" (Vine, Unger and White say, "This word refers to the Ten Commandments as a solemn divine charge or duty. In particular, it represents those commandments as written on the tablets and existing as a reminder and 'testimony' of Israel's relationship and responsibility to God."[1190]) "are very sure" (Landes says "be reliable, faithful; be permanent, endure"[1191]). "Holiness becometh thine house, O Lord, forever" (Holladay and Kohler say "a holy thing, a thing to which holiness adheres and which must thus be treated with care."[1192] Spurgeon says, "The teaching and the character of God are both unaltered. God has not admitted evil to dwell with Him; He will not tolerate it in His house; He is eternally its enemy and is forever the sworn friend of holiness. The church must remain unchanged and forever be holiness unto the Lord...."Jehovah reigns" is the first word and the main doctrine of the Psalm, and holiness is the final result; a due esteem for the great King will lead us to adopt a behavior becoming His royal presence."[1193]).

Homily

"This Psalm is the prelude to the remarkable group of 'theocratic' Psalms 95–100, and should be studied in connection with them."[1194] Albert Barnes states, "The author of this psalm is unknown, and there is nothing by which we can determine this, or its date, or the occasion on which it was written."[1195] Plumer nonetheless says that David is the most likely composer.[1196]

The song points to the one far-off divine event, to which the whole creation moves—the arrival and reign of Messiah on earth. The song was prepared to be sung when He comes to earth to reign as King of Kings and Lord of Lords. So think Charles Spurgeon, Adam Clarke, John Gill, Matthew Henry, William McDonald, the commentators of the King James Version Study Bible, and others. John Gill states, "The subject of the psalm is the kingdom of God; not of nature and providence, but of grace; the kingdom of Messiah."[1197] Hindson and Kroll write, "Here we see the majesty of the divine Sovereign as His program moves unimpeded through history, from creation to consummation."[1198] Matthew Henry wrote, "It relates both to the kingdom of His providence, by which He upholds and governs the world, and especially to the kingdom of His grace, by which He secures the church, sanctifies and preserves it. The administration of both these kingdoms is put into the hands of the Messiah, and to Him, doubtless, the prophet here bears witness, and to His kingdom."[1199]

William MacDonald wrote, "The songs that will be sung when Jesus is crowned LORD are all ready—and this is one of them. It anticipates the glorious day when Israel's Messiah proclaims Himself King. He will be clothed with majesty, in contrast to the lowly grace which characterized Him at His First Advent. He will openly clothe Himself with the strength that is needed to reign over the world. And world conditions will then be established on a firm, stable basis, no longer subject to vast moral and political convulsions."[1200]

Though an anticipatory Psalm of Christ's kingdom on earth, its description of Him is yet true as He rules from the throne of Heaven.

Christ reigns personally. "The Lord reigneth." Although Jesus Christ reigns presently in Heaven, one day He will reign from the throne of earth. Paul declares, "For the Lord himself shall descend from heaven with a shout, with the voice of the archangel, and with the trump of God" (1 Thessalonians 4:16). God will not send an angel, but His son to rule. Christ came the first time to suffer and die upon a Cross for man's sin. He comes the second time to celebrate that victory won over sin, Satan and the world. He came the first time as the suffering servant of Isaiah 53. The next time He comes it will be as the King of Kings, and Lord of Lords.

Christ reigns majestically. "He is clothed in majesty." Majesty means "loftiness."[1201] It depicts supreme and sovereign status.[1202] John Gill says Christ "is clothed with...all the regalia and ensigns of royalty; seated on a throne of glory, with a crown of pure gold on His head, a scepter of righteousness in His hand, and arrayed with robes of honor and majesty; so that His appearance at His kingdom will be very splendid."[1203] "In Psalms such as this one, the eternal and sovereign reign of God is stressed."[1204]

> Majesty,
> Kingdom authority
> Flow from His throne
> Unto His own;
> His anthem raise.
>
> Majesty,
> Worship His majesty;
> Unto Jesus be all glory
> Honor and praise. ~ Jack Hayford (1987)

Christ reigns mightily. "He is clothed with strength." King Jesus possesses the power to reign triumphantly over His foes. His power is incomparable and unconquerable. Presently from Heaven's throne He thus reigns, thwarting evil, saving sinners, vindicating His name and protecting saints. Pray that His power may be even more greatly unleashed and manifested. See Revelation 11:17. *Wherewith he hath girded himself.* Spurgeon says, "As men gird up their loins for running or working, so the Lord appears in the eyes of His people to be preparing for action, girt with His omnipotence. Strength always dwells in the Lord Jehovah, but He hides His power full often, until, in answer to His children's cries, He puts on strength, assumes the throne, and defends His own. It should be a constant theme for prayer, that in our day the reign of the Lord may be conspicuous, and His power displayed in His church and on her behalf. 'Thy kingdom come' should be our daily prayer; that the Lord Jesus does actually reign should be our daily praise."[1205] He reigns powerfully, presently upon Heaven's throne, but one day He shall from earth's.

Christ reigns permanently. "Thy throne is established from old." Matthew Henry says, "God's right to rule the world is founded in His making it; He that gave being to it, no doubt, may give law to it, and so His title to the government is incontestable."[1206] Gill says, "Christ was set up and anointed as King from everlasting; He had a kingdom appointed and prepared for Him so early; and His throne, which is prepared in the heavens, is an established one; it is for ever and ever; His kingdom is an everlasting kingdom; of His government, and the increase of it, there is no end."[1207] See Hebrews 1:8; 1 Timothy 6:15–16 and Isaiah 9:7.

Christ reigns triumphantly. "The Lord on high is mightier than the noise of many waters." Matthew Henry comments, "they [His foes] cannot disturb His rest or rule; they cannot defeat His designs and purposes. Observe, the power of the church's enemies is but as the noise of many waters; there is more of sound than substance in it."[1208] Though disturbed, be not rattled by the mighty noise of the tumultuous waves of trouble and adversity Satan designs to "rock your boat." It is only a lot of "hype" that at best can frighten. See Psalm 65:7. Jesus can calm the wind and waves that rock the boat of our lives, saying, "Peace be still." See Mark 4:38–39. Satan and the demons are making a lot of "noise," but it is all empty boasts and threats. They are already defeated. Christ is the winner. When Christ returns, all that noise will be forever silenced. 'Even so come, King Jesus.' See Revelation 22:20.

When King Jesus comes to live with us again,
He will show His righteous love to every man.
Wars and strife will all be passed;
There'll be peace on earth at last,
When King Jesus comes to live with us again.

~ The Oak Ridge Boys

Whatever your circumstance, battle, strife, temptation, persecution or fear, remember that Christ reigns! He not only will reign upon His return to earth the second time, but presently reigns, able to conquer the enemy that assails the castle of your life. We are more than conquerors through Him, so be encouraged and take hope. Matthew Henry says, "The unlimited sovereignty and irresistible power of the great Jehovah are very encouraging to the people of God in reference to all the noises and hurries they meet with in this world."[1209] Also Christ reigns over the uprising of evil ("the floods lift up their waves"). Evil is escalating, and righteousness is being driven back. But Christ reigns. And with Him reigning as the Almighty King, the world cannot win. Ultimately evil will be the one driven back and forever banished, and peace and holiness will permeate the earth. This God's Word promises, and it is true and sure. See Psalm 93:5.

The Bottom Line: Take hope, for Christ reigns. Be encouraged, for Christ reigns. He will protect you from the *waves of hostility* of the enemy that beat upon life's boat, making sure the anchor holds. His Word with promises of deliverance and provision in the time of calamity or trouble is from "everlasting" true, thus dependable. See Hebrews 6:19. Nonbelievers are part of the troublesome waves. Jude says they are "raging waves of the sea, foaming out their own shame; wandering stars, to whom is reserved the blackness of darkness for ever" (Jude 13). The roaring "noise" of the enemy of God that denounces the right and truth and promotes atheism and licentiousness is only that, just "noise," and soon will be silenced when King Jesus comes to earth again. See Psalm 29:10 and Psalm 46:1–2.

48. Comfort for Troubling and Anxious Thoughts   Psalm 94:19

"In the multitude of my thoughts within me thy comforts delight my soul."—Psalm 94:19.

In the "multitude" (Vine, Unger and White say "to be heavy, weighty, burdensome, dull....Whenever *kabed* is used, it reflects the idea of 'weightiness,' or that which is added to something else."[1210] Thomas says "multitude, abundance, greatness."[1211]) of my "thoughts within me" (Swanson says "troubled thoughts, anxious thoughts, i.e., the processing of information which causes distress and anxiety in one's mind and heart [Psalm 94:19; 139:23]"[1212] Barnes says, "The idea seems to be that in the great number of thoughts which passed through his mind, so many of them perplexing, anxious, burdensome, so many of them vain and profitless, so many of them that seemed to come and go without any aim or object..."[1213]).

"Thy" (The Psalmist says God personally came in care to silence them and render solace.) "comforts" (Wilson says, "The origin of the root seems to reflect the idea of 'breathing deeply,' hence the physical display of one's feelings, usually sorrow, compassion, or comfort."[1214] Swanson says "that which causes encouragement, implying hope"[1215]).

"Delight my soul" (Swanson says "take joy in, delight in, i.e., have a feeling or attitude of taking pleasure in and having fondness for an object."[1216] Rawlinson says, "Internal comfort is given by God himself to the perplexed and troubled in spirit, whereby they are 'delighted,' or, rather, 'soothed and solaced.'"[1217] Plumer says, "The word rendered *delight* very strongly expresses refreshment and gratification."[1218]).

Homily

W. S. Plumer writes, "The authorship cannot be known, though David may have written it....All attempts to give it a historic occasion have been failures."[1219] The Psalm is included in the kingship psalms (Psalm 93–100). The Jewish Mishnah reveals it was sung on Wednesday's.

The Psalmist beckons God to avenge His cause and people by punishing the wicked (Psalm 94:1–11). Jacopo Sadoleto says, "David does not pray, neither should we pray, that God would take vengeance on the wicked in the same way that men, inflamed with anger and hatred, are wont often to avenge themselves of their enemies, but that He would punish them after His own divine manner and measure."[1220] In the second stanza of the Psalm (Psalm 94:12–15), the Psalmist cites the blessing of chastisement. See Deuteronomy 7:5; 2 Samuel 7:14, 15; Job 5:17; Psalm 89:32, 33; Proverbs 3:12. Matthew Henry says "The afflictions of the saints are fatherly chastenings, designed for their instruction, reformation, and improvement."[1221] W. A. Criswell states, "During a time of chastisement, man often needs help in understanding the purposes of God. God's revelation, i.e., in this instance 'your law,' or the Pentateuch, gives helpful instruction through which a man gains wisdom and grows into godliness (Proverbs 13:24; Heb. 12:5–11)."[1222]

In the third stanza (Psalm 94:16–23), the Psalmist exclaims confidence in the Lord's power and willingness to intervene in the believer's behalf, granting help "against the workers of iniquity" (Psalm 94:16). He says, "But the LORD is my defense; and my God is the rock of my refuge" (Psalm 94:22). The Psalmist knows that in God's time the wicked will be judged justly for their evil deeds. The wicked will not escape divine judgment, though it appears they shall and think they shall. See Psalm 94:7 and Psalm 94:23.

In the multitude of my thoughts. The Psalmist was weighted down with troubling and anxious thoughts of doubt and confusion regarding God's failure to execute swift judgment upon the wicked. He couldn't understand why God allowed the wicked to boast of their evil conduct without fear of divine jeopardy (Psalm 94:4, 7), engage in hideous conduct (Psalm 94:5–6), and afflict His people (Psalm 94:5) without immediate punishment (Psalm 94:3). Christians are bombarded with 'multitudes of thoughts' that are burdensome and troublesome, designed to cause shipwreck. We must not give place to the Devil by entertaining or believing the destructive thoughts, but rather expel them immediately in Jesus' name. See Ephesians 4:27. Paul exhorts the believer to bring "into captivity every thought to the obedience of Christ" (2 Corinthians 10:5).

Thy comforts. Men seek escape from haunting thoughts in strong drink, hard drugs, prescription drugs, and suicide. But escape is to be known only through Jesus Christ. He provides the "balm of Gilead" (soothing and cheering comfort) to distressed, hurting, grieving and doubting hearts. See Luke 17:11–19 and Jeremiah 8:22. Matthew Henry says, "The world's comforts give but little delight to the soul when it is hurried with melancholy thoughts; they are songs to a heavy heart. But God's comforts will reach the soul, and not the fancy only, and will bring with them that peace and that pleasure which the smiles of the world cannot give and which the frowns of the world cannot take away."[1223]

Within me thy comforts delight my soul. What are the "comforts" of the Lord to anxious and troublesome thoughts? They are the *comforting* promises of God as revealed in Holy Scripture. See 2 Peter 1:4. God's promises should be fastened to the mind so that in times of troublesome thoughts they may be recalled to put the injurious thoughts to flight. Cherish the promises of God and allow them to expel the negative thoughts that choke out joy and peace. Second, muse upon biblical truths. Spurgeon says, "When I am tossed to and fro with various reasonings, distractions, questionings, and forebodings, I will fly to my true rest, for 'thy comforts delight my soul.' From my sinful thoughts, my vain thoughts, my sorrowful thoughts, my griefs, my cares, my conflicts, I will hasten to the Lord; He has divine comforts, and these will not only console but actually delight me. How sweet are the comforts of the Spirit! Who can muse upon eternal love, immutable purposes, covenant promises, finished redemption, the risen Savior, His union with His people, the coming glory, and such like themes, without feeling his heart leaping with joy? The little world within is, like the great world without, full of confusion and strife; but when Jesus enters it, and whispers, 'Peace be unto you,' there is a calm."[1224] Charles Simeon states, "These are as marrow and fatness to their souls; and, nourished by these, they not only bear with patience, but glory and exult in, all their trials. Encouraged by these promises, they are content to go into the furnace, assured that they shall come forth, at last, purified as gold."[1225]

The "thy comforts" also are thoughts of God's person and attributes. To remember that God's love is unfailing, that He constantly watches over His children and works good out of the bad that happens to them, brings solace in times of troubling thoughts. The 'comforts of the Lord' are also the remembrances of His loving-kindness and the manifold blessings He has showered upon you. "Hitherto the Lord has helped me." Therefore I am assured of His help now. See Psalm 94:22.

Many wanton thoughts may be prevented by daily meditating upon the Word of God. Darkness cannot cohabitat with the Light of the World. Sit tight on your thoughts. In times of mental distress, take a good dose of Heaven's medicine; saturate the mind with the comforting thoughts and promises of God.

The saint's comfort also is the ministry of the Holy Spirit. "Afflictions are seasons when God for the most part manifests Himself to the souls of His people. The Son of Man then walks most visibly with them, when they are put into the furnace for His sake. In the mount of difficulty and trial He will be seen. In His people's extremity He vouchsafes to them His richest communications, imparting to them His Holy Spirit, as a Comforter, to witness their adoption into His family, and to seal them unto the day of redemption."[1226] See John 14:26.

The Bottom Line: Comforting thoughts from the Lord will "delight" the soul. They will soothe and cheer the soul. They will restore the soul. They will keep the soul in "perfect peace" (Isaiah 26:3). They will encourage the soul. They will give the soul "songs in the night." See 1 Peter 5:7 and Philippians 4:6–7. Oswald Chambers wrote, "Your mind is the greatest gift God has given you, and it ought to be devoted entirely to Him. You should seek to be 'bringing every thought into captivity to the obedience of Christ' (2 Corinthians 10:5). This will be one of the greatest assets of your faith when a time of trial comes, because then your faith and the Spirit of God will work together."[1227]

49. Harden Not Your Heart — Psalm 95:8–11

"Harden not your heart, as in the provocation, and as in the day of temptation in the wilderness: When your fathers tempted me, proved me, and saw my work. Forty years long was I grieved with this generation, and said, It is a people that do err in their heart, and they have not known my ways: Unto whom I sware in my wrath that they should not enter into my rest."—Psalm 95:8–11.

"Harden not your heart" (Tate says "be rebellious/disobedient/stubborn"[1228]) as in the "provocation" (Swanson says "*Meribah*: site in

Kadesh Barnea where Moses drew water from a rock [Numbers 20:13, 24; Deuteronomy 33:8; Psalm 95:8; 106:32]"[1229] Tate says, "Meribah is literally 'contention' or 'controversy.'"[1230] Barnes says "contention. The original is 'Meribah.' See Exodus 17:7, where the original words *Meribah,* rendered here 'provocation,' and *Massah,* rendered here 'temptation,' are retained in the translation."[1231] Simeon says, "As Israel hardened themselves against God when His messages were sent them by Moses, so do many now harden themselves against the word preached by the ministers of Christ. They 'puff at' all the judgments denounced against them"[1232]).

AND as in the "day of temptation in the wilderness" (*Massah* connotes "testing" or "tempting."[1233] See Deuteronomy 6:16 and 9:22). When "your fathers [ancestors] tempted me, proved me" ("To test metals by placing them in the fire, a melting process; to examine." Rawlinson says "'tested Me'—put My power and goodness to the proof."[1234] Kirkpatrick says, "The Israelites tempted and tried God by faithless doubts of His goodness and arbitrary demands that He should prove His power."[1235] Swanson says "test, try, probe, examine, assay, i.e., to try and learn the genuineness of an object by examination, and observing reaction to a standard."[1236]).

AND "saw my work" (Poole says "both My works of mercy, which gave them abundant cause to trust Me; and My works of justice, for which they had reason to fear and please Me. Heb. *my work,* to wit, that great and stupendous work of bringing My people out of Egypt with a strong hand, and of conducting them safely through the Red Sea into the wilderness, and of destroying the Egyptians. For not many more of God's great works were done before they came to Meribah."[1237] Kirkpatrick says, "Though they had just had proof of God's power and goodwill in the Exodus, it had not taught them to trust Him."[1238]).

"Forty years long" (Benson says, "Nor did they cease their discontented murmurings and distrust of Me; but persisted in their stubborn infidelity and disobedience for the space of forty years."[1239]) was I "grieved" (Barnes says "means properly to loathe, to nauseate, to be disgusted with. It is translated 'loathe' in Ezekiel 6:9; 20:43; 36:31; and 'grieved' in Psalm 119:158; 139:21. It is here expressive of the strong abhorrence which God had of their conduct."[1240]) with this "generation" (the generation that tested God in the wilderness.) AND said, It is a people that "do err in their heart" (The Israelites, like a drunkard [the intoxicated], staggered, wandered about, straying from God's law and paths.[1241]).

AND they have "not known" (Poole says "to wit, with a practical and useful knowledge, as that word commonly notes in Scripture. They did not rightly understand, nor duly consider, nor seriously lay to heart; they remain ignorant after all My teachings and discoveries of Myself to them."[1242]) "my ways" (To speak of God's "ways" frequently refers to His law, statutes, commandments.[1243]). Unto whom I "sware" (Swanson says "promise, take an oath, adjure, i.e., make a promise to do something, or affirm the truth of a statement, with sanctions to follow if the conditions are not met [Ezekiel 21:28]; swear an oath, make a sworn promise."[1244]).

"In my wrath" (Harris, Archer and Waltke say "is used to express the Lord's attitude of anger toward the covenant people when they have sinned, e.g., Moses (Deuteronomy 1:37), Aaron (Deuteronomy 9:20), the people (Deuteronomy 9:8). Men acknowledge God's prerogative, but plead that He not continue to be angry."[1245]).

That they should not enter "into my rest" (Rawlinson says, "The 'rest' originally intended was that of Canaan, when 'the Lord gave rest unto Israel from all their enemies round about' (Joshua 23:1). But Canaan was a type of the heavenly rest; and the warning given to the Israel of his day by the present Psalmist is to be regarded as a warning that, if they followed in the steps of their forefathers, they might miss of that final and crowning 'rest,' which, after the wilderness of this world is traversed, still 'remaineth for the people of God' [see Hebrews 3:7–19; 4:1–9]."[1246] Barnes says, "Unbelief shut them out; and this fact is properly made use of here, and in Hebrews 3, as furnishing a solemn warning to all not to be unbelieving and rebellious, since the consequence of unbelief and rebellion must be to exclude us from the kingdom of Heaven, the true place of 'rest.'"[1247]).

Homily

Psalm 95 is attributed to David by the writer of Hebrews (4:7) and is Messianic, reflecting the Jews' rejection of Christ. M. E. Tate says, "Perhaps the key passage for Psalm 95:8 is Exodus 17:7: 'And he called the name of the place Massah and Meribah, because of the faultfinding of the children of Israel, and because they put the LORD to the proof by saying, "Is the LORD among us or not?"' The testing of the Meribah-generation was the questioning of the reality of the presence of Yahweh. 'The oracular [prophetic, prophetical] warning is saying not only "Do not be rebellious as your fathers were about the waters of Meribah," but it is also saying "Do not question the presence of God here today, as your fathers questioned it at Massah.""'[1248] These words would be spoken in a ceremony unto the worshippers gathered by a leader who called for fresh obedience to the Lord.[1249]

Harden not your heart. "Be not willfully, wantonly, repeatedly, obstinately rebellious. Let the example of that unhappy generation [the Israelites in the wilderness wanderings] serve as a beacon; do not repeat the offenses which have already more than enough provoked the Lord."[1250] Spurgeon describes the hardened heart: "Considerations that used to thrill me and make my flesh creep are now put before me, but I seem like a piece of steel—nay, I do not even rust under the word; I am unimpressible. Harvests have dried me; summers have parched me; age has shriveled my soul....Harvests and summers leave us worse if they do not see us mend....Oh, for grace to repent at once, ere yet the wax has cooled and the seal is set forever."[1251] Charles Stanley says, "The hardening of the heart is not a one-time act. It is the result of a gradual progression in which sin and the conviction of the Holy Spirit are ignored. The hardened heart has no desire for the things of God."[1252] John Gill says, "Respect seems to be had here [Psalm 95] to the hardness of heart in the Jews in the times of Christ and His apostles, which the Holy Ghost foresaw, and here dehorts from; who, notwithstanding the clear evidence of Jesus being the Messiah, from prophecy, from miracles, from doctrines, from the gifts of the Spirit, etc., yet hardened their hearts against Him, rebelled against light, and would not receive, but reject him."[1253]

As in the day of temptation in the wilderness. Matthew Henry remarks, "Days of temptation are days of provocation. Nothing is more offensive to God than disbelief of His promise and despair of the performance of it because of some difficulties that seem to lie in the way. The more experience we have had of the power and goodness of God, the greater is our sin if we distrust Him. What, to tempt Him in the wilderness, where we live upon Him! This is as ungrateful as it is absurd and unreasonable. Hardness of heart is at the bottom of all our distrusts of God and quarrels with Him. That is a hard heart which receives not the impressions of divine discoveries and conforms not to the intentions of the divine will, which will not melt, which will not bend."[1254]

The hardening of the heart is gradual. It develops slowly over a period of time in being obstinate to God's Word and ways. Man is reproved for sin, yet he continues unrepentant and unchanged. George Lawson says, "He despises a merciful appointment of God for his recovery and tramples upon precious pearls. He refuses to bow before the Lord and...puts off his intended repentance until judgment comes upon him unexpectedly and he is ruined forever! The reproofs which he received will then be like hot thunderbolts to him, and the remembrance of them will feed the worm that never dies."[1255]

The hardening of the heart is grievous to God. The Lord is nauseated, disgusted with the believer that is bent to backsliding, heedless to His commands and invitation to repent and be restored. See Revelation 2:16 and Revelation 3:15–20. It also is grievous to him that hardens his heart. The true Christian that is obstinate and stubborn in refusal to obey the Lord is the most miserable, unhappy and depressed Christian on earth. To be reproved with the chastening rod of God without repentance is to incur the worst of soul pain and anguish and perhaps physical affliction. See Psalm 94:12. To deny the *transformed* conscience regarding convictions and conduct produces inescapable anguish and guilt. The wayward believer learns from bitter experience that "the way of transgressors is hard" (Proverbs 13:5).

Solomon warned, "He, that being often reproved hardeneth his neck, shall suddenly be destroyed, and that without remedy" (Proverbs 29:1). H. A. Ironside states, "Hardening the neck is a figure taken from the manner in which a refractory bullock turns away from and avoids the yoke. In this way, men, in their obstinacy, persistently refuse to heed reproof, and set their wills stubbornly against what would be for their own best interests, thus insuring their destruction. God is gracious and long-suffering, slow to anger, and doth not afflict willingly nor grieve the children of men. Yet even *His* patience with the unrepentant comes to an end at last. He will plead and strive and warn till it is manifest the heart is fully set upon having its own way. Then He leaves the hardened soul to its doom, giving it up to sudden destruction. Many are the scriptural examples of this, but I only remind the reader of Korah, Dathan, and Abiram; of Belshazzar; and of Jezebel."[1256] See Hebrews 3:8.

> There is a time, I know not when;
>   A place, I know not where;
> Which marks the destiny of men
>   To Heaven or despair.
>
> How long may men go on in sin?
>   How long will God forbear?
> Where does hope end, and where begins
>   The confines of despair?
>
> One answer from those skies is sent:
>   "Ye who from God depart,
> While it is called today, repent,
>   And harden not your heart. ~ Author unknown

Spurgeon wrote, "It will be a serious evil if you do. Under the sound of love's entreaties, within ear-shot of mercy's imploring tones, the sinner is hardening his heart. Sad work to harden one's heart against one's own welfare! Shall any man do this and go unpunished?...This dreadful sin can be committed in a great many ways. Some harden their hearts by a resolution not to feel, some by wishing to wait, some by getting into evil company. This sin will bring with it the most fearful consequences. 'He sware in His wrath, they shall not enter into My rest!' You wish to rest at last, you long to rest even now. But it cannot be till you yield to God. You are not at peace now, and you never will be if you harden your hearts....Remember that it is a time limited (Hebrews 4:7). Today will not last for ever; a day is but a day. When days are longest, shadows fall at last and night comes on. The longest life soon wanes into the evening of old age, and old age hastens to the sunset of the tomb."[1257]

The Bottom Line: Avoid the sin of the Israelites in the wilderness, King Saul and others. Stay alert, sensitive and obedient to the promptings of the Lord. Immediately repent of sin upon participation in it. Maintain a walk in righteousness and holiness. Refrain from partial or halfhearted allegiance to the Lord. For the unsaved, the time to be saved is the very moment of conviction to be saved.

50. Christ Cometh Soon   Psalm 96:13

"Before the LORD: for he cometh, for he cometh to judge the earth: he shall judge the world with righteousness, and the people with his truth."—Psalm 96:13.

"Before the Lord" (That is, at the second coming of Christ the "heavens rejoice," "the earth is glad," the sea will "roar," the trees and all in the field will sing with joy, because that for which they have groaned has now arrived. See Romans 8:22. Henry says "that the days of the Messiah will be joyful days, and, as far as His grace and government are submitted to, will bring joy along with them."[1258]) "for he cometh" (At some point in history Christ will come to earth the second time for His bride, the church.) "for he cometh" (Gill says, "'For he cometh, for he cometh'; which is repeated to show the certainty of Christ's coming, and the importance of it, and the just reason there was for the above joy and gladness on account of it."[1259]).

"To judge the earth" (Gill says "to judge the earth; the inhabitants of it, small and great, high and low, rich and poor, bond and free, quick and dead, righteous and wicked; when all works, words, and thoughts, good and bad, will be brought to account; and every man will be judged, as those shall be, with or without the grace of God."[1260] Christ's judgment determines man's eternal destiny, Heaven or Hell.) He shall judge the world with "righteousness, and all the people with his truth" (Spurgeon says, "All the world will be under the jurisdiction of this great Judge, and before His bar all will be summoned to appear. At this moment He is on the road, and the hour of His coming draweth nigh....*He shall judge the world with righteousness*. His essential rectitude will determine all causes and cases; there will be no bribery and corruption there, neither can error or failure be found in His decisions. *And the people with his truth*, or rather 'the nations in faithfulness.' Honesty, veracity, integrity will rule

238

upon his judgment seat. No nation shall be favored there, and none be made to suffer through prejudice."[1261]).

Homily

First Chronicles 16:23–33 indicates that David is most likely the Psalm's author. Or its occasion may have been associated with Israel's return from Babylonian exile.[1262] "The joyous feelings, the glorious expectations, the marked repetition (both in matter and style) of the later prophecies of Isaiah, their rhythmical character suggesting that they were intended for liturgical purposes, combine to identify them with this period."[1263]

Albert Barnes says of Psalm 96:11–13: "The 'language' is such as would properly refer to the anticipated reign of the Messiah, as a reign of righteousness, and is such language as is frequently employed in the Old Testament to denote the character of His reign. There is no reason to doubt that this Psalm may be 'designed' to describe the reign of the Messiah, and that the Psalmist in this language may have looked forward to that future kingdom of righteousness and peace."[1264] W. A. Criswell states, "This latter part of the Psalm should be interpreted Messianically, for the future judgment and sovereign rule spoken of here find fulfillment only in the universal reign of Christ. Even the earth itself will rejoice at His coming (Romans 8:19–22)."[1265] Martin Luther wrote, "This is a prophecy concerning the kingdom of Christ, and the spreading of the Gospel over the whole world and before every creature; which Gospel will be a word of joy and thanksgiving, of peace, of rejoicing, and of a continued sacrifice of praise."[1266] Jennings and Lowe state, "In a certain sense all these Psalms [Psalms 95–100] may be styled Messianic, for they present to us ardent hopes of a Divine manifestation, which were fulfilled in the person of Jesus Christ."[1267] William McDonald states the Psalm cites seventeen different ways of praising God revealed in crisp commands.[1268]

Then shall all the trees of the wood rejoice. See Psalm 96:12. At the coming of Christ Jesus to earth for the redeemed, all of nature will burst into resounding joy in welcome. See Psalm 96:11–12. Nature supplies the "music"; the saints provide the "song." What a glorious day that will be when King Jesus returns!

Forest and flower exclaim,
Mountain and meadow the same,
All earth and heaven proclaim,
    Jesus is coming again. ~ John W. Peterson (1972)

For He cometh. Jesus promised to return for His bride, the church of the redeemed. See John 14:1–6. The time and date for Jesus' return for the church is set, but known only to God. "But of that day and hour knoweth no man, no, not the angels of heaven, but my Father only" (Matthew 24:36). There are in excess of 320 references to the Second Coming in the New Testament; one of every twenty-five verses reference this event. See 2 Thessalonians 1:7–8; Matthew 25:31; 1 Thessalonians 5:2–3; Titus 2:13; Matthew 24:42–51; and 1Thessalonians 4:13–18.

There are two phases of the coming of Christ. The first is the "Rapture" in which Jesus comes *for* the saints and meets them in the *air*. It is at this time the saint will be changed in the twinkling of an eye to be like Jesus (1 Corinthians 15:51–52), receive rewards at the Judgment Seat (1 Corinthians 4:5), and *partake* of the Marriage Supper of the Lamb. See Revelation 19:7–10. The second phase is when He comes *with* His saints to *earth* to set up His Kingdom of 1,000 years, known as the Millennial reign. See Revelation 19:11–15.

He shall judge the world. In every courtroom in America there is a judge who sits on a bench and makes people accept responsibility for their actions. At Christ's coming, He will do the same. See Hebrews 9:27. The judgment will be just and fair to all, based upon His truth. See Psalm 96:13. The Bible does not speak of a general judgment for all mankind. There will be two judgments: one for the believer (Judgment Seat of Christ, 2 Corinthians 5:9–10) and one for the unbeliever (Great White Throne, Revelation 20:11–15). The Christian is not judged with regard to salvation, but conduct and service. See 1 Corinthians 3:11–15. Results of this judgment determine the Christian's reward. See Revelation 22:12 and Revelation 4:10. The unbeliever at the Great White Throne will be judged according to his sin and rejection of Christ as Lord and Savior and will receive the condemnation of eternal torment in Hell. See Revelation 21:8. Man's eternal destiny is forever sealed or settled at Christ's appearing. Knowing not the day or hour that He may come, it behooves you to make preparation as if He may come today.

Say among the heathen that the LORD reigneth. See Psalm 96:10. Proclaim to the world that Jesus Christ reigns, urging man to bow in submission to His Lordship. Tell man to set his house in order, for Christ is coming again. Allan Harman wrote "Psalm 96 is a call to all nations to praise the LORD, and forms part of *the missionary outlook of the Old Testament.* This praise is not to take place just within Israel, but also among the Gentile nations as well (v. 10). It is an anticipation of the worldwide mission of the Christian church (Matthew 28:16–20)."[1269]

> Lift up the trumpet, and loud let it ring:
> > Jesus is coming again!
> Cheer up, ye pilgrims; be joyful and sing:
> > Jesus is coming again!
>
> Echo it, hilltops; proclaim it, ye plains:
> > Jesus is coming again!
> Coming in glory, the Lamb that was slain,
> > Jesus is coming again!
>
> Heavings of earth, tell the vast, wondering throng:
> > Jesus is coming again!
> Tempests and whirlwinds, the anthem prolong:
> > Jesus is coming again! ~ George E. Lee (1872)

John Angell James (an English Nonconformist clergyman and writer in the eighteenth century) said, "We do not think enough of Christ's Second Coming. What would be said of the wife who, when her husband was away in another country, could be happy without him, and be contented to think rarely of him. On the contrary, the loving wife longs for her husband's return. Oh, when will he come back! is her frequent exclamation. Wife of the Lamb, church of the Savior, where is thy Lord? Is this thy blessed hope, as it was that of the primitive church? O Christian, are these not wanting here? Every morsel of that bread thou eatest at the [Lord's Supper] table, every drop of [grape juice] thou drinkest, is the voice of Christ saying to thee, I will come again, and receive you to myself; and should draw forth thy longing desires, Come, Lord Jesus; even so, come quickly."[1270]

The Bottom Line: Billy Graham stated, "We are to wait for the coming of Christ with patience. We are to watch with anticipation. We are to work with zeal. We are to prepare with urgency. Scripture says Christ is coming when you're least expecting Him—coming as a thief. He said, 'Be prepared. Get Ready. Prepare to meet thy God. Are you prepared?'"[1271]

51. That Which Christ Has Sown for the Redeemed   Psalm 97:11

"Light is sown for the righteous, and gladness for the upright in heart."—Psalm 97:11.

"Light" (Swanson says "i.e., that which is contrasted to darkness [Genesis 1:3], note: in some contexts with the associative meaning of guidance, health, life, prosperity, enlightened judgment, and other positive things."[1272] Bratcher and Reyburn say "a figure for God's salvation, His goodness, His blessing on His people."[1273]) is "sown" (to scatter or disperse as with seed into a cultivated field with anticipation of reaping its corresponding harvest.[1274] Jennings and Lowe say "the figure being that of light sown as a seed, even now germinating, and about eventually to spring up for the righteous."[1275] See Psalm 126:6) "for the righteous" (Vine, Unger and White say "to be righteous, be in the right, be justified, be just."[1276] The righteous are those made righteous in the New Birth through Jesus Christ. See 2 Corinthians 5:21 and Romans 3:22.)

AND "gladness" (Swanson says "joy, gladness, delight, i.e., a feeling or attitude of joyful happiness and cheerfulness [Psalm 51:8], note: in some contexts this is a response to, or manifestation of, worship to God and so transcendent even of unfavorable circumstances."[1277] Barnes says "is parallel to the word *light.* Joy or gladness is sown for the righteous; that is, arrangements are made for producing joy, as preparations are made by sowing seed for a harvest. The world is full of arrangements for conferring happiness on the righteous."[1278] Rawlinson says "the irrepressible joy which comes from a sense of His favor and protection."[1279]) for the "upright in heart" (The person that is pleasing to the Lord; one that walks straight as contrasted to crooked.).

Homily

Adam Clarke said, "Who the author was is uncertain; it is much in the spirit of David's finest compositions."[1280] Dilday and Kennedy state, "Presumably the return of Israel from exile was the background."[1281] Allan Harman conjectures the song was written after the division of the kingdom following Solomon's death.[1282] The author of Hebrews quotes a portion of Psalm 97:7, attributing it to Jesus Christ and making it Messianic in that regard (Hebrews 1:6). Calvin says, "The description which we have of the kingdom of God in this Psalm does not apply to the state of it under the law. We may infer, accordingly, that it contains a prediction of that kingdom of Christ, which was erected upon the introduction of the Gospel."[1283] Charles Simeon states, "This psalm, whatever was the particular occasion on which it was written, undoubtedly refers to the kingdom of the Messiah, in which the whole creation has abundant reason to rejoice. To him it is expressly applied in the Epistle to the Hebrews, even to his incarnation: 'When Jehovah bringeth in the First-begotten into the world, he saith, And let all the angels of God worship him.'"[1284]

Ultimately the *Light* that is sown for the righteous is Jesus. See Psalm 97:11. As the sun but rises to rid the blackness of night, just so He has risen from the dead to extinguish the darkness of sin and its consequences upon the righteous, scattering joy, peace, hope and contentment upon their path even in times of distress and calamity. He is the divine seed that produces abundant and eternal life. See John 12:24.

Light is sown. Not only does it refer to Jesus who is the Light of the World, but also to the seeds of exceedingly great joy and gladness that He has sown in the pathway of the righteous (His children) through His death and resurrection. Matthew Henry says, "Those that rejoice in Christ Jesus, and in His exaltation, have fountains of joy treasured up for them, which will be opened sooner or later....The subjects of Christ's kingdom are told to expect tribulation in the world. They must suffer by its malice, and must not share in its mirth; yet let them know, to their comfort, that light is sown for them; it is designed and prepared for them."[1285]

That which is sown will sprout. The farmer that sows good seed in fertile soil will reap its fruit. Spurgeon notes, "All along their [Christians'] pathway it [Light] is strewn. Their night is almost over, their day is coming, the morning already advancing with rosy steps is sowing the earth with orient pearls. The full harvest of delight is not yet ours, but it is sown for us; it is springing; it will yet appear in fullness. This is only for those who are right before the Lord in His own righteousness; for all others the blackness of darkness is reserved."[1286] Albert Barnes says that the seed (Light) that has been sown "will spring up around the righteous, and he shall reap that which light tends to produce—happiness, intelligence, and peace. The figure of sowing light is an unusual one, but the meaning is plain. It is that the righteous will not always be in darkness; that there is in preparation for him a harvest of joy; that it will as certainly be produced as a harvest will from grain that is sown; that though there may be present calamities, there will be ultimate peace and triumph."[1287] Adam Clarke remarks, "The Divine light in the soul of man is a seed which takes root, and springs up and increases thirty, sixty, and a hundred fold. Gladness is also a seed: it is sown, and, if carefully improved and cultivated, will also multiply itself into thousands. Every grace of God is a seed which he intends should produce a thousand fold in the hearts of genuine believers." [1288]

In summary. Though at times that which is sown (Light) is hidden in the ground, it yet will rise up with full blossoms of joy, peace, happiness and hope to bless the redeemed of the Lord. The righteous have reaped the fruit of the "Light" in part, but the day is coming when they shall reap its harvest in full (the second coming of Christ). In this knowledge the believer takes comfort. Until Christ comes, let them that love the Lord "hate evil" (hate, despise sin of all kind in self and others universally), "rejoice in the Lord" (in gratitude for the "Light," fruit of salvation sown and harvested through the death, burial and resurrection of Jesus that has been scattered upon the pathway to Heaven in part but will be known in full at His coming) and give thanks in "remembrance of his holiness" ("the infinite purity, rectitude, and perfection of the divine nature"[1289]; the holiness of His person, life and actions [flawless; perfect; just]). Albert

Barnes says, "The highest source of joy for man is that there is a God, and that God is exactly what He is: pure and holy."[1290] See Psalm 97:10 and 12.

The Bottom Line: "The Gospel of Jesus, wherever it goes, sows the whole earth with joy for believers, for these are the people who are righteous before the Lord."[1291] Adam Clarke remarks, "However distressed or persecuted the righteous and the upright may be, it shall not be always so. As surely as the grain that is sown in the earth shall vegetate and bring forth its proper fruit in its season, so surely shall light, prosperity and gladness, comfort and peace, be communicated to [God's people]. They also will spring up in due time."[1292] See Isaiah 58 and 60. Upon Christ's return believers will experience in full that which they know presently in part, not only with regard to knowledge, but joy, peace, holiness and happiness.

52. Let's Just Praise the Lord   Psalm 98

"O sing unto the LORD a new song; for he hath done marvellous things: his right hand, and his holy arm, hath gotten him the victory. The LORD hath made known his salvation: his righteousness hath he openly shewed in the sight of the heathen. He hath remembered his mercy and his truth toward the house of Israel: all the ends of the earth have seen the salvation of our God. Make a joyful noise unto the LORD, all the earth: make a loud noise, and rejoice, and sing praise. Sing unto the LORD with the harp; with the harp, and the voice of a psalm. With trumpets and sound of cornet make a joyful noise before the LORD, the King. Let the sea roar, and the fulness thereof; the world, and they that dwell therein. Let the floods clap their hands: let the hills be joyful together Before the LORD; for he cometh to judge the earth: with righteousness shall he judge the world, and the people with equity."—Psalm 98.

O sing unto the Lord a "new song" (Holladay and Kohler say "new, fresh."[1293] Spurgeon says, "We had a new song before [Psalm 96] because the Lord was coming, but now we have another new song because He has come, and seen and conquered."[1294] Henry says, "'Sing a most excellent song, the best song you have.' Let the song of Christ's love be like Solomon's on that subject, a song of songs. A song of praise, for redeeming love is a new song, such a song as had not been sung before; for this is a mystery which was hidden from ages and generations"[1295]).

"For he hath done marvelous things" (Vine, Unger and White say "to be marvelous, be extraordinary, be beyond one's power to do, do wonderful acts....the extraordinary aspects, of God's dealings with His people (Exodus 15:11; Psalm 77:11; Isaiah 29:14). The Messianic title, 'marvel of a counselor' (Isaiah 9:6; KJV, RSV, 'wonderful counselor'), points toward God's Anointed continuing the marvelous acts of God."[1296]) "his right hand and his holy arm" (The marvelous works God performed by His power alone. They were devised and executed solely by Him.) hath gotten him the "victory" (deliverance, salvation).

The Lord hath made "known his salvation" (Vine, Unger and White say "to know, regard, recognize, pay attention to, be acquainted with."[1297] Rawlinson says "i.e., 'has manifested his power to save.'"[1298]) his "righteousness hath he openly showed" (Holladay and Kohler say "blameless behavior, honesty (of the whole being)."[1299] The Lord's "goodness and mercy [in] justifying sinners and making them righteous through faith in Christ"[1300] (salvation of sinners) was not done in a corner. It is no secret what God hath wrought through Christ Jesus. See Acts 26:26. *Openly showed*. Landes says "to uncover; to be exposed, reveal oneself"[1301]).

"In the sight of the heathen" (Barnes says "the nations; or, so that the nations could see it; that is, the nations outside of Palestine. His acts were so public—so remarkable—that surrounding nations could learn what was His true character. Thus it was when He delivered His people from Egyptian bondage; and thus also frequently in the history of His people"[1302]—and in the salvific work of Jesus.)

He hath "remembered his mercy" (Barnes says, "The idea is, that God had called to mind His promise of mercy to His people; that He had not suffered it to pass out of His recollection; that He had kept His word."[1303] See Luke 1:72. *Mercy*. Vincent, Unger and White say "loving-kindness; steadfast love; grace; mercy; faithfulness; goodness; devotion"[1304]).

AND "his truth" (Clarke says "faithfully accomplishing what He had promised. All this was fulfilled under the Gospel."[1305] God kept His promise to send the Messiah into the world to save His people from their sin.) "toward the house of Israel" (His people) "all the ends of the earth" (quoted from Isaiah 52:10, on which Poole says "all nations of the world shall with astonishment behold the wonderful work of God, first in bringing His people out of Babylon, and afterwards in their redemption by Christ."[1306] Gill says "either Christ Himself, who is the salvation or Savior of God's appointing, providing, and sending; or the salvation which He has wrought out, the Gospel declaring it; which has been sent throughout the world; and many in all parts of it, even in the most distant parts of it, in the very ends of it, have been made to see the nature, want, worth, and value of it; not every individual person in the world, but some in the several parts, and in the remote corners of it, whither the Gospel has been or will be sent."[1307]) have seen the "salvation of our God" (the deliverance of man from the captivity of sin through the death and resurrection of His Son, Jesus Christ).

"Make a joyful noise unto the Lord" (White, Harris and Archer say "to shout, raise a sound, cry out. The primary meaning is 'to raise a noise' by shouting or with an instrument, especially a horn (Numbers 10:7) or the traditional ram's horn, the 'shofar' (Joshua 6:5)."[1308] Rawlinson says, "God is to be praised heartily—with a loud and ringing voice. The body is to unite with the soul in giving Him thanks, and to perform its part vigorously and with zeal [Psalm 5:3; Psalm 66:1; Psalm 81:1; Psalm 95:1, 2; Psalm 100:1.]"[1309]) "all the earth" (The totality of earth, everything is to join in the praising of God.[1310]) "make a loud noise" (Strong says "to break out (in joyful sound):—break (forth, forth into joy), make a loud noise."[1311]).

AND "rejoice, and sing praise" (Swanson says "sing for joy, i.e., make loud public melodic and rhythmic words, with a focus on the joy it expresses."[1312]). Sing unto the Lord with "the harp; with the harp" (Rawlinson says "i.e., 'with a harp accompaniment.' It is fitting that in the praises of God, instrumental music should be joined with vocal melody."[1313]).

AND "the voice of a Psalm" (Barnes says "the voice in singing; a musical voice. Let it not be mere instrumental music, but let that be accompanied with the voice uttering intelligible sounds or words"[1314]).

With "trumpets" (The long straight trumpet that mainly was used to assemble the people together for worship or battle[1315]). AND sound of "cornet" (Rawlinson says, "The *shophâr* is the ordinary curved or rounded trumpet or horn."[1316]).

"Make a joyful noise before the Lord, the King" (Jamieson, Fausset and Brown say, "Hail Him as your sovereign; and while, with every aid to demonstrate zeal and joy, intelligent creatures are invited to praise, as in Psalm 96:11–13, inanimate nature is also summoned to honor Him who triumphs and rules in righteousness and equity."[1317]).

"Let the sea roar, and the fullness thereof; the world, and they that dwell therein." (The sea and its vastness and fullness is beckoned to join the saints in the praise of God, as are the world and its inhabitants; all living things.) "Let the floods clap their hands" (only time used here in Scripture. Brown, Driver and Briggs say "stream, river."[1318] Spurgeon says, "The rolling rivers, the tidal estuaries, the roaring cataracts, are here summoned to pay their homage, and to clap their hands, as men do when they greet their sovereign with acclamation."[1319]) let the "hills be joyful together" (Spurgeon says "or in concert with the floods. Silent as are the mighty mountains, let them forget themselves, and burst forth into a sublime uproariousness of mirth."[1320]).

Before the Lord; for "he cometh to judge the earth: with righteousness shall he judge the world, and the people with equity" (Hengstenberg says, "God by His righteous judgment will bring the whole earth from a state of sorrow into a state of salvation and joy."[1321] Gill says God will judge the world "'with equity', or 'uprightnesses'; in the most upright manner, according to the strictest rules of justice and judgment."[1322] At the second coming of Christ all peoples will be judged justly based upon their response to God's provision of salvation in Jesus Christ).

Homily

"The authorship of this is probably the same as that of several Psalms immediately preceding."[1323] Perhaps its backdrop was the return of Israel from captivity.[1324] It is Messianic in nature. Allan Harman writes, "There is clearly a focus too on the final coming of the Lord, when the Lord Jesus will return to gather His people and to judge the whole world (Matthew 25:31–46)."[1325] George Horne cites the Psalm as an "evangelical hymn" in which "the prophet extols the miracles, the victory, the salvation, the righteousness, the mercy, and truth of the Redeemer."[1326] David exhorts man and nature to praise God for the mighty, miraculous and merciful things He has done, especially in the provision of salvation. "As Hengstenberg has observed, the first section of this Psalm declares the reason why there should be joy, this second section declares how the joy is to be expressed, and the third declares who are to rejoice."[1327]

We are told to praise God with loud, shouting voices, the singing of a new song, with the accompaniment of musical instruments and with Psalms (a musical voice in singing[1328]). Believers are to unite in praise with the roaring, turbulent rivers ("and the fullness thereof"), the gigantic mountains and "the world, and they that dwell therein" (all the inhabitants of earth) in exalting the glorious name of the Lord. Spurgeon says, "You might condense the gospel message into this joyful invitation: "Come and learn how to sing to the Lord a new song! Come and find peace, rest, joy, and all your souls can desire. Come and eat what is good and let your soul delight!"...The gospel is a source of joy to those who proclaim it, for to us who are less than all the saints is this grace given that we should preach among the Gentiles the unsearchable riches of Christ."[1329] Amen.

> Thou flowing water pure and clear,
> Make music for thy Lord to hear,
> Oh, praise Him! Alleluia!
> Thou fire so masterful and bright
> That gives to man both warmth and light,
> Oh, praise Him! Oh, praise Him!
> Alleluia! Alleluia! Alleluia!
>
> And all ye men of tender heart,
> Forgiving others, take your part;
> Oh, sing ye, alleluia!
> Ye who long pain and sorrow bear,
> Praise God and on Him cast your care.
> Oh, praise Him; Oh, praise Him.
> Alleluia! Alleluia! Alleluia!

Let all things their Creator bless
And worship Him in humbleness;
Oh, praise Him, alleluia!
Praise, praise the Father, praise the Son,
And praise the Spirit, three in one.
Oh, praise Him; Oh, praise Him.
Alleluia! Alleluia! Alleluia! ~ St. Francis of Assisi (1225)

For He hath done marvelous things. All of creation ought to praise the Lord for the wondrous things He hath wrought. The word *marvelous* "is used primarily with God as its subject, expressing actions that are beyond the bounds of human powers or expectations."[1330] See Psalm 118:23 and Psalm 9:1. Matthew Henry said, "The Redeemer has overcome all difficulties in the way of our redemption, and was not discouraged by the services or sufferings appointed him. Let us praise Him for the discoveries made to the world of the work of redemption; His salvation and His righteousness fulfilling the prophecies and promises of the Old Testament. In pursuance of this design, God raised up His Son Jesus to be not only a Light to lighten the Gentiles, but the glory of His people Israel."[1331]

Spurgeon declared, "Jesus, our King, has lived a marvelous life, died a marvelous death, risen by a marvelous resurrection, and ascended marvelously into Heaven. By His divine power He has sent forth the Holy Spirit doing marvels, and by that sacred energy His disciples have also wrought marvelous things and astonished all the earth."[1332] The wondrous, supernatural acts in behalf of man that God has done have put a "new song" in their heart that flows through the lips (the regenerated, redeemed). Matthew Henry says, "Surely it behooves us to inquire whether His holy arm hath gotten the victory in our hearts, over the power of Satan, unbelief, and sin? If this be our happy case, we shall exchange all light songs of vanity for songs of joy and thanksgiving; our lives will celebrate the Redeemer's praise."[1333]

Praise Him for the victory won in salvation. *His right hand, and His holy arm, hath gotten him the victory.* Salvation was wrought and accomplished solely by God's power. He needed no assistance, nor received any. Christ is Victor, making possible man's forgiveness with God and deliverance from the clutches of Satan and sin.

> Love lifted me!
> Love lifted me!
> When nothing else could help,
> Love lifted me. ~ James Rowe (1866–1933)

Praise Him for making known His salvation. *The Lord hath made known his salvation.* Spurgeon says God hath revealed His salvation "by the coming of Jesus and by the outpouring of the Holy Ghost, by whose power the Gospel was preached among the Gentiles....In God's own light His light is seen. He must reveal His Son in us, or we shall be unable to discern Him."[1334] *He hath openly showed salvation in the sight of the heathen.* Salvation was conspicuously wrought on the cross that all peoples of the world may know of God's loving-kindness for man. It was not done in the dark, nor was it kept a secret. In witnessing to Festus, Paul said, "I...speak forth the words of truth and soberness. For the king knoweth of these things, before whom also I speak freely: for I am persuaded that none of these things are hidden from him; for this thing was not done in a corner" (Acts 26:25–26). Nor has the message of the cross been hidden from any man.

> It is no secret what God can do.
> What He's done for others He'll do for you.
> With arms wide open He'll pardon you.
> It is no secret what God can do. ~ Stuart Hamblen (1949)

Praise Him for keeping His promise to His people and all peoples of the earth. *He hath remembered His mercy.* God fulfilled His promise to exhibit loving-kindness and grace to all the inhabitants of earth in sending His Son Jesus into the world to accomplish the means of their salvation. See 1 John 2:2 and Romans 10:12.

In commeration of Spurgeon's twenty-fifth anniversary as pastor at the Metropolitan Tabernacle, he said, "If the Lord has blessed us, let us shake off any idea of ascribing praise to ourselves, as Paul shook off the viper from his hand. We are mere vanity, and to us belongs shame.

This is our possession—the only dowry [inheritance] our fathers have left to us. What are we that the Lord should bless us? Did I bring a soul to Christ the other day? I bless the Holy Spirit who helped me by His power to do so divine a deed. Did I bear testimony for the truth but yesterday? I bless Him who is the faithful and true witness, that at His feet I learned how to be true and by His Spirit was enabled to be brave."[1335] Psalm 115:1 says, "Not unto us, O LORD, not unto us, but unto thy name give glory, for thy mercy, and for thy truth's sake."

The Bottom Line: Make your life an orchestration of continual praise unto Christ Jesus for that which He endured, even death upon the cross to purchase your salvation. The converts' "new song" is that of the soul that has been set free from Satan's captivity and sin's power and penalty. *Thy praise, O Lord, will be continually upon my lips.* See Psalm 34:1.

53. The Holiness of God and Man   Psalm 99:5

"Exalt ye the LORD our God, and worship at his footstool; for he is holy."—Psalm 99:5.

"Exalt" (Swanson says "to raise up, to lift up. To be great, have triumph, honor, i.e., have elevation of status."[1336]) ye the "LORD our God" (Barnes says, "The meaning is, Let his name be, as it were, lifted up on high, so as to be conspicuous or seen from afar. Let it be done with a lofty voice; let it be with ascriptions of praise."[1337]).

AND "worship" (Swanson says to "bow down, prostrate oneself, i.e., take a stance of bowing low in an act of respect or honor."[1338]) "at his footstool" (Barnes says, "By humble prostration at His feet. The footstool is that on which the feet rest when one is sitting, and the reference here is to the footstool on which the feet of a king rested when he sat on his throne or chair of state."[1339] MacArthur says, "In general, this is a metaphor for the Temple in Jerusalem [Isaiah 60:13; Lamentations 2:1]; but more specifically, for the ark of the covenant [1 Chronicles 28:2]. Footstools were included with the thrones of the kings of Israel [2 Chronicles 9:18]."[1340]).

For "he is holy" (Swanson says "holy, i.e., pertaining to being unique and pure in the sense of superior moral qualities and possessing certain essential divine qualities in contrast with what is human."[1341]).

Homily

The title for Psalm 99 is "The Holiness of God" and its composer is *likely* David. Spurgeon called Psalm 99 "'The Holy, Holy, Holy Psalm,' for the word 'holy' is the conclusion and the refrain of its three main divisions."[1342] J. J. Stewart Perowne wrote, "In this Psalm not only the righteous sway of the King, but His awful holiness forms the subject of praise."[1343] George Horne states, "The prophet celebrates the reign of Messiah, and the submission of His enemies; His exaltation, holiness, power, and justice."[1344] A. F. Kirkpatrick said, "Jehovah's fresh proclamation of His sovereignty is once more the initial watchword, as in Psalms 93 and 97 (Psalm 96:10), and doubtless this Psalm belongs to the same period. Its distinctive idea is expressed in the threefold refrain (Psalm 99:3, 5, 9). It is a call to all nations, and especially to His own people, to worship Jehovah as the thrice Holy God. The unceasing adoration which is evoked in Heaven by the contemplation of the absolute moral perfection of God (Isaiah 6:3) should find an echo upon earth."[1345]

Three times in its short text (vv. 3, 5, 9) the attribute of God's holiness is mentioned. God's holiness is foundational in understanding the character of God and His dealing with man. All of God's attributes are precious jewels, but that of holiness is the crown jewel. Jerry Bridges said, "Holiness is the perfection of all [God's] other attributes. His power is holy power; His mercy is holy mercy; His wisdom is holy wisdom. It is His holiness more than any other attribute that makes Him worthy of our praise."[1346]

Isaiah, in seeing God seated upon the throne of Heaven, heard one seraph cry out to another, "Holy, Holy, Holy is the LORD of hosts" (Isaiah 6:3). Benson rightly says that God's "holiness should strike an awe upon us, as it doth on the angels themselves, Isaiah 6:2–3."[1347] God is the thrice "holy" reigning Monarch of the entire world. Note that although the seraphim could have cried out, "Powerful, Powerful, Powerful is the Lord of hosts" or reference to any other attribute, but he did not. That in itself speaks of the loftiness of God's holiness. Bratcher and Reyburn comment that *holy* "is used to describe the divine nature, the essential attribute that makes God what He is, the conviction that there is an 'otherness' to God, a mode of being which is different from that of all living creatures and which makes him unique. In various places in the Bible, several consequences are drawn from this central fact, the main one being that of reverence, awe, fear that a person feels when confronted by the holy God; the feeling of unworthiness, of inferiority, before the awesome mystery of the God of Israel."[1348]

> Holy, holy, holy! Lord God Almighty!
>   Early in the morning our song shall rise to thee.
> Holy, holy, holy! Merciful and mighty,
>   God in three Persons, blessed Trinity!
> ~ Reginald Heber (1826)

In light of God's holiness, man is to "worship" Him in awe and reverence. He is to prostrate himself in humility in His holy presence. This attitude is absent in much of the worship in our "closets" and "churches." Spurgeon says, "When He reveals Himself in Christ Jesus, as our reconciled God who allows us to approach even to His throne, it becomes us to unite earnestness and humility, joy and adoration."[1349]

We are extolled to worship God at his "footstool." Albert Barnes states this "denotes the deepest humility and the profoundest prostration and reverence. It is as if we could not look on His face, or on His throne, or on His gorgeous and magnificent robes, but bowed our heads in lowly reverence, and deemed it sufficient honor to lie low before that on which His feet rested. To show the dignity and majesty of God, the earth itself is represented as being merely His footstool; as being, in comparison with the Heaven—the place of His seat—His "throne," only as the footstool is as compared with the splendid chair of state."[1350] J. M. Boice says, "This is the only way we can approach God to worship Him. We 'worship at His footstool' because it is only on the basis of the shed blood, pointing to the poured-out blood of Jesus Christ, that we can approach the holy God."[1351]

Exalt ye the Lord our God. Matthew Henry comments, "When we draw nigh to God to worship Him, our hearts ought to be filled with high thoughts of Him, and we ought to exalt Him in our souls. And the more we abase ourselves, and the more prostrate we are before God, the more we exalt Him."[1352]

Worship the Lord in holiness of heart. "O worship the LORD in the beauty of holiness: fear before him, all the earth" (Psalm 96:9). Spurgeon remarks, "Beauty of architecture and apparel He does not regard; moral and spiritual beauty is that in which His soul delighteth. Worship must not be rendered to God in a slovenly, sinful, superficial manner; we must be reverent, sincere, earnest, and pure in heart both in our prayers and praises. Purity is the white linen of the Lord's choristers, righteousness is the comely garment of His priests, holiness is the royal apparel of His servants."[1353]

J. C. Ryle says, "Holiness is the habit of being of one mind with God, according as we find His mind described in Scripture. It is the habit of agreeing in God's judgment; hating what He hates, loving what He loves and measuring everything in this world by the standard of His Word. He who most entirely agrees with God, he is the most holy man."[1354] Holiness involves separation from all that contaminates and defiles. See Matthew 5:8; Romans 12:1 and 1 Thessalonians 4:7. The writer of Hebrews says that 'without holiness no man shall see God' (Hebrews 12:14b). The text does not refer to the "imputed holiness" one receives from God at conversion that makes him "righteous" through and in Christ Jesus, but to practical holiness (not perfect but growing) that is manifested in heart and conduct. As one is to "follow peace," he is to pursue "holiness." Without holiness, man is inapt to enjoy communion with the Lord. See Hebrews 12:14a.

Spurgeon, in the sermon *Holiness Demanded,* says, (1 "Thou art no friend to true holiness, but an utter stranger to it unless the past causes thee profound sorrow, and sends thee to thy knees to weep and hope that God, for Christ's sake, has blotted it out. (2 And I am quite sure that you know nothing of true holiness if you can look forward to any future indulgence of sensual appetites with a certain degree of delightful anticipation....(3 That man is not right with God who would not do the same in the dark that he would do in the light; who does not feel, 'If every eye should look upon me, I would not be different from what I am when no eye gazes upon me; that which keeps me right is not the judgment and opinions of men, but the eye of the Omnipresent, and the heart of the Lord who loves me.'...(4 There must be an absence of the vital principle of godliness when we can become partakers of other men's sins by applauding or joining with them in the approval of them."[1355]

To the anxious one desirous to know whether or not he is holy, Spurgeon states: "Now if our text said that without perfection of holiness no man could have any communion with Christ, it would shut every one of us out, for no one who knows his own heart ever pretends to be perfectly conformed to God's will. It does not say, 'Perfection of holiness,' mark, but 'holiness.' This holiness is a thing of growth."[1356] It is to say, "I am not the holy man I want to be or should be but am *growing*, moving in that direction even if it be at a snail's pace."

The *professing* Christian that *delights* in sinful pleasure habitually without remorse or repentance has no fellowship with God and never has had it. See 1 John 2:4, 15, 19 and Amos 2:3. Paul asks three pressing rhetorical questions: "What fellowship hath righteousness with unrighteousness? and what communion hath light with darkness? And what concord hath Christ with Belial? or what part hath he that believeth with an infidel?" (2 Corinthians 6:14–15). May he that has a pretentious profession of faith (clearly manifested by a contradictory lifestyle to that of the true believer and that taught in Holy Scripture) realize yet his unregenerate estate and be genuinely converted. See Matthew 7:21–23.

The Bottom Line: Spurgeon says, "In holiness God is more clearly seen than in anything else, save in the Person of Christ Jesus the Lord, of whose life such holiness is but a repetition."[1357] Sinclair Ferguson wrote, "God's holiness means He is separate from sin. But holiness in God also means wholeness. God's holiness is His 'God-ness.' It is His being God in all that it means for Him to be God. To meet God in His holiness, therefore, is to be altogether overwhelmed by the discovery that He is God, and not man."[1358]

54. A Thanksgiving Psalm   Psalm 100:1–5

"Make a joyful noise unto the LORD, all ye lands. Serve the LORD with gladness: come before his presence with singing. Know ye that the LORD he is God: it is he that hath made us, and not we ourselves; we are his people, and the sheep of his pasture. Enter into his gates with thanksgiving, and into his courts with praise: be thankful unto him, and bless his name. For the LORD is good; his mercy is everlasting; and his truth endureth to all generations."—Psalm 100.

"Make a joyful noise" (to cry out, to cheer, and to give a great shout) unto the Lord, "all ye lands" (the totality of earth). "Serve" (Swanson says "work, labor, do, i.e., expend considerable energy and intensity in a task or function."[1359]) the Lord with "gladness" (Swanson says "joy, gladness, delight, i.e., a feeling or attitude of joyful happiness and cheerfulness [Psalm 51:10], note: in some contexts this is a response to, or manifestation of, worship to God."[1360]): come before his presence with "singing" (Gesenius and Tregelles say "shouting for joy [Job 3:7; 20:5; Psalm 63:7]"[1361]).

"Know ye" (Rawlinson says, "be sure—'recognize the fact as a certainty.'"[1362]) "that the Lord he is God" (Benson says, *"Jehovah, He is God*—The only living and true God; a being infinitely perfect, self-existent, and self- sufficient; and the fountain of all being; the first cause and last end of all things."[1363]) "it is he that hath made us, and not we ourselves" (Barnes says, "The Hebrew is, 'He made us,' and this expresses the exact idea. The fact that He is the Creator proves that He is God, since no one but God can perform the work of creation. The highest idea that we can form of power is that which is evinced in an act of creation; that is, in causing anything to exist where there was nothing before. Every created thing, therefore, is a proof of the existence of God; the immensity of the universe is an illustration of the greatness of His power."[1364] Benson says, "It is He that hath made us—Not only by creation, but by regeneration, which is also called a creation, because by it we are made His people."[1365]) "we are his people" (All mankind is the sole property of God, for He created us). AND "the sheep of his pasture" (Henry says, "He that made us maintains us, and gives us all good things richly to enjoy."[1366]).

"Enter into his gates" (Rawlinson says, "The mention of 'gates' and 'courts' points primarily to the temple worship, but the reference may be, as Professor Alexander suggests, 'typical or metaphorical' rather than literal, and may extend to all the faithful and to all places of worship."[1367]) "with thanksgiving" (Swanson says "a confession of thankfulness, i.e., to speak works of personal praise."[1368] Whitaker, Brown and Driver say "give praise to…, praise rendered by acknowledging and abandoning sin."[1369]).

AND into "his courts with praise" (Barnes says, "The 'courts' were literally the open spaces which surrounded the tabernacle or temple. It was in these that worship was celebrated, and not in the tabernacle or temple."[1370]) be "thankful unto him" (Vine, Unger and White say "to confess, praise, give thanks."[1371]) AND "bless his name" (Oswalt, Harris, Archer and Waltke say "to kneel, bless, praise, salute."[1372]).

For the Lord is "good" (Barnes says, "In the former verses, His claim to adoration is founded on the fact that He is the 'Creator,' and has, as such, a right to our service; in this verse, the claim is asserted on account of His moral character."[1373]) "his mercy is everlasting" (Vine, Unger and White say "loving-kindness; steadfast love; grace; mercy; faithfulness; goodness; devotion"[1374]).

AND "his truth endureth" (Swanson says "faithfulness, trustworthiness, steadiness, entrusted, i.e., a state or condition of being dependable to a person or standard. Honesty, i.e., a state of being completely truthful."[1375] Spurgeon says, "Our heart leaps for joy as we bow before One who has never broken His word or changed His purpose. Resting on His sure word, we feel that joy which is here commanded, and in the strength of it we come into His presence even now, and speak good of His name."[1376]) to "all generations" (His unfailing love is offered to every member of every "family-line" until Christ returns.).

Homily

W. S. Plumer states, "The Arabic gives David as author. This is probably but not certainly correct. There is nothing in it forbidding us to regard the sweet singer of Israel as the composer."[1377] It is a psalm of Thanksgiving. "It is commonly referred to as the 'Old Hundredth,' after the name of the stately tune to which it is often sung. This tune was composed by Louis Bourgeois and first appeared in the French Genevan Psalter of 1551."[1378]

> Praise God, from whom all blessings flow;
> Praise Him, all creatures here below;
> Praise Him above, ye heav'nly host;
> Praise Father, Son, and Holy Ghost.
> Amen.

Serve the Lord with gladness. Spurgeon said, "Service coupled with cheerfulness is heart-service, and therefore true. Take away joyful willingness from the Christian, and you have removed the test of his sincerity....Cheerfulness is the support of our strength; in the joy of the Lord are we strong."[1379] See Nehemiah 8:10.

Enter his gates with thanksgiving. The Psalmist cites seven reasons to render praise unto the Lord.

(1 *The Lord is God.* Jehovah is the true and self-existent God, worthy alone of man's adoration and worship.

(2 *It is He that hath made us.* God is creator of man and all that exists.

(3 *We are His people.* As creator of man, He is man's owner who deserves man's praise and worship and submissive obedience in service. As "owner," He has the right to govern our lives. The Christian is "twice" the property of God (creation and the "new creation" in Christ Jesus).

(4 *The sheep of His pasture.* Albert Barnes wrote, "As the shepherd owns the flock, so God is our owner; as the shepherd guards his flock and provides for it, so God guards us and provides for us."[1380] See Psalm 23.

(5 *For the Lord is good.* God is holy and righteous in character, incapable of wrong and forever just in His dealings with man.

(6 *His mercy is everlasting.* God's unfailing love and grace is steadfast from one generation to the next.

259

(7 *His truth endureth for all generations.* Albert Barnes comments, "We could not love and honor a God who was not true to His promises, and who did not Himself love the truth; we could not honor one who was changeable and flexible—who loved one thing in one generation and a different thing in the next; who in one age was the friend of truth, and in the next the patron of falsehood. It is the just foundation for praise to God—our God—that he is essentially and always—in all worlds, and in all the generations of people—toward all in the universe—a Being of unchangeable benevolence, mercy, and truth. Such a God is worthy to be had in universal reverence; such a God is worthy of universal praise."[1381]

> I will enter His gates with thanksgiving in my heart;
> I will enter His courts with praise.
> I will say this is the day that the Lord has made.
> I will rejoice for He has made me glad.
> ~ Leona Von Brethorst (1976)

Man's praise and thanksgiving to God includes making a loud cheering noise, exhibit of great delight and joy, and jubilant singing. See Psalm 100:1–2. W. S. Plumer states, "The singing required must be with joyful lips, with a joyful voice, with triumphing as the word is rendered in Psalm 63:5; Job 3:7; 20:5. Nothing is more offensive to God than that we bow the head like a bulrush and give way to sadness and gloom, when we are called to joyful thanksgiving."[1382]

W. S. Plumer wrote, "Church music should be solemn; for it is an [awesome] thing to worship God. It should be simple, that the mass of the people may join in it. It should be in good taste, that we may not dishonor God with hideous sounds."[1383] Chrysostom said of sacred music, "Nothing so lifteth up the soul, so looseth it from the chains of the body, and giveth it a contempt for all earthly things."[1384] Augustine declared, "How freely was I made to weep by these hymns and spiritual songs, transported by the voice of the congregation sweetly singing;—the melody of their voices filled my ear, and divine truth was poured into my heart. Then burned the flame of sacred devotion in my soul, and gushing tears flowed from my eyes, as well they might."[1385]

Not only does praise encompass singing, but confession. Vine, Unger, and White state "An affirmation or confession of God's undeserved kindness throws man's unworthiness into sharp relief. Hence, a confession of sin may be articulated in the same breath as a confession of faith or praise and thanksgiving....God is even to be praised for His judgments, by which He awakens repentance (Psalm 51:4). So one is not surprised to find praises in penitential contexts, and vice versa (1 Kings 8:33ff; Nehemiah 9:2ff.; Daniel 9:4ff). If praise inevitably entails confession of sin, the reverse is also true: the sure word of forgiveness elicits praise and thanksgiving on the confessor's part. This wells up almost automatically from the new being of the repentant person."[1386]

The Bottom Line: Praise flows from the soul that has experienced the goodness of the Lord in salvation and caring supervision and provision ("sheep of his pasture"). The redeemed "enter his courts" humbly and contritely to "bless his name" (ascribing honor and praise to the Lord).

[1] Plumer, W. S. *Studies in the Book of Psalms: Being a Critical and Expository Commentary, with Doctrinal and Practical Remarks on the Entire Psalter.* (Philadelphia; Edinburgh: J. B. Lippincott Company; A & C Black, 1872), 7.

[2] Hamilton, William W. *Sermons on Books of the Bible: Vol. 2.* (Nashville: Broadman Press, 1925), 35–36.

[3] Hastings, James. *The Great Texts of the Bible: Job to Psalm 23.* (New York: Charles Scribner's Sons, 1913), Psalm 1:1.

[4] Bonar, A. A. *Christ and His Church in the Book of Psalms.* (New York: Robert Carter & Brothers, 1860), v.

[5] Perowne, J. J. S. *The Book of Psalms: A New Translation, with Introductions and Notes, Explanatory and Critical, Fifth Edition, Revised, Vol. 1.* (London; Cambridge: George Bell and Sons; Deighton Bell and Co., 1883), 29.

[6] https://www.yosemite.com/yosemite-in-two-days/, accessed November 21, 2018. The author adapted an illustration shared by Craig C. Broyles in *Psalms: New International Biblical Commentary,* Vol. 11, p. 1.

[7] Spurgeon, C. H. *Psalms.* (Wheaton, IL: Crossway Books, 1993), 11.

[8] Brueggemann, W. *Spirituality of the Psalms.* (Minneapolis: Fortress Press, 2002), vii.

[9] Criswell, W. A. Ed., *The Criswell Study Bible,* Psalms (Introduction). (Nashville: Thomas Nelson Publishers, 1979), 640.

[10] Freedman D. N., A. C. Myers, & A. B. Beck, Eds. *Eerdmans Dictionary of the Bible.* (Grand Rapids, MI: W. B. Eerdmans, 2000), 1093. (J. L.Crenshaw, in Psalms, Book of)

[11] Ibid.

[12] Elwell, W. A. and P. W. Comfort. *Tyndale Bible Dictionary.* (Wheaton, IL: Tyndale House Publishers, 2001), 1093.

[13] Mills, Watson and Richard Wilson, Eds., *Mercer Commentary on the Bible.* (Macon, GA: Mercer University Press, 1995), 431.

[14] Lockyer, Herbert, Sr. *Psalms: A Devotional Commentary,* Psalm 119. (Grand Rapids: Kregel Publications, 1993), 535, 537.

[15] Spurgeon, C. H. *Psalms.* (Wheaton, IL: Crossway Books, 1993), 8–9.

[16] Stott, John. *Favorite Psalms.* (Grand Rapids: Baker Books, 1988), 5.

[17] Henry, M. *Matthew Henry's Commentary on the Whole Bible: Complete and Unabridged in One Volume.* (Peabody: Hendrickson, 1994), 743.

[18] VanGemeren, Willem A. *The Expositor's Bible Commentary,* Psalms. (Grand Rapids: Zondervan, 1991), Introduction.

[19] Perowne, J. J. S. *The Book of Psalms: A New Translation, with Introductions and Notes, Explanatory and Critical, Fifth Edition, Revised, Vol. 1.* (London; Cambridge: George Bell and Sons; Deighton Bell and Co., 1883), 22.

[20] Lucado, M. *Life Lessons from the Inspired Word of God*: Book of Psalms. (Dallas, TX: Word Pub., 1997), 7–9.

[21] Plumer, W. S. *Studies in the Book of Psalms: Being a Critical and Expository Commentary, with Doctrinal and Practical Remarks on the Entire Psalter.* (Philadelphia; Edinburgh: J. B. Lippincott Company; A & C Black, 1872), 8.

[22] Ibid., 5.

[23] Ibid.

[24] *The Spurgeon Study Bible.* (Nashville: Holman Bible Publishers, 2017), 689.

[25] Coffman's Commentaries on the Bible, Psalms, (Introduction).

[26] Kirkpatrick, A. F. (Ed.). *The Cambridge Bible for Schools and Colleges,* Psalms. (Cambridge: Cambridge University Press, 1914), xi.

[27] VanGemeren, Willem A. *The Expositor's Bible Commentary,* Psalms. (Grand Rapids: Zondervan, 1991), 18.

[28] Ibid.

[29] Mills, Watson and Richard Wilson, Eds., *Mercer Commentary on the Bible.* (Macon, GA: Mercer University Press, 1995), 331.

[30] Fraser, James H. *The Authenticity of the Psalm Titles.* Submitted in partial fulfillment of requirements for the degree of Master of Theology in Grace Theological Seminary, May 1984. https://faculty.gordon.edu/hu/bi/ted_hildebrandt/otesources/19-psalms/text/books/frazer-pstitles/frazer-pstitles.pdf, accessed November 24, 2018.

[31] Ibid.

[32] Watts, J. Walsh. *Old Testament Teaching.* (Nashville: Broadman Press, 1967), 150–151.

[33] Plumer, W. S. *Studies in the Book of Psalms: Being a Critical and Expository Commentary, with Doctrinal and Practical Remarks on the Entire Psalter.* (Philadelphia; Edinburgh: J. B. Lippincott Company; A & C Black, 1872), 11.

[34] Ibid., 78.

[35] Kirkpatrick, A. F. (Ed.). *The Cambridge Bible for Schools and Colleges,* Psalms. (Cambridge: Cambridge University Press, 1914), 37.

[36] Swindoll, Chuck. "Psalms." https://www.insight.org/resources/bible/the-wisdom-books/psalms, accessed November 24, 2018.

[37] Criswell, W. A. Ed., *The Criswell Study Bible,* Psalms (Introduction). (Nashville: Thomas Nelson Publishers, 1979), 640.

[38] Elwell, W. A. and P. W. Comfort. *Tyndale Bible Dictionary.* (Wheaton, IL: Tyndale House Publishers, 2001), 1093–1094.

[39] Horne, G. *A Commentary on the Book of Psalms.* (New York: Robert Carter & Brothers, 1856), 12.

[40] Keil & Delitzsch. Commentary on the Old Testament: Volume 5. (Peabody, Massachusetts: Hendrickson Publishers, 2006), 28.

[41] Tholuck, A. *A Translation and Commentary of the Book of Psalms: For the Use of the Ministry and Laity of the Christian Church,* (J. I. Mombert, Trans.). (Philadelphia: William S. & Alfred Martien, 1858), 2.

[42] Kirkpatrick, A. F. (Ed.). *The Cambridge Bible for Schools and Colleges,* Psalms. (Cambridge: Cambridge University Press, 1914), xcvi.

[43] Criswell, W. A., P. Patterson, E. R. Clendenen, D. L. Akin, M. Chamberlin, D. K. Patterson, and J. Pogue (Eds.). Believer's Study Bible, (electronic ed.). (Nashville: Thomas Nelson, 1991), Ps. 1:1.

[44] Ironside, H. A. Studies in Book One of the Psalms. (New York: Loizeaux Brothers, 1951), Introduction.

[45] Keil & Delitzsch. Commentary on the Old Testament: Volume 5. (Peabody, Massachusetts: Hendrickson Publishers, 2006), 46.

[46] Ibid.

[47] "Psalms of Trust: Living Real Life in the Real World," 7. https://docplayer.net/88840979-Psalms-of-trust-living-real-life-in-the-real-world.html, accessed October 2, 2018.

[48] Ironside, H. A. Studies in Book One of the Psalms. (New York: Loizeaux Brothers, 1951), Psalm 2:1–12.

[49] Eskew, Harry and Hugh T. McElrath, *Sing With Understanding.* (Nashville: Broadman Press, 1980), 45.

[50] Tholuck, A. *A Translation and Commentary of the Book of Psalms: For the Use of the Ministry and Laity of the Christian Church,* (J. I. Mombert, Trans.). (Philadelphia: William S. & Alfred Martien, 1858), 2.

[51] Harman, A. *Psalms: A Mentor Commentary (Vol. 1–2).* (Ross-shire, Great Britain: Mentor, 2011), 92–93.

[52] Ibid., 93.

[53] Ibid.

[54] Ibid.

[55] https://www.vocabulary.com/articles/chooseyourwords/indict-indite/, accessed August 19, 2018.

[56] Plumer, W. S. *Studies in the Book of Psalms: Being a Critical and Expository Commentary, with Doctrinal and Practical Remarks on the Entire Psalter.* (Philadelphia; Edinburgh: J. B. Lippincott Company; A & C Black, 1872), 5.

[57] Henry, M. *Matthew Henry's Commentary on the Whole Bible: Complete and Unabridged in One Volume.* (Peabody: Hendrickson, 1994), 743.

[58] McGee, J. V. *Thru the Bible Commentary: Poetry* (Psalms 1–41) (electronic ed., Vol. 17). (Nashville: Thomas Nelson, 1991), ix.

[59] https://www.studylight.org/commentaries/isn/psalms.html, accessed March 28, 2019.

[60] Ironside, Harry. *Notes on Selected Books*, 16.

[61] Bonar, A. A. *Christ and His Church in the Book of Psalms.* (New York: Robert Carter & Brothers, 1860), xi.

[62] Criswell, W. A., P. Patterson, E. R. Clendenen, D. L. Akin, M. Chamberlin, D. K. Patterson, and J. Pogue (Eds.). Believer's Study Bible, (electronic ed.). (Nashville: Thomas Nelson, 1991), Ps. 1:1.

[63] Keil & Delitzsch. Commentary on the Old Testament: Volume 5. (Peabody, Massachusetts: Hendrickson Publishers, 2006), 28.

[64] Carroll, B. H. *An Interpretation of the English Bible: The Poetical Books of the Bible.* (Nashville: Broadman Press, 1948), 138.

[65] Ibid., 139–143.

[66] Horne, G. *A Commentary on the Book of Psalms.* (New York: Robert Carter & Brothers, 1856), 19.

[67] Exell, Joseph S. Ed. *The Biblical Illustrator,* Introduction to the Psalms.

[68] Ibid.

[69] Boice, J. M. *Psalms 1–41: An Expositional Commentary.* (Grand Rapids, MI: Baker Books, 2005), 254.

[70] Ironside, H. A. *Studies on Book One of the Psalms*. (Neptune, NJ: Loizeaux Brothers, 1952), 195–196.

[71] Carroll, B. H. *An Interpretation of the English Bible: The Poetical Books of the Bible.* (Nashville: Broadman Press, 1948), 123.

[72] Ibid.

[73] VanGemeren, Willem A. *The Expositor's Bible Commentary,* Psalms. (Grand Rapids: Zondervan, 1991), 5.

[74] Lucado, M. *Life Lessons from the Inspired Word of God*: Book of Psalms. (Dallas, TX: Word Pub., 1997), 7–9.

[75] McGee, J. V. *Thru the Bible Commentary: Poetry* (Psalms 1–41) (electronic ed., Vol. 17). (Nashville: Thomas Nelson, 1991), viii.

[76] Perowne, J. J. S. *The Book of Psalms: A New Translation, with Introductions and Notes, Explanatory and Critical, Fifth Edition, Revised, Vol. 1.* (London; Cambridge: George Bell and Sons; Deighton Bell and Co., 1883), 25.

[77] Spurgeon, C. H. *Commenting and Commentaries.* (London: Passmore & Alabaster, 1890), 1.

[78] Nichols, J. W. H. *Musings in the Psalms.* (Galaxie Software, 2005), 12.

[79] Kirkpatrick, A. F. (Ed.). *The Cambridge Bible for Schools and Colleges,* Psalms. (Cambridge: Cambridge University Press, 1914), appendix. (Several passages

included are not formally introduced as quotations though taken straight from the Psalms.)

[80] Bratcher, R. G. and W. D. Reyburn. *A Translator's Handbook on the Book of Psalms.* (New York: United Bible Societies, 1991), 468.

[81] Plumer, W. S. *Studies in the Book of Psalms: Being a Critical and Expository Commentary, with Doctrinal and Practical Remarks on the Entire Psalter.* (Philadelphia; Edinburgh: J. B. Lippincott Company; A & C Black, 1872), 555.

[82] Spence-Jones, H. D. M. (Ed.). *Psalms,* (Vol. 1). (London; New York: Funk & Wagnalls Company, 1909), 394.

[83] Barnes, Albert. Notes on the Psalms, Critical, Explanatory and Practical. (New York: Harper & Brothers, 1868), Psalm 37:4.

[84] Gill, John. *The John Gill Exposition of the Entire Bible,* Psalm 51:1.

[85] Kirkpatrick, A. F. (Ed.). *The Cambridge Bible for Schools and Colleges,* Psalms. (Cambridge: Cambridge University Press, 1914), Psalm 51:1.

[86] Benson, Joseph. *The Holy Bible With Notes, Critical, Explanatory and Practical.* (London: J. Kershaw, 1825), Psalm 51:1.

[87] https://biblehub.com/commentaries/ellicott/psalms/51.htm, accessed May 18, 2018.

[88] Benson, Joseph. *The Holy Bible With Notes, Critical, Explanatory and Practical.* (London: J. Kershaw, 1825), Psalm 51:1.

[89] https://biblehub.com/commentaries/poole/psalms/51.htm, accessed May 18, 2018.

[90] Harman, A. *Psalms: A Mentor Commentary (Vol. 1–2).* (Ross-shire, Great Britain: Mentor, 2011), 399.

[91] Jennings, A. C., and W. H. Lowe. *The Psalms, with Introductions and Critical Notes* (Second Edition, Vol. 1). (London: Macmillan and Co., 1884), 238.

[92] Bratcher, R. G. and W. D. Reyburn. *A Translator's Handbook on the Book of Psalms.* (New York: United Bible Societies, 1991), 468.

[93] https://biblehub.com/commentaries/ellicott/psalms/51.htm, accessed May 18, 2018.

[94] Jennings, A. C., and W. H. Lowe. *The Psalms, with Introductions and Critical Notes* (Second Edition, Vol. 1). (London: Macmillan and Co., 1884), 238.

[95] Bratcher, R. G. and W. D. Reyburn. *A Translator's Handbook on the Book of Psalms.* (New York: United Bible Societies, 1991), 468.

[96] Spence-Jones, H. D. M. (Ed.). *Psalms,* (Vol. 1). (London; New York: Funk & Wagnalls Company, 1909), 394.

[97] Barnes, Albert. Notes on the Psalms, Critical, Explanatory and Practical. (New York: Harper & Brothers, 1868), Psalm 51:2.

[98] Gill, John. *The John Gill Exposition of the Entire Bible,* Psalm 51:2.

[99] Bratcher, R. G. and W. D. Reyburn. *A Translator's Handbook on the Book of Psalms.* (New York: United Bible Societies, 1991), 468.

[100] Spence-Jones, H. D. M. (Ed.). *Psalms,* (Vol. 1). (London; New York: Funk & Wagnalls Company, 1909), 394.

[101] Benson, Joseph. *The Holy Bible With Notes, Critical, Explanatory and Practical.* (London: J. Kershaw, 1825), Psalm 51:4.

[102] Barnes, Albert. Notes on the Psalms, Critical, Explanatory and Practical. (New York: Harper & Brothers, 1868), Psalm 51:4.

[103] https://biblehub.com/commentaries/poole/psalms/51.htm, accessed May 18, 2018.

[104] Smith, James. *Handfuls on Purpose, Vol. 4, Series Eleven,* 119.

[105] Ironside, H. A. *Studies on Book One of the Psalms.* (Neptune, NJ: Loizeaux Brothers, 1952), 3–4.

[106] Plumer, W. S. *Studies in the Book of Psalms: Being a Critical and Expository Commentary, with Doctrinal and Practical Remarks on the Entire Psalter.* (Philadelphia; Edinburgh: J. B. Lippincott Company; A & C Black, 1872), 555.

[107] *The Spurgeon Study Bible.* (Nashville: Holman Bible Publishers, 2017), 734.

[108] Ibid.

[109] Horne, G. *A Commentary on the Book of Psalms.* (New York: Robert Carter & Brothers, 1856), 192.

[110] Tate, M. E. *Psalms 51–100 (Vol. 20).* (Dallas: Word, Incorporated, 1998), 5.

[111] Ibid.

[112] Kirkpatrick, A. F. (Ed.). *The Cambridge Bible for Schools and Colleges,* Psalms. (Cambridge: Cambridge University Press, 1914), Psalm 51:1.

[113] Ibid.

[114] Spence-Jones, H. D. M. (Ed.). *Psalms,* (Vol. 1). (London; New York: Funk & Wagnalls Company, 1909), 394.

[115] Gill, John. *The John Gill Exposition of the Entire Bible,* Psalm 51:2.

[116] Plumer, W. S. *Studies in the Book of Psalms: Being a Critical and Expository Commentary, with Doctrinal and Practical Remarks on the Entire Psalter.* (Philadelphia; Edinburgh: J. B. Lippincott Company; A & C Black, 1872), 556.

[117] Ibid.

[118] Barnes, Albert. Notes on the Psalms, Critical, Explanatory and Practical. (New York: Harper & Brothers, 1868), Psalm 51:3.

[119] Horne, G. *A Commentary on the Book of Psalms.* (New York: Robert Carter & Brothers, 1856), 191.

[120] Plumer, W. S. *Studies in the Book of Psalms: Being a Critical and Expository Commentary, with Doctrinal and Practical Remarks on the Entire Psalter.* (Philadelphia; Edinburgh: J. B. Lippincott Company; A & C Black, 1872), 557.

[121] Chambers, Oswald. *My Utmost For His Highest,* November 19.

122 Alexander, J. A. *The Psalms Translated and Explained.* (Edinburgh: Andrew Elliot; James Thin, 1864), 231.

123 Criswell, W. A., P. Patterson, E. R. Clendenen, D. L. Akin, M. Chamberlin, D. K. Patterson, and J. Pogue (Eds.). Believer's Study Bible, (electronic ed.). (Nashville: Thomas Nelson, 1991), Ps. 51:1.

124 Spurgeon, C. H. *Psalms.* (Wheaton, IL: Crossway Books, 1993), 210.

125 Alexander, J. A. *The Psalms Translated and Explained.* (Edinburgh: Andrew Elliot; James Thin, 1864), 230.

126 Barnes, Albert. Notes on the Psalms, Critical, Explanatory and Practical. (New York: Harper & Brothers, 1868), Psalm 51:1.

127 Ibid.

128 Clarke, Adam. *Clarkes' Commentary and Critical Notes*, Psalm 51:1.

129 Gill, John. *The John Gill Exposition of the Entire Bible,* Psalm 51:1.

130 Alexander, J. A. *The Psalms Translated and Explained.* (Edinburgh: Andrew Elliot; James Thin, 1864), 230.

131 Henry, M. *Matthew Henry's Commentary on the Whole Bible: Complete and Unabridged in One Volume.* (Peabody: Hendrickson, 1994), 786.

132 Hamilton, William W. *Sermons on the Books of the Bible,* (Vol. 3), 96.

133 Barnes, Albert. Notes on the Psalms, Critical, Explanatory and Practical. (New York: Harper & Brothers, 1868), Psalm 51:3.

134 https://www.christianquotes.info/quotes-by-topic/quotes-about-repentance/#ixzz5FtCNO7Mr, accessed May 18, 2018.

135 Alexander, J. A. *The Psalms Translated and Explained.* (Edinburgh: Andrew Elliot; James Thin, 1864), 232.

136 Ibid.

137 Spurgeon, C. H. *Psalms.* (Wheaton, IL: Crossway Books, 1993), 212.

138 Horne, G. *A Commentary on the Book of Psalms.* (New York: Robert Carter & Brothers, 1856), 193.

139 Benson, Joseph. *The Holy Bible With Notes, Critical, Explanatory and Practical.* (London: J. Kershaw, 1825), Psalm 51:10.

140 Alexander, J. A. *The Psalms Translated and Explained.* (Edinburgh: Andrew Elliot; James Thin, 1864), 232.

141 Smith, James. *Handfuls on Purpose, Vol. 4, Series Eleven,* 121.

142 Vine, W. E., M. F. Unger, & W. White, Jr. *Vine's Complete Expository Dictionary of Old and New Testament Words (Vol. 1).* (Nashville, TN: T. Nelson, 1996), 203.

143 https://biblehub.com/commentaries/poole/psalms/51.htm, accessed May 18, 2018.

144 Spence-Jones, H. D. M. (Ed.). *Psalms,* (Vol. 1). (London; New York: Funk & Wagnalls Company, 1909), Psalm 51:12.

[145] Horne, G. *A Commentary on the Book of Psalms.* (New York: Robert Carter & Brothers, 1856), 193.

[146] Perowne, J. J. S. *The Book of Psalms; A New Translation, with Introductions and Notes, Explanatory and Critical* (Fifth Edition, Revised, Vol. 1). (London; Cambridge: George Bell and Sons; Deighton Bell and Co., 1883), 437.

[147] Alexander, J. A. *The Psalms Translated and Explained.* (Edinburgh: Andrew Elliot; James Thin, 1864), 233.

[148] Perowne, J. J. S. *The Book of Psalms; A New Translation, with Introductions and Notes, Explanatory and Critical* (Fifth Edition, Revised, Vol. 1). (London; Cambridge: George Bell and Sons; Deighton Bell and Co., 1883), 437.

[149] Barnes, Albert. Notes on the Psalms, Critical, Explanatory and Practical. (New York: Harper & Brothers, 1868), Psalm 51:13.

[150] Perowne, J. J. S. *The Book of Psalms; A New Translation, with Introductions and Notes, Explanatory and Critical* (Fifth Edition, Revised, Vol. 1). (London; Cambridge: George Bell and Sons; Deighton Bell and Co., 1883), 437–438.

[151] Spurgeon, C. H. *The Treasury of David.* (Grand Rapids, Michigan: Kregel Publications, 2004), Psalm 51:15.

[152] Swindoll, Charles. *David: A Man of Passion & Destiny.* (Dallas: Word Publishing Company, 1997), 224–225.

[153] Matthew Henry's Concise Commentary, Psalm 51:3.

[154] Barnes, Albert. Notes on the Psalms, Critical, Explanatory and Practical. (New York: Harper & Brothers, 1868), Psalm 51:3.

[155] https://biblehub.com/commentaries/ellicott/psalms/51.htm, accessed May 18, 2018.

[156] Ross, A. P. In Walvoord, J. F. and R. B. Zuck (Eds.). *The Bible Knowledge Commentary: An Exposition of the Scriptures* (Vol. 1, Psalms). (Wheaton, IL: Victor Books, 1985), 795.

[157] Benson, Joseph. *The Holy Bible With Notes, Critical, Explanatory and Practical.* (London: J. Kershaw, 1825), Psalm 51:15.

[158] Jamieson, R., A. R. Fausset, & D. Brown. *Commentary Critical and Explanatory on the Whole Bible* (Vol. 1). (Oak Harbor, WA: Logos Research Systems, Inc., 1997), Psalm 51:10.

[159] Barnes, Albert. Notes on the Psalms, Critical, Explanatory and Practical. (New York: Harper & Brothers, 1868), Psalm 51:10.

[160] Swindoll, Charles. *David: A Man of Passion & Destiny.* (Dallas: Word Publishing Company, 1997), 231.

[161] Ibid., 233.

[162] Ibid.

[163] https://www.christianquotes.info/quotes-by-topic/quotes-about-repentance/#ixzz5FtDlom5Z, accessed May 18, 2018.

[164] Ibid.

[165] https://witzend.wordpress.com/tag/psalm-51/, accessed May 18, 2018.

[166] VanGemeren, Willem A. *The Expositor's Bible Commentary,* Psalms. (Grand Rapids: Zondervan, 1991), 385.

[167] Bratcher, R. G. and W. D. Reyburn. *A Translator's Handbook on the Book of Psalms.* (New York: United Bible Societies, 1991), 479.

[168] Barnes, Albert. Notes on the Psalms, Critical, Explanatory and Practical. (New York: Harper & Brothers, 1868), Psalm 52:2.

[169] Kirkpatrick, A. F. (Ed.). *The Cambridge Bible for Schools and Colleges,* Psalms. (Cambridge: Cambridge University Press, 1914), Psalm 52:2.

[170] https://biblehub.com/commentaries/poole/psalms/52.htm, accessed May 18, 2018.

[171] Clarke, Adam. *Clarkes' Commentary and Critical Notes*, Psalm 52:2.

[172] Kirkpatrick, A. F. (Ed.). *The Cambridge Bible for Schools and Colleges,* Psalms. (Cambridge: Cambridge University Press, 1914), Psalm 52:3.

[173] Barnes, Albert. Notes on the Psalms, Critical, Explanatory and Practical. (New York: Harper & Brothers, 1868), Psalm 52:3.

[174] Spence-Jones, H. D. M. (Ed.). *Psalms,* (Vol. 1). (London; New York: Funk & Wagnalls Company, 1909), 407.

[175] Gill, John. *The John Gill Exposition of the Entire Bible,* Psalm 52:3.

[176] https://biblehub.com/commentaries/poole/psalms/52.htm, accessed May 18, 2018.

[177] https://biblehub.com/commentaries/ellicott/psalms/52.htm, accessed May 18, 2018.

[178] Spurgeon, C. H. *Psalms.* (Wheaton, IL: Crossway Books, 1993), 216.

[179] Spence-Jones, H. D. M. (Ed.). *Psalms,* (Vol. 1). (London; New York: Funk & Wagnalls Company, 1909), 408.

[180] The NET Bible Notes Bible, First Edition Notes. (Richardson, TX: Biblical Studies Press, 2006), Psalm 52:4.

[181] Jennings, A. C., and W. H. Lowe. *The Psalms, with Introductions and Critical Notes* (Second Edition, Vol. 1). (London: Macmillan and Co., 1884), 244.

[182] Spurgeon, C. H. *Psalms.* (Wheaton, IL: Crossway Books, 1993), 216.

[183] Barnes, Albert. Notes on the Psalms, Critical, Explanatory and Practical. (New York: Harper & Brothers, 1868), Psalm 52:3.

[184] Henry, M. *Matthew Henry's Commentary on the Whole Bible: Complete and Unabridged in One Volume.* (Peabody: Hendrickson, 1994), 819.

[185] Plumer, W. S. *Studies in the Book of Psalms: Being a Critical and Expository Commentary, with Doctrinal and Practical Remarks on the Entire Psalter.* (Philadelphia; Edinburgh: J. B. Lippincott Company; A & C Black, 1872), 566.

186 Barclay, W. (Ed.). *The Daily Study Bible Series,* The Letters of James and Peter. (Philadelphia: Westminster John Knox Press, 1976), 112.

187 Spurgeon, C. H. *Faith's Checkbook.* (New Kensington, Pa.: Whitaker House, 2002), November 16.

188 Swindoll, Chuck. Job: A Man of Heroic Endurance. (Nashville: WPublishing Group, 2004), 163.

189 Allen, Kerry James, Ed., *Exploring the Mind and Heart of the Prince of Preachers.* (Oswego, IL: Fox River Press, 2005), 450.

190 Wiersbe, W. W. *With the Word Bible Commentary.* (Nashville: Thomas Nelson, 1991), Ps. 69:1.

191 Plumer, W. S. *Studies in the Book of Psalms: Being a Critical and Expository Commentary, with Doctrinal and Practical Remarks on the Entire Psalter.* (Philadelphia; Edinburgh: J. B. Lippincott Company; A & C Black, 1872), 573.

192 Gill, John. *The John Gill Exposition of the Entire Bible,* Romans 3:12.

193 Clarke, Adam. *Clarkes' Commentary and Critical Notes*, Psalm 14:1.

194 Barnes' Notes on the Bible, Romans 3:12.

195 Bengel's Gnomen, Romans 3:12.

196 Smith, James. *Handfuls on Purpose, Vol. 4, Series Eleven,* 115.

197 Blanchard, John. *Whatever Happened to Hell?* (Evangelical Press, 2005), 154.

198 Criswell, W. A. Ed., *The Criswell Study Bible,* Psalms (Introduction). (Nashville: Thomas Nelson Publishers, 1979), 1 John 2:2.

199 *Crossroads.* Issue 7, 16.

200 Spurgeon, C. H. *The Treasury of David.* (Grand Rapids, Michigan: Kregel Publications, 2004), Psalm 53.

201 Gill, John. *The John Gill Exposition of the Entire Bible,* Psalm 54:2.

202 Spurgeon, C. H. *Psalms.* (Wheaton, IL: Crossway Books, 1993), 219.

203 Plumer, W. S. *Studies in the Book of Psalms: Being a Critical and Expository Commentary, with Doctrinal and Practical Remarks on the Entire Psalter.* (Philadelphia; Edinburgh: J. B. Lippincott Company; A & C Black, 1872), 576.

204 Ibid.

205 Boice, J. M. *Psalms 1–41: An Expositional Commentary.* (Grand Rapids, MI: Baker Books, 2005), 453.

206 Clarke, Adam. *Clarkes' Commentary and Critical Notes*, Psalm 54:1.

207 Henry, Matthew. *Matthew Henry's Concise Bible Commentary,* Psalm 54:2.

208 Spurgeon, C. H. *Psalms.* (Wheaton, IL: Crossway Books, 1993), 219.

209 Plumer, W. S. *Studies in the Book of Psalms: Being a Critical and Expository Commentary, with Doctrinal and Practical Remarks on the Entire Psalter.* (Philadelphia; Edinburgh: J. B. Lippincott Company; A & C Black, 1872), 574–575.

210 Spurgeon, C. H. *Psalms.* (Wheaton, IL: Crossway Books, 1993), 219.

[211] MacArthur, John. *The Keys to Spiritual Growth.* (Wheaton: Crossway Books, 1991), 123.

[212] Rogers, Adrian. "The Privilege of Prayer." Lwf.org, accessed November 30, 2011.

[213] Hutson, Curtis, Ed., *Great Preaching on Prayer.* (Murfreesboro, Tenn.: Sword of the Lord Publishers, 1988), 45.

[214] Keller, Tim. *Prayer: Experiencing Awe and Intimacy with God,* 68.

[215] Taken from "Answers to Prayer"—From *George Müller's Narratives.*

[216] Spurgeon, C. H. *Morning and Evening,* October 18 (Morning).

[217] Plumer, W. S. *Studies in the Book of Psalms: Being a Critical and Expository Commentary, with Doctrinal and Practical Remarks on the Entire Psalter.* (Philadelphia; Edinburgh: J. B. Lippincott Company; A & C Black, 1872), 576–577.

[218] Maclaren, Alexander. *The Expositor's Bible:* The Psalms. (New York: Scriptura Press, 2015), Psalm 54:2.

[219] E. M. Bounds Quotes. https://prayer-coach.com/2010/01/15/prayer-quotes-e-m-bounds/, accessed May 19, 2018.

[220] Barnes, Albert. Notes on the Psalms, Critical, Explanatory and Practical. (New York: Harper & Brothers, 1868), Psalm 55:13.

[221] *Merriam-Webster's Collegiate Dictionary* (10th ed.). (Springfield, MA: Merriam-Webster, 1996).

[222] Barnes, Albert. Notes on the Psalms, Critical, Explanatory and Practical. (New York: Harper & Brothers, 1868), Psalm 55:13.

[223] Spurgeon, C. H. *The Treasury of David.* (Grand Rapids, Michigan: Kregel Publications, 2004), Psalm 55:12.

[224] Plumer, W. S. *Studies in the Book of Psalms: Being a Critical and Expository Commentary, with Doctrinal and Practical Remarks on the Entire Psalter.* (Philadelphia; Edinburgh: J. B. Lippincott Company; A & C Black, 1872), 581.

[225] https://biblehub.com/commentaries/poole/psalms/55.htm, accessed May 19, 2018.

[226] Gill, John. *The John Gill Exposition of the Entire Bible,* Psalm 55:12.

[227] https://biblehub.com/commentaries/poole/psalms/55.htm, accessed May 19, 2018.

[228] Spurgeon, C. H. *Psalms.* (Wheaton, IL: Crossway Books, 1993), 224.

[229] Barnes, Albert. Notes on the Psalms, Critical, Explanatory and Practical. (New York: Harper & Brothers, 1868), Psalm 55:13.

[230] Plumer, W. S. *Studies in the Book of Psalms: Being a Critical and Expository Commentary, with Doctrinal and Practical Remarks on the Entire Psalter.* (Philadelphia; Edinburgh: J. B. Lippincott Company; A & C Black, 1872), 581.

[231] Ibid.

[232] Ibid.

[233] Perowne, J. J. S. *The Book of Psalms; A New Translation, with Introductions and Notes, Explanatory and Critical* (Fifth Edition, Revised, Vol. 1). (London; Cambridge: George Bell and Sons; Deighton Bell and Co., 1883), 455.

[234] Spurgeon, C. H. *Psalms*. (Wheaton, IL: Crossway Books, 1993), 224.

[235] Plumer, W. S. *Studies in the Book of Psalms: Being a Critical and Expository Commentary, with Doctrinal and Practical Remarks on the Entire Psalter.* (Philadelphia; Edinburgh: J. B. Lippincott Company; A & C Black, 1872), 581.

[236] Kirkpatrick, A. F. (Ed.). *The Cambridge Bible for Schools and Colleges,* Psalms. (Cambridge: Cambridge University Press, 1914), Psalm 55:14.

[237] Plumer, W. S. *Studies in the Book of Psalms: Being a Critical and Expository Commentary, with Doctrinal and Practical Remarks on the Entire Psalter.* (Philadelphia; Edinburgh: J. B. Lippincott Company; A & C Black, 1872), 581.

[238] Maclaren, Alexander. *The Expositor's Bible:* The Psalms. (New York: Scriptura Press, 2015), Psalm 55:12.

[239] Exell, Joseph S. Ed. *The Biblical Illustrator,* Psalm 55:12–15.

[240] Henry, M. *Matthew Henry's Commentary on the Whole Bible: Complete and Unabridged in One Volume.* (Peabody: Hendrickson, 1994), 822.

[241] Spurgeon, C. H. "The Cause and Cure of a Wounded Spirit," April 16, 1885. http://www.ccel.org, accessed December 8, 2013.

[242] Spurgeon, C. H. "Healing for the Wounded." November 11, 1855. http://www.spurgeon.org, accessed June 28, 2014.

[243] Swindoll, Charles. *David: A Man of Passion & Destiny.* (Dallas: Word Publishing Company, 1997), 243.

[244] Ibid., 247.

[245] Plumer, W. S. *Studies in the Book of Psalms: Being a Critical and Expository Commentary, with Doctrinal and Practical Remarks on the Entire Psalter.* (Philadelphia; Edinburgh: J. B. Lippincott Company; A & C Black, 1872), 586.

[246] Henry, Matthew. *Matthew Henry's Concise Bible Commentary,* Psalm 55:12.

[247] Plumer, W. S. *Studies in the Book of Psalms: Being a Critical and Expository Commentary, with Doctrinal and Practical Remarks on the Entire Psalter.* (Philadelphia; Edinburgh: J. B. Lippincott Company; A & C Black, 1872), 589.

[248] Barnes, Albert. Notes on the Psalms, Critical, Explanatory and Practical. (New York: Harper & Brothers, 1868), Psalm 56:8.

[249] Ibid.

[250] Perowne, J. J. S. *The Book of Psalms; A New Translation, with Introductions and Notes, Explanatory and Critical* (Fifth Edition, Revised, Vol. 1). (London; Cambridge: George Bell and Sons; Deighton Bell and Co., 1883), 463.

[251] Barnes, Albert. Notes on the Psalms, Critical, Explanatory and Practical. (New York: Harper & Brothers, 1868), Psalm 56:8.

252 Tate, M. E. *Psalms 51–100 (Vol. 20).* (Dallas: Word, Incorporated, 1998), 71.

253 Maclaren, Alexander. *The Expositor's Bible:* The Psalms. (New York: Scriptura Press, 2015), Psalm 56:8.

254 Dilday, R. H., Jr., and J. H. Kennedy. The Teacher's Bible Commentary, Psalms, (Paschall, H. F. and H. H. Hobbs, Eds.) (Nashville: Broadman and Holman Publishers, 1972), 316.

255 Spurgeon, C. H. *Morning and Evening,* November 3.

256 Henry, Matthew. *Matthew Henry's Concise Bible Commentary,* Psalm 56:8.

257 Gill, John. *The John Gill Exposition of the Entire Bible,* Psalm 56:8.

258 Ross, A. P. In Walvoord, J. F. and R. B. Zuck (Eds.). *The Bible Knowledge Commentary: An Exposition of the Scriptures* (Vol. 1, Psalms). (Wheaton, IL: Victor Books, 1985), 835–836.

259 Henry, M. *Matthew Henry's Commentary on the Whole Bible: Complete and Unabridged in One Volume.* (Peabody: Hendrickson, 1994), 824.

260 Maclaren, Alexander. *The Expositor's Bible:* The Psalms. (New York: Scriptura Press, 2015), Psalm 56:8.

261 Plumer, W. S. *Studies in the Book of Psalms: Being a Critical and Expository Commentary, with Doctrinal and Practical Remarks on the Entire Psalter.* (Philadelphia; Edinburgh: J. B. Lippincott Company; A & C Black, 1872), 592.

262 Card, Michael. *A Sacred Sorrow,* 11.

263 Gill, John. *The John Gill Exposition of the Entire Bible,* Psalm 56:8.

264 Henry, M. *Matthew Henry's Commentary on the Whole Bible: Complete and Unabridged in One Volume.* (Peabody: Hendrickson, 1994), 824.

265 VanGemeren, Willem A. *The Expositor's Bible Commentary,* Psalms. (Grand Rapids: Zondervan, 1991), Psalm 56:8. The author adapted.

266 Chilcote, Paul Wesley. *John & Charles Wesley: Selections From Their Writings and Hymns.* (Woodstock, Vermont: SkyLight Paths Publishing, 2011), 56.

267 Ibid.

268 Plumer, W. S. *Studies in the Book of Psalms: Being a Critical and Expository Commentary, with Doctrinal and Practical Remarks on the Entire Psalter.* (Philadelphia; Edinburgh: J. B. Lippincott Company; A & C Black, 1872), 592.

269 Harman, A. *Psalms: A Mentor Commentary (Vol. 1–2).* (Ross-shire, Great Britain: Mentor, 2011), 431.

270 Google Dictionary.

271 Clarke, Adam. *Clarkes' Commentary and Critical Notes,* Psalm 56:8.

272 Gill, John. *The John Gill Exposition of the Entire Bible,* Psalm 57:6.

273 Plumer, W. S. *Studies in the Book of Psalms: Being a Critical and Expository Commentary, with Doctrinal and Practical Remarks on the Entire Psalter.* (Philadelphia; Edinburgh: J. B. Lippincott Company; A & C Black, 1872), 595.

[274] https://biblehub.com/commentaries/poole/psalms/57.htm, accessed May 22, 2018.

[275] Spurgeon, C. H. *Psalms.* (Wheaton, IL: Crossway Books, 1993), 233

[276] Clarke, Adam. *Clarkes' Commentary and Critical Notes*, Psalm 57 (Introduction).

[277] Spurgeon, C. H. *Morning and Evening,* May 03.

[278] Spurgeon, C. H. *Faith's Checkbook.* (New Kensington, Pa.: Whitaker House, 2002), November 10.

[279] VanGemeren, Willem A. *The Expositor's Bible Commentary,* Psalms. (Grand Rapids: Zondervan, 1991), Psalm 57:7.

[280] Spurgeon, C. H. *Faith's Checkbook.* (New Kensington, Pa.: Whitaker House, 2002), November 10.

[281] *The Spurgeon Study Bible.* (Nashville: Holman Bible Publishers, 2017), 737.

[282] Tate, M. E. *Psalms 51–100 (Vol. 20).* (Dallas: Word, Incorporated, 1998), 82.

[283] Kirkpatrick, A. F. (Ed.). *The Cambridge Bible for Schools and Colleges,* Psalms. (Cambridge: Cambridge University Press, 1914), Psalm 58:1.

[284] Jamieson, R., A. R. Fausset, & D. Brown. *Commentary Critical and Explanatory on the Whole Bible* (Vol. 1). (Oak Harbor, WA: Logos Research Systems, Inc., 1997), Psalm 58:1.

[285] Spence-Jones, H. D. M. (Ed.). *Psalms,* (Vol. 2). (London; New York: Funk & Wagnalls Company, 1909), 9.

[286] Barnes, Albert. Notes on the Psalms, Critical, Explanatory and Practical. (New York: Harper & Brothers, 1868), Psalm 58:1.

[287] Ibid.

[288] Benson, Joseph. *The Holy Bible With Notes, Critical, Explanatory and Practical.* (London: J. Kershaw, 1825), Psalm 58:1.

[289] Spence-Jones, H. D. M. (Ed.). *Psalms,* (Vol. 2). (London; New York: Funk & Wagnalls Company, 1909), 9.

[290] Bratcher, R. G. and W. D. Reyburn. *A Translator's Handbook on the Book of Psalms.* (New York: United Bible Societies, 1991), 516.

[291] Alexander, J. A. *The Psalms Translated and Explained.* (Edinburgh: Andrew Elliot; James Thin, 1864), 256.

[292] Ibid.

[293] Plumer, W. S. *Studies in the Book of Psalms: Being a Critical and Expository Commentary, with Doctrinal and Practical Remarks on the Entire Psalter.* (Philadelphia; Edinburgh: J. B. Lippincott Company; A & C Black, 1872), 603.

[294] Ibid.

[295] Spence-Jones, H. D. M. (Ed.). *Psalms,* (Vol. 2). (London; New York: Funk & Wagnalls Company, 1909), 9.

296 Barnes, Albert. Notes on the Psalms, Critical, Explanatory and Practical. (New York: Harper & Brothers, 1868), Psalm 58:4.

297 Plumer, W. S. *Studies in the Book of Psalms: Being a Critical and Expository Commentary, with Doctrinal and Practical Remarks on the Entire Psalter.* (Philadelphia; Edinburgh: J. B. Lippincott Company; A & C Black, 1872), 600.

298 Barnes, Albert. Notes on the Psalms, Critical, Explanatory and Practical. (New York: Harper & Brothers, 1868), Psalm 58:4.

299 Ibid.

300 Spurgeon, C. H. *Psalms.* (Wheaton, IL: Crossway Books, 1993), 235.

301 Barnes, Albert. Notes on the Psalms, Critical, Explanatory and Practical. (New York: Harper & Brothers, 1868), Psalm 58:5.

302 Dilday, R. H., Jr., and J. H. Kennedy. The Teacher's Bible Commentary, Psalms, (Paschall, H. F. and H. H. Hobbs, Eds.) (Nashville: Broadman and Holman Publishers, 1972), 317.

303 Spence-Jones, H. D. M. (Ed.). *Psalms,* (Vol. 2). (London; New York: Funk & Wagnalls Company, 1909), 10.

304 Plutarch. *Plutarch's Lives.* (New York: Harper Brothers, 1872), 421.

305 http://www.selfgovernment.us/news/james-garfield-if-congress-is-corrupt-it-is-because-we-tolerate-it, accessed May 22, 2018.

306 Spence-Jones, H. D. M. (Ed.). *Psalms,* (Vol. 2). (London; New York: Funk & Wagnalls Company, 1909), 11–12.

307 Jennings, A. C., and W. H. Lowe. *The Psalms, with Introductions and Critical Notes* (Second Edition, Vol. 1). (London: Macmillan and Co., 1884), 274.

308 Barnes, Albert. Notes on the Psalms, Critical, Explanatory and Practical. (New York: Harper & Brothers, 1868), Psalm 59:1.

309 Ibid., Psalm 59:2.

310 Harman, A. *Psalms: A Mentor Commentary (Vol. 1–2).* (Ross-shire, Great Britain: Mentor, 2011), 442.

311 Barnes, Albert. Notes on the Psalms, Critical, Explanatory and Practical. (New York: Harper & Brothers, 1868), Psalm 59:3.

312 Spurgeon, C. H. *Psalms.* (Wheaton, IL: Crossway Books, 1993), 237.

313 Plumer, W. S. *Studies in the Book of Psalms: Being a Critical and Expository Commentary, with Doctrinal and Practical Remarks on the Entire Psalter.* (Philadelphia; Edinburgh: J. B. Lippincott Company; A & C Black, 1872), 606.

314 Barnes, Albert. Notes on the Psalms, Critical, Explanatory and Practical. (New York: Harper & Brothers, 1868), Psalm 59:4.

315 Ibid.

316 Spurgeon, C. H. *Psalms.* (Wheaton, IL: Crossway Books, 1993), 238.

317 Harman, A. *Psalms: A Mentor Commentary (Vol. 1–2).* (Ross-shire, Great Britain: Mentor, 2011), 442.

[318] Barnes, Albert. Notes on the Psalms, Critical, Explanatory and Practical. (New York: Harper & Brothers, 1868), Psalm 59:4.

[319] Spence-Jones, H. D. M. (Ed.). *Psalms,* (Vol. 2). (London; New York: Funk & Wagnalls Company, 1909), 12.

[320] Spurgeon, C. H. *Psalms.* (Wheaton, IL: Crossway Books, 1993), 237.

[321] *Geneva Study Bible,* Psalm 59:1.

[322] Maclaren, Alexander. *Expositions of Holy Scripture, vol. 3: The Psalms, Isaiah 1–48.* (Grand Rapids, MI: Eerdmans, 1959), part 2, 61.

[323] Spurgeon, C. H. *Psalms.* (Wheaton, IL: Crossway Books, 1993), 239.

[324] Clarke, Adam. *Clarkes' Commentary and Critical Notes*, Psalm 60:4.

[325] Spurgeon, C. H. *Psalms.* (Wheaton, IL: Crossway Books, 1993), 244.

[326] Barnes, Albert. Notes on the Psalms, Critical, Explanatory and Practical. (New York: Harper & Brothers, 1868), Psalm 60:4.

[327] Plumer, W. S. *Studies in the Book of Psalms: Being a Critical and Expository Commentary, with Doctrinal and Practical Remarks on the Entire Psalter.* (Philadelphia; Edinburgh: J. B. Lippincott Company; A & C Black, 1872), 614.

[328] Barnes, Albert. Notes on the Psalms, Critical, Explanatory and Practical. (New York: Harper & Brothers, 1868), Psalm 60:4

[329] Spurgeon, C. H. *The Treasury of David.* (Grand Rapids, Michigan: Kregel Publications, 2004), Psalm 60:4.

[330] Jennings, A. C., and W. H. Lowe. *The Psalms, with Introductions and Critical Notes* (Second Edition, Vol. 1). (London: Macmillan and Co., 1884), 283.

[331] Spurgeon, C. H. *The Treasury of David.* (Grand Rapids, Michigan: Kregel Publications, 2004), Psalm 60.

[332] Ibid., Psalm 60:3.

[333] Harman, A. *Psalms: A Mentor Commentary (Vol. 1–2).* (Ross-shire, Great Britain: Mentor, 2011), 447.

[334] Boice, J. M. *Psalms 42–106: An Expositional Commentary.* (Grand Rapids, MI: Baker Books, 2005), 496.

[335] Ibid.

[336] Spurgeon, C. H. *The Treasury of David.* (Grand Rapids, Michigan: Kregel Publications, 2004), Psalm 60:4.

[337] Henry, M. *Matthew Henry's Commentary on the Whole Bible: Complete and Unabridged in One Volume.* (Peabody: Hendrickson, 1994), 828.

[338] Gill, John. *The John Gill Exposition of the Entire Bible,* Psalm 60:4.

[339] Spurgeon, C. H. "Our Banner" (Sermon # 2979), *Metropolitan Tabernacle Pulpit,* 1863.

[340] Ibid.

[341] Jennings, A. C., and W. H. Lowe. *The Psalms, with Introductions and Critical Notes* (Second Edition, Vol. 1). (London: Macmillan and Co., 1884), 286.

342 Spence-Jones, H. D. M. (Ed.). *Psalms,* (Vol. 2). (London; New York: Funk & Wagnalls Company, 1909), 17.

343 Barnes' Notes on the Bible, Psalm 61:2.

344 Jennings, A. C., and W. H. Lowe. *The Psalms, with Introductions and Critical Notes* (Second Edition, Vol. 1). (London: Macmillan and Co., 1884), 286–287.

345 Spurgeon, C. H. *Psalms.* (Wheaton, IL: Crossway Books, 1993), 247.

346 Plumer, W. S. *Studies in the Book of Psalms: Being a Critical and Expository Commentary, with Doctrinal and Practical Remarks on the Entire Psalter.* (Philadelphia; Edinburgh: J. B. Lippincott Company; A & C Black, 1872), 620.

347 Henry, M. *Matthew Henry's Commentary on the Whole Bible: Complete and Unabridged in One Volume.* (Peabody: Hendrickson, 1994), 829.

348 https://biblehub.com/commentaries/poole/psalms/61.htm, accessed September 29, 2018.

349 Gill, John. *The John Gill Exposition of the Entire Bible,* Psalm 61:2.

350 Barnes, Albert. Notes on the Psalms, Critical, Explanatory and Practical. (New York: Harper & Brothers, 1868), Psalm 61:4.

351 Benson, Joseph. *The Holy Bible With Notes, Critical, Explanatory and Practical.* (London: J. Kershaw, 1825), Psalm 61:4.

352 The NET Bible Notes Bible, First Edition Notes. (Richardson, TX: Biblical Studies Press, 2006), Psalm 61:4.

353 Jennings, A. C., and W. H. Lowe. *The Psalms, with Introductions and Critical Notes* (Second Edition, Vol. 1). (London: Macmillan and Co., 1884), 287.

354 Ibid., 286.

355 Harman, A. *Psalms: A Mentor Commentary (Vol. 1–2).* (Ross-shire, Great Britain: Mentor, 2011), 452.

356 Exell, Joseph S. Ed. *The Biblical Illustrator,* Psalm 61:2.

357 Spurgeon, C. H. *The Treasury of David.* (Grand Rapids, Michigan: Kregel Publications, 2004), Psalm 61:1.

358 Exell, Joseph S. Ed. *The Biblical Illustrator,* Psalm 61.

359 Spurgeon, C. H. "The High Rock" (Sermon # 2728). *New Park Street Chapel,* 1859. https://www.spurgeongems.org/vols46-48/chs2728.pdf, accessed September 29, 2018.

360 Harman, A. *Psalms: A Mentor Commentary (Vol. 1–2).* (Ross-shire, Great Britain: Mentor, 2011), 453.

361 Bratcher, R. G. and W. D. Reyburn. *A Translator's Handbook on the Book of Psalms.* (New York: United Bible Societies, 1991), 542.

362 Spurgeon, C. H. *The Treasury of David.* (Grand Rapids, Michigan: Kregel Publications, 2004), Psalm 62:5.

363 Barnes, Albert. Notes on the Psalms, Critical, Explanatory and Practical. (New York: Harper & Brothers, 1868), Psalm 62:5.

[364] Plumer, W. S. *Studies in the Book of Psalms: Being a Critical and Expository Commentary, with Doctrinal and Practical Remarks on the Entire Psalter.* (Philadelphia; Edinburgh: J. B. Lippincott Company; A & C Black, 1872), 625.
[365] Harman, A. *Psalms: A Mentor Commentary (Vol. 1–2).* (Ross-shire, Great Britain: Mentor, 2011), 459.
[366] Bratcher, R. G. and W. D. Reyburn. *A Translator's Handbook on the Book of Psalms.* (New York: United Bible Societies, 1991), 116.
[367] Gill, John. *The John Gill Exposition of the Entire Bible,* Psalm 62:5.
[368] Clarke, Adam. *Clarkes' Commentary and Critical Notes*, Psalm 62 (Introduction).
[369] Henry, M. *Matthew Henry's Commentary on the Whole Bible: Complete and Unabridged in One Volume.* (Peabody: Hendrickson, 1994), 830.
[370] Ibid.
[371] Kirkpatrick, A. F. (Ed.). *The Cambridge Bible for Schools and Colleges,* Psalms. (Cambridge: Cambridge University Press, 1914), Psalm 62:1.
[372] Dilday, R. H., Jr., and J. H. Kennedy. The Teacher's Bible Commentary, Psalms, (Paschall, H. F. and H. H. Hobbs, Eds.) (Nashville: Broadman and Holman Publishers, 1972), 318.
[373] Spurgeon, C. H. *Psalms.* (Wheaton, IL: Crossway Books, 1993), 252.
[374] Maclaren, Alexander. *Expositions of Holy Scripture, vol. 3: The Psalms, Isaiah 1–48.* (Grand Rapids, MI: Eerdmans, 1959), Psalm 62:1, 5.
[375] Plumer, W. S. *Studies in the Book of Psalms: Being a Critical and Expository Commentary, with Doctrinal and Practical Remarks on the Entire Psalter.* (Philadelphia; Edinburgh: J. B. Lippincott Company; A & C Black, 1872), 628.
[376] *The Spurgeon Study Bible.* (Nashville: Holman Bible Publishers, 2017), 740.
[377] Chambers, Oswald. *My Utmost For His Highest,* October 11 and *If You Will Ask,* Chapter 5.
[378] Wiersbe, W. W. *With the Word Bible Commentary.* (Nashville: Thomas Nelson, 1991), Ps. 37:1.
[379] Spurgeon, C. H. *Morning and Evening,* February 28 (Morning).
[380] Barnes, Albert. Notes on the Psalms, Critical, Explanatory and Practical. (New York: Harper & Brothers, 1868), Psalm 63:8.
[381] https://biblehub.com/commentaries/poole/psalms/63.htm, accessed November 20, 2018.
[382] Barnes, Albert. Notes on the Psalms, Critical, Explanatory and Practical. (New York: Harper & Brothers, 1868), Psalm 63:8.
[383] Harman, A. *Psalms: A Mentor Commentary (Vol. 1–2).* (Ross-shire, Great Britain: Mentor, 2011), 464.
[384] Henry, M. *Matthew Henry's Commentary on the Whole Bible: Complete and Unabridged in One Volume.* (Peabody: Hendrickson, 1994), 831.

385 Franz, Gordon. "Psalm 63: Longing to Worship the LORD While in the Wilderness," June 10, 2011. http://www.biblearchaeology.org/post/2011/06/10/Psalm-63-Longing-to-Worship-the-LORD-While-in-the-Wilderness.aspx, accessed November 20, 2018.

386 Barnes, Albert. Notes on the Psalms, Critical, Explanatory and Practical. (New York: Harper & Brothers, 1868), Psalm 63 (Introduction).

387 Ibid., Psalm 63:8.

388 Ibid.

389 Henry, M. *Matthew Henry's Commentary on the Whole Bible: Complete and Unabridged in One Volume.* (Peabody: Hendrickson, 1994), 832.

390 Plumer, W. S. *Studies in the Book of Psalms: Being a Critical and Expository Commentary, with Doctrinal and Practical Remarks on the Entire Psalter.* (Philadelphia; Edinburgh: J. B. Lippincott Company; A & C Black, 1872), 632.

391 Ibid.

392 Ibid.

393 Ibid.

394 Wiersbe, Warren. *The Best of A. W. Tozer.* (Grand Rapids: Baker Book House, 1978), 15–16.

395 Plumer, W. S. *Studies in the Book of Psalms: Being a Critical and Expository Commentary, with Doctrinal and Practical Remarks on the Entire Psalter.* (Philadelphia; Edinburgh: J. B. Lippincott Company; A & C Black, 1872), 634.

396 Ibid.

397 Kirkpatrick, A. F. (Ed.). *The Cambridge Bible for Schools and Colleges,* 2 Samuel. (Cambridge: Cambridge University Press, 1914), 2 Samuel 5:17.

398 Cowman, L. B. *Streams in the Desert,* (Grand Rapids: Zondervan, 1999), January 21.

399 Henry, M. *Matthew Henry's Commentary on the Whole Bible: Complete and Unabridged in One Volume.* (Peabody: Hendrickson, 1994), 832.

400 Wiersbe, Warren. *The Best of A. W. Tozer.* (Grand Rapids: Baker Book House, 1978), 17.

401 Plumer, W. S. *Studies in the Book of Psalms: Being a Critical and Expository Commentary, with Doctrinal and Practical Remarks on the Entire Psalter.* (Philadelphia; Edinburgh: J. B. Lippincott Company; A & C Black, 1872), 636.

402 Barnes, Albert. Notes on the Psalms, Critical, Explanatory and Practical. (New York: Harper & Brothers, 1868), Psalm 64:3.

403 Spurgeon, C. H. *Psalms.* (Wheaton, IL: Crossway Books, 1993), 259.

404 Jamieson, R., A. R. Fausset, & D. Brown. *Commentary Critical and Explanatory on the Whole Bible* (Vol. 1). (Oak Harbor, WA: Logos Research Systems, Inc., 1997), Psalm 64:3.

405 Clarke, Adam. *Clarkes' Commentary and Critical Notes,* Psalm 64:3.

Exposition of the Psalms

[406] Bratcher, R. G. and W. D. Reyburn. *A Translator's Handbook on the Book of Psalms.* (New York: United Bible Societies, 1991), 553.

[407] Kirkpatrick, A. F. (Ed.). *The Cambridge Bible for Schools and Colleges,* Psalms. (Cambridge: Cambridge University Press, 1914), Psalm 64:4.

[408] Spence-Jones, H. D. M. (Ed.). *Psalms,* (Vol. 2). (London; New York: Funk & Wagnalls Company, 1909), 26.

[409] Barnes, Albert. Notes on the Psalms, Critical, Explanatory and Practical. (New York: Harper & Brothers, 1868), Psalm 64:4.

[410] Bratcher, R. G. and W. D. Reyburn. *A Translator's Handbook on the Book of Psalms.* (New York: United Bible Societies, 1991), 553.

[411] Spurgeon, C. H. *Psalms.* (Wheaton, IL: Crossway Books, 1993), 259.

[412] Plumer, W. S. *Studies in the Book of Psalms: Being a Critical and Expository Commentary, with Doctrinal and Practical Remarks on the Entire Psalter.* (Philadelphia; Edinburgh: J. B. Lippincott Company; A & C Black, 1872), 637.

[413] Dilday, R. H., Jr., and J. H. Kennedy. The Teacher's Bible Commentary, Psalms, (Paschall, H. F. and H. H. Hobbs, Eds.) (Nashville: Broadman and Holman Publishers, 1972), 319.

[414] Bratcher, R. G. and W. D. Reyburn. *A Translator's Handbook on the Book of Psalms.* (New York: United Bible Societies, 1991), 553.

[415] https://biblehub.com/commentaries/ellicott/psalms/64.htm, accessed May 25, 2018.

[416] Kirkpatrick, A. F. (Ed.). *The Cambridge Bible for Schools and Colleges,* Psalms. (Cambridge: Cambridge University Press, 1914), Psalm 64:5.

[417] Spence-Jones, H. D. M. (Ed.). *Psalms,* (Vol. 2). (London; New York: Funk & Wagnalls Company, 1909), 26.

[418] https://biblehub.com/commentaries/ellicott/psalms/64.htm, accessed May 25, 2018.

[419] Kirkpatrick, A. F. (Ed.). *The Cambridge Bible for Schools and Colleges,* Psalms. (Cambridge: Cambridge University Press, 1914), Psalm 64:5.

[420] Bratcher, R. G. and W. D. Reyburn. *A Translator's Handbook on the Book of Psalms.* (New York: United Bible Societies, 1991), 554.

[421] Barnes, Albert. Notes on the Psalms, Critical, Explanatory and Practical. (New York: Harper & Brothers, 1868), Psalm 64:6.

[422] Kirkpatrick, A. F. (Ed.). *The Cambridge Bible for Schools and Colleges,* Psalms. (Cambridge: Cambridge University Press, 1914), Psalm 64:6.

[423] Clarke, Adam. *Clarkes' Commentary and Critical Notes*, Psalm 64:6.

[424] Barnes, Albert. Notes on the Psalms, Critical, Explanatory and Practical. (New York: Harper & Brothers, 1868), Psalm 64:6.

[425] Plumer, W. S. *Studies in the Book of Psalms: Being a Critical and Expository Commentary, with Doctrinal and Practical Remarks on the Entire Psalter.* (Philadelphia; Edinburgh: J. B. Lippincott Company; A & C Black, 1872), 637.

[426] Bratcher, R. G. and W. D. Reyburn. *A Translator's Handbook on the Book of Psalms.* (New York: United Bible Societies, 1991), 554.

[427] Barnes, Albert. Notes on the Psalms, Critical, Explanatory and Practical. (New York: Harper & Brothers, 1868), Psalm 64:7.

[428] Plumer, W. S. *Studies in the Book of Psalms: Being a Critical and Expository Commentary, with Doctrinal and Practical Remarks on the Entire Psalter.* (Philadelphia; Edinburgh: J. B. Lippincott Company; A & C Black, 1872), 637.

[429] Clarke, Adam. *Clarkes' Commentary and Critical Notes*, Psalm 64:7.

[430] Jennings, A. C., and W. H. Lowe. *The Psalms, with Introductions and Critical Notes* (Second Edition, Vol. 1). (London: Macmillan and Co., 1884), 296.

[431] Clarke, Adam. *Clarkes' Commentary and Critical Notes*, Psalm 64 (Introductin).

[432] Plumer, W. S. *Studies in the Book of Psalms: Being a Critical and Expository Commentary, with Doctrinal and Practical Remarks on the Entire Psalter.* (Philadelphia; Edinburgh: J. B. Lippincott Company; A & C Black, 1872), 636.

[433] Spurgeon, C. H. *Spurgeon's Gems.* (New York: Sheldon and Co., 1859), 155.

[434] Moody, D. L. *The D. L. Moody Book: A Living Daily Message from the Words of D. L. Moody.* (Chicago: Fleming H. Revell Company, 1900), 205–206.

[435] Baggarly, H. M. *Tulia Herald.* Tulia, Texas, Feb. 4, 1954.

[436] Allen, Kerry James, Ed., *Exploring the Mind and Heart of the Prince of Preachers.* (Oswego, IL: Fox River Press, 2005), 450.

[437] Moody, D. L. *The D. L. Moody Book: A Living Daily Message from the Words of D. L. Moody.* (Chicago: Fleming H. Revell Company, 1900), 205-206.

[438] John MacArthur. "The Blasphemous Sin of Defaming Others," Part 2, http://www.gty.org/resources/sermons/59-27, accessed August 2, 2014.

[439] Swindoll, Chuck. Job: A Man of Heroic Endurance. (Nashville: WPublishing Group, 2004), 179.

[440] Spurgeon, C. H. *The Treasury of David.* (Grand Rapids, Michigan: Kregel Publications, 2004), Psalm 7:1.

[441] Barnes, Albert. Notes on the Psalms, Critical, Explanatory and Practical. (New York: Harper & Brothers, 1868), Psalm 65:2.

[442] Spence-Jones, H. D. M. (Ed.). *Psalms,* (Vol. 2). (London; New York: Funk & Wagnalls Company, 1909), 29.

[443] https://biblehub.com/commentaries/poole/psalms/65.htm, accessed May 25, 2018.

[444] Barnes, Albert. Notes on the Psalms, Critical, Explanatory and Practical. (New York: Harper & Brothers, 1868), Psalm 65:2.

445 Plumer, W. S. *Studies in the Book of Psalms: Being a Critical and Expository Commentary, with Doctrinal and Practical Remarks on the Entire Psalter.* (Philadelphia; Edinburgh: J. B. Lippincott Company; A & C Black, 1872), 641.
446 Kirkpatrick, A. F. (Ed.). *The Cambridge Bible for Schools and Colleges,* Psalms. (Cambridge: Cambridge University Press, 1914), Psalm 65:2.
447 Spurgeon, C. H. *Psalms.* (Wheaton, IL: Crossway Books, 1993), 262.
448 Gill, John. *The John Gill Exposition of the Entire Bible,* Psalm 65:2.
449 https://www.crosswalk.com/faith/spiritual-life/inspiring-quotes/31-prayer-quotes-be-inspired-and-encouraged.html, accessed May 25, 2018.
450 Barnes, Albert. Notes on the Psalms, Critical, Explanatory and Practical. (New York: Harper & Brothers, 1868), Psalm 65:2.
451 Spurgeon, C. H. *Psalms.* (Wheaton, IL: Crossway Books, 1993), 262.
452 VanGemeren, Willem A. *The Expositor's Bible Commentary,* Psalms. (Grand Rapids: Zondervan, 1991), Psalm 65:3.
453 Spurgeon, C. H. *Psalms.* (Wheaton, IL: Crossway Books, 1993), 263.
454 Barnes, Albert. Notes on the Psalms, Critical, Explanatory and Practical. (New York: Harper & Brothers, 1868), Psalm 65:5.
455 https://www.azquotes.com/quote/544914, accessed May 25, 2018.
456 Plumer, W. S. *Studies in the Book of Psalms: Being a Critical and Expository Commentary, with Doctrinal and Practical Remarks on the Entire Psalter.* (Philadelphia; Edinburgh: J. B. Lippincott Company; A & C Black, 1872), 646.
457 Cowman, L. B. *Streams in the Desert,* (Grand Rapids: Zondervan, 1999), January 24.
458 Truett, George W. *A Quest For Souls.* (New York: Harper & Brothers Publishers, 1917), 7.
459 Spurgeon, C. H. "Crowning Blessings Ascribed to God" (Sermon #1475), May 18, 1879.
460 Barnes, Albert. Notes on the Psalms, Critical, Explanatory and Practical. (New York: Harper & Brothers, 1868), Psalm 66:16.
461 Harman, A. *Psalms: A Mentor Commentary (Vol. 1–2).* (Ross-shire, Great Britain: Mentor, 2011), 485.
462 Ibid.
463 Alexander, J. A. *The Psalms Translated and Explained.* (Edinburgh: Andrew Elliot; James Thin, 1864), 278.
464 Jennings, A. C., and W. H. Lowe. *The Psalms, with Introductions and Critical Notes* (Second Edition, Vol. 1). (London: Macmillan and Co., 1884), 305.
465 Harman, A. *Psalms: A Mentor Commentary (Vol. 1–2).* (Ross-shire, Great Britain: Mentor, 2011), 481.
466 Henry, M. *Matthew Henry's Commentary on the Whole Bible: Complete and Unabridged in One Volume.* (Peabody: Hendrickson, 1994), 836.

[467] Plumer, W. S. *Studies in the Book of Psalms: Being a Critical and Expository Commentary, with Doctrinal and Practical Remarks on the Entire Psalter.* (Philadelphia; Edinburgh: J. B. Lippincott Company; A & C Black, 1872), 654–655.

[468] Harman, A. *Psalms: A Mentor Commentary (Vol. 1–2).* (Ross-shire, Great Britain: Mentor, 2011), 485.

[469] Barnes, Albert. Notes on the Psalms, Critical, Explanatory and Practical. (New York: Harper & Brothers, 1868), Psalms 66:16.

[470] Spurgeon, C. H. *Psalms.* (Wheaton, IL: Crossway Books, 1993), 270.

[471] Exell, Joseph S. Ed. *The Biblical Illustrator,* Psalm 66:16.

[472] Johnston, Thomas P. *The Gift of the Evangelist and Revival.* (unpublished notes), 419.

[473] Cowman, L. B. *Streams in the Desert,* (Grand Rapids: Zondervan, 1999), Feburary 6.

[474] Ibid., March 24.

[475] Harman, A. *Psalms: A Mentor Commentary (Vol. 1–2).* (Ross-shire, Great Britain: Mentor, 2011), 486.

[476] Swanson, J. *Dictionary of Biblical Languages with Semantic Domains: Hebrew (Old Testament)* (electronic ed.). (Oak Harbor: Logos Research Systems, Inc., 1997).

[477] Barnes, Albert. Notes on the Psalms, Critical, Explanatory and Practical. (New York: Harper & Brothers, 1868), Psalm 66:18.

[478] Ibid.

[479] Henry, M. *Matthew Henry's Commentary on the Whole Bible: Complete and Unabridged in One Volume.* (Peabody: Hendrickson, 1994), 837.

[480] Clarke, Adam. *Clarkes' Commentary and Critical Notes*, Psalm 66:18.

[481] Horne, G. *A Commentary on the Book of Psalms.* (New York: Robert Carter & Brothers, 1856), 226.

[482] Chambers, Oswald. *My Utmost For His Highest,* August 24.

[483] Clarke, Adam. *Clarkes' Commentary and Critical Notes*, Psalm 66:19.

[484] Plumer, W. S. *Studies in the Book of Psalms: Being a Critical and Expository Commentary, with Doctrinal and Practical Remarks on the Entire Psalter.* (Philadelphia; Edinburgh: J. B. Lippincott Company; A & C Black, 1872), 653.

[485] Alexander, J. A. *The Psalms Translated and Explained.* (Edinburgh: Andrew Elliot; James Thin, 1864), 281.

[486] Spurgeon, C. H. *Psalms.* (Wheaton, IL: Crossway Books, 1993), 271.

[487] Ibid.

[488] Tate, M. E. *Psalms 51–100 (Vol. 20).* (Dallas: Word, Incorporated, 1998), 157.

[489] Ibid.

[490] Bratcher, R. G. and W. D. Reyburn. *A Translator's Handbook on the Book of Psalms.* (New York: United Bible Societies, 1991), 297.

[491] Tate, M. E. *Psalms 51–100 (Vol. 20).* (Dallas: Word, Incorporated, 1998), 157.

[492] Ibid.

[493] Alexander, J. A. *The Psalms Translated and Explained.* (Edinburgh: Andrew Elliot; James Thin, 1864), 282.

[494] Tate, M. E. *Psalms 51–100 (Vol. 20).* (Dallas: Word, Incorporated, 1998), 157.

[495] Clarke, Adam. *Clarkes' Commentary and Critical Notes,* Psalm 67:2.

[496] Ibid.

[497] Clarke, Adam. *Clarkes' Commentary and Critical Notes,* Psalm 67 (Introduction).

[498] Jennings, A. C., and W. H. Lowe. *The Psalms, with Introductions and Critical Notes* (Second Edition, Vol. 1). (London: Macmillan and Co., 1884), 308–309.

[499] Spurgeon, C. H. *The Treasury of David.* (Grand Rapids, Michigan: Kregel Publications, 2004), Psalm 67:3.

[500] Henry, Matthew. *Matthew Henry's Concise Bible Commentary,* Psalm 67:1.

[501] https://djameskennedy.org/devotional-detail/20150225-a-checklist-for-your-prayer-life, accessed May 9, 2017.

[502] Ryle, J. C. "A Call to Prayer," www.gracegems.org, accessed May 9, 2017.

[503] https://www.crosswalk.com/faith/spiritual-life/inspiring-quotes/31-prayer-quotes-be-inspired-and-encouraged.html, accessed May 26, 2018.

[504] https://wmpl.org/quote/, accessed May 26, 2018.

[505] Ironside, H. A. *Studies on Book One of the Psalms.* (Neptune, NJ: Loizeaux Brothers, 1952), Psalm 2.

[506] Ibid.

[507] https://wmpl.org/quote/, accessed May 26, 2018.

[508] https://wmpl.org/quote/without-prayer-even/, accessed May 26, 2018.

[509] Plumer, W. S. *Studies in the Book of Psalms: Being a Critical and Expository Commentary, with Doctrinal and Practical Remarks on the Entire Psalter.* (Philadelphia; Edinburgh: J. B. Lippincott Company; A & C Black, 1872), 662.

[510] Alexander, J. A. *The Psalms Translated and Explained.* (Edinburgh: Andrew Elliot; James Thin, 1864), 284.

[511] Barnes, Albert. Notes on the Psalms, Critical, Explanatory and Practical. (New York: Harper & Brothers, 1868), Psalm 68:5.

[512] Kirkpatrick, A. F. (Ed.). *The Cambridge Bible for Schools and Colleges,* Psalms. (Cambridge: Cambridge University Press, 1914), Psalm 68:5.

[513] Plumer, W. S. *Studies in the Book of Psalms: Being a Critical and Expository Commentary, with Doctrinal and Practical Remarks on the Entire Psalter.* (Philadelphia; Edinburgh: J. B. Lippincott Company; A & C Black, 1872), 662.

514 Spence-Jones, H. D. M. (Ed.). *Psalms,* (Vol. 2). (London; New York: Funk & Wagnalls Company, 1909), 43.

515 Jennings, A. C., and W. H. Lowe. *The Psalms, with Introductions and Critical Notes* (Second Edition, Vol. 1). (London: Macmillan and Co., 1884), 312.

516 Harman, A. *Psalms: A Mentor Commentary (Vol. 1–2).* (Ross-shire, Great Britain: Mentor, 2011), 491.

517 Plumer, W. S. *Studies in the Book of Psalms: Being a Critical and Expository Commentary, with Doctrinal and Practical Remarks on the Entire Psalter.* (Philadelphia; Edinburgh: J. B. Lippincott Company; A & C Black, 1872), 660.

518 Ibid.

519 Ibid.

520 Barnes, Albert. Notes on the Psalms, Critical, Explanatory and Practical. (New York: Harper & Brothers, 1868), Psalm 68:5.

521 Henry, M. *Matthew Henry's Commentary on the Whole Bible: Complete and Unabridged in One Volume.* (Peabody: Hendrickson, 1994), 1007.

522 Plumer, W. S. *Studies in the Book of Psalms: Being a Critical and Expository Commentary, with Doctrinal and Practical Remarks on the Entire Psalter.* (Philadelphia; Edinburgh: J. B. Lippincott Company; A & C Black, 1872), 670.

523 Ibid.

524 Henry, M. *Matthew Henry's Commentary on the Whole Bible: Complete and Unabridged in One Volume.* (Peabody: Hendrickson, 1994), 838.

525 Gill, John. *The John Gill Exposition of the Entire Bible,* Psalm 68:5.

526 Ibid., Psalm 69:4.

527 Ibid.

528 Ibid.

529 Henry, M. *Matthew Henry's Commentary on the Whole Bible: Complete and Unabridged in One Volume.* (Peabody: Hendrickson, 1994), 841.

530 Spurgeon, C. H. *Psalms.* (Wheaton, IL: Crossway Books, 1993), 286.

531 Benson, Joseph. *The Holy Bible With Notes, Critical, Explanatory and Practical.* (London: J. Kershaw, 1825), Psalm 69:21.

532 Barnes, Albert. Notes on the Psalms, Critical, Explanatory and Practical. (New York: Harper & Brothers, 1868), Psalm 69:21.

533 Vincent's Word Studies, Romans 11:9.

534 Wesley's Explanatory Notes, Romans 11:9-10.

535 Expository Notes with Practical Observations on the New Testament, Romans 11:9–10.

536 Gill, John. *The John Gill Exposition of the Entire Bible,* Acts 1:20.

537 Harman, A. *Psalms: A Mentor Commentary (Vol. 1–2).* (Ross-shire, Great Britain: Mentor, 2011), 505.

---

[538] Boice, J. M. *Psalms 42–106: An Expositional Commentary*. (Grand Rapids, MI: Baker Books, 2005), 569.

[539] Ibid.

[540] Gaebelein's Annotated Bible, Psalm 69.

[541] Boice, J. M. *Psalms 42–106: An Expositional Commentary*. (Grand Rapids, MI: Baker Books, 2005), 569.

[542] Spurgeon, C. H. *The Treasury of David*. (Grand Rapids, Michigan: Kregel Publications, 2004), Psalm 70:1.

[543] Ibid.

[544] VanGemeren, Willem A. *The Expositor's Bible Commentary,* Psalms. (Grand Rapids: Zondervan, 1991), Psalm 70:1–5.

[545] Spurgeon, C. H. *Psalms*. (Wheaton, IL: Crossway Books, 1993), 294.

[546] Bratcher, R. G. and W. D. Reyburn. *A Translator's Handbook on the Book of Psalms*. (New York: United Bible Societies, 1991), 608.

[547] Ibid.

[548] Spurgeon, C. H. *Psalms*. (Wheaton, IL: Crossway Books, 1993), 294.

[549] Ross, A. P. In Walvoord, J. F. and R. B. Zuck (Eds.). *The Bible Knowledge Commentary: An Exposition of the Scriptures* (Vol. 1, Psalms). (Wheaton, IL: Victor Books, 1985), 845.

[550] Spurgeon, C. H. *Psalms*. (Wheaton, IL: Crossway Books, 1993), 294.

[551] Bratcher, R. G. and W. D. Reyburn. *A Translator's Handbook on the Book of Psalms*. (New York: United Bible Societies, 1991), 609.

[552] *Merriam-Webster's Collegiate Dictionary* (10th ed.). (Springfield, MA: Merriam-Webster, 1996).

[553] Spurgeon, C. H. *Psalms*. (Wheaton, IL: Crossway Books, 1993), 294.

[554] Henry, M. *Matthew Henry's Commentary on the Whole Bible: Complete and Unabridged in One Volume*. (Peabody: Hendrickson, 1994), 844.

[555] Ross, A. P. In Walvoord, J. F. and R. B. Zuck (Eds.). *The Bible Knowledge Commentary: An Exposition of the Scriptures* (Vol. 1, Psalms). (Wheaton, IL: Victor Books, 1985), 822.

[556] Spence-Jones, H. D. M. (Ed.). *Psalms,* (Vol. 2). (London; New York: Funk & Wagnalls Company, 1909), 58.

[557] Craigie, P. C. *Psalms 1–50*, (Vol. 19). (Dallas: Word, Incorporated, 1998), 303.

[558] Exell, Joseph S. Ed. *The Biblical Illustrator,* Psalm 70.

[559] Hunter, William. "The Great Physician" (hymn).

[560] Scaer, David P. "The Concept of *Anfechtung* in Luther's Thought." *Concordia Theological Quarterly,* Vol. 47, No. 1, January, 1983.

[561] Collver, Albert B. "A Mighty Fortress," October 1, 2015. https://lutheranreformation.org/history/a-mighty-fortress/, accessed May 27, 2018.

[562] Hastings, James. *The Great Texts of the Bible: Job to Psalm 23.* (New York: Charles Scribner's Sons, 1913), 122.

[563] Cowman, L. B. *Streams in the Desert,* (Grand Rapids: Zondervan, 1999), January 21.

[564] Bratcher, R. G. and W. D. Reyburn. *A Translator's Handbook on the Book of Psalms.* (New York: United Bible Societies, 1991), 613.

[565] Ibid.

[566] Harman, A. *Psalms: A Mentor Commentary (Vol. 1–2).* (Ross-shire, Great Britain: Mentor, 2011), 521.

[567] Alexander, J. A. *The Psalms Translated and Explained.* (Edinburgh: Andrew Elliot; James Thin, 1864), 9.

[568] Spurgeon C. H., "God's Innumerable Mercies" (Sermon #3022), October 22, 1868.

[569] Plumer, W. S. *Studies in the Book of Psalms: Being a Critical and Expository Commentary, with Doctrinal and Practical Remarks on the Entire Psalter.* (Philadelphia; Edinburgh: J. B. Lippincott Company; A & C Black, 1872), 692.

[570] Spurgeon, C. H. *The Treasury of David.* (Grand Rapids, Michigan: Kregel Publications, 2004), Psalm 71:9.

[571] Barnes, Albert. Notes on the Psalms, Critical, Explanatory and Practical. (New York: Harper & Brothers, 1868), Psalm 71:9.

[572] Taken from the author's book *Aging Honorably and Happily,* 2017.

[573] Spurgeon, C. H. "The Remembrance of Christ," (sermon), January 7, 1855. http://www.spurgeon.org/sermons/0002.php, accessed February 6, 2017.

[574] Spurgeon, C. H. *Morning and Evening,* November 17 (Evening).

[575] https://www.christianquotes.info/top-quotes/22-motivating-quotes-about-prayer/#axzz4XwcXBYxu, accessed February 6, 2017.

[576] Ibid.

[577] Spurgeon, C. H. "The God of the Aged" (sermon # 81). May 25, 1856 at the New Park Street Chapel, Southwark.

[578] Barnes, Albert. Notes on the Psalms, Critical, Explanatory and Practical. (New York: Harper & Brothers, 1868), Psalm 72:1.

[579] Spurgeon, C. H. *Psalms.* (Wheaton, IL: Crossway Books, 1993), 301.

[580] Spence-Jones, H. D. M. (Ed.). *Psalms,* (Vol. 2). (London; New York: Funk & Wagnalls Company, 1909), 65.

[581] Spurgeon, C. H. *Psalms.* (Wheaton, IL: Crossway Books, 1993), 302.

[582] Cited in Josh McDowell, *Evidence for Christianity,* 205. Bracket added by author.

[583] Spence-Jones, H. D. M. (Ed.). *Psalms,* (Vol. 2). (London; New York: Funk & Wagnalls Company, 1909), 66.

584 Barnes, Albert. Notes on the Psalms, Critical, Explanatory and Practical. (New York: Harper & Brothers, 1868), Psalm 72:15.
585 Ibid.
586 Ibid.
587 Spurgeon, C. H. *Psalms.* (Wheaton, IL: Crossway Books, 1993), 304.
588 Gill, John. *The John Gill Exposition of the Entire Bible,* Psalm 72:15.
589 Barnes, Albert. Notes on the Psalms, Critical, Explanatory and Practical. (New York: Harper & Brothers, 1868), Psalm 72:15.
590 Benson, Joseph. *The Holy Bible With Notes, Critical, Explanatory and Practical.* (London: J. Kershaw, 1825), Psalm 72:17.
591 Spurgeon, C. H. *Psalms.* (Wheaton, IL: Crossway Books, 1993), 305.
592 Benson, Joseph. *The Holy Bible With Notes, Critical, Explanatory and Practical.* (London: J. Kershaw, 1825), Psalm 72:17,
593 Carroll, B. H. *An Interpretation of the English Bible: The Poetical Books of the Bible.* (Nashville: Broadman Press, 1948), 121.
594 Henry, Matthew. *Matthew Henry's Concise Bible Commentary,* Psalm 72.
595 Barnes, Albert. Notes on the Psalms, Critical, Explanatory and Practical. (New York: Harper & Brothers, 1868), Psalm 72:1.
596 Spurgeon, C. H. *The Treasury of David.* (Grand Rapids, Michigan: Kregel Publications, 2004), Psalm 72:4.
597 Alexander, J. A. *The Psalms Translated and Explained.* (Edinburgh: Andrew Elliot; James Thin, 1864), 302.
598 Henry, M. *Matthew Henry's Commentary on the Whole Bible: Complete and Unabridged in One Volume.* (Peabody: Hendrickson, 1994), 847.
599 Henry, Matthew. *Matthew Henry's Concise Bible Commentary,* Psalm 72:18–20.
600 Barnes, Albert. Notes on the Psalms, Critical, Explanatory and Practical. (New York: Harper & Brothers, 1868), Psalm 72:15.
601 Clarke, Adam. *Clarkes' Commentary and Critical Notes*, Psalm 72:20.
602 Gill, John. *The John Gill Exposition of the Entire Bible,* Psalm 72:20.
603 Perowne, J. J. S. *The Book of Psalms; A New Translation, with Introductions and Notes, Explanatory and Critical* (Fifth Edition, Revised, Vol. 1). (London; Cambridge: George Bell and Sons; Deighton Bell and Co., 1883), 594.
604 Henry, Matthew. *Matthew Henry's Concise Bible Commentary,* Psalm 72:2–17.
605 Bratcher, R. G. and W. D. Reyburn. *A Translator's Handbook on the Book of Psalms.* (New York: United Bible Societies, 1991), 633.
606 Plumer, W. S. *Studies in the Book of Psalms: Being a Critical and Expository Commentary, with Doctrinal and Practical Remarks on the Entire Psalter.* (Philadelphia; Edinburgh: J. B. Lippincott Company; A & C Black, 1872), 709.

[607] Ibid.

[608] Clarke, Adam. *Clarkes' Commentary and Critical Notes*, Psalm 73:3.

[609] Barnes, Albert. Notes on the Psalms, Critical, Explanatory and Practical. (New York: Harper & Brothers, 1868), Psalm 73:4.

[610] Spurgeon, C. H. *Psalms.* (Wheaton, IL: Crossway Books, 1993), 306–307.

[611] Barnes, Albert. Notes on the Psalms, Critical, Explanatory and Practical. (New York: Harper & Brothers, 1868), Psalm 73:5.

[612] Benson, Joseph. *The Holy Bible With Notes, Critical, Explanatory and Practical.* (London: J. Kershaw, 1825), Psalm 73:5.

[613] Spence-Jones, H. D. M. (Ed.). *Psalms,* (Vol. 2). (London; New York: Funk & Wagnalls Company, 1909), 71.

[614] Benson, Joseph. *The Holy Bible With Notes, Critical, Explanatory and Practical.* (London: J. Kershaw, 1825), Psalm 73:18.

[615] Spence-Jones, H. D. M. (Ed.). *Psalms,* (Vol. 2). (London; New York: Funk & Wagnalls Company, 1909), 72.

[616] Barnes, Albert. Notes on the Psalms, Critical, Explanatory and Practical. (New York: Harper & Brothers, 1868), Psalm 73:19.

[617] Alexander, J. A. *The Psalms Translated and Explained.* (Edinburgh: Andrew Elliot; James Thin, 1864), 306–307.

[618] Exell, Joseph S. Ed. *The Biblical Illustrator,* Psalm 73.

[619] Boice, J. M. *Psalms 42–106: An Expositional Commentary.* (Grand Rapids, MI: Baker Books, 2005), 612.

[620] Jennings, A. C., and W. H. Lowe. *The Psalms, with Introductions and Critical Notes* (Second Edition, Vol. 2). (London: Macmillan and Co., 1884), 1.

[621] Hamilton, William W. *Sermons on the Books of the Bible,* (Vol. 3), 258.

[622] Henry, M. *Matthew Henry's Commentary on the Whole Bible: Complete and Unabridged in One Volume.* (Peabody: Hendrickson, 1994), 847.

[623] Watkinson, William L. *Mistaken Signs.* (London: T. Woolmer, 1882), 66.

[624] Maclaren, Alexander. *Expositions of Holy Scripture, vol. 3: The Psalms, Isaiah 1–48.* (Grand Rapids, MI: Eerdmans, 1959), Deuteronomy 33:25.

[625] Spence-Jones, H. D. M. (Ed.). *Psalms,* (Vol. 2). (London; New York: Funk & Wagnalls Company, 1909), 77.

[626] Bratcher, R. G. and W. D. Reyburn. *A Translator's Handbook on the Book of Psalms.* (New York: United Bible Societies, 1991), 647.

[627] Kirkpatrick, A. F. (Ed.). *The Cambridge Bible for Schools and Colleges,* Psalms. (Cambridge: Cambridge University Press, 1914), Psalm 74:1.

[628] Bratcher, R. G. and W. D. Reyburn. *A Translator's Handbook on the Book of Psalms.* (New York: United Bible Societies, 1991), 647.

[629] Barnes, Albert. Notes on the Psalms, Critical, Explanatory and Practical. (New York: Harper & Brothers, 1868), Psalm 74:2.

[630] Ibid.

[631] Ibid.

[632] https://biblehub.com/commentaries/ellicott/psalms/74.htm, accessed May 29, 2018.

[633] Ibid.

[634] Spence-Jones, H. D. M. (Ed.). *Psalms,* (Vol. 2). (London; New York: Funk & Wagnalls Company, 1909), 82.

[635] Ibid.

[636] Spurgeon, C. H. *Psalms.* (Wheaton, IL: Crossway Books, 1993), 314.

[637] Barnes, Albert. Notes on the Psalms, Critical, Explanatory and Practical. (New York: Harper & Brothers, 1868), Psalm 74:6.

[638] Benson, Joseph. *The Holy Bible With Notes, Critical, Explanatory and Practical.* (London: J. Kershaw, 1825), Psalm 74:7.

[639] Ibid.

[640] https://biblehub.com/commentaries/poole/psalms/74.htm, accessed May 29, 2018.

[641] Spence-Jones, H. D. M. (Ed.). *Psalms,* (Vol. 2). (London; New York: Funk & Wagnalls Company, 1909), 83.

[642] Jamieson, R., A. R. Fausset, & D. Brown. *Commentary Critical and Explanatory on the Whole Bible* (Vol. 1). (Oak Harbor, WA: Logos Research Systems, Inc., 1997), 369.

[643] Spence-Jones, H. D. M. (Ed.). *Psalms,* (Vol. 2). (London; New York: Funk & Wagnalls Company, 1909), 83.

[644] Harman, A. *Psalms: A Mentor Commentary (Vol. 1–2).* (Ross-shire, Great Britain: Mentor, 2011), 559.

[645] Jennings, A. C., and W. H. Lowe. *The Psalms, with Introductions and Critical Notes* (Second Edition, Vol. 2). (London: Macmillan and Co., 1884), 8.

[646] Kirkpatrick, A. F. (Ed.). *The Cambridge Bible for Schools and Colleges,* Psalms. (Cambridge: Cambridge University Press, 1914), Psalm 74 (Introduction).

[647] Harman, A. *Psalms: A Mentor Commentary (Vol. 1–2).* (Ross-shire, Great Britain: Mentor, 2011), 559.

[648] Henry, M. *Matthew Henry's Commentary on the Whole Bible: Complete and Unabridged in One Volume.* (Peabody: Hendrickson, 1994), 850.

[649] Spurgeon, C. H. *Psalms.* (Wheaton, IL: Crossway Books, 1993), 313.

[650] Bratcher, R. G. and W. D. Reyburn. *A Translator's Handbook on the Book of Psalms.* (New York: United Bible Societies, 1991), 658.

[651] Spurgeon, C. H. *Psalms.* (Wheaton, IL: Crossway Books, 1993), 319.

[652] Plumer, W. S. *Studies in the Book of Psalms: Being a Critical and Expository Commentary, with Doctrinal and Practical Remarks on the Entire Psalter.* (Philadelphia; Edinburgh: J. B. Lippincott Company; A & C Black, 1872), 729.

653 Tate, M. E. *Psalms 51–100 (Vol. 20)*. (Dallas: Word, Incorporated, 1998), 256.

654 Spence-Jones, H. D. M. (Ed.). *Psalms,* (Vol. 2). (London; New York: Funk & Wagnalls Company, 1909), 91.

655 Spurgeon, C. H. *Psalms*. (Wheaton, IL: Crossway Books, 1993), 319.

656 Barnes, Albert. Notes on the Psalms, Critical, Explanatory and Practical. (New York: Harper & Brothers, 1868), Psalm 75:1.

657 Spence-Jones, H. D. M. (Ed.). *Psalms,* (Vol. 2). (London; New York: Funk & Wagnalls Company, 1909), 91.

658 Plumer, W. S. *Studies in the Book of Psalms: Being a Critical and Expository Commentary, with Doctrinal and Practical Remarks on the Entire Psalter.* (Philadelphia; Edinburgh: J. B. Lippincott Company; A & C Black, 1872), 729.

659 Alexander, J. A. *The Psalms Translated and Explained.* (Edinburgh: Andrew Elliot; James Thin, 1864), 318.

660 Harman, A. *Psalms: A Mentor Commentary (Vol. 1–2).* (Ross-shire, Great Britain: Mentor, 2011), 567.

661 Plumer, W. S. *Studies in the Book of Psalms: Being a Critical and Expository Commentary, with Doctrinal and Practical Remarks on the Entire Psalter.* (Philadelphia; Edinburgh: J. B. Lippincott Company; A & C Black, 1872), 731.

662 Buttrick, George Arthur, Ed. *The Interpreters Bible* Vol. IV. (Nashville: Abingdon Press, 1952), 401.

663 Coffman's Commentaries on the Bible, Psalms, Psalm 75:1.

664 Halley, Henry H. *Halley's Bible Handbook.* (Grand Rapids: Zondervan, 1965) 244.

665 Jennings, A. C., and W. H. Lowe. *The Psalms, with Introductions and Critical Notes* (Second Edition, Vol. 2). (London: Macmillan and Co., 1884), 21.

666 Harman, A. *Psalms: A Mentor Commentary (Vol. 1–2).* (Ross-shire, Great Britain: Mentor, 2011), 568.

667 Spurgeon, C. H. *The Treasury of David.* (Grand Rapids, Michigan: Kregel Publications, 2004), Psalm 75:1.

668 Hutson, Curtis. *Great Preaching on Thanksgiving.* (Murfreesboro: Sword of the Lord Publishers, 1987), 36.

669 Henry, M. *Matthew Henry's Commentary on the Whole Bible: Complete and Unabridged in One Volume.* (Peabody: Hendrickson, 1994), 852.

670 https://www.crosswalk.com/faith/spiritual-life/inspiring-quotes/30-christian-quotes-about-thankfulness.html, accessed May 29, 2018.

671 Harman, A. *Psalms: A Mentor Commentary (Vol. 1–2).* (Ross-shire, Great Britain: Mentor, 2011), 570.

672 https://www.crosswalk.com/faith/spiritual-life/inspiring-quotes/30-christian-quotes-about-thankfulness.html, accessed May 29, 2018.

[673] Plumer, W. S. *Studies in the Book of Psalms: Being a Critical and Expository Commentary, with Doctrinal and Practical Remarks on the Entire Psalter.* (Philadelphia; Edinburgh: J. B. Lippincott Company; A & C Black, 1872), 729.

[674] Hamilton, William W. *Sermons on the Books of the Bible,* (Vol. 4), 75.

[675] Plumer, W. S. *Studies in the Book of Psalms: Being a Critical and Expository Commentary, with Doctrinal and Practical Remarks on the Entire Psalter.* (Philadelphia; Edinburgh: J. B. Lippincott Company; A & C Black, 1872), 733

[676] Kirkpatrick, A. F. (Ed.). *The Cambridge Bible for Schools and Colleges,* Psalms. (Cambridge: Cambridge University Press, 1914), Psalm 76:1.

[677] Benson Commentary, Psalm 76:1.

[678] Bratcher, R. G. and W. D. Reyburn. *A Translator's Handbook on the Book of Psalms.* (New York: United Bible Societies, 1991), 664.

[679] Spence-Jones, H. D. M. (Ed.). *Psalms,* (Vol. 1). (London; New York: Funk & Wagnalls Company, 1909), 101.

[680] Barnes' Notes on the Bible, Psalm 76:2.

[681] VanGemeren, Willem A. *The Expositor's Bible Commentary,* Psalms. (Grand Rapids: Zondervan, 1991), 495.

[682] Ibid.

[683] Barnes' Notes on the Bible, Psalm 76:2.

[684] Spence-Jones, H. D. M. (Ed.). *Psalms,* (Vol. 1). (London; New York: Funk & Wagnalls Company, 1909), 101.

[685] Barnes' Notes on the Bible, Psalm 76:3.

[686] Tate, M. E. *Psalms 51–100 (Vol. 20).* (Dallas: Word, Incorporated, 1998), 261.

[687] Ibid.

[688] Plumer, W. S. *Studies in the Book of Psalms: Being a Critical and Expository Commentary, with Doctrinal and Practical Remarks on the Entire Psalter.* (Philadelphia; Edinburgh: J. B. Lippincott Company; A & C Black, 1872), 734.

[689] Spurgeon, C. H. *Psalms.* (Wheaton, IL: Crossway Books, 1993), 322.

[690] https://biblehub.com/commentaries/poole/psalms/76.htm, accessed May 31, 2018.

[691] Spence-Jones, H. D. M. (Ed.). *Psalms,* (Vol. 1). (London; New York: Funk & Wagnalls Company, 1909), 102.

[692] Bratcher, R. G. and W. D. Reyburn. *A Translator's Handbook on the Book of Psalms.* (New York: United Bible Societies, 1991), 666.

[693] Spurgeon, C. H. *Psalms.* (Wheaton, IL: Crossway Books, 1993), 322.

[694] Spence-Jones, H. D. M. (Ed.). *Psalms,* (Vol. 1). (London; New York: Funk & Wagnalls Company, 1909), 102.

[695] Ibid.

[696] Benson Commentary, Psalm 76:6.

[697] Alexander, J. A. *The Psalms Translated and Explained.* (Edinburgh: Andrew Elliot; James Thin, 1864), 322.

[698] Benson Commentary, Psalm 76:7.

[699] Barnes' Notes on the Bible, Psalm 76:7.

[700] Bratcher, R. G. and W. D. Reyburn. *A Translator's Handbook on the Book of Psalms.* (New York: United Bible Societies, 1991), 667.

[701] Spurgeon, C. H. *Psalms.* (Wheaton, IL: Crossway Books, 1993), 322.

[702] Spence-Jones, H. D. M. (Ed.). *Psalms,* (Vol. 1). (London; New York: Funk & Wagnalls Company, 1909), 102.

[703] Barnes' Notes on the Bible, Psalm 76:8.

[704] Spence-Jones, H. D. M. (Ed.). *Psalms,* (Vol. 1). (London; New York: Funk & Wagnalls Company, 1909), 102.

[705] Barnes' Notes on the Bible, 1 Peter 5:8.

[706] https://biblehub.com/commentaries/poole/1_peter/5.htm, accessed May 31, 2018.

[707] Plumer, W. S. *Studies in the Book of Psalms: Being a Critical and Expository Commentary, with Doctrinal and Practical Remarks on the Entire Psalter.* (Philadelphia; Edinburgh: J. B. Lippincott Company; A & C Black, 1872), 736.

[708] Ibid.

[709] Henry, M. *Matthew Henry's Commentary on the Whole Bible: Complete and Unabridged in One Volume.* (Peabody: Hendrickson, 1994), 853.

[710] Spurgeon, C. H. *Faith's Checkbook.* (New Kensington, Pa.: Whitaker House, 2002), November 10.

[711] Dilday, R. H., Jr., and J. H. Kennedy. *Psalms.* In H. F. Paschall and H. H. Hobbs (Eds.). *The Teacher's Bible Commentary.* (Nashville: Broadman and Holman Publishers, 1972), 324.

[712] Spurgeon, C. H. *Faith's Checkbook.* (New Kensington, Pa.: Whitaker House, 2002), November 10.

[713] Barnes' Notes on the Bible, Psalm 77:1.

[714] Spence-Jones, H. D. M. (Ed.). *Psalms,* (Vol. 1). (London; New York: Funk & Wagnalls Company, 1909), 110.

[715] Spurgeon, C. H. *Psalms.* (Wheaton, IL: Crossway Books, 1993), 324.

[716] Plumer, W. S. *Studies in the Book of Psalms: Being a Critical and Expository Commentary, with Doctrinal and Practical Remarks on the Entire Psalter.* (Philadelphia; Edinburgh: J. B. Lippincott Company; A & C Black, 1872), 738.

[717] Gill, John. *The John Gill Exposition of the Entire Bible,* Psalm 77:1.

[718] Spurgeon, C. H. *Psalms.* (Wheaton, IL: Crossway Books, 1993), 324.

[719] Barnes' Notes on the Bible, Psalm 77:2.

[720] Gill, John. *The John Gill Exposition of the Entire Bible,* Psalm 77:2.

[721] Barnes' Notes on the Bible, Psalm 77:2.

[722] Clarke, Adam. *Clarkes' Commentary and Critical Notes*, Psalm 77:2.

[723] Ibid.

[724] Benson Commentary, Psalm 77:3.

[725] Barnes' Notes on the Bible, Psalm 77:3.

[726] Plumer, W. S. *Studies in the Book of Psalms: Being a Critical and Expository Commentary, with Doctrinal and Practical Remarks on the Entire Psalter.* (Philadelphia; Edinburgh: J. B. Lippincott Company; A & C Black, 1872), 738.

[727] Ibid.

[728] Ibid.

[729] Jennings, A. C., and W. H. Lowe. *The Psalms, with Introductions and Critical Notes* (Second Edition, Vol. 1). (London: Macmillan and Co., 1884), 28.

[730] Harman, A. *Psalms: A Mentor Commentary (Vol. 1–2).* (Ross-shire, Great Britain: Mentor, 2011), 575.

[731] Brueggemann, W. *Spirituality of the Psalms.* (Minneapolis: Fortress Press, 2002), xiii.

[732] Henry, M. *Matthew Henry's Commentary on the Whole Bible: Complete and Unabridged in One Volume.* (Peabody: Hendrickson, 1994), 854.

[733] Boice, J. M. *Psalms 42–106: An Expositional Commentary.* (Grand Rapids, MI: Baker Books, 2005), 715.

[734] Rogers, Adrian P. "Can God Be Trusted in Your Troubles?" Sermon Notes, (Job 13:15), The Adrian Rogers Legacy Collection. Database © 2011 WORDsearch Corp.

[735] Wiersbe, W. W. *Be Obedient.* (Wheaton, IL: Victor Books, 1991, 41.

[736] Henry, M. *Matthew Henry's Commentary on the Whole Bible: Complete and Unabridged in One Volume.* (Peabody: Hendrickson, 1994), 854.

[737] Plumer, W. S. *Studies in the Book of Psalms: Being a Critical and Expository Commentary, with Doctrinal and Practical Remarks on the Entire Psalter.* (Philadelphia; Edinburgh: J. B. Lippincott Company; A & C Black, 1872), 739.

[738] Barnes' Notes on the Bible, Psalm 77:2.

[739] Gill, John. *The John Gill Exposition of the Entire Bible,* Psalm 77:7.

[740] Ibid.

[741] Spurgeon, C. H. *Psalms.* (Wheaton, IL: Crossway Books, 1993), 326.

[742] Henry, Matthew. *Matthew Henry's Concise Bible Commentary,* Psalm 77:11.

[743] Criswell, W. A. "The Unchanging Christ," The Daily Word, November 24, 2018.

[744] Hastings, James. *The Great Texts of the Bible: Job to Psalm 23.* (New York: Charles Scribner's Sons, 1913), 121.

[745] Simeon, C. *Horae Homileticae: Psalms, LXXIII–CL (Vol. 6).* (London: Samuel Holdsworth, 1836), 186.

[746] Exell, Joseph S. Ed. *The Biblical Illustrator,* Psalm 77:1 (God's ear open to the cry of the needy).

[747] Spurgeon, C. H. "Refusing to Be Comforted" (Sermon No. 2578), March 18, 1883.

[748] Bonar, A. A. *Christ and His Church in the Book of Psalms.* (New York: Robert Carter & Brothers, 1860), 230–231.

[749] www.azquotes.com/quotes/topics/dark-night-of-the-soul.htm, accessed May 31, 2018.

[750] Lewis, C. S. *The Problem with Pain.* (San Francisco: Harper San Francisco, 2001), 14.

[751] Plumer, W. S. *Studies in the Book of Psalms: Being a Critical and Expository Commentary, with Doctrinal and Practical Remarks on the Entire Psalter.* (Philadelphia; Edinburgh: J. B. Lippincott Company; A & C Black, 1872), 742.

[752] Brueggemann, W. *Spirituality of the Psalms*. (Minneapolis: Fortress Press, 2002), xiii.

[753] Hamilton, William W. *Sermons on the Books of the Bible,* (Vol. 2), 190.

[754] Spence-Jones, H. D. M. (Ed.). *Psalms,* (Vol. 1). (London; New York: Funk & Wagnalls Company, 1909), 123.

[755] Ibid.

[756] Bratcher, R. G. and W. D. Reyburn. *A Translator's Handbook on the Book of Psalms.* (New York: United Bible Societies, 1991), 681.

[757] Clarke, Adam. *Clarkes' Commentary and Critical Notes*, Psalm 78:2.

[758] Plumer, W. S. *Studies in the Book of Psalms: Being a Critical and Expository Commentary, with Doctrinal and Practical Remarks on the Entire Psalter.* (Philadelphia; Edinburgh: J. B. Lippincott Company; A & C Black, 1872), 746.

[759] Clarke, Adam. *Clarkes' Commentary and Critical Notes*, Psalm 78:2.

[760] Ibid.

[761] Kirkpatrick, A. F. (Ed.). *The Cambridge Bible for Schools and Colleges,* Psalms. (Cambridge: Cambridge University Press, 1914), Psalm 78:2.

[762] Barnes' Notes on the Bible, Psalm 49:4.

[763] Spurgeon, C. H. *Psalms.* (Wheaton, IL: Crossway Books, 1993), 329.

[764] Spence-Jones, H. D. M. (Ed.). *Psalms,* (Vol. 1). (London; New York: Funk & Wagnalls Company, 1909), 124.

[765] Spurgeon, C. H. *Psalms.* (Wheaton, IL: Crossway Books, 1993), 329.

[766] Bratcher, R. G. and W. D. Reyburn. *A Translator's Handbook on the Book of Psalms.* (New York: United Bible Societies, 1991), 682.

[767] Ibid., 85.

[768] Spence-Jones, H. D. M. (Ed.). *Psalms,* (Vol. 1). (London; New York: Funk & Wagnalls Company, 1909), 123.

769 Boice, J. M. *Psalms 42–106: An Expositional Commentary.* (Grand Rapids, MI: Baker Books, 2005), 646–647.

770 Spence-Jones, H. D. M. (Ed.). *Psalms,* (Vol. 1). (London; New York: Funk & Wagnalls Company, 1909), 133.

771 Spurgeon, C. H. *Psalms.* (Wheaton, IL: Crossway Books, 1993), 329.

772 Boice, J. M. *Psalms 42–106: An Expositional Commentary.* (Grand Rapids, MI: Baker Books, 2005), 646.

773 Hamilton, William W. *Sermons on the Books of the Bible,* (Vol. 5), 240.

774 Dilday, R. H., Jr., and J. H. Kennedy. *Psalms.* In H. F. Paschall and H. H. Hobbs (Eds.). *The Teacher's Bible Commentary.* (Nashville: Broadman and Holman Publishers, 1972), 325.

775 Plumer, W. S. *Studies in the Book of Psalms: Being a Critical and Expository Commentary, with Doctrinal and Practical Remarks on the Entire Psalter.* (Philadelphia; Edinburgh: J. B. Lippincott Company; A & C Black, 1872), 763–764).

776 Harman, A. *Psalms: A Mentor Commentary (Vol. 1–2).* (Ross-shire, Great Britain: Mentor, 2011), 604.

777 Swanson, J. *Dictionary of Biblical Languages with Semantic Domains: Hebrew (Old Testament)* (electronic ed.). (Oak Harbor: Logos Research Systems, Inc., 1997).

778 Perowne, J. J. S. *The Book of Psalms: A New Translation, with Introductions and Notes, Explanatory and Critical, Fifth Edition, Revised, Vol. 1.* (London; Cambridge: George Bell and Sons; Deighton Bell and Co., 1883), 80.

779 Harris, R. L., G. L. Archer, Jr., and B. K. Waltke (Eds.). *Theological Wordbook of the Old Testament* (electronic ed.). L. J. Coppes, 433 לָלַד. (Chicago: Moody Press, 1999), 190.

780 Brown, F., S. R. Driver, and C. A. Briggs. *Enhanced Brown-Driver-Briggs Hebrew and English Lexicon.* (Oxford: Clarendon Press, 1977), 447.

781 Strong, J. *The New Strong's Dictionary of Hebrew and Greek Words.* (Nashville: Thomas Nelson, 1996).

782 Strong, J. *A Concise Dictionary of the Words in the Greek Testament and the Hebrew Bible.* (Vol. 2). (Bellingham, WA: Logos Bible Software, 2009), 57.

783 Spence-Jones, H. D. M. (Ed.). *Psalms,* (Vol. 1). (London; New York: Funk & Wagnalls Company, 1909), 146.

784 Spurgeon, C. H. *Psalms.* (Wheaton, IL: Crossway Books, 1993), 346.

785 Gill, John. *The John Gill Exposition of the Entire Bible,* Psalm 79:8.

786 Tozer, A. W. *I Talk Back to the Devil,* 12–13.

787 Ibid.

788 Steadman, Ray. "The Scars of Sin." https://www.raystedman.org/thematic-studies/doctrinal-topics/the-scars-of-sin, accessed June 2, 2018.

789 Benson Commentary, Psalm 80:3.

790 Bratcher, R. G. and W. D. Reyburn. *A Translator's Handbook on the Book of Psalms.* (New York: United Bible Societies, 1991), 297.

791 Gill, John. *The John Gill Exposition of the Entire Bible,* Psalm 80:3.

792 Nichols, J. W. H. *Musings in the Psalms.* (Galaxie Software, 2005), 55.

793 Boice, J. M. *Psalms 42–106: An Expositional Commentary.* (Grand Rapids, MI: Baker Books, 2005), 660.

794 MacArthur, J., Jr. (Ed.). *The MacArthur Study Bible,* (electronic ed.). (Nashville, TN: Word Pub, 1997), 814.

795 Spence-Jones, H. D. M. (Ed.). *Psalms,* (Vol. 1). (London; New York: Funk & Wagnalls Company, 1909), 156.

796 Clarke, Adam. *Clarkes' Commentary and Critical Notes*, Psalm 80.

797 Benson Commentary, Psalm 80:3.

798 Harman, A. *Psalms: A Mentor Commentary (Vol. 1–2).* (Ross-shire, Great Britain: Mentor, 2011), 607.

799 Ibid.

800 Henry, M. *Matthew Henry's Commentary on the Whole Bible: Complete and Unabridged in One Volume.* (Peabody: Hendrickson, 1994), 860.

801 Plumer, W. S. *Studies in the Book of Psalms: Being a Critical and Expository Commentary, with Doctrinal and Practical Remarks on the Entire Psalter.* (Philadelphia; Edinburgh: J. B. Lippincott Company; A & C Black, 1872), 772.

802 Ibid.

803 Henry, M. *Matthew Henry's Commentary on the Whole Bible: Complete and Unabridged in One Volume.* (Peabody: Hendrickson, 1994), 860.

804 https://www.biblestudytools.com/commentaries/robertsons-word-pictures/acts/acts-2-38.html, accessed June 2, 2018.

805 https://www.christianquotes.info/quotes-by-topic/quotes-about-repentance/#ixzz5HJV7Xj6G, accessed June 2, 2018.

806 Carroll, B. H. "Revival Messages: The Inspiration of the Bible," http://nashpublications. com/wp-content/uploads/2013/10/Baptist_History/Old_Baptist_Books/Revival-Sermons-BHCarroll.pdf, accessed October 24, 2018.

807 Tate, M. E. *Psalms 51–100 (Vol. 20).* (Dallas: Word, Incorporated, 1998), 314.

808 Ibid.

809 https://www.christianquotes.info/quotes-by-topic/quotes-about-repentance/#ixzz5HJTnYpl3, accessed June 2, 2018.

810 Spurgeon, C. H. *Psalms.* (Wheaton, IL: Crossway Books, 1993), 348.

811 https://www.christianquotes.info/quotes-by-topic/quotes-about-repentance/#ixzz5HJUWzZ2b, accessed June 2, 2018.

812 Spence-Jones, H. D. M. (Ed.). *Psalms,* (Vol. 1). (London; New York: Funk & Wagnalls Company, 1909), 167.

[813] Bratcher, R. G. and W. D. Reyburn. *A Translator's Handbook on the Book of Psalms.* (New York: United Bible Societies, 1991), 721.

[814] Spurgeon, C. H. *The Treasury of David.* (Grand Rapids, Michigan: Kregel Publications, 2004), Psalm 81:1.

[815] Spence-Jones, H. D. M. (Ed.). *Psalms,* (Vol. 1). (London; New York: Funk & Wagnalls Company, 1909), 167.

[816] Barnes' Notes on the Bible, Psalm 81:2.

[817] Kirkpatrick, A. F. (Ed.). *The Cambridge Bible for Schools and Colleges,* Psalms. (Cambridge: Cambridge University Press, 1914), Psalm 81:2.

[818] Spence-Jones, H. D. M. (Ed.). *Psalms,* (Vol. 1). (London; New York: Funk & Wagnalls Company, 1909), 167.

[819] Tate, M. E. *Psalms 51–100 (Vol. 20).* (Dallas: Word, Incorporated, 1998), 318.

[820] Ibid.

[821] Bratcher, R. G. and W. D. Reyburn. *A Translator's Handbook on the Book of Psalms.* (New York: United Bible Societies, 1991), 721.

[822] Kirkpatrick, A. F. (Ed.). *The Cambridge Bible for Schools and Colleges,* Psalms. (Cambridge: Cambridge University Press, 1914), Psalm 81:2.

[823] Benson Commentary, Psalm 81:4.

[824] Kirkpatrick, A. F. (Ed.). *The Cambridge Bible for Schools and Colleges,* Psalms. (Cambridge: Cambridge University Press, 1914), Psalm 81:4.

[825] Tate, M. E. *Psalms 51–100 (Vol. 20).* (Dallas: Word, Incorporated, 1998), 323.

[826] https://biblehub.com/commentaries/poole/psalms/81.htm, accessed June 4, 2019.

[827] Jennings, A. C., and W. H. Lowe. *The Psalms, with Introductions and Critical Notes* (Second Edition, Vol. 1). (London: Macmillan and Co., 1884), 48.

[828] Spurgeon, C. H. *The Treasury of David.* (Grand Rapids, Michigan: Kregel Publications, 2004), Psalm 81:5.

[829] Barnes' Notes on the Bible, Psalm 81:6.

[830] https://biblehub.com/commentaries/poole/psalms/81.htm, accessed June 4, 2019.

[831] Barnes' Notes on the Bible, Psalm 81:7.

[832] Kirkpatrick, A. F. (Ed.). *The Cambridge Bible for Schools and Colleges,* Psalms. (Cambridge: Cambridge University Press, 1914), Psalm 81:7.

[833] Spence-Jones, H. D. M. (Ed.). *Psalms,* (Vol. 1). (London; New York: Funk & Wagnalls Company, 1909), 168.

[834] Clarke, Adam. *Clarkes' Commentary and Critical Notes*, Psalm 81 (Introduction).

[835] VanGemeren, Willem A. *The Expositor's Bible Commentary,* Psalms. (Grand Rapids: Zondervan, 1991), Psalm 81:1.

[836] Boice, J. M. *Psalms 42–106: An Expositional Commentary.* (Grand Rapids, MI: Baker Books, 2005), 668.

[837] Barnes' Notes on the Bible, John 4:23.

[838] https://biblehub.com/commentaries/ellicott/john/4.htm, accessed June 4, 2018.

[839] Benson Commentary, John 4:23.

[840] https://www.renewingworshipnc.org/2017/08/02/quotes-by-tozer/, accessed June 4, 2018.

[841] Spurgeon, C. H. *The Treasury of David.* (Grand Rapids, Michigan: Kregel Publications, 2004), Psalm 81:1.

[842] Plumer, W. S. *Studies in the Book of Psalms: Being a Critical and Expository Commentary, with Doctrinal and Practical Remarks on the Entire Psalter.* (Philadelphia; Edinburgh: J. B. Lippincott Company; A & C Black, 1872), 778.

[843] Hastings, James. *The Great Texts of the Bible: Job to Psalm 23.* (New York: Charles Scribner's Sons, 1913), 116.

[844] Plumer, W. S. *Studies in the Book of Psalms: Being a Critical and Expository Commentary, with Doctrinal and Practical Remarks on the Entire Psalter.* (Philadelphia; Edinburgh: J. B. Lippincott Company; A & C Black, 1872), 778.

[845] https://www.renewingworshipnc.org/2017/08/02/quotes-by-tozer/, accessed June 4, 2018.

[846] Henry, M. *Matthew Henry's Commentary on the Whole Bible: Complete and Unabridged in One Volume.* (Peabody: Hendrickson, 1994), 861.

[847] Plumer, W. S. *Studies in the Book of Psalms: Being a Critical and Expository Commentary, with Doctrinal and Practical Remarks on the Entire Psalter.* (Philadelphia; Edinburgh: J. B. Lippincott Company; A & C Black, 1872), 777.

[848] Alexander, J. A. *The Psalms Translated and Explained.* (Edinburgh: Andrew Elliot; James Thin, 1864), 348.

[849] Barnes' Notes on the Bible, Psalm 81:14.

[850] Alexander, J. A. *The Psalms Translated and Explained.* (Edinburgh: Andrew Elliot; James Thin, 1864), 348.

[851] Barnes' Notes on the Bible, Psalm 81:14.

[852] Ibid., Psalm 81:15.

[853] Plumer, W. S. *Studies in the Book of Psalms: Being a Critical and Expository Commentary, with Doctrinal and Practical Remarks on the Entire Psalter.* (Philadelphia; Edinburgh: J. B. Lippincott Company; A & C Black, 1872), 778.

[854] Barnes' Notes on the Bible, Psalm 81:15.

[855] Benson Commentary, Psalm 81:16.

[856] Barnes' Notes on the Bible, Psalm 81;16.

[857] Whittier, John Greenleaf. *Bartlett's Familiar Quotations,* 13th ed. (Boston: Little, Brown and Company), 527.

858 Barnes' Notes on the Bible, Psalm 81:13.

859 Jamieson, R., A. R. Fausset, & D. Brown. *Commentary Critical and Explanatory on the Whole Bible* (Vol. 1). (Oak Harbor, WA: Logos Research Systems, Inc., 1997), Psalm 81:13–16.

860 Spurgeon, C. H. *Psalms.* (Wheaton, IL: Crossway Books, 1993), 354.

861 Henry, M. *Matthew Henry's Commentary on the Whole Bible: Complete and Unabridged in One Volume.* (Peabody: Hendrickson, 1994), 862.

862 Maclaren, Alexander. *The Expositor's Bible:* The Psalms. (New York: Scriptura Press, 2015), 422.

863 Chambers, Oswald. *My Utmost For His Highest,* June 2.

864 Simeon, C. *Horae Homileticae: Psalms, LXXIII–CL (Vol. 6).* (London: Samuel Holdsworth, 1836), 63–64.

865 Henry, Matthew. *Matthew Henry's Concise Bible Commentary,* Psalm 81:16.

866 Barnes' Notes on the Bible, Psalm 82:1.

867 Jamieson, R., A. R. Fausset, & D. Brown. *Commentary Critical and Explanatory on the Whole Bible* (Vol. 1). (Oak Harbor, WA: Logos Research Systems, Inc., 1997), Psalm 82:1.

Criswell, W. A., P. Patterson, E. R. Clendenen, D. L. Akin, M. Chamberlin, D. K. Patterson, and J. Pogue (Eds.). Believer's Study Bible, (electronic ed.). (Nashville: Thomas Nelson, 1991), Ps. 82:1.

869 Benson Commentary, Psalm 82:2.

870 Spence-Jones, H. D. M. (Ed.). *Psalms,* (Vol. 1). (London; New York: Funk & Wagnalls Company, 1909), 177.

871 Benson Commentary, Psalm 82:2.

872 Gill, John. *The John Gill Exposition of the Entire Bible,* Psalm 82:4.

873 Barnes' Notes on the Bible, Psalm 82:5.

874 Ibid.

875 Gill, John. *The John Gill Exposition of the Entire Bible,* Psalm 82:5.

876 Kirkpatrick, A. F. (Ed.). *The Cambridge Bible for Schools and Colleges,* Psalms. (Cambridge: Cambridge University Press, 1914), Psalm 82:6.

877 Benson Commentary, Psalm 8

878 Spence-Jones, H. D. M. (Ed.). *Psalms,* (Vol. 1). (London; New York: Funk & Wagnalls Company, 1909), 178.

879 Spurgeon, C. H. *Psalms.* (Wheaton, IL: Crossway Books, 1993), 356.

880 The NET Bible Notes Bible, First Edition Notes. (Richardson, TX: Biblical Studies Press, 2006), Ps. 82:8.

881 Barnes' Notes on the Bible, Psalm 82:8.

882 Gill, John. *The John Gill Exposition of the Entire Bible,* Psalm 82 (Introduction).

883 Dilday, R. H., Jr., and J. H. Kennedy. *Psalms.* In H. F. Paschall and H. H. Hobbs (Eds.). *The Teacher's Bible Commentary.* (Nashville: Broadman and Holman Publishers, 1972), 327.

884 Jennings, A. C., and W. H. Lowe. *The Psalms, with Introductions and Critical Notes* (Second Edition, Vol. 1). (London: Macmillan and Co., 1884), 61.

885 Maclaren, Alexander. *The Expositor's Bible:* The Psalms. (New York: Scriptura Press, 2015), 428.

886 Ibid.

887 Spence-Jones, H. D. M. (Ed.). *Psalms,* (Vol. 1). (London; New York: Funk & Wagnalls Company, 1909), 181.

888 Harman, A. *Psalms: A Mentor Commentary (Vol. 1–2).* (Ross-shire, Great Britain: Mentor, 2011), 620.

889 Henry, M. *Matthew Henry's Commentary on the Whole Bible: Complete and Unabridged in One Volume.* (Peabody: Hendrickson, 1994), 863.

890 Spurgeon, C. H. *Psalms.* (Wheaton, IL: Crossway Books, 1993), 355.

891 Horne, G. *A Commentary on the Book of Psalms.* (New York: Robert Carter & Brothers, 1856), 297–298.

892 Plumer, W. S. *Studies in the Book of Psalms: Being a Critical and Expository Commentary, with Doctrinal and Practical Remarks on the Entire Psalter.* (Philadelphia; Edinburgh: J. B. Lippincott Company; A & C Black, 1872), 785.

893 Ibid.

894 Ibid.

895 VanGemeren, Willem A. *The Expositor's Bible Commentary,* Psalms. (Grand Rapids: Zondervan, 1991), Psalm 82:5–7.

896 Horne, G. *A Commentary on the Book of Psalms.* (New York: Robert Carter & Brothers, 1856), 297.

897 Plumer, W. S. *Studies in the Book of Psalms: Being a Critical and Expository Commentary, with Doctrinal and Practical Remarks on the Entire Psalter.* (Philadelphia; Edinburgh: J. B. Lippincott Company; A & C Black, 1872), 785.

898 Hyman, Hon. Michael B. *Bench & Bar,* June 2016, vol. 46, no. 9.

899 Plumer, W. S. *Studies in the Book of Psalms: Being a Critical and Expository Commentary, with Doctrinal and Practical Remarks on the Entire Psalter.* (Philadelphia; Edinburgh: J. B. Lippincott Company; A & C Black, 1872), 785.

900 Henry, M. *Matthew Henry's Commentary on the Whole Bible: Complete and Unabridged in One Volume.* (Peabody: Hendrickson, 1994), 864.

901 Plumer, W. S. *Studies in the Book of Psalms: Being a Critical and Expository Commentary, with Doctrinal and Practical Remarks on the Entire Psalter.* (Philadelphia; Edinburgh: J. B. Lippincott Company; A & C Black, 1872), 787.

902 Alexander, J. A. *The Psalms Translated and Explained.* (Edinburgh: Andrew Elliot; James Thin, 1864), 352.

[903] Harman, A. *Psalms: A Mentor Commentary (Vol. 1–2).* (Ross-shire, Great Britain: Mentor, 2011), 624.
[904] Benson Commentary, Psalm 83:1.
[905] Jamieson, R., A. R. Fausset, & D. Brown. *Commentary Critical and Explanatory on the Whole Bible* (Vol. 1). (Oak Harbor, WA: Logos Research Systems, Inc., 1997), 372.
[906] Spence-Jones, H. D. M. (Ed.). *Psalms,* (Vol. 1). (London; New York: Funk & Wagnalls Company, 1909), 184.
[907] Jennings, A. C., and W. H. Lowe. *The Psalms, with Introductions and Critical Notes* (Second Edition, Vol. 1). (London: Macmillan and Co., 1884), 67. (Various views as to the Psalm's possible historical occasion are cited in detail.)
[908] Kirkpatrick, A. F. (Ed.). *The Cambridge Bible for Schools and Colleges,* Psalms. (Cambridge: Cambridge University Press, 1914), Psalm 83 (Introduction).
[909] *The Spurgeon Study Bible.* (Nashville: Holman Bible Publishers, 2017), 762.
[910] Benson Commentary, John 11:3.
[911] Ibid.
[912] Barnes' Notes on the Bible, John 11:3.
[913] Benson Commentary, John 11:3.
[914] Maclaren, Alexander. *Expositions of Holy Scripture: St. John.* (Woodstock, Ontario: Devoted Publishing, 2017), 171.
[915] Benson Commentary, John 11:45.
[916] Chambers, Oswald. *My Utmost For His Highest,* October 11.
[917] Spurgeon, C. H. *Psalms.* (Wheaton, IL: Crossway Books, 1993), 356–357.
[918] Henry, M. *Matthew Henry's Commentary on the Whole Bible: Complete and Unabridged in One Volume.* (Peabody: Hendrickson, 1994), 864.
[919] Jennings, A. C., and W. H. Lowe. *The Psalms, with Introductions and Critical Notes* (Second Edition, Vol. 1). (London: Macmillan and Co., 1884), 74.
[920] Henry, M. *Matthew Henry's Commentary on the Whole Bible: Complete and Unabridged in One Volume.* (Peabody: Hendrickson, 1994), 866.
[921] Spence-Jones, H. D. M. (Ed.). *Psalms,* (Vol. 1). (London; New York: Funk & Wagnalls Company, 1909), 192.
[922] Kirkpatrick, A. F. (Ed.). *The Cambridge Bible for Schools and Colleges,* Psalms. (Cambridge: Cambridge University Press, 1914), Psalm 84:10.
[923] Henry, Matthew. *Matthew Henry's Concise Bible Commentary,* Psalm 84:8–12.
[924] Barnes' Notes on the Bible, Psalm 84:10.
[925] Spurgeon, C. H. *Psalms.* (Wheaton, IL: Crossway Books, 1993), 362.
[926] Gill, John. *The John Gill Exposition of the Entire Bible,* Psalm 84:10.
[927] Spurgeon, C. H. *The Treasury of David,* Psalm 84:10.

[928] Spurgeon, C. H. *The Treasury of David.* (Grand Rapids, Michigan: Kregel Publications, 2004), Psalm 84.

[929] Jennings, A. C., and W. H. Lowe. *The Psalms, with Introductions and Critical Notes* (Second Edition, Vol. 1). (London: Macmillan and Co., 1884), 73.

[930] Plumer, W. S. *Studies in the Book of Psalms: Being a Critical and Expository Commentary, with Doctrinal and Practical Remarks on the Entire Psalter.* (Philadelphia; Edinburgh: J. B. Lippincott Company; A & C Black, 1872), 794.

[931] Jennings, A. C., and W. H. Lowe. *The Psalms, with Introductions and Critical Notes* (Second Edition, Vol. 1). (London: Macmillan and Co., 1884), 74.

[932] Barnes' Notes on the Bible, Psalm 84:10.

[933] Spurgeon, C. H. *Psalms.* (Wheaton, IL: Crossway Books, 1993), 362.

[934] Simeon, C. *Horae Homileticae: Psalms, LXXIII–CL (Vol. 6).* (London: Samuel Holdsworth, 1836), 72.

[935] Spurgeon, C. H. *Psalms.* (Wheaton, IL: Crossway Books, 1993), 362.

[936] http://www.quoteschristian.com/church2.html, accessed June 6, 2018.

[937] Simeon, C. *Horae Homileticae: Psalms, LXXIII–CL (Vol. 6).* (London: Samuel Holdsworth, 1836), 69–70.

[938] Jennings, A. C., and W. H. Lowe. *The Psalms, with Introductions and Critical Notes* (Second Edition, Vol. 1). (London: Macmillan and Co., 1884), 75.

[939] Henry, M. *Matthew Henry's Commentary on the Whole Bible: Complete and Unabridged in One Volume.* (Peabody: Hendrickson, 1994), 866.

[940] Spurgeon, C. H. *Morning and Evening,* December 14 (Morning).

[941] Simeon, C. *Horae Homileticae: Psalms, LXXIII–CL (Vol. 6).* (London: Samuel Holdsworth, 1836), 73.

[942] Kirkpatrick, A. F. (Ed.). *The Cambridge Bible for Schools and Colleges,* Psalms. (Cambridge: Cambridge University Press, 1914), Psalm 85:6.

[943] Barnes' Notes on the Bible, Psalm 85:6.

[944] Soanes, C., and A. Stevenson, (Eds.). *Concise Oxford English Dictionary,* (11th ed.). (Oxford: Oxford University Press, 2004).

[945] Swanson, J. *Dictionary of Biblical Languages with Semantic Domains: Hebrew (Old Testament)* (electronic ed.). (Oak Harbor: Logos Research Systems, Inc., 1997).

[946] Spence-Jones, H. D. M. (Ed.). *Psalms,* (Vol. 1). (London; New York: Funk & Wagnalls Company, 1909), 203.

[947] Criswell, W. A., P. Patterson, E. R. Clendenen, D. L. Akin, M. Chamberlin, D. K. Patterson, and J. Pogue (Eds.). Believer's Study Bible, (electronic ed.). (Nashville: Thomas Nelson, 1991), Ps. 85:6.

[948] Vine, W. E., M. F. Unger, & W. White, Jr. *Vine's Complete Expository Dictionary of Old and New Testament Words (Vol. 1).* (Nashville, TN: T. Nelson, 1996), 219.

[949] Ibid., 142.

[950] Swanson, J. *Dictionary of Biblical Languages with Semantic Domains: Hebrew (Old Testament)* (electronic ed.). (Oak Harbor: Logos Research Systems, Inc., 1997).

[951] BYBHV, Psalm 85:8.

[952] Benson Commentary, Psalm 85:8.

[953] Vine, W. E., M. F. Unger, & W. White, Jr. *Vine's Complete Expository Dictionary of Old and New Testament Words (Vol. 1).* (Nashville, TN: T. Nelson, 1996), 173.

[954] Swanson, J. *Dictionary of Biblical Languages with Semantic Domains: Hebrew (Old Testament)* (electronic ed.). (Oak Harbor: Logos Research Systems, Inc., 1997).

[955] Barnes' Notes on the Bible, Psalm 85:8.

[956] Kirkpatrick, A. F. (Ed.). *The Cambridge Bible for Schools and Colleges,* Psalms. (Cambridge: Cambridge University Press, 1914), Psalm 85:9.

[957] Benson Commentary, Psalm 85:9.

[958] Kirkpatrick, A. F. (Ed.). *The Cambridge Bible for Schools and Colleges,* Psalms. (Cambridge: Cambridge University Press, 1914), Psalm 85:9.

[959] Alexander, J. A. *The Psalms Translated and Explained.* (Edinburgh: Andrew Elliot; James Thin, 1864), 358.

[960] Drummond, Lewis. *The Canvass Cathedral.* (Word Publishing, 2003), 428.

[961] Spurgeon, C. H. *The Sword and Trowel,* December, 1866.

[962] www.vitalchristianity.org/docs/New%20Articles/Revivial-Requirement2.pdf, accessed May 10, 2014.

[963] Barnes' Notes on the Bible, Psalm 85:6.

[964] Spurgeon, C. H. *Sermons Preached and Revised.* (London: Passmore and Alabaster, 1877), 404.

[965] Exell, Joseph S. Ed. *The Biblical Illustrator,* Psalm 85:6.

[966] Burns, James. *The Laws of Revival.* (Minneapolis: World Wide Productions, 1993), 33.

[967] Christianity.com, "Jeremy Lanphier Led Prayer Revival," accessed May 10, 2014; www.christianexaminer.com, "Evangelism Is Not Reserved for Just a Select Few Christ Followers," Greg Laurie, accessed May 10, 2014.

[968] Spurgeon, C. H. *"Marvelous Lovingkindness"* (Sermon #2702), October 20, 1881.

[969] Spurgeon, C. H. *Psalms.* (Wheaton, IL: Crossway Books, 1993), 364–365.

[970] Spurgeon, C. H. *The Sword and Trowel,* December, 1866.

[971] Chambers, Oswald. *My Utmost For His Highest,* November 23.

[972] Smith, Shelton, Ed. *Great Preaching on Revivals.* (Murfreesboro, TN: Sword of the Lord Publishers, 1997), Preface.

[973] Aitken, W. Hay. *Mission Sermons*, 1st series, 220.

[974] Gill, John. *The John Gill Exposition of the Entire Bible,* Psalm 86:5.

[975] Ibid.

[976] Gesenius, W., and S. P. Tregelles. *Gesenius' Hebrew and Chaldee Lexicon to the Old Testament Scriptures.* (Bellingham, WA: Logos Bible Software, 2003), 739.

[977] Criswell, W. A., P. Patterson, E. R. Clendenen, D. L. Akin, M. Chamberlin, D. K. Patterson, and J. Pogue (Eds.). Believer's Study Bible, (electronic ed.). (Nashville: Thomas Nelson, 1991), Ps. 86:1.

[978] Spurgeon, C. H. *The Treasury of David.* (Grand Rapids, Michigan: Kregel Publications, 2004), Psalm 86:5.

[979] Dilday, R. H., Jr., and J. H. Kennedy. *Psalms.* In H. F. Paschall and H. H. Hobbs (Eds.). *The Teacher's Bible Commentary.* (Nashville: Broadman and Holman Publishers, 1972), 328.

[980] Spurgeon, C. H. *The Treasury of David.* (Grand Rapids, Michigan: Kregel Publications, 2004), Psalm 86:5.

[981] Henry, M. *Matthew Henry's Commentary on the Whole Bible: Complete and Unabridged in One Volume.* (Peabody: Hendrickson, 1994), 868.

[982] Ibid.

[983] Bunyan, John. *The Commemorative Edition of the Works of John Bunyan,* Volume 2. (London: The London Printing and Publishing Company, 1859), 1206.

[984] Barnes' Notes on the Bible, Psalm 86:7.

[985] Spence-Jones, H. D. M. (Ed.). *Psalms,* (Vol. 1). (London; New York: Funk & Wagnalls Company, 1909), 214.

[986] Dilday, R. H., Jr., and J. H. Kennedy. *Psalms.* In H. F. Paschall and H. H. Hobbs (Eds.). *The Teacher's Bible Commentary.* (Nashville: Broadman and Holman Publishers, 1972), 328.

[987] Barnes' Notes on the Bible, Psalm 86:7.

[988] Gesenius, W., and S. P. Tregelles. *Gesenius' Hebrew and Chaldee Lexicon to the Old Testament Scriptures.* (Bellingham, WA: Logos Bible Software, 2003), 619.

[989] Ibid., 544.

[990] Ibid.

[991] Spurgeon, C. H. *The Treasury of David.* (Grand Rapids, Michigan: Kregel Publications, 2004), Psalm 86:17.

[992] Gill, John. *The John Gill Exposition of the Entire Bible,* Psalm 86:17.

[993] Ibid., Psalm 86:7.

[994] Criswell, W. A., P. Patterson, E. R. Clendenen, D. L. Akin, M. Chamberlin, D. K. Patterson, and J. Pogue (Eds.). Believer's Study Bible, (electronic ed.). (Nashville: Thomas Nelson, 1991), Ps. 86:8.

[995] Plumer, W. S. *Studies in the Book of Psalms: Being a Critical and Expository Commentary, with Doctrinal and Practical Remarks on the Entire Psalter.* (Philadelphia; Edinburgh: J. B. Lippincott Company; A & C Black, 1872), 811.

[996] Jensen, Gordon. www.namethathymn.com, accessed April 22, 2013.

[997] Spurgeon, C. H. *The Treasury of David.* (Grand Rapids, Michigan: Kregel Publications, 2004), Psalm 86:7.

[998] Barnes' Notes on the Bible, Psalm 86:7.

[999] Boice, J. M. *Psalms 42–106: An Expositional Commentary.* (Grand Rapids, MI: Baker Books, 2005), 703.

[1000] Ibid.

[1001] Spence-Jones, H. D. M. (Ed.). *Psalms,* (Vol. 1). (London; New York: Funk & Wagnalls Company, 1909), 221.

[1002] Packer, J. I. *Knowing God.* (Downers Grove, IL: InterVarsity Press, 1993), 41–42.

[1003] *The Spurgeon Study Bible.* (Nashville: Holman Bible Publishers, 2017), 713.

[1004] Cowman, L. B. *Streams in the Desert,* (Grand Rapids: Zondervan, 1999), January 25.

[1005] Plumer, W. S. *Studies in the Book of Psalms: Being a Critical and Expository Commentary, with Doctrinal and Practical Remarks on the Entire Psalter.* (Philadelphia; Edinburgh: J. B. Lippincott Company; A & C Black, 1872), 814.

[1006] Alexander, J. A. *The Psalms Translated and Explained.* (Edinburgh: Andrew Elliot; James Thin, 1864), 364.

[1007] Spurgeon, C. H. *The Treasury of David.* (Grand Rapids, Michigan: Kregel Publications, 2004), Psalm 87:3.

[1008] Plumer, W. S. *Studies in the Book of Psalms: Being a Critical and Expository Commentary, with Doctrinal and Practical Remarks on the Entire Psalter.* (Philadelphia; Edinburgh: J. B. Lippincott Company; A & C Black, 1872), 812.

[1009] Plumer, W. S. *Studies in the Book of Psalms: Being a Critical and Expository Commentary, with Doctrinal and Practical Remarks on the Entire Psalter.* (Philadelphia; Edinburgh: J. B. Lippincott Company; A & C Black, 1872), 813.

[1010] Ibid.

[1011] Kirkpatrick, A. F. (Ed.). *The Cambridge Bible for Schools and Colleges,* Psalms. (Cambridge: Cambridge University Press, 1914), Psalm 87 (Introduction).

[1012] Benson Commentary, Psalm 87:3.

[1013] Henry, M. *Matthew Henry's Commentary on the Whole Bible: Complete and Unabridged in One Volume.* (Peabody: Hendrickson, 1994), 869.

[1014] Spurgeon, C. H. *The Treasury of David.* (Grand Rapids, Michigan: Kregel Publications, 2004), Psalm 87:2.

1015 Simeon, C. *Horae Homileticae: Psalms, LXXIII–CL (Vol. 6).* (London: Samuel Holdsworth, 1836), 98.
1016 Nichols, J. W. H. *Musings in the Psalms.* (Galaxie Software, 2005), 61.
1017 Barnes' Notes on the Bible, Revelation 21:2.
1018 Gill, John. *The John Gill Exposition of the Entire Bible,* Revelation 21:2.
1019 Spurgeon, C. H. *Morning and Evening,* April 20, (Morning).
1020 Little, Paul. *Know What You Believe.* (Wheaton, Illinois: Victor Books, 1979), 189.
1021 Wiersbe, W. W. *With the Word Bible Commentary.* (Nashville: Thomas Nelson, 1991), Ps. 48:1.
1022 Gill, John. *The John Gill Exposition of the Entire Bible,* Psalm 88:1.
1023 Spence-Jones, H. D. M. (Ed.). *Psalms,* (Vol. 1). (London; New York: Funk & Wagnalls Company, 1909), 230.
1024 Holladay, W. L., and L. Köhler. *A Concise Hebrew and Aramaic Lexicon of the Old Testament.* (Leiden: Brill, 2000), 308.
1025 Barnes' Notes on the Bible, Psalm 88:2.
1026 Swanson, J. *Dictionary of Biblical Languages with Semantic Domains: Hebrew (Old Testament)* (electronic ed.). (Oak Harbor: Logos Research Systems, Inc., 1997).
1027 Harris, R. L., G. L. Archer, Jr., and B. K. Waltke (Eds.). *Theological Wordbook of the Old Testament* (electronic ed.). L. J. Coppes, 1293 נגד. (Chicago: Moody Press, 1999), 551.
1028 Barnes' Notes on the Bible, Psalm 88:3.
1029 Spurgeon, C. H. *The Treasury of David.* (Grand Rapids, Michigan: Kregel Publications, 2004), Psalm 88:3.
1030 Ibid., Psalm 88:4.
1031 Swanson, J. *Dictionary of Biblical Languages with Semantic Domains: Hebrew (Old Testament)* (electronic ed.). (Oak Harbor: Logos Research Systems, Inc., 1997).
1032 Bratcher, R. G. and W. D. Reyburn. *A Translator's Handbook on the Book of Psalms.* (New York: United Bible Societies, 1991), 764.
1033 Barnes' Notes on the Bible, Psalm 88:5.
1034 Bratcher, R. G. and W. D. Reyburn. *A Translator's Handbook on the Book of Psalms.* (New York: United Bible Societies, 1991), 765.
1035 Kirkpatrick, A. F. (Ed.). *The Cambridge Bible for Schools and Colleges,* Psalms. (Cambridge: Cambridge University Press, 1914), Psalm 88:5.
1036 Barnes' Notes on the Bible, Psalm 88:5.
1037 Landes, G. M. *Building Your Biblical Hebrew Vocabulary: Learning Words by Frequency and Cognate,* (Vol. 41). (Atlanta, GA: Society of Biblical Literature, 2001), 77.

[1038] Spence-Jones, H. D. M. (Ed.). *Psalms,* (Vol. 1). (London; New York: Funk & Wagnalls Company, 1909), 230.

[1039] Ibid.

[1040] Barnes' Notes on the Bible, Psalm 88:7.

[1041] Ibid.

[1042] Kirkpatrick, A. F. (Ed.). *The Cambridge Bible for Schools and Colleges,* Psalms. (Cambridge: Cambridge University Press, 1914), Psalm 88:7.

[1043] Swanson, J. *Dictionary of Biblical Languages with Semantic Domains: Hebrew (Old Testament)* (electronic ed.). (Oak Harbor: Logos Research Systems, Inc., 1997).

[1044] Barnes' Notes on the Bible, Psalm 88:8.

[1045] Holladay, W. L., and L. Köhler. *A Concise Hebrew and Aramaic Lexicon of the Old Testament.* (Leiden: Brill, 2000), 157.

[1046] Swanson, J. *Dictionary of Biblical Languages with Semantic Domains: Hebrew (Old Testament)* (electronic ed.). (Oak Harbor: Logos Research Systems, Inc., 1997).

[1047] Kirkpatrick, A. F. (Ed.). *The Cambridge Bible for Schools and Colleges,* Psalms. (Cambridge: Cambridge University Press, 1914), Psalm 88:9.

[1048] Spurgeon, C. H. *The Treasury of David.* (Grand Rapids, Michigan: Kregel Publications, 2004), Psalm 88:9.

[1049] Plumer, W. S. *Studies in the Book of Psalms: Being a Critical and Expository Commentary, with Doctrinal and Practical Remarks on the Entire Psalter.* (Philadelphia; Edinburgh: J. B. Lippincott Company; A & C Black, 1872), 818.

[1050] Leupold, H. C. *Exposition of the Psalms.* (Grand Rapids: Baker, 1969), 626–27.

[1051] Perowne, J. J. S. *The Book of Psalms: A New Translation, with Introductions and Notes, Explanatory and Critical, Fifth Edition, Revised, Vol. 1.* (London; Cambridge: George Bell and Sons; Deighton Bell and Co., 1883), 140.

[1052] Jennings, A. C., and W. H. Lowe. *The Psalms, with Introductions and Critical Notes* (Second Edition, Vol. 1). (London: Macmillan and Co., 1884), 94.

[1053] Henry, M. *Matthew Henry's Commentary on the Whole Bible: Complete and Unabridged in One Volume.* (Peabody: Hendrickson, 1994), 870.

[1054] Boice, J. M. *Psalms 42–106: An Expositional Commentary.* (Grand Rapids, MI: Baker Books, 2005), 716.

[1055] *The Spurgeon Study Bible.* (Nashville: Holman Bible Publishers, 2017), 765.

[1056] Ibid.

[1057] Plumer, W. S. *Studies in the Book of Psalms: Being a Critical and Expository Commentary, with Doctrinal and Practical Remarks on the Entire Psalter.* (Philadelphia; Edinburgh: J. B. Lippincott Company; A & C Black, 1872), 818.

[1058] Spence-Jones, H. D. M. (Ed.). *Psalms,* (Vol. 1). (London; New York: Funk & Wagnalls Company, 1909), 231.

[1059] Kidner, Derek. *Psalms 73–150: A Commentary on Books III–V of the Psalms.* (Downers Grove, Ill.: InterVarsity, 1975), 316.

[1060] Spurgeon, C. H. *The Treasury of David.* (Grand Rapids, Michigan: Kregel Publications, 2004), Psalm 88:1.

[1061] Boice, J. M. *Psalms 42–106: An Expositional Commentary.* (Grand Rapids, MI: Baker Books, 2005), 719.

[1062] Criswell, W. A. "Glory Out of Suffering." W. A. Criswell Sermon Library. Daily Word, November 15, 2018.

[1063] Kidner, Derek. *Psalms 73–150: A Commentary on Books III–V of the Psalms.* (Downers Grove, Ill.: InterVarsity, 1975), 316.

[1064] Vine, W. E., M. F. Unger, & W. White, Jr. *Vine's Complete Expository Dictionary of Old and New Testament Words (Vol. 1).* (Nashville, TN: T. Nelson, 1996), 130.

[1065] Swanson, J. *Dictionary of Biblical Languages with Semantic Domains: Hebrew (Old Testament)* (electronic ed.). (Oak Harbor: Logos Research Systems, Inc., 1997).

[1066] Harman, A. *Psalms: A Mentor Commentary (Vol. 1–2).* (Ross-shire, Great Britain: Mentor, 2011), 660.

[1067] Spurgeon, C. H. *The Treasury of David.* (Grand Rapids, Michigan: Kregel Publications, 2004), Psalm 89:15.

[1068] https://biblehub.com/commentaries/poole/psalms/89.htm, accessed June 13, 2018.

[1069] Gill, John. *The John Gill Exposition of the Entire Bible,* Psalm 89:16.

[1070] Swanson, J. *Dictionary of Biblical Languages with Semantic Domains: Hebrew (Old Testament)* (electronic ed.). (Oak Harbor: Logos Research Systems, Inc., 1997).

[1071] Henry, M. *Matthew Henry's Commentary on the Whole Bible: Complete and Unabridged in One Volume.* (Peabody: Hendrickson, 1994), 872.

[1072] Spurgeon, C. H. *The Treasury of David.* (Grand Rapids, Michigan: Kregel Publications, 2004), Psalm 89:16.

[1073] Gill, John. *The John Gill Exposition of the Entire Bible,* Psalm 89:16.

[1074] Plumer, W. S. *Studies in the Book of Psalms: Being a Critical and Expository Commentary, with Doctrinal and Practical Remarks on the Entire Psalter.* (Philadelphia; Edinburgh: J. B. Lippincott Company; A & C Black, 1872), 825.

[1075] Kirkpatrick, A. F. (Ed.). *The Cambridge Bible for Schools and Colleges,* Psalms. (Cambridge: Cambridge University Press, 1914), Psalm 89 (Introduction).

[1076] https://biblehub.com/library/maclaren/expositions_of_holy_scripture_j/
continual_sunshine.htm, accessed June 13, 2018.

[1077] Alexander, J. A. *The Psalms Translated and Explained.* (Edinburgh: Andrew Elliot; James Thin, 1864), 373.

[1078] Henry, M. *Matthew Henry's Commentary on the Whole Bible: Complete and Unabridged in One Volume.* (Peabody: Hendrickson, 1994), 872.

[1079] Smith, James. *Handfuls on Purpose,* Vol. 4, Series Ten, 280.

[1080] Plumer, W. S. *Studies in the Book of Psalms: Being a Critical and Expository Commentary, with Doctrinal and Practical Remarks on the Entire Psalter.* (Philadelphia; Edinburgh: J. B. Lippincott Company; A & C Black, 1872), 828.

[1081] Barnes' Notes on the Bible, Psalm 90:4.

[1082] Kirkpatrick, A. F. (Ed.). *The Cambridge Bible for Schools and Colleges, Psalms.* (Cambridge: Cambridge University Press, 1914), Psalm 90:4.

[1083] Barnes' Notes on the Bible, Psalm 90:4.

[1084] Thomas, R. L. *New American Standard Hebrew-Aramaic and Greek Dictionaries: updated edition.* (Anaheim: Foundation Publications, Inc., 1998).

[1085] Gesenius, W., and S. P. Tregelles. *Gesenius' Hebrew and Chaldee Lexicon to the Old Testament Scriptures.* (Bellingham, WA: Logos Bible Software, 2003), 840).

[1086] Holladay, W. L., and L. Köhler. *A Concise Hebrew and Aramaic Lexicon of the Old Testament.* (Leiden: Brill, 2000), 304.

[1087] Spurgeon, C. H. *The Treasury of David.* (Grand Rapids, Michigan: Kregel Publications, 2004), Psalm 90:6.

[1088] Swanson, J. *Dictionary of Biblical Languages with Semantic Domains: Hebrew (Old Testament)* (electronic ed.). (Oak Harbor: Logos Research Systems, Inc., 1997).

[1089] Vine, W. E., M. F. Unger, & W. White, Jr. *Vine's Complete Expository Dictionary of Old and New Testament Words (Vol. 1).* (Nashville, TN: T. Nelson, 1996), 296.

[1090] Kirkpatrick, A. F. (Ed.). *The Cambridge Bible for Schools and Colleges, Psalms.* (Cambridge: Cambridge University Press, 1914), Psalm 90:7.

[1091] Spurgeon, C. H. *The Treasury of David.* (Grand Rapids, Michigan: Kregel Publications, 2004), Psalm 90:7.

[1092] *Logos Exegetical Guide,* Psalm 90:8.

[1093] Spurgeon, C. H. *The Treasury of David.* (Grand Rapids, Michigan: Kregel Publications, 2004), Psalm 90:7.

[1094] Swanson, J. *Dictionary of Biblical Languages with Semantic Domains: Hebrew (Old Testament)* (electronic ed.). (Oak Harbor: Logos Research Systems, Inc., 1997).

[1095] Harris, R. L., G. L. Archer, Jr., and B. K. Waltke (Eds.). *Theological Wordbook of the Old Testament* (electronic ed.). R. L. Harris, 1629 עָלַם. (Chicago: Moody Press, 1999), 671.

[1096] Swanson, J. *Dictionary of Biblical Languages with Semantic Domains: Hebrew (Old Testament)* (electronic ed.). (Oak Harbor: Logos Research Systems, Inc., 1997).

[1097] Barnes' Notes on the Bible, Psalm90:9.

[1098] Kirkpatrick, A. F. (Ed.). *The Cambridge Bible for Schools and Colleges, Psalms.* (Cambridge: Cambridge University Press, 1914), Psalm 90:9.

[1099] Carroll, B. H. *An Interpretation of the English Bible: The Poetical Books of the Bible.* (Nashville: Broadman Press, 1948), 109.

[1100] Barnes' Notes on the Bible, Psalm 90:10.

[1101] Ibid.

[1102] https://biblehub.com/commentaries/poole/psalms/90.htm, accessed June 13, 2018.

[1103] Gesenius, W., and S. P. Tregelles. *Gesenius' Hebrew and Chaldee Lexicon to the Old Testament Scriptures.* (Bellingham, WA: Logos Bible Software, 2003), 639.

[1104] Swanson, J. *Dictionary of Biblical Languages with Semantic Domains: Hebrew (Old Testament)* (electronic ed.). (Oak Harbor: Logos Research Systems, Inc., 1997).

[1105] Gesenius, W., and S. P. Tregelles. *Gesenius' Hebrew and Chaldee Lexicon to the Old Testament Scriptures.* (Bellingham, WA: Logos Bible Software, 2003), 162.

[1106] Barnes' Notes on the Bible, Psalm 90:10.

[1107] Alexander, J. A. *The Psalms Translated and Explained.* (Edinburgh: Andrew Elliot; James Thin, 1864), 382.

[1108] Vine, W. E., M. F. Unger, & W. White, Jr. *Vine's Complete Expository Dictionary of Old and New Testament Words (Vol. 1).* (Nashville, TN: T. Nelson, 1996), 130.

[1109] Benson Commentary, Psalm 90:11.

[1110] https://biblehub.com/commentaries/poole/psalms/90.htm, accessed June 13, 2018.

[1111] https://biblehub.com/commentaries/ellicott/psalms/90.htm, accessed June 13, 2018.

[1112] Benson Commentary, Psalm 90:12.

[1113] Barnes' Notes on the Bible, Psalm 90:12.

[1114] Harman, A. *Psalms: A Mentor Commentary (Vol. 1–2).* (Ross-shire, Great Britain: Mentor, 2011), 669.

[1115] Plumer, W. S. *Studies in the Book of Psalms: Being a Critical and Expository Commentary, with Doctrinal and Practical Remarks on the Entire Psalter.* (Philadelphia; Edinburgh: J. B. Lippincott Company; A & C Black, 1872), 841.

[1116] Barnes' Notes on the Bible, Psalm90:9.

[1117] Ibid., Psalm 90:10.

[1118] Packer, J. I. *Knowing God.* (Downers Grove, IL: InterVarsity Press, 1993), 211.

[1119] Benson Commentary, Psalm 90:12.

[1120] Henry, M. *Matthew Henry's Commentary on the Whole Bible: Complete and Unabridged in One Volume.* (Peabody: Hendrickson, 1994), 876.

[1121] Plumer, W. S. *Studies in the Book of Psalms: Being a Critical and Expository Commentary, with Doctrinal and Practical Remarks on the Entire Psalter.* (Philadelphia; Edinburgh: J. B. Lippincott Company; A & C Black, 1872), 845–846).

[1122] Gesenius, W., and S. P. Tregelles. *Gesenius' Hebrew and Chaldee Lexicon to the Old Testament Scriptures.* (Bellingham, WA: Logos Bible Software, 2003), 313.

[1123] Barnes' Notes on the Bible, Psalm 91:14.

[1124] Harris, R. L., G. L. Archer, Jr., and B. K. Waltke (Eds.). *Theological Wordbook of the Old Testament* (electronic ed.). (Chicago: Moody Press, 1999), 724.

[1125] Spurgeon, C. H. *The Treasury of David.* (Grand Rapids, Michigan: Kregel Publications, 2004), Psalm 91:14.

[1126] https://biblehub.com/commentaries/poole/psalms/91.htm, accessed June 13, 2018.

[1127] Holladay, W. L., and L. Köhler. *A Concise Hebrew and Aramaic Lexicon of the Old Testament.* (Leiden: Brill, 2000), 349.

[1128] Vine, W. E., M. F. Unger, & W. White, Jr. *Vine's Complete Expository Dictionary of Old and New Testament Words (Vol. 1).* (Nashville, TN: T. Nelson, 1996), 130.

[1129] Gill, John. *The John Gill Exposition of the Entire Bible,* Psalm 91:14.

[1130] Swanson, J. *Dictionary of Biblical Languages with Semantic Domains: Hebrew (Old Testament)* (electronic ed.). (Oak Harbor: Logos Research Systems, Inc., 1997).

[1131] Ibid.

[1132] Spurgeon, C. H. *The Treasury of David.* (Grand Rapids, Michigan: Kregel Publications, 2004), Psalm 91:15.

[1133] Vine, W. E., M. F. Unger, & W. White, Jr. *Vine's Complete Expository Dictionary of Old and New Testament Words (Vol. 1).* (Nashville, TN: T. Nelson, 1996), 101.

[1134] Spurgeon, C. H. *The Treasury of David.* (Grand Rapids, Michigan: Kregel Publications, 2004), Psalm 91:16.

[1135] https://biblehub.com/commentaries/poole/psalms/91.htm, accessed June 13, 2018.

[1136] Spence-Jones, H. D. M. (Ed.). *Psalms,* (Vol. 1). (London; New York: Funk & Wagnalls Company, 1909), 269.

[1137] Clarke, Adam. *Clarkes' Commentary and Critical Notes*, Psalm 91:16.

[1138] Ibid., Introduction.

[1139] Simeon, C. *Horae Homileticae: Psalms, LXXIII–CL (Vol. 6).* (London: Samuel Holdsworth, 1836), 141.

[1140] Jennings, A. C., and W. H. Lowe. *The Psalms, with Introductions and Critical Notes* (Second Edition, Vol. 1). (London: Macmillan and Co., 1884), 128.

[1141] Henry, M. *Matthew Henry's Commentary on the Whole Bible: Complete and Unabridged in One Volume.* (Peabody: Hendrickson, 1994), 877.

[1142] https://biblehub.com/sermons/auth/maclaren/the_answer_to_trust.htm, accessed June 13, 2018.

[1143] Spurgeon, C. H. *Morning and Evening,* January 24 (Morning).

[1144] Spurgeon, C. H. *The Treasury of David.* (Grand Rapids, Michigan: Kregel Publications, 2004), Psalm 91:15.

[1145] https://biblehub.com/commentaries/poole/psalms/91.htm, accessed June 13, 2018.

[1146] Simeon, C. *Horae Homileticae: Psalms, LXXIII–CL (Vol. 6).* (London: Samuel Holdsworth, 1836), 143.

[1147] Henry, M. *Matthew Henry's Commentary on the Whole Bible: Complete and Unabridged in One Volume.* (Peabody: Hendrickson, 1994), 877.

[1148] Gill, John. *The John Gill Exposition of the Entire Bible,* Psalm 91:15.

[1149] Henry, M. *Matthew Henry's Commentary on the Whole Bible: Complete and Unabridged in One Volume.* (Peabody: Hendrickson, 1994), 878.

[1150] Ibid.

[1151] Simeon, C. *Horae Homileticae: Psalms, LXXIII–CL (Vol. 6).* (London: Samuel Holdsworth, 1836), 143.

[1152] Hamilton, William W. *Sermons on the Books of the Bible,* (Vol. 3), 212.

[1153] Barnes' Notes on the Bible, Psalm 92:12.

[1154] Swanson, J. *Dictionary of Biblical Languages with Semantic Domains: Hebrew (Old Testament)* (electronic ed.). (Oak Harbor: Logos Research Systems, Inc., 1997).

[1155] https://biblehub.com/commentaries/poole/psalms/92.htm, accessed June 13, 2018.

[1156] Barnes' Notes on the Bible, Psalm 92:12.

[1157] Holladay, W. L., and L. Köhler. *A Concise Hebrew and Aramaic Lexicon of the Old Testament.* (Leiden: Brill, 2000), 385.

[1158] Gill, John. *The John Gill Exposition of the Entire Bible,* Psalm 92:13.

[1159] Benson Commentary, Psalm 92:13.

[1160] Ibid.

[1161] https://biblehub.com/commentaries/poole/psalms/92.htm, accessed June 13, 2018.

[1162] Gill, John. *The John Gill Exposition of the Entire Bible,* Psalm 82:14.

[1163] Spence-Jones, H. D. M. (Ed.). *Psalms,* (Vol. 1). (London; New York: Funk & Wagnalls Company, 1909), 283.

[1164] Spurgeon, C. H. *The Treasury of David.* (Grand Rapids, Michigan: Kregel Publications, 2004), Psalm 92:15.

[1165] Ross, A. P. In Walvoord, J. F. and R. B. Zuck (Eds.). *The Bible Knowledge Commentary: An Exposition of the Scriptures* (Vol. 1, Psalms). (Wheaton, IL: Victor Books, 1985), 806.

[1166] Brown, F., S. R. Driver, and C. A. Briggs. *Enhanced Brown-Driver-Briggs Hebrew and English Lexicon.* (Oxford: Clarendon Press, 1977), 732.

[1167] Spurgeon, C. H. *The Treasury of David.* (Grand Rapids, Michigan: Kregel Publications, 2004), Psalm 92:15.

[1168] Plumer, W. S. *Studies in the Book of Psalms: Being a Critical and Expository Commentary, with Doctrinal and Practical Remarks on the Entire Psalter.* (Philadelphia; Edinburgh: J. B. Lippincott Company; A & C Black, 1872), 856.

[1169] Ibid.

[1170] Jennings, A. C., and W. H. Lowe. *The Psalms, with Introductions and Critical Notes* (Second Edition, Vol. 1). (London: Macmillan and Co., 1884), 129.

[1171] Ibid.

[1172] Henry, M. *Matthew Henry's Commentary on the Whole Bible: Complete and Unabridged in One Volume.* (Peabody: Hendrickson, 1994), 879.

[1173] Spurgeon, C. H. *The Treasury of David.* (Grand Rapids, Michigan: Kregel Publications, 2004), Psalm 92:15.

[1174] Barnes' Notes on the Bible, Matthew 21:8.

[1175] Lannom, Gloria W. "The Remarkable and Useful Date Palm." https://www.eduplace.com/science/hmxs/ls/modc/cricket/sect2cc.shtml, accessed June 13, 2018.

[1176] Simeon, C. *Horae Homileticae: Psalms, LXXIII–CL (Vol. 6).* (London: Samuel Holdsworth, 1836), 147.

[1177] Dabbs, Amy. "Palm Trees a Lifeline; Many Creatures Find Shelter, Food," July 29, 2016. https://www.postandcourier.com/features/home_and_garden/palm-trees-a-lifeline-many-creatures-find-shelter-food/article_2370b386-3e98-52dd-a667-2897cbaaf858.html, accessed June 13, 2018.

[1178] Barnes' Notes on the Bible, Psalm 92:14.

[1179] Benson Commentary, Psalm 93:1.

[1180] Swanson, J. *Dictionary of Biblical Languages with Semantic Domains: Hebrew (Old Testament)* (electronic ed.). (Oak Harbor: Logos Research Systems, Inc., 1997).

[1181] Clarke, Adam. *Clarkes' Commentary and Critical Notes*, Psalm 93:1.

[1182] Barnes' Notes on the Bible, Psalm 93:1.

[1183] Spurgeon, C. H. *The Treasury of David.* (Grand Rapids, Michigan: Kregel Publications, 2004), Psalm 93:1.

[1184] Landes, G. M. *Building Your Biblical Hebrew Vocabulary: Learning Words by Frequency and Cognate,* (Vol. 41). (Atlanta, GA: Society of Biblical Literature, 2001), 55.

[1185] Spence-Jones, H. D. M. (Ed.). *Psalms,* (Vol. 1). (London; New York: Funk & Wagnalls Company, 1909), 294.

[1186] Swanson, J. *Dictionary of Biblical Languages with Semantic Domains: Hebrew (Old Testament)* (electronic ed.). (Oak Harbor: Logos Research Systems, Inc., 1997).

[1187] Kirkpatrick, A. F. (Ed.). *The Cambridge Bible for Schools and Colleges,* Psalms. (Cambridge: Cambridge University Press, 1914), Psalm 93:3.

[1188] Barnes' Notes on the Bible, Psalm 93:3.

[1189] https://biblehub.com/commentaries/poole/psalms/93.htm, accessed June 16, 2018.

[1190] Vine, W. E., M. F. Unger, & W. White, Jr. *Vine's Complete Expository Dictionary of Old and New Testament Words (Vol. 1).* (Nashville, TN: T. Nelson, 1996), 260.

[1191] Landes, G. M. *Building Your Biblical Hebrew Vocabulary: Learning Words by Frequency and Cognate,* (Vol. 41). (Atlanta, GA: Society of Biblical Literature, 2001), 59.

[1192] Holladay, W. L., and L. Köhler. *A Concise Hebrew and Aramaic Lexicon of the Old Testament.* (Leiden: Brill, 2000), 314.

[1193] Spurgeon, C. H. *The Treasury of David.* (Grand Rapids, Michigan: Kregel Publications, 2004), Psalm 93:5.

[1194] Kirkpatrick, A. F. (Ed.). *The Cambridge Bible for Schools and Colleges,* Psalms. (Cambridge: Cambridge University Press, 1914), Psalm 93 (Introduction).

[1195] Barnes' Notes on the Bible, Psalm 93 (Introduction).

[1196] Plumer, W. S. *Studies in the Book of Psalms: Being a Critical and Expository Commentary, with Doctrinal and Practical Remarks on the Entire Psalter.* (Philadelphia; Edinburgh: J. B. Lippincott Company; A & C Black, 1872), 861.

[1197] Hindson, E. E., and W. M. Kroll, (Eds.). *KJV Bible Commentary*. (Nashville: Thomas Nelson, 1994), 1104.

[1198] Ibid.

[1199] Henry, M. *Matthew Henry's Commentary on the Whole Bible: Complete and Unabridged in One Volume*. (Peabody: Hendrickson, 1994), 879.

[1200] MacDonald, W. *Believer's Bible Commentary: Old and New Testaments,* (A. Farstad, Ed.) (Nashville: Thomas Nelson, 1995), 692–693.

[1201] Barnes' Notes on the Bible, Psalm 93:1.

[1202] *Webster's New Universal Unabridged Dictionary*. (New York: Barnes & Noble Books, 1996), 1161.

[1203] Gill, John. *The John Gill Exposition of the Entire Bible,* Psalm 93:1.

[1204] Harman, A. *Psalms: A Mentor Commentary (Vol. 1–2)*. (Ross-shire, Great Britain: Mentor, 2011), 688.

[1205] Spurgeon, C. H. *The Treasury of David*. (Grand Rapids, Michigan: Kregel Publications, 2004), Psalm 93:1.

[1206] Henry, M. *Matthew Henry's Commentary on the Whole Bible: Complete and Unabridged in One Volume*. (Peabody: Hendrickson, 1994), 879.

[1207] Gill, John. *The John Gill Exposition of the Entire Bible,* Psalm 93:2.

[1208] Henry, M. *Matthew Henry's Commentary on the Whole Bible: Complete and Unabridged in One Volume*. (Peabody: Hendrickson, 1994), 879.

[1209] Ibid.

[1210] Vine, W. E., M. F. Unger, & W. White, Jr. *Vine's Complete Expository Dictionary of Old and New Testament Words (Vol. 1)*. (Nashville, TN: T. Nelson, 1996), 101.

[1211] Thomas, R. L. *New American Standard Hebrew-Aramaic and Greek Dictionaries: updated edition*. (Anaheim: Foundation Publications, Inc., 1998).

[1212] Swanson, J. *Dictionary of Biblical Languages with Semantic Domains: Hebrew (Old Testament)* (electronic ed.). (Oak Harbor: Logos Research Systems, Inc., 1997).

[1213] Barnes' Notes on the Bible, Psalm 94:19.

[1214] Harris, R. L., G. L. Archer, Jr., and B. K. Waltke (Eds.). *Theological Wordbook of the Old Testament* (electronic ed.). M. R. Wilson. (Chicago: Moody Press, 1999), 570.

[1215] Swanson, J. *Dictionary of Biblical Languages with Semantic Domains: Hebrew (Old Testament)* (electronic ed.). (Oak Harbor: Logos Research Systems, Inc., 1997).

[1216] Ibid.

[1217] Spence-Jones, H. D. M. (Ed.). *Psalms,* (Vol. 1). (London; New York: Funk & Wagnalls Company, 1909), 301.

[1218] Plumer, W. S. *Studies in the Book of Psalms: Being a Critical and Expository Commentary, with Doctrinal and Practical Remarks on the Entire Psalter.* (Philadelphia; Edinburgh: J. B. Lippincott Company; A & C Black, 1872), 868.

[1219] Ibid., 865.

[1220] Spurgeon, C. H. *The Treasury of David.* (Grand Rapids, Michigan: Kregel Publications, 2004), Psalm 94:1 (Explanatory Notes and Quaint Sayings).

[1221] Henry, M. *Matthew Henry's Commentary on the Whole Bible: Complete and Unabridged in One Volume.* (Peabody: Hendrickson, 1994), 880.

[1222] Criswell, W. A., P. Patterson, E. R. Clendenen, D. L. Akin, M. Chamberlin, D. K. Patterson, and J. Pogue (Eds.). Believer's Study Bible, (electronic ed.). (Nashville: Thomas Nelson, 1991), Ps. 94:12.

[1223] Henry, M. *Matthew Henry's Commentary on the Whole Bible: Complete and Unabridged in One Volume.* (Peabody: Hendrickson, 1994), 881.

[1224] Spurgeon, C. H. *The Treasury of David.* (Grand Rapids, Michigan: Kregel Publications, 2004), Psalm 94:19.

[1225] Simeon, C. *Horae Homileticae: Psalms, LXXIII–CL (Vol. 6).* (London: Samuel Holdsworth, 1836), 152.

[1226] Ibid., 152–153.

[1227] Chambers, Oswald. *My Utmost For His Highest,* February 11.

[1228] Tate, M. E. *Psalms 51–100 (Vol. 20).* (Dallas: Word, Incorporated, 1998), 502.

[1229] Swanson, J. *Dictionary of Biblical Languages with Semantic Domains: Hebrew (Old Testament)* (electronic ed.). (Oak Harbor: Logos Research Systems, Inc., 1997).

[1230] Tate, M. E. *Psalms 51–100 (Vol. 20).* (Dallas: Word, Incorporated, 1998), 502.

[1231] Barnes' Notes on the Bible, Psalm 95:8.

[1232] Simeon, C. *Horae Homileticae: Psalms, LXXIII–CL (Vol. 6).* (London: Samuel Holdsworth, 1836), 155.

[1233] Barnes' Notes on the Bible, Psalm 95:8.

[1234] Spence-Jones, H. D. M. (Ed.). *Psalms,* (Vol. 1). (London; New York: Funk & Wagnalls Company, 1909), 311.

[1235] Kirkpatrick, A. F. (Ed.). *The Cambridge Bible for Schools and Colleges, Psalms.* (Cambridge: Cambridge University Press, 1914), Psalm 95:9.

[1236] Swanson, J. *Dictionary of Biblical Languages with Semantic Domains: Hebrew (Old Testament)* (electronic ed.). (Oak Harbor: Logos Research Systems, Inc., 1997).

[1237] https://biblehub.com/commentaries/poole/psalms/95.htm, accessed June 16, 2018.

[1238] Kirkpatrick, A. F. (Ed.). *The Cambridge Bible for Schools and Colleges, Psalms.* (Cambridge: Cambridge University Press, 1914), Psalm 95:9.

[1239] Benson Commentary, Psalm 95:10.

[1240] Barnes' Notes on the Bible, Psalm 95:10.

[1241] Whitaker, R., F. Brown, and S. R. Driver. *The Abridged Brown-Driver-Briggs Hebrew-English Lexicon of the Old Testament: Based on the Lexicon of Wilhelm Gesenius.* (Boston; New York: Houghton, Mifflin and Company, 1906).

[1242] https://biblehub.com/commentaries/poole/psalms/95.htm, accessed June 16, 2018.

[1243] Ibid.

[1244] Swanson, J. *Dictionary of Biblical Languages with Semantic Domains: Hebrew (Old Testament)* (electronic ed.). (Oak Harbor: Logos Research Systems, Inc., 1997).

[1245] Harris, R. L., G. L. Archer, Jr., and B. K. Waltke (Eds.). *Theological Wordbook of the Old Testament* (electronic ed.). (Chicago: Moody Press, 1999), 58.

[1246] Spence-Jones, H. D. M. (Ed.). *Psalms,* (Vol. 1). (London; New York: Funk & Wagnalls Company, 1909), 312.

[1247] Barnes' Notes on the Bible, Psalm 95:11.

[1248] Tate, M. E. *Psalms 51–100 (Vol. 20).* (Dallas: Word, Incorporated, 1998), 502.

[1249] Harman, A. *Psalms: A Mentor Commentary (Vol. 1–2).* (Ross-shire, Great Britain: Mentor, 2011), 699.

[1250] Spurgeon, C. H. *The Treasury of David.* (Grand Rapids, Michigan: Kregel Publications, 2004), Psalm 95:8.

[1251] Spurgeon, C. H. *Sermons for Special Days and Occasions.* (Grand Rapids: Zondervan Publishing House, 1966), 184.

[1252] Stanley, Charles. *Handbook for Christian Living.* (Nashville: Thomas Nelson, 2008), 248.

[1253] Gill, John. *The John Gill Exposition of the Entire Bible,* Psalm 95:8.

[1254] Henry, M. *Matthew Henry's Commentary on the Whole Bible: Complete and Unabridged in One Volume.* (Peabody: Hendrickson, 1994), 882.

[1255] Lawson, George, Proverbs 29:1.

[1256] Ironside, H. A. *Notes on the Book of Proverbs.* (Neptune, NJ: Loizeaux Bros, 1908), 414–415.

[1257] Spurgeon, C. H. "Today! Today! Today!'" (Sermon # 1551), August 1, 1880.

[1258] Henry, M. *Matthew Henry's Commentary on the Whole Bible: Complete and Unabridged in One Volume.* (Peabody: Hendrickson, 1994), 884.

[1259] Gill, John. *The John Gill Exposition of the Entire Bible,* Psalm 96:13.

[1260] Ibid.

[1261] Spurgeon, C. H. *The Treasury of David.* (Grand Rapids, Michigan: Kregel Publications, 2004), Psalm 96:13.

[1262] Dilday, R. H., Jr., and J. H. Kennedy. *Psalms.* In H. F. Paschall and H. H. Hobbs (Eds.). *The Teacher's Bible Commentary.* (Nashville: Broadman and Holman Publishers, 1972), 333.

[1263] Jennings, A. C., and W. H. Lowe. *The Psalms, with Introductions and Critical Notes* (Second Edition, Vol. 1). (London: Macmillan and Co., 1884), 150.

[1264] Barnes' Notes on the Bible, Psalm 96:13.

[1265] Criswell, W. A., P. Patterson, E. R. Clendenen, D. L. Akin, M. Chamberlin, D. K. Patterson, and J. Pogue (Eds.). Believer's Study Bible, (electronic ed.). (Nashville: Thomas Nelson, 1991), Ps. 96:10–13.

[1266] Plumer, W. S. *Studies in the Book of Psalms: Being a Critical and Expository Commentary, with Doctrinal and Practical Remarks on the Entire Psalter.* (Philadelphia; Edinburgh: J. B. Lippincott Company; A & C Black, 1872), 878.

[1267] Jennings, A. C., and W. H. Lowe. *The Psalms, with Introductions and Critical Notes* (Second Edition, Vol. 1). (London: Macmillan and Co., 1884), 149.

[1268] MacDonald, W. *Believer's Bible Commentary: Old and New Testaments,* (A. Farstad, Ed.) (Nashville: Thomas Nelson, 1995), 695.

[1269] Harman, A. *Psalms: A Mentor Commentary (Vol. 1–2).* (Ross-shire, Great Britain: Mentor, 2011), 701.

[1270] https://www.dailychristianquote.com/tag/second-coming/, accessed June 16, 2018.

[1271] "Jesus Is Coming Soon? 7 Quotes About Second Coming from Billy Graham" | Newsmax.com, accessed June 16, 2018.

[1272] Swanson, J. *Dictionary of Biblical Languages with Semantic Domains: Hebrew (Old Testament)* (electronic ed.). (Oak Harbor: Logos Research Systems, Inc., 1997).

[1273] Bratcher, R. G. and W. D. Reyburn. *A Translator's Handbook on the Book of Psalms.* (New York: United Bible Societies, 1991), 843.

[1274] Barnes' Notes on the Bible, Psalm 97:11.

[1275] Jennings, A. C., and W. H. Lowe. *The Psalms, with Introductions and Critical Notes* (Second Edition, Vol. 1). (London: Macmillan and Co., 1884), 159.

[1276] Vine, W. E., M. F. Unger, & W. White, Jr. *Vine's Complete Expository Dictionary of Old and New Testament Words (Vol. 1).* (Nashville, TN: T. Nelson, 1996), 205.

[1277] Swanson, J. *Dictionary of Biblical Languages with Semantic Domains: Hebrew (Old Testament)* (electronic ed.). (Oak Harbor: Logos Research Systems, Inc., 1997).

[1278] Barnes' Notes on the Bible, Psalm 97:11.

[1279] Spence-Jones, H. D. M. (Ed.). *Psalms,* (Vol. 1). (London; New York: Funk & Wagnalls Company, 1909), 330.

[1280] Clarke, Adam. *Clarkes' Commentary and Critical Notes*, Psalm 97 (Introduction).

[1281] Dilday, R. H., Jr., and J. H. Kennedy. *Psalms.* In H. F. Paschall and H. H. Hobbs (Eds.). *The Teacher's Bible Commentary.* (Nashville: Broadman and Holman Publishers, 1972), 333.

[1282] Harman, A. *Psalms: A Mentor Commentary (Vol. 1–2).* (Ross-shire, Great Britain: Mentor, 2011), 708.

[1283] Plumer, W. S. *Studies in the Book of Psalms: Being a Critical and Expository Commentary, with Doctrinal and Practical Remarks on the Entire Psalter.* (Philadelphia; Edinburgh: J. B. Lippincott Company; A & C Black, 1872), 882.

[1284] Simeon, C. *Horae Homileticae: Psalms, LXXIII–CL (Vol. 6).* (London: Samuel Holdsworth, 1836), 169.

[1285] Henry, M. *Matthew Henry's Commentary on the Whole Bible: Complete and Unabridged in One Volume.* (Peabody: Hendrickson, 1994), 885.

[1286] Spurgeon, C. H. *The Treasury of David.* (Grand Rapids, Michigan: Kregel Publications, 2004), Psalm 97:11.

[1287] Barnes' Notes on the Bible, Psalm 97:11.

[1288] Clarke, Adam. *Clarkes' Commentary and Critical Notes*, Psalm 97:11.

[1289] Henry, M. *Matthew Henry's Commentary on the Whole Bible: Complete and Unabridged in One Volume.* (Peabody: Hendrickson, 1994), 885.

[1290] Barnes' Notes on the Bible,, Psalm 97:12.

[1291] Spurgeon, C. H. *The Treasury of David.* (Grand Rapids, Michigan: Kregel Publications, 2004), Psalm 97:11.

[1292] Plumer, W. S. *Studies in the Book of Psalms: Being a Critical and Expository Commentary, with Doctrinal and Practical Remarks on the Entire Psalter.* (Philadelphia; Edinburgh: J. B. Lippincott Company; A & C Black, 1872), 886.

[1293] Holladay, W. L., and L. Köhler. *A Concise Hebrew and Aramaic Lexicon of the Old Testament.* (Leiden: Brill, 2000), 96.

[1294] Spurgeon, C. H. *The Treasury of David.* (Grand Rapids, Michigan: Kregel Publications, 2004), Psalm 98:1.

[1295] Henry, M. *Matthew Henry's Commentary on the Whole Bible: Complete and Unabridged in One Volume.* (Peabody: Hendrickson, 1994), 885.

[1296] Vine, W. E., M. F. Unger, & W. White, Jr. *Vine's Complete Expository Dictionary of Old and New Testament Words (Vol. 1).* (Nashville, TN: T. Nelson, 1996), 149.

[1297] Ibid., 130.

[1298] Spence-Jones, H. D. M. (Ed.). *Psalms,* (Vol. 1). (London; New York: Funk & Wagnalls Company, 1909), 340.

[1299] Holladay, W. L., and L. Köhler. *A Concise Hebrew and Aramaic Lexicon of the Old Testament.* (Leiden: Brill, 2000), 303.

[1300] Benson Commentary, Psalm 98:2.

[1301] Landes, G. M. *Building Your Biblical Hebrew Vocabulary: Learning Words by Frequency and Cognate,* (Vol. 41). (Atlanta, GA: Society of Biblical Literature, 2001), 61.

[1302] Barnes' Notes on the Bible, Psalm 98:2.

[1303] Ibid., Psalm 98:3

[1304] Vine, W. E., M. F. Unger, & W. White, Jr. *Vine's Complete Expository Dictionary of Old and New Testament Words (Vol. 1).* (Nashville, TN: T. Nelson, 1996), 142.

[1305] Clarke, Adam. *Clarkes' Commentary and Critical Notes*, Psalm 98:3.

[1306] https://biblehub.com/commentaries/poole/isaiah/52.htm, accessed June 18, 2018.

[1307] Gill, John. *The John Gill Exposition of the Entire Bible,* Psalm 98:3.

[1308] Harris, R. L., G. L. Archer, Jr., and B. K. Waltke (Eds.). *Theological Wordbook of the Old Testament* (electronic ed.). W. White, 2135 רֵעַ. (Chicago: Moody Press, 1999), 839.

[1309] Spence-Jones, H. D. M. (Ed.). *Psalms,* (Vol. 1). (London; New York: Funk & Wagnalls Company, 1909), 340.

[1310] Holladay, W. L., and L. Köhler. *A Concise Hebrew and Aramaic Lexicon of the Old Testament.* (Leiden: Brill, 2000), 156–157.

[1311] Strong, J. *A Concise Dictionary of the Words in the Greek Testament and the Hebrew Bible.* (Vol. 2). (Bellingham, WA: Logos Bible Software, 2009), 96.

[1312] Swanson, J. *Dictionary of Biblical Languages with Semantic Domains: Hebrew (Old Testament)* (electronic ed.). (Oak Harbor: Logos Research Systems, Inc., 1997).

[1313] Spence-Jones, H. D. M. (Ed.). *Psalms,* (Vol. 1). (London; New York: Funk & Wagnalls Company, 1909), 340.

[1314] Barnes' Notes on the Bible, Psalm 98:5.

[1315] Ibid., Psalm 98:6.

[1316] Spence-Jones, H. D. M. (Ed.). *Psalms,* (Vol. 1). (London; New York: Funk & Wagnalls Company, 1909), 340.

[1317] Jamieson, R., A. R. Fausset, & D. Brown. *Commentary Critical and Explanatory on the Whole Bible* (Vol. 1). (Oak Harbor, WA: Logos Research Systems, Inc., 1997), 375.

[1318] Brown, F., S. R. Driver, and C. A. Briggs. *Enhanced Brown-Driver-Briggs Hebrew and English Lexicon.* (Oxford: Clarendon Press, 1977), 625.

[1319] Spurgeon, C. H. *The Treasury of David.* (Grand Rapids, Michigan: Kregel Publications, 2004), Psalm 98:8.

[1320] Ibid.

[1321] Spence-Jones, H. D. M. (Ed.). *Psalms,* (Vol. 1). (London; New York: Funk & Wagnalls Company, 1909), 341.

[1322] Gill, John. *The John Gill Exposition of the Entire Bible,* Psalm 98:9.

[1323] Plumer, W. S. *Studies in the Book of Psalms: Being a Critical and Expository Commentary, with Doctrinal and Practical Remarks on the Entire Psalter.* (Philadelphia; Edinburgh: J. B. Lippincott Company; A & C Black, 1872), 887.

[1324] Dilday, R. H., Jr., and J. H. Kennedy. *Psalms.* In H. F. Paschall and H. H. Hobbs (Eds.). *The Teacher's Bible Commentary.* (Nashville: Broadman and Holman Publishers, 1972), 334.

[1325] Harman, A. *Psalms: A Mentor Commentary (Vol. 1–2).* (Ross-shire, Great Britain: Mentor, 2011), 711.

[1326] Horne, G. *A Commentary on the Book of Psalms.* (New York: Robert Carter & Brothers, 1856), 351.

[1327] Jennings, A. C., and W. H. Lowe. *The Psalms, with Introductions and Critical Notes* (Second Edition, Vol. 1). (London: Macmillan and Co., 1884), 161.

[1328] Barnes' Notes on the Bible, Psalm 98:5.

[1329] *The Spurgeon Study Bible.* (Nashville: Holman Bible Publishers, 2017), 773.

[1330] Vine, W. E., M. F. Unger, & W. White, Jr. *Vine's Complete Expository Dictionary of Old and New Testament Words (Vol. 1).* (Nashville, TN: T. Nelson, 1996), 149.

[1331] Henry, Matthew. *Matthew Henry's Concise Bible Commentary,* Psalm 98:1.

[1332] Spurgeon, C. H. *The Treasury of David.* (Grand Rapids, Michigan: Kregel Publications, 2004), Psalm 98:1.

[1333] Henry, Matthew. *Matthew Henry's Concise Bible Commentary,* Psalm 98:1.

[1334] Spurgeon, C. H. *The Treasury of David.* (Grand Rapids, Michigan: Kregel Publications, 2004), Psalm 98:2.

[1335] Spurgeon, C. H. "Crowning Blessings Ascribed to God" (Sermon #1475), May 18, 1879. (The second sermon in commemoration of the completion of 25 years of his ministry in the midst of the church assembling in the Tabernacle).

[1336] Swanson, J. *Dictionary of Biblical Languages with Semantic Domains: Hebrew (Old Testament)* (electronic ed.). (Oak Harbor: Logos Research Systems, Inc., 1997).

[1337] Barnes' Notes on the Bible, Psalm 99:5.

[1338] Swanson, J. *Dictionary of Biblical Languages with Semantic Domains: Hebrew (Old Testament)* (electronic ed.). (Oak Harbor: Logos Research Systems, Inc., 1997).

[1339] Barnes' Notes on the Bible, Psalm 99:5.

[1340] MacArthur, J., Jr. (Ed.). *The MacArthur Study Bible,* (electronic ed.). (Nashville, TN: Word Pub, 1997), 830.

[1341] Swanson, J. *Dictionary of Biblical Languages with Semantic Domains: Hebrew (Old Testament)* (electronic ed.). (Oak Harbor: Logos Research Systems, Inc., 1997).

[1342] Spurgeon, C. H. *The Treasury of David.* (Grand Rapids, Michigan: Kregel Publications, 2004), Psalm 99 (Introduction).

[1343] Boice, J. M. *Psalms 42–106: An Expositional Commentary.* (Grand Rapids, MI: Baker Books, 2005), 804.

[1344] Horne, G. *A Commentary on the Book of Psalms.* (New York: Robert Carter & Brothers, 1856), 352.

[1345] Kirkpatrick, A. F. (Ed.). *The Cambridge Bible for Schools and Colleges, Psalms.* (Cambridge: Cambridge University Press, 1914), Psalm 99 (Introduction).

[1346] https://www.christianquotes.info/top-quotes/20-amazing-quotes-about-gods-holiness/#ixzz5lom3wHPA, accessed June 18, 2018.

[1347] Benson Commentary, Psalm 99:5.

[1348] Bratcher, R. G. and W. D. Reyburn. *A Translator's Handbook on the Book of Psalms.* (New York: United Bible Societies, 1991), 849.

[1349] Spurgeon, C. H. *The Treasury of David.* (Grand Rapids, Michigan: Kregel Publications, 2004), Psalm 99:5.

[1350] Barnes' Notes on the Bible, Psalm 99:5.

[1351] Boice, J. M. *Psalms 42–106: An Expositional Commentary.* (Grand Rapids, MI: Baker Books, 2005), 807.

[1352] Henry, M. *Matthew Henry's Commentary on the Whole Bible: Complete and Unabridged in One Volume.* (Peabody: Hendrickson, 1994), 886.

[1353] Spurgeon, C. H. *The Treasury of David.* (Grand Rapids, Michigan: Kregel Publications, 2004), Psalm 96:9.

[1354] Ryle, J. C. "Holiness," Sermon. <iclnet.org/pub/resources/text/history/spurgeon/web/ryle.holiness.html – 49k>, accessed June 19, 2018.

[1355] Spurgeon, C. H. "Holiness Demanded," Sermon #2902, Delivered at the Metropolitan Tabernacle, Newington, 1862.

[1356] Ibid.

[1357] https://www.christianquotes.info/top-quotes/20-amazing-quotes-about-gods-holiness/#ixzz5lonD4aoW, accessed June 18, 2018.

[1358] https://www.christianquotes.info/top-quotes/20-amazing-quotes-about-gods-holiness/#ixzz5loncfgtt, accessed June 18, 2018.

[1359] Swanson, J. *Dictionary of Biblical Languages with Semantic Domains: Hebrew (Old Testament)* (electronic ed.). (Oak Harbor: Logos Research Systems, Inc., 1997).

[1360] Ibid.

[1361] Gesenius, W., and S. P. Tregelles. *Gesenius' Hebrew and Chaldee Lexicon to the Old Testament Scriptures.* (Bellingham, WA: Logos Bible Software, 2003), 771.

[1362] Spence-Jones, H. D. M. (Ed.). *Psalms,* (Vol. 1). (London; New York: Funk & Wagnalls Company, 1909), 352.

[1363] Benson Commentary, Psalm 100:3.

[1364] Barnes' Notes on the Bible, Psalm 105:3.

[1365] Benson Commentary, Psalm 105:3.

[1366] Henry, M. *Matthew Henry's Commentary on the Whole Bible: Complete and Unabridged in One Volume.* (Peabody: Hendrickson, 1994), 887.

[1367] Spence-Jones, H. D. M. (Ed.). *Psalms,* (Vol. 1). (London; New York: Funk & Wagnalls Company, 1909), 353.

[1368] Swanson, J. *Dictionary of Biblical Languages with Semantic Domains: Hebrew (Old Testament)* (electronic ed.). (Oak Harbor: Logos Research Systems, Inc., 1997).

[1369] Whitaker, R., F. Brown, and S. R. Driver. *The Abridged Brown-Driver-Briggs Hebrew-English Lexicon of the Old Testament: Based on the Lexicon of Wilhelm Gesenius.* (Boston; New York: Houghton, Mifflin and Company, 1906).

[1370] Barnes' Notes on the Bible, Psalm 100:4.

[1371] Vine, W. E., M. F. Unger, & W. White, Jr. *Vine's Complete Expository Dictionary of Old and New Testament Words (Vol. 1).* (Nashville, TN: T. Nelson, 1996), 44.

[1372] Harris, R. L., G. L. Archer, Jr., and B. K. Waltke (Eds.). *Theological Wordbook of the Old Testament* (electronic ed.). J. N. Oswalt, 285 בָּרַךְ. (Chicago: Moody Press, 1999), 132. Oswalt, J. N. (1999).

[1373] Barnes' Notes on the Bible, Psalm 100:5.

[1374] Vine, W. E., M. F. Unger, & W. White, Jr. *Vine's Complete Expository Dictionary of Old and New Testament Words (Vol. 1).* (Nashville, TN: T. Nelson, 1996), 142.

[1375] Swanson, J. *Dictionary of Biblical Languages with Semantic Domains: Hebrew (Old Testament)* (electronic ed.). (Oak Harbor: Logos Research Systems, Inc., 1997).

[1376] Spurgeon, C. H. *The Treasury of David.* (Grand Rapids, Michigan: Kregel Publications, 2004), Psalm 100:5.

[1377] Plumer, W. S. *Studies in the Book of Psalms: Being a Critical and Expository Commentary, with Doctrinal and Practical Remarks on the Entire Psalter.* (Philadelphia; Edinburgh: J. B. Lippincott Company; A & C Black, 1872), 895.

[1378] Harman, A. *Psalms: A Mentor Commentary (Vol. 1–2).* (Ross-shire, Great Britain: Mentor, 2011), 719–720.

[1379] Spurgeon, C. H. *Morning and Evening,* January 9 (Evening).

[1380] Barnes' Notes on the Bible, Psalm 100:3.

[1381] Ibid. Psalm 100:5

[1382] Plumer, W. S. *Studies in the Book of Psalms: Being a Critical and Expository Commentary, with Doctrinal and Practical Remarks on the Entire Psalter.* (Philadelphia; Edinburgh: J. B. Lippincott Company; A & C Black, 1872), 896.

[1383] Ibid., 897.

[1384] Ibid.

[1385] Ibid.

[1386] Vine, W. E., M. F. Unger, & W. White, Jr. *Vine's Complete Expository Dictionary of Old and New Testament Words (Vol. 1).* (Nashville, TN: T. Nelson, 1996), 45.

CPSIA information can be obtained
at www.ICGtesting.com
Printed in the USA
BVHW030342250919
559324BV00002B/9/P

9 781878 127365